A TIGER RULES THE MOUNTAIN

A TIGER RULES THE MOUNTAIN

CAMBODIA'S PURSUIT OF DEMOCRACY

GORDON CONOCHIE

MONASH
UNIVERSITY
PUBLISHING

Published by Monash University Publishing
Matheson Library Annexe
40 Exhibition Walk
Monash University
Clayton, Victoria 3800, Australia
publishing.monash.edu

Monash University Publishing: the discussion starts here

Gordon Conochie © Copyright 2023
Gordon Conochie reserves the right to be known as the author of the work.

All rights reserved. Apart from any uses permitted by Australia's *Copyright Act 1968*, no part of this book may be reproduced by any process without prior written permission from the copyright owners. Enquiries should be directed to the publisher.

Reasonable attempts have been made to locate copyright holders, and any potential infringement of copyright is accidental. Should any infringement be suspected, contact Monash University Publishing.

Read more about the making of *A Tiger Rules the Mountain*,
plus see images and videos, at www.atigerrules.com

9781922633903 (paperback)
9781922633910 (pdf)
9781922633927 (epub)
Cover design by Tom William Francis, Pineapple Design
Cover image by Erika Piñeros
Text design and typesetting by Typography Studio
Author photograph by Claire Wilcock

Printed in Australia by Griffin Press

CONTENTS

Author's Note — ix
Timeline of Key Events — x
The People You'll Meet (In Order of Appearance) — xiii

PART I: 2013–2015

1. Change at the Corner — 1
2. Injustice Burns — 4
3. The Man in Charge — 12
4. To the Rescue — 21
5. Shifting Currents — 27
6. Election Eve — 39
7. Ghosts and Nobodies — 44
8. Drop by Drop, the Bucket Fills — 48
9. Veng Sreng Street — 57
10. The Third Hand — 66
11. A Culture of Dialogue — 70
12. Dialogue Unravels — 77

PART II: 2015–2017

13. A Game of Chess — 87
14. Here Is My Son — 97

15.	*Khnorng*	102
16.	A Slave to One Side	108
17.	Rule of Law	113
18.	The Man in the White Shirt with a Black Heart	121
19.	The Rise of Rozeth	129
20.	A Transfer of Power	135
21.	To Catch a Tiger	142
22.	Radio Silence	146
23.	*Chhob*	155
24.	Clearing the Table	161
25.	Flattened	164
26.	What the West Fails to See	168

PART III: 2018

27.	Clean Fingers	183
28.	Charm Offensive	189
29.	Pressure	199
30.	Your Aim Is One	208
31.	Endgame	212
32.	Election Day	223
33.	The Numbers	229
34.	Cambodia Changing	236
35.	Hun Sen's Right to Rule	242
36.	The Sacrifice of Sin Rozeth	250
37.	Playing with Coal	254
38.	Cambodia's Way	260

PART IV: 2022

39.	Candelight	271
40.	A Chicken House	276
41	The Elephant and a Mouse	281
42.	Enmity Returns	287
43.	Chapter Two	291
	Postscript	301
	Acknowledgements	305
	Notes	307

AUTHOR'S NOTE

I lived in Cambodia for a total of nearly three years between 2012 and 2022, the period that is the focus of this book, working with government, United Nations and international aid agencies, and local charities. I returned multiple times to gather information and conduct interviews, greatly supported by Cambodian friends who made introductions for me.

I became conversationally fluent in Khmer, the main language in Cambodia, but mostly used an interpreter to assist when interviews were conducted in Khmer. Some Cambodians chose to converse in English, and I have tried to keep their quotes as spoken, only editing to assist understanding. To protect identities as agreed, pseudonyms are used for some people, and I have, on occasion, been deliberately vague in describing them and their roles.

I employed two Cambodians experienced in research to assist in gathering information and translating documents. They, as well as some other Cambodians who have worked in research or social development, reviewed certain sections of the text to ensure that I interpreted and explained cultural aspects accurately. This was of great assistance and their recommendations will hopefully help the reader learn more about the people and the country, in addition to its politics. References throughout the text to dollars relate to US dollars, the dominant reserve currency.

I have written this as a narrative, rather than as a conventional academic text, because it is as much about the people as the political events, and I want to give readers the chance to know them like I do. However, I have followed academic conventions of rigour in terms of citations, and have a reference list of over 1200 documents – books, journal articles, official reports and newspaper articles.

I conducted more than 200 in-depth interviews, usually interviewing the same person multiple times. It is these people who form the heart of this book. You will hear them share how those dichotomous twins of idealism and pragmatism, of freedom and power, and of hope and fear, are pitched against each other, in a wrestle for the future of Cambodia.

TIMELINE OF KEY EVENTS

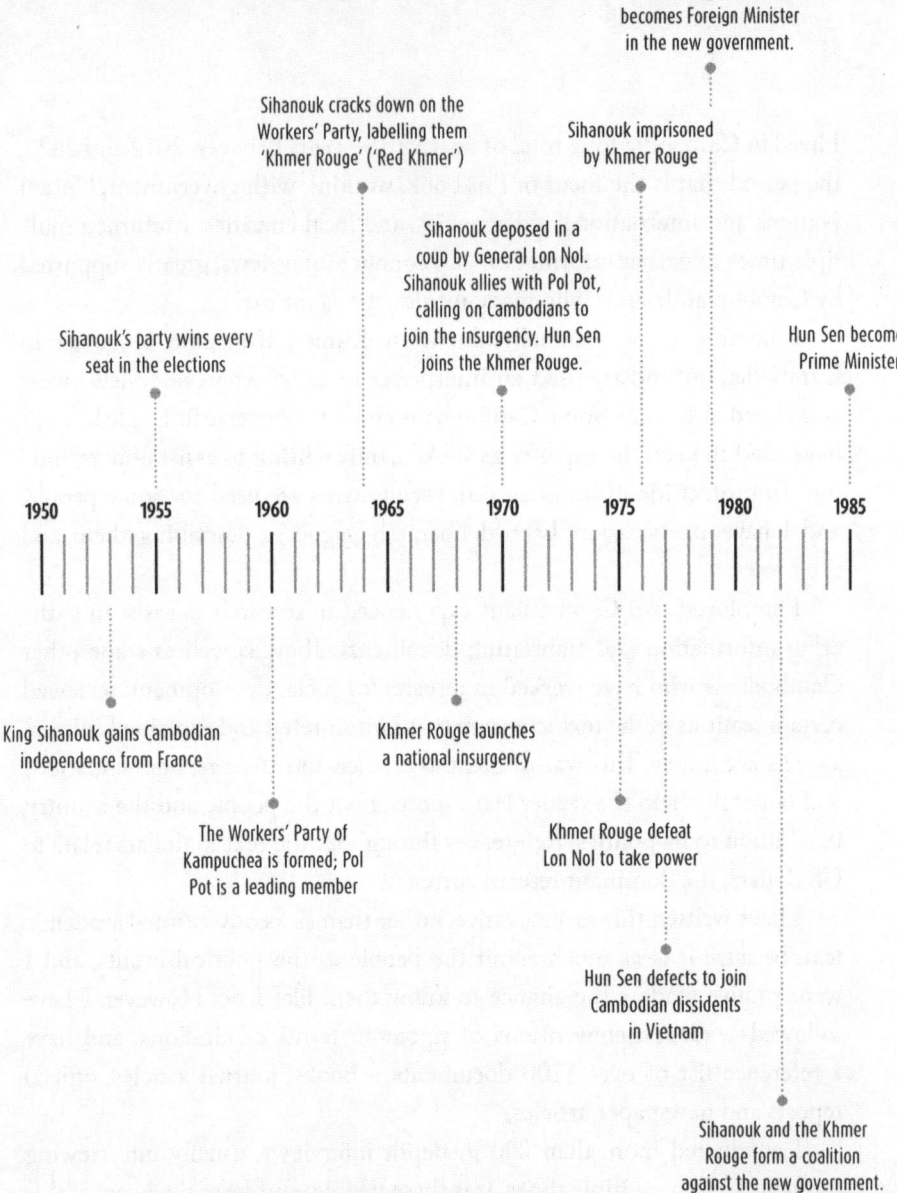

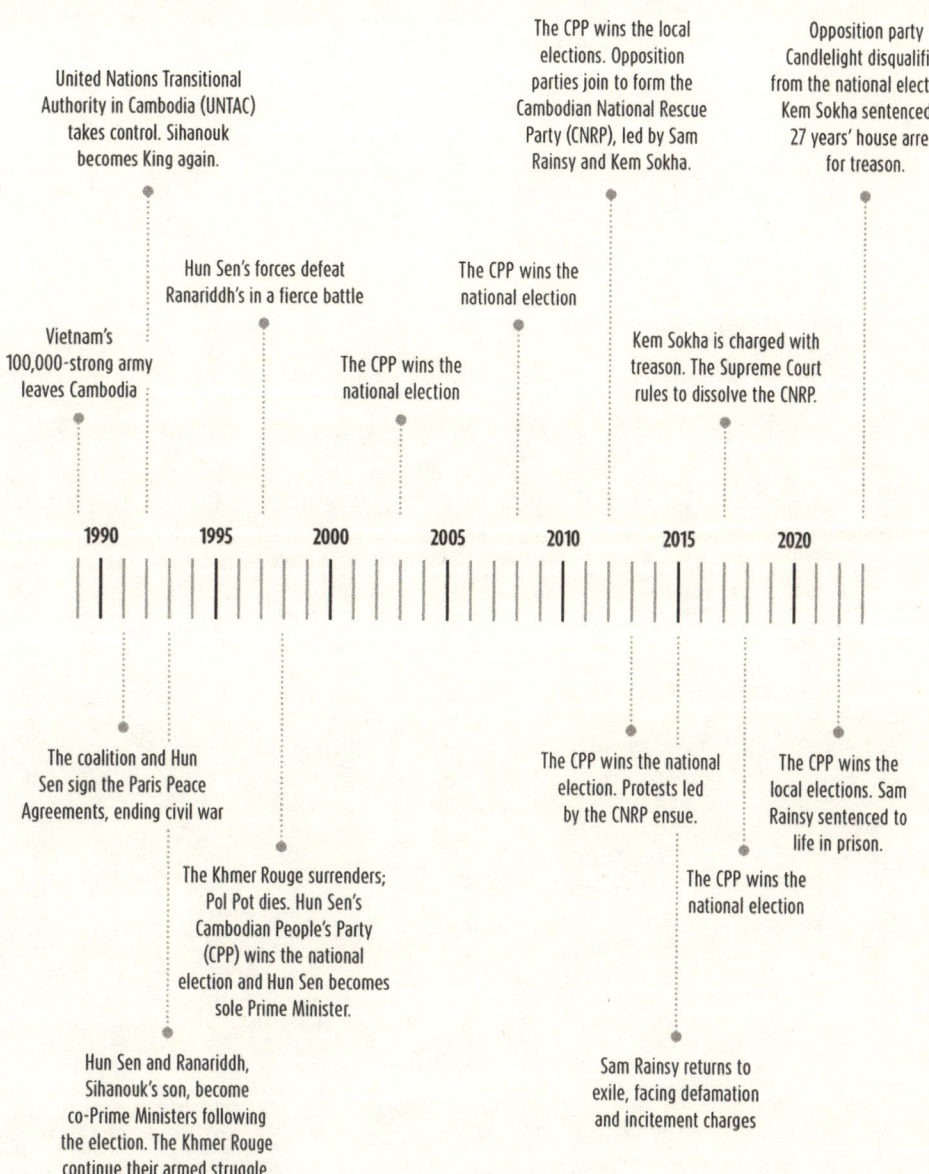

THE PEOPLE YOU'LL MEET
(IN ORDER OF APPEARANCE)

Neary: worked for a charity supporting people with land rights issues

May Titthara: *The Phnom Penh Post* journalist; *Khmer Times* editor; friend of Chut Wutty

Chut Wutty: prominent environmental campaigner

Phorn Bopha: *Cambodia Daily* journalist

Hun Sen: Prime Minister and leader of the Cambodian People's Party (CPP)

Kimsorn: CPP local organiser in Banteay Meanchey

Kannitha: former colleague; married mother of two; long-term supporter of Sam Rainsy

Sam Rainsy: founder and President of the Cambodian National Rescue Party (CNRP)

Kem Sokha: founder and Deputy President of the CNRP

Rotha and Soveacha: friends who joined the CNRP's 2013 election campaign

Chamroeun: joined the CNRP's 2013 election campaign; previously worked in government; married father of two

Rithisak: grew up in a refugee camp during the civil war of the 1980s

Leap: senior official for an international organisation in Cambodia

Sophal: CNRP supporter; neighbour of Kimsorn

Ou Ritthy: founder of Politikoffee, a weekly forum that discusses politics and youth-related issues; former election observer for the Committee for Free and Fair Elections in Cambodia; friend of Kem Ley

Kunthea: garment factory worker; trade union official; married mother of three

Channa: garment factory worker; married mother of two

Rong Chhun: President of the Cambodian Independent Teachers' Association; President of the Cambodian Confederation of Unions

Soeng Sen Karuna: human rights worker, Cambodian Human Rights and Development Association (ADHOC)

Hang Puthea: National Election Committee member; former Executive Director, Neutral and Impartial Committee for Free and Fair Elections in Cambodia

Dav Ansan: Under-Secretary of State in the Ministry of Industry, Science and Technology; Central Committee Member of the Union of the Youth Federations of Cambodia

Maly: former university lecturer now working in social development; studied in Australia

Sreyleak: midwife who studied abroad; husband owns a garage

Phirun: senior civil servant

Nay Vanda: imprisoned ADHOC human rights worker

Ny Sokha: imprisoned ADHOC human rights worker

Yeang Sothearin: *Radio Free Asia* journalist

Kem Ley: prominent political commentator; founder of the Grassroots Democratic Party

Sin Rozeth: Commune Council Chief in O'Char, Battambang, CNRP

Chen Sokngeng: Commune Council Chief in Sala Kamreuk, Siem Reap, CNRP; youngest Commune Council Chief in Cambodia

Huy Vannak: President of the Union of Journalist Federations of Cambodia; Secretary of State, Ministry of Interior

Chea Chiv: Battambang Province Leader, CNRP

Kosal: director in a government ministry; member of the CPP

Khemera: director in a government ministry; member of the CPP

Yeng Virak: President, Grassroots Democratic Party

Davuth: leader of a charity; CPP supporter

Channary: CPP supporter

Chang Phalla: Commune Council Chief in Pdao Chum, Kampong Thom, Candlelight Party

Yab Yot: Commune Council Chief in Kraya, Kampong Thom, Candlelight Party

PART I
2013–2015

'Drop by drop, the bucket fills.'
តក់ៗពេញបំពង់

Cambodian proverb

CHAPTER 1
CHANGE AT THE CORNER

It was early July 2013, and hints of freshness had returned after Cambodia's hot season. Dusk was turning to night as Neary and I ordered handmade noodles at a busy intersection near Phnom Penh's riverside.

The streets closest to the river belong to tourists, indulging their desires for cheap beer, seedy nightlife and local women, but just 400 metres from the river is the old centre of Phnom Penh, where Cambodians live amid tightly packed apartments, crowded markets and restaurants serving an array of rice and noodle dishes. There, as in much of Phnom Penh, the streets buzz with an energy that courses through the city.

Neary nodded for us to settle into our bowls of noodles and began telling me the story of the night she was born.

It was February 1980 and Phnom Penh had been relatively peaceful since the murderous Khmer Rouge regime lost control of Cambodia the year before. But on this night, the crack of gunfire was heard in the moonlit sky. Neary's mother, panting and heaving in labour, froze. *No*, she thought to herself, *the savage Khmer Rouge cannot be retaking the capital just as my baby is entering the world.*

The terror the Khmer Rouge had wrought, beyond the imagination of most, still tormented Neary's mother. She had slaved in work camps for four years, seeing friends and relatives slowly expire. She lived while around her two million died.

The gunfire continued and so did the cries of Neary's mother. Her little girl was about to be born and not even the prospect of the Khmer Rouge's return could stop that. It was only afterwards, when cradling Neary in her arms, that she realised the gunfire was not the Khmer Rouge, but her neighbours shooting wildly into the air to celebrate Chinese New Year.

The Khmer Rouge never did retake Phnom Penh, but their ghosts lingered in Neary's early years. Her family's small apartment looked onto the notorious S-21 prison, now a museum of genocide. Cambodians still fear that spirits haunt this place, causing nightmares that make people twist in their sleep and dogs howl at shadows long into the night. Neary never seemed afraid of demons, though, or even the darker side of human nature. A diminutive woman, her rounded cheeks, wide grin and soft brown eyes draw warmth from whoever she is with. Perhaps because she was born in a time of pain, Neary grew up determined to help people find peace.

By 2013, Neary was working for a charity that supported communities whose land had been taken by wealthy tycoons with powerful connections. She would travel down mud roads in far-flung villages and see children in rags living in wooden shacks. She would hear stories of violent evictions and court rulings denying local people claim to land they had lived on for decades as Vietnamese loggers and rapacious rubber companies tore up ancient forests. Neary often worked away from home in remote areas for days at a time, and with every homecoming her narrow shoulders seemed more sloped. Sometimes, in the evening, we would hire a boat to sail down the Mekong or sit in a rooftop bar to feel the breeze, as much to cleanse Neary from her trip as to cool us from the heat.

A division was being carved between rural Cambodia and bustling Phnom Penh. While the capital was modernising, with air-conditioned cafés and free wi-fi, most rural Cambodians lived without electricity and measured wealth by whether they owned a cow. The inequality was becoming stark as more young people were moving from rural Cambodia to find work in the capital. Locals gaped as corrupt officials and business tycoons flaunted their Lexus cars, gauche jewellery and disdain for the rules that others had to abide by. The rich were lording it over the masses.

Sitting back in our plastic chairs, noodles consumed, Neary and I watched the life around us. Twenty-somethings whizzed past, enjoying last moments of freedom before returning home to their families. The most popular motorbike – or moto, as they are known in Cambodia – is the small Honda Dream 125, upon which two, three or even four young people will ride together. Driving abreast, groups of friends chatted about the latest Preap Sovath song, where they were going to eat, or their new smartphone.

We began to hear shouts from young moto riders as they crossed the intersection – one would shout something and another would quickly respond. I couldn't quite catch what they were saying amid the revving engines and beeping horns. I looked to Neary for help. Smiling, she leaned over and whispered what they were shouting: 'Change.'

Just a few minutes later, we saw a small convoy of motos, maybe five or ten, driving through the streets. The lead moto had a passenger carrying a loudspeaker, who shouted *'Doe, min doe?'* ('Change, no change?') The motos following yelled *'Doe!'* in response.

It did not need to be explained what change they wanted. The national election was only a few weeks away and these young people wanted a new government.

The waitress in the restaurant stepped out to see what the shouting was about. She spoke to Neary, releasing her anger at the ruling party and the corruption within it. She was incensed by crooked officials with their big cars who would talk down to her as a lowly restaurant worker. She was proud that she earned her money while they had stolen theirs. I had never heard such open dissent about the government, especially between two strangers, in Cambodia. I was used to the hesitation that my colleagues would show when we ate lunch together, only risking talk of politics in hushed tones.

Every lunchtime, my male colleagues and I would eat together at the same restaurant on a street corner. It had plastic tables and chairs on bare earth, set around a giant tree that reached through the tin roof. Our female colleagues would usually go home or eat lunch they had brought with them in the office. Conversation was usually in Khmer, but my colleagues would take the time to explain in English if I struggled to follow. Generally they would talk about work and family life, but sometimes they would talk about what was happening in the news. I noticed that whenever they spoke about politics they would do so quietly, with their heads bowed, looking down at their food. There was an air of discontent, but the overriding sense was of resignation. They didn't like the taste of what the government was serving, but they didn't see any way of changing it. Instead, it burned in their throat.

CHAPTER 2
INJUSTICE BURNS

May Titthara was in primary school when his uncle returned from the Soviet Union to visit his family. Sitting in the corner of his small wooden home, Titthara heard the adults talk, but his eyes were fixed on his uncle's leather messenger bag. He had never seen one before, let alone the camera sticking out the top of it. Titthara, surrounded by rice farmers, could not help but ask what it was his uncle did. Titthara had no idea what a journalist was, but staring at that bag and camera, he knew that he wanted to become one too.

Titthara arrived in Phnom Penh after graduating from high school, a rare achievement in his rural province of Svay Rieng during the 1990s. University after university rejected him, though, so Titthara enrolled in a certificate-level course in journalism and devoured Cambodia's English-language newspapers every night after class.

'At first, I don't know how to write,' Titthara explained. 'I always read newspapers from the US, and *The Cambodia Daily* and *The Phnom Penh Post*, so I learnt to write in the Western way. If I write in Khmer, people think I am crazy. My style is like a foreigner's way. Use a lot of colour to describe everything – you don't need to use a picture.'

Titthara's style soon attracted *The Phnom Penh Post*, and he ended up becoming their star reporter.

'I love investigative journalism a lot. The first time, I never know how to write investigative [stories],' he said. 'I just write breaking news and then a lot of feature stories. I work with foreigners and they said that I did a lot of investigative journalism. I said "No, I don't know," but it seems I was.'

Titthara's investigations took him on a journey to Thailand in 2008, where he uncovered a network trafficking Cambodian men to work as fishermen slaves there. The small boy besotted by a camera was now the winner of an Asian journalism award, although he had kept his floppy brown hair and plump cheeks. Four years later, Titthara was one of the few journalists to report Human Rights Watch's allegation that Cambodia's leaders were protecting military and police officials guilty of 300 politically motivated killings in the preceding twenty years. Titthara's opening line read: 'Systematic extra-judicial killings were directed and executed for decades by death squads established under Prime Minister Hun Sen's regime and run by men who are now some of the highest-ranking members of government, a report released yesterday alleges.'[1]

Titthara became indignant as he explained what happened next, his high-pitched voice rising further. 'On local TV, they say I am not educated and name me [as opposition to the government]. I had two letters from the Prime Minister's cabinet and I get one from Mok Chito.'

Mok Chito is a high-ranking general in the Ministry of Interior who was identified in Titthara's article as being involved in multiple killings. After being shown the article, an enraged Chito allegedly stood at his desk bellowing, 'Who is May Titthara?!?' Officials were sent to visit the upstart journalist. 'His staff came to my office showing me a gun,' recalled Titthara, 'and a [man on a] moto a followed me around all of the time.'

Needing to lie low, Titthara returned home to his parents in rural Svay Rieng. They did not even know he was a journalist until they saw him being criticised on television. Titthara was not to be deterred for long, though, and he quickly broke another story in 2012 that would reverberate around Cambodia.

It was February, at the start of Cambodia's hot season, when the Governor of the city of Bavet stepped out of an expensive car wearing a khaki police-style uniform, raised his gun and started shooting into the crowd of protesting garment factory workers. Young women scattered in panic. One was shot in the back as she ran away, suffering multiple injuries as the bullet burst out of her side. A second woman was hit in the arm, and a bullet tore through the lung of a third, just missing her heart, causing her to vomit blood. The Governor shot four more times before his gun jammed. Flanked by a police officer and a bodyguard, he jumped into a waiting black Toyota Camry and sped off.[2]

That morning, the three women, aged between eighteen and twenty-three, had been demonstrating along with 6000 other garment factory workers in the hope of increasing their monthly wage of $66. They wanted an extra 50 cents a day for food and $10 per month to cover costs of getting to the out-of-town factory. The factory workers had been in a desperate mood after the government advised companies to give only a third of what the strikers wanted, so they hurled rocks at the factory, smashing its windows.[3]

Bavet is in Svay Rieng province, and May Titthara immediately set off to report on the event. The city was swirling with eyewitness reports that the shooter was the Governor, but no warrant for his arrest was issued, despite there being CCTV footage of the incident.[4] Through a relationship with an official, Titthara obtained leaked documents implicating the Governor, but he was still unable to name him publicly as the shooter.

As the speculation over the incident intensified, the Minister of Interior, Sar Kheng, often seen as an internal competitor to Prime Minister Hun Sen, advised the media that there was enough evidence to charge a suspect.[5] He stopped short of naming the suspect, but Titthara was determined to draw it out of him.

Titthara learned that Sar Kheng would be attending a conference at the opulent colonial-era Le Royal Hotel in Phnom Penh and found his car outside waiting for the event to finish. Titthara asked Sar Kheng's driver which side of the car the Minister would get into, and Titthara stood there, on the right side, waiting to ask his question. 'So, I plan to ask him a straight question, yes or no. He comes out, I just ask him yes-no question – I know that he will not explain. "I hear people say that the Governor opened fire on the garment factory workers: is it true?" He said yes and then got inside.'

Titthara had his story, and *The Phnom Penh Post* could tell all Cambodia what most in Bavet already knew: in front of multiple eye-witnesses, the Governor had shot three young women who were running away from him in broad daylight.[6]

Rather than arrest him, police reportedly visited the three women in hospital, offering them up to $1000 – more than an annual salary – in return for not filing a complaint, but they all refused. One family member said that the officials 'looked down on my sister's life like a chicken'.[7]

The extent of injuries suffered and Titthara's reporting of the mounting evidence increased pressure on police to act, but the Governor's political connections were strong. Over ten months, the courts repeatedly summoned the three victims to provide evidence of their complaint while the Governor remained absent.

Eventually, the court decided that the case would not proceed to trial, leaving the three women devastated. One of them, Nuth Sakhorn, could not comprehend how the Governor 'shot us like animals but is not guilty', while another, Buot Chenda, commented, 'The intention of court is to release the guilty suspect. It is so difficult in our country between poor and powerful people.'[8] Titthara saw that locals simmered with rage: 'People, they got angry. All workers in Svay Rieng, they are angry. During that time, if they saw him [the Governor] in Bavet town, they would kill him.'

The women now feared for their safety, due to the police intimidation.[9] Cambodia's Community Legal Education Centre funded an appeal, but the cause seemed lost as witnesses were scared into silence and dozens of police and local authorities defended the now former Governor, proclaiming his innocence.[10] Only one man refused to bend.

Long Phorn was a local deputy police chief who told the court that he was standing seven metres away when he saw the former Governor shoot at the workers. Titthara explained that Long Phorn, having sworn to tell the truth in court, feared karmic retribution if he lied. Phorn withstood police officers following him, watching his house and threatening his neighbours and family. He could not be swayed even when challenged in court by the former Governor himself.[11] Phorn had dared to do what few others thought possible, and Titthara was full of admiration.

A few weeks after breaking that story, Titthara was deep in Cambodia's Cardamom Mountains, investigating illegal logging. Titthara had met a former employee of Conservation International who claimed he had proof that forestry administration and military police officials, whose salaries were funded by Conservation International, were taking bribes to allow large-scale illegal logging.

In the small village of O'Som in Cambodia's west, Titthara saw a forest he described as 'completely gutted ... [only] stumps and eroded soil in a charred, barren landscape'.[12] The rosewood trees had all gone, as had the *m'reach preu* (yellow vine) tree, whose bark can produce safrole, which is used in pesticides and methamphetamines.

Viewing photographs of a ledger recording bribes, Titthara determined that forestry rangers had received $5757 in one month for allowing illegal loggers to pass – a sum five times the average annual income for a Cambodian. A local villager confessed to Titthara that he used to work in a factory that would send ten trucks of rosewood to Vietnam each day. The villager lived in the factory, along with seventy other workers – they were not permitted to leave for fear they would speak too freely. Titthara uncovered a web of corruption, which included the chief ranger, who had 'lost' illegally felled rosewood confiscated by volunteer patrols. The rosewood was worth more than $10,000, and local people said that a company called Timber Green was buying it.[13]

In the dark of night, Titthara watched a policeman at a checkpoint shine a flashlight at a timber truck and then allow it to pass unimpeded. Titthara made notes while the local driver he had hired began to wonder who his new employer was. Interrupting Titthara, the driver asked him why he had visited so many people and was writing things down. Misjudging the situation, Titthara explained his investigation, which caused the driver to explode: 'Do you know who I am?! My brother is the police chief here!' Titthara was sure that he would be killed in O'Som that night.

Not knowing what to do as the driver raced off, Titthara phoned one of his best friends, Chut Wutty, Cambodia's foremost environmental campaigner. 'I said, "I think that I will die." He said that I should go to buy a new SIM card and put it in my phone.' Titthara followed Wutty's instructions. 'I go to my guesthouse. I speak to the boy, he was a ladyboy, at reception. It is dark, night – I don't have time to ride anywhere. So I give him $10 and swap from Room 1 to 2 and tell him that if people ask for me, tell them that I have left.'

Titthara then packed his bag and walked out of the hotel to show anybody watching that he was leaving. Having crossed the road and walked out of sight, he doubled back, entering the hotel through a small back entrance. Titthara sat breathlessly in Room 2, listening while a group of six policemen arrived with guns to search Room 1.

'I can hear them, they do not check number 2,' explained Titthara. 'The ladyboy said, "Relax, he is not here. He is gone." They do not believe him, though. So they go out and buy beer and sit outside at the front. They drink, drink, drink. And then about 11pm, they leave. I try to talk to the ladyboy. I say that I need to leave and ask if he can get me a moto. I cannot go back to Koh Kong past O'Som, so I need to go the jungle way from Koh Kong to Pursat. I reach Pursat early morning, around 6.00am or 7.00am. I give that moto-taxi driver $200. He saved my life.' Titthara mimicked stuffing all the notes from his wallet in the hand of the taxi driver. His infectious laugh returned at his own good fortune. 'Lucky me! Even Wutty, he is so scared, he could not reach me. But the next day I call him, tell him that I survived.'

Titthara and Wutty, despite their contrasting personalities, had formed a close bond after Titthara had accompanied him to investigate illegal logging. 'Sometimes we don't have food, sometimes just one small thing to share. I don't know why he is so brave. In the jungle he had nothing and he tried to block the loggers. He look like the soldier because he had been a soldier. He was very strict. When with him, you do not drink. His activists –

no drinking. And when we reach the time – go! "It is time, we need to go!" For me that is fine. He never drinks, but he used to drink with me one time.' Titthara smiled at corrupting the disciplined, single-minded Wutty.

⁕

Chut Wutty had been campaigning since 2001 to preserve Cambodia's rapidly disappearing forests, becoming a thorn in the side of loggers and complicit government officials. His unflinching gaze was accentuated by high, sharp cheekbones. Often wearing a wide-brimmed cowboy hat, a rarity in Cambodia, Wutty resembled the fearsome gunslinger played by Lee Van Cleef in *The Good, The Bad and The Ugly*.

In 2000, just under half of Cambodia was covered in trees, with huge tracts of thick, dense forest that was home to elephants, tigers, bears, rare monkeys and giant ibis. Cambodia's 2001 *Land Law* enabled the government to lease state-owned land to private companies for up to ninety-nine years. By 2011, the government had leased 2 million hectares of land for economic development concessions and a further 1.9 million hectares for mining developments. Over one-fifth of the country had been leased, with millions paid that didn't always reach the national accounts.[14]

Developers quickly set about logging the prized hardwood forests. One tycoon reputedly earned $227 million from one concession alone, selling rosewood to Vietnam and China at $20,000 per cubic metre.[15] Cambodia's forests were disappearing at an alarming rate. Sixty-five thousand hectares were cleared in 2009, 125,000 hectares in 2010, and the same in 2011. Nowhere was safe as the government reclassified protected national parks for development. Even a wildlife sanctuary was 90 per cent deforested.[16]

It wasn't just the trees that were being cut down; lives were altered too. Half a million people were forcibly moved from where they farmed, hunted and gathered.[17] In deals with military leaders, soldiers were employed by private companies to raze villages and throw people off their land. A fourteen-year-old girl was killed by machine-gun fire as troops stormed one village in the province of Kratie, otherwise known for majestic sunsets over the Mekong and sightings of rare river dolphins.[18]

Wutty led protests all over the country. In April 2012, he took two young journalists from *The Cambodia Daily*, Phorn Bopha and Olesia Plohkii, to witness illegal logging in the forests of Cambodia's Cardamom Mountains. Wutty suspected Timber Green, the same company Titthara had investigated, of illegally logging yellow vine trees and warned the journalists to move quickly so that they could get in and out before trouble arrived.

Wutty and the journalists entered the forest, seeing stacks of yellow vine logs, and began to take photos and speak to villagers. They returned to their car after ten minutes, but two military policemen and a Timber Green security guard soon arrived, all carrying AK-47 machine guns.

The military police and security guard, wearing soldiers' khaki, demanded that Wutty and the journalists go with them to meet their boss. Wutty refused. The men became angry and confiscated one of the cameras, accidentally striking Bopha in the face as they did. Tempers frayed and a scuffle broke out. The men took a second camera, which they began inspecting, allowing Wutty and the journalists to jump in the car. Tragically, the engine spluttered and failed to start.

Plokhii, a Canadian, got out to jumpstart the car, but each time Wutty started the ignition, a soldier, with gun pointed, would reach in and turn the key. Finally, the soldier relented and the engine motored into life. Wutty called Plokhii to close the bonnet and get in quickly. Trembling, she walked around to the front passenger seat. As she opened the door, she heard the crack of shots and threw herself to the ground. When she looked up, Wutty was slumped in the driver's seat, with blood seeping from his stomach. His cowboy hat lay on the red dirt next to the car.[19] A soldier also lay dead in front of the car.

Plokhii and Bopha tried in vain to save Wutty's life before looking up to see themselves surrounded by soldiers who would not let them leave. A nearby villager gave Bopha his phone so she could call *The Cambodia Daily*'s editor, and she wrote her editor's phone number on her stomach so people knew who to contact if she was killed.[20] The two young journalists watched as more soldiers arrived, one of them running towards his colleague slain in the dirt and weeping at his side. Nearby, Wutty's body lay alone.

Neither journalist saw who fired the shots, and contradictory versions were floated by authorities. In each version, it was the dead solider, In Rattana, who killed Wutty, possibly inadvertently, and then either killed himself or was killed by a Timber Green security guard, the son of a former forestry administration chief.[21]

Police investigations proceeded slowly and without information being shared with Wutty's family. When the court finally opened on the security guard's trial, the judge astonished everybody by declaring that the investigation into Chut Wutty's death had ended three months earlier because the presumed perpetrator, In Rattana, was dead. The family's anger was fuelled by their belief that it was not In Rattana who was responsible for the killing.[22]

I asked Titthara if he thought Wutty's death resulted from a tragic escalation of unplanned events. Titthara let out a long 'Noooooo,' adamant that I not acquit the system that killed him. 'I don't think it was a situation just out of control, because they make a crackdown.' His expression turned serious as he sought to convince me. 'During that time, one of the people in the court – a prosecutor but he loves Wutty – he tells Wutty, "Don't go to the forest. They plan something." So [Wutty] stayed in Phnom Penh and he had to use his phone to organise the activists. Talk to them, tell them what to do. He survived. But two months later … So I think that thing that happened to him is not accident. Not accident.'

Hundreds of people flocked to Chut Wutty's funeral and many others went to the site of his killing, as Cambodians mourned a man who had inspired city dwellers and rural farmers alike to care for Cambodia's forests. Titthara ruminated, 'I find people who work with nature … I feel that they fall in love. Even though my home is very small, I try to plant many trees now. Wutty did not care about money. He could have been rich and got a lot of money from loggers. So I'm very proud of him.'

During lunchtime conversations at my workplace, a colleague would quietly mention the shootings at Bavet or the killing of Chut Wutty, to which my other colleagues would murmur their dismay. During these brief exchanges about politics, they would hesitate before saying the Prime Minister's name or avoid it altogether. People acted as though the government had an ear in every conversation, and some said that through their network of informers they did. You would look at the man sitting at the table next to you, check over your shoulder and then inch your head closer to whisper.

CHAPTER 3

THE MAN IN CHARGE

Hun Sen peered at his watch. It was 2.00 am and he, along with four of his most trusted soldiers, were taking their first nervous steps into Vietnam. Days earlier, dozens of their Khmer Rouge comrades had been spirited away as Pol Pot purged in a paranoid frenzy, fearing enemies within. Hun Sen, commander of Khmer Rouge forces at the Vietnamese border, had failed to wrestle disputed land from Cambodia's historic enemies and knew that his own arrest was imminent.

The five men trod carefully through the dark but never encountered the Vietnamese border troops they expected. As the sun rose across the rice paddies, Hun Sen ordered his men to dispense with their weapons and keep walking, hoping to stumble across villagers who could help them. They eventually met some workers returning from a rubber plantation who took them to their village office, where soldiers detained them for questioning, not believing that Sen, aged only twenty-five, could be the commander of thousands of men.

Sen and his men were not the only Khmer Rouge defectors who had sought Vietnamese refuge. They were also joined by Cambodians who had been in exile since before the Khmer Rouge had seized power in 1975. Together, they tried to persuade their Vietnamese hosts to rid Cambodia of the murderous Khmer Rouge, but Vietnam's leaders were hesitant. It was only after the Khmer Rouge launched a swathe of attacks killing hundreds of Vietnamese villagers that an infuriated Vietnamese army chief finally met Sen to hear his proposals for how Vietnam could help overthrow Pol Pot.[1]

It took another year of planning and prompting, during which there were more Khmer Rouge attacks, before Vietnam fully committed to overthrowing Pol Pot. On 25 December 1978, a massive Vietnamese army of 100,000 troops invaded Cambodia, assisted by a much smaller Cambodian force, with Sen as one of its leaders. Within two weeks, the Khmer Rouge had fled to the mountain jungles and a new Vietnamese-backed government was installed in Phnom Penh, with the youthful Sen appointed as Foreign Minister. Hun Sen was still only thirty-two years old when, in January 1985, following the death of his predecessor, the Cambodian Communist Party and its Vietnamese backers selected him to become Prime Minister.

The new Prime Minister did not govern a united country, however. He controlled only 80 per cent of the nation, despite the ongoing presence of 100,000 Vietnamese soldiers to support him. Throughout the 1980s, Cambodia was beset by civil war, with Hun Sen on one side, backed by Vietnam and the Soviet Union, and a coalition of Cambodia's former King and the Khmer Rouge on the other, backed by America and China. Western governments and China refused to recognise Sen as Cambodia's Prime Minister, instead viewing him as a Vietnamese stooge – a caricature known for ill-fitting suits and a crudely made fake eye that replaced the one lost fighting for the Khmer Rouge.[2] America and China's manoeuvring meant that, throughout the 1980s, the UN officially recognised a coalition of the Khmer Rouge and former King Sihanouk as Cambodia's official government.

It was in the home of the French Ambassador to Angola that the first steps towards peace were taken. The Ambassador's wife was Cambodian and knew that Sen was visiting Angola – in the early 1980s, it was a communist country too. Knowing that her husband could not engage in formal diplomatic talks with Sen, she invited him and his colleagues to dinner, during which she asked if he would agree to peace talks with Sihanouk, who was being supported by the West.

With the unravelling of the Soviet Union and cash-strapped Vietnam wanting to withdraw its soldiers, Sen was willing to talk, as he knew that Cambodia needed the support of the West to rebuild his devastated country. The former King, much loved in Cambodia for having won independence from France in the 1950s, was not so inclined, refusing to talk with Sen until his Vietnamese backers withdrew all of their soldiers. The Ambassador's wife persevered; in late 1987, she heard that Sihanouk would be visiting France. Now working in Paris as a medical doctor, she surprised Sihanouk as he landed at Charles de Gaulle airport and persuaded him to meet her the following day at his opulent hotel. They talked continuously, not stopping for lunch, as he peppered her with questions about Hun Sen and the situation inside Cambodia. After six hours, Sihanouk was satisfied, sat back and told her that she could tell Hun Sen they should meet.[3]

By the late 1980s, Hun Sen, whose initial salary as Foreign Minister was ten kilograms of rice and six kilograms of maize, had become by many accounts 'an outstanding politician' with deeply informed views on international affairs.[4] After the demise of his communist patrons – Vietnam withdrew its soldiers in 1989, as the Soviet Union could no longer provide support – Hun Sen visited America, where he impressed congressmen, the media and government officials with his 'poise', 'aplomb' and ability to hold court in meetings.[5] *The New York Times* reported that the 'Vietnamese puppet' had become 'an articulate and unintimidated prime minister'.[6]

One journalist who interviewed Sen at his home outside Phnom Penh found him playing his weekly game of Cambodian chess with friends. Cambodian chess, called *ouk*, is even more ponderous than international chess. The queen can only move one square at a time; the bishop is similarly limited. Pawns cannot move two spaces on a first move, nor can they perform en passant. Losing at Cambodian chess is akin to coming face-to-face with a python – you don't know the danger you are in until you feel the pressure tightening inexorably, and you find yourself unable to move. Sen told the journalist that he was 'happiest when playing chess'. Watching his games, she noticed that he never lost.[7]

King Sihanouk and Prime Minister Sen finally clinked glasses and inked the Paris Peace Agreements in 1991, which allowed the UN to hold an election to decide who should rule Cambodia. The United Nations Transitional Authority in Cambodia (UNTAC), with more than 20,000 military and administrative personnel from forty-six countries, officially administered Cambodia during 1992 and 1993 and was responsible for organising the election. However, while UNTAC's Tower of Babel tried to coordinate itself while administering a country whose language it did not speak, the government bureaucracy, police and military, established by and owing loyalty to Hun Sen, continued to run the day-to-day affairs of Cambodia.

Hun Sen's party, the Cambodian People's Party (CPP), prepared for the upcoming elections by removing statues of Lenin from classrooms and public buildings, disavowing the Vietnamese-tainted communism and embracing the liberal, multi-party democracy that the UN had promised Cambodians.[8] Having been Prime Minister for eight years and boasting a party membership and resources that dwarfed all other parties, Hun Sen was widely expected to win the election.

His main competition was the royalist FUNCINPEC party, headed by one of King Sihanouk's sons, Prince Ranariddh. 'FUNCINPEC' is a

French acronym of National United Front for an Independent, Neutral, Peaceful and Cooperative Cambodia. Ranariddh benefitted greatly from his father's popularity, and his party won fifty-eight seats while Hun Sen's CPP came second, with fifty-one. The election was meant to create a universally accepted government but, in a 120-seat National Assembly, FUNCINPEC had fallen three seats short of a majority.

Hun Sen had lost but he wasn't beaten, and the world was to witness how he reacted when his authority was threatened. Hun Sen rejected the election result, attacking the UN's administration of the elections and arguing that ballot boxes had been tampered with. Allies of Hun Sen then declared that seven provinces would secede from Cambodia if FUNCINPEC formed the government, and forced UN peacekeepers to withdraw from these areas at gunpoint.[9]

Seeing an opportunity to increase his influence as King sitting above two quarrelling factions, Sihanouk proposed that Ranariddh and Hun Sen serve as co-Prime Ministers in a coalition government. They both agreed – Ranariddh somewhat reluctantly – and Sen ordered the secessionists to stand down, making Cambodia the only country to ever have two prime ministers at the same time.[10]

There is an old Cambodian proverb that one mountain cannot have two tigers, and neither Sen nor Ranariddh were content with the compromise of sharing power.[11] Both parties retained their own armed forces as well as controlling different parts of official government forces. The atmosphere in Cambodia was one of mistrust and competition, played out in a country where everyone in power had guns and tanks.

CPP and FUNCINPEC forces clashed in February 1997, and in May the CPP confiscated a large shipment of arms destined for FUNCINPEC. Tensions rose when two FUNCINPEC soldiers were killed by the CPP in a gunfight, and both sides began to manoeuvre troops in and around Phnom Penh.[12] Parents stockpiled food and banned children from going outside, while others rushed to stay with family in the countryside.[13]

Hun Sen was counselled by Chea Sim, President of the CPP and the National Assembly, to approach FUNCINPEC with restraint and in a spirit of conciliation. This advice was widely supported by the CPP Central Committee, which chose to elect more of Chea Sim's supporters to the committee, rejecting many of Hun Sen's nominees as the party divided along two factions.[14] Hun Sen chose to ignore the older Sim, and pushed for the removal of Ranariddh's parliamentary immunity so that he could be tried in a military court for smuggling arms. Both sides hunkered down, preparing troops and devising battle plans. Conflict became inevitable; it was just a matter of who would emerge from the fray alive.[15]

The morning after government officials were strangely absent from an American Independence Day celebration at the US Embassy, fierce fighting broke out at FUNCINPEC's military base near Phnom Penh's airport. Hun Sen was dealt a blow when Chea Sim and his supporters, which included the military chief, refused to mobilise regiments under their command. Sen managed to persuade individual generals to rouse their soldiers but still went into battle with only half of the CPP's troops.

For the next two days, T-55 tanks roamed the streets and mortars shelled buildings as Hun Sen crushed the ineptly commanded FUNCINPEC forces. FUNCINPEC's Secretary of State for the Interior was shot dead in the grounds of the Interior Ministry, and Ranariddh's top military adviser was allegedly executed in Hun Sen's personal compound after having his tongue ripped out. *The Washington Post* reported that forty senior FUNCINPEC officials were shot in the head, execution-style. Hundreds more were killed during the fighting, including four who were displayed on the streets with their eyes gouged out.[16]

When the dust settled, it was Hun Sen who was left standing as the leader of Cambodia. FUNCINPEC had been destroyed and Chea Sim, fearing Hun Sen would turn his forces on him, conceded that Hun Sen could appoint new leaders, ones devoutly loyal to him, in the military and police.[17] Sim remained as President of the CPP but tensions within the party continued to increase as Sen's power grew. Then, in 2004, under pressure over his refusal to sign a law that would make it easier for Sen to control appointments to key positions in government, Sim's house was surrounded with dozens of armed police to force the ageing man onto a plane to Bangkok. Once out of the country, Sim's deputy signed the law, marking Sim's final demise and Sen's ascent to absolute power.[18]

Hun Sen had come a long way from a poor, rural upbringing, but it is a past he never forgets. He prides himself on having risen from Cambodia's soil and has described his political philosophy as based on 'knowing reality', mulling that it may take the rest of his life to 'get people out of this poverty'.[19] A colleague of mine, Chhay, told me that the only reason he survived the Khmer Rouge regime, unlike his parents and all his siblings, was because he had a strong spoon. During communal mealtimes, he and many other young children would be trying to eat from the same bowl and would clank their spoons against each other as they fought for scraps of food. Some children had thin metal spoons that bent or even snapped in the fight, but five-year-old Chhay's spoon was resolute. It was because of this spoon that he survived, and others became skeletons in the dirt. This was the reality that Hun Sen knew his countrymen had endured. While foreign governments and aid agencies wanted to promote human rights, a free press, an independent judiciary and a strong civil society – trappings of democracy – Hun Sen decided that before all else, people needed stronger spoons.[20]

After UNTAC, foreign governments, primarily America and Japan and others through the UN, poured billions of dollars into Cambodia, enabling the Cambodian government to embark on a huge infrastructure program. In the 1980s, classes were often taught in the shade of the village's biggest tree, but by 2012 there were over 11,000 schools.[21] Health centres, albeit rudimentary, were built around the country, and roads enabled villagers to access them, and schools, and markets, even during heavy rains of the wet season. The mighty Mekong was conquered in 2001 when a 1500-metre bridge, the first to traverse the river in Cambodia, was opened, enabling eastern and western Cambodia to be connected by road.

These physical emblems of development impressed Cambodians. America's International Republican Institute conducted eight surveys between 2006 and 2012 and 80 per cent of Cambodians consistently responded that Cambodia was heading in the right direction.[22] Chhay jokingly imitated his elderly in-laws effusing about progress under Hun Sen: 'Oh, so much better. In the past we have war, never have school, never have food, never have. Much better now – have pagoda!'[23] Cambodians, especially older ones, liked the spoons they were being given.

One man in awe of Cambodia's transformation was Phan Kimsorn, who lives on the outskirts of Sisophon town, near the Thai border, and has led CPP campaigning in his neighbourhood and surrounding area. Kimsorn has lived there since 1979, just after the Khmer Rouge government was overthrown, and remembers it being full of Vietnamese soldiers during the 1980s, protecting its residents from a surrounding countryside full of Khmer Rouge guerrillas. Now a major trading town, trucks rumble down the wide roads, kicking up clouds of dust, and thousands of motorbikes rev in the streets.

I met Kimsorn at his house, a traditional wooden dwelling on stilts with a recent concrete extension to add a ground floor. Behind the house were tall sugarcane plants that he sold to supplement his income as a moto-taxi driver and seller of second-hand motos. A few chickens, including an orange-brown cockerel, pecked at the ground around us. He was eager to talk about his support for Hun Sen's CPP, even missing a party meeting to do so, and screwed up his eyes in concentration when I was talking, before lighting up when it was his turn to speak.

'What are the things you like about Hun Sen?' I asked.

'Because during the Khmer Rouge period, no one except Hun Sen comes to rescue Cambodian people. We have to be grateful to him for having saved us.'

'Has he managed the country well?'

'Yes, development increases. Even bridges across the rivers have been constructed. Previously ... it was difficult to travel. And roads are also convenient. I can even go to Phnom Penh with safety at night time. That is why people like him.'

At that moment, he proudly whisked away a *krama* (Cambodian sarong) to reveal the family's colour television, proclaiming that everybody had one now.

Kimsorn deferred questions about what the government should do in the future, suggesting that such weighty considerations were above him but that Hun Sen knew what was right for the country.[24]

Kimsorn was not alone in trusting Hun Sen after the poverty rate halved in a decade. Most people in 2012 believed that the CPP was the best party for creating jobs, improving education, fighting crime, protecting the sacred monarchy and building roads.[25] Kimsorn was unconcerned by his own admission that, despite an overall lift in living standards, the divide between rich and poor had sharpened. For him, it was the natural order of things.

Hun Sen's dominance was not a natural outcome, however. During elections in the 1990s, the CPP machine played on the fear that many rural, uneducated Cambodians had of government authorities. The Village Chief, appointed by the CPP, would reportedly gather all voting cards, hold them for a few days, and then give them back, implying that some advanced technological magic had occurred that would enable authorities to know how they voted.[26] A more chilling tactic reported was for the Village Chief to ask villagers to pledge an oath of allegiance to the CPP and then drink a glass of water with a bullet in it. That same bullet, they were told, would later kill them if they did not vote as they had pledged.[27] During the 2012 local commune election, I was with a colleague, Kannitha, when we saw CPP officials going house to house. They would give money, food and *kramas* to people who in return would promise to vote for them. I asked Kannitha why certain houses were being passed by and she explained that opposition activists are cut off from the CPP's largesse. Indeed, villages that had the temerity to vote for the opposition at previous elections would find their roads remaining untarmacked and schools suffering disrepair as punishment for their failure to acquiesce.

As well as receiving gifts, villagers would be called to practise how to vote – understandable given the country's high illiteracy rates. But I was told that all participants would practise by voting for the CPP, never any other party.

Huge signs, emblazoned with 'the Cambodian People's Party', appeared on roads throughout the country advertising the schools, hospitals and pagodas that had been built, often with no mention of the aid money that contributed to these developments. Some schools were named after Hun Sen or other CPP leaders, reminding parents and students who to be grateful to as they were told that Hun Sen had built Cambodia. Teachers I knew, and indeed any person working for a government body or the public service, would be called to meetings during which their bosses would tell them that the CPP had saved Cambodia from the Khmer Rouge, bringing peace, stability and development, all of which would be at risk if the CPP wasn't in government.

By October 2012, following King Sihanouk's passing due to age and illness, Hun Sen had become embedded as the country's father figure and dominant authority. He enjoyed lecturing an assembled crowd, wagging his right forefinger to thrust home an argument, while adjusting his rectangular-shaped glasses with his other hand. Once slender, even wiry, at sixty he boasted a paunch that had grown in tandem with his power. Cambodia was still poor, but Hun Sen's suits were now immaculately tailored, and he owned mansions in every province of the country, with a wealth reported to be hundreds of millions of American dollars.[28] In those 2012 local elections I saw the CPP campaigning in, Sen won easily, meaning that the CPP controlled 97 per cent of all local commune councils as well as the National Assembly and the Senate.

The CPP's continued rise was not greeted with universal celebration, though – certainly not in Phnom Penh, where in the 2012 elections 30 per cent of people voted for the Sam Rainsy Party, even though its leader, Sam Rainsy, was in forced exile for fear of arrest or death.[29] The atmosphere in my office was muted, and my colleagues would pick at their lunch, saying little. I remember Kannitha being the most deflated, feeling let down by her compatriots. In possession of a quick mind, a quick wit and a quick tongue, she had worked full-time since returning to Cambodia from studying at an overseas university (working full-time is less usual for mothers in Cambodia), and it was she, not her husband, who took the family car to work. Kannitha was frustrated that people would sell their vote for a *krama*, some MSG or rice. She understood the pull of the CPP for older people, because it had defeated the Khmer Rouge, but she wanted people to care about what was happening in Cambodia now, not thirty-five years previously. She listened to the television despondently as Hun Sen, already the world's longest serving Prime Minister, talked about ruling for another thirty years.

CHAPTER 4
TO THE RESCUE

Sam Rainsy stepped onto a chair in the middle of Wat Botum park in Phnom Penh and began treating 200 of his followers to a tirade on corrupt judges whose scales of justice were tipped by bribes. It was only 8.30am but the humidity of Cambodia's hot season was already causing beads of sweat on his forehead to trickle into his eyes. Feeling faint, he cut his speech short and gave way to a mother of two whose house had been confiscated as part of an illegal land deal that a judge refused to annul unless she paid him. Caught in a flow of invective, neither she nor Rainsy noticed the ring of policemen collectively take a few steps back from the crowd. Moments later, she was upended from the chair as a blast tore through at the feet of Rainsy's supporters. Rainsy felt somebody push him in the back, forcing him to the ground just before another grenade exploded. Dazed and sandwiched between concrete paving and a prone body, he heard a woman shout to his wife, 'Your husband is dead! Your husband is dead!' The ground then shook with the explosions of two more grenades.

Rainsy rolled the heavy body away and saw the lifeless eyes of his loyal bodyguard staring skywards. He struggled to his feet, covered in blood and choking in the smoke, trying to make sense of the bodies strewn in front of him. One woman, lying beside a sugarcane juice cart where the third grenade had exploded, writhed in agony, both feet blown off. A thirteen-year-old boy, still clutching his protest sign, was pinned to the ground by shrapnel in his legs and arms.

One of Rainsy's security men saw a grenade-thrower run towards a nearby pagoda and sprinted after him. Rainsy's man shouted to soldiers outside the pagoda to stop him, but they let the thrower pass. The soldiers, members of Hun Sen's elite Bodyguard Unit, then pointed their guns at Rainsy's man. Dumbfounded, he came to a standstill and felt a whack to the back of his head that knocked him unconscious. The grenade-thrower, and his two accomplices, made it safely back to Hun Sen's compound near the pagoda. No arrests were made, despite sixteen people dying, including two children, and 150 being wounded.[1]

Four years earlier, in 1993, Sam Rainsy had been appointed Finance Minister by FUNCINPEC, but was sacked after opposing a corrupt land deal and publicly accusing Hun Sen and FUNCINPEC's Ranariddh of complicity in widescale illegal logging.[2] Thrown out of FUNCINPEC and ejected from Parliament, Rainsy decided to establish his own party, which, by the time of the grenade attack in 1997, was quickly garnering support among garment workers and the educated classes of Phnom Penh.

Rotha was the administrative manager where I worked and was often responsible for ordering the food we shared at lunchtimes. But it was not just ordering lunch that people trusted Rotha with; he was also given responsibility for taking care of the staff's mutual savings scheme. Given that people trusted Rotha more than they did banks, it was unsurprising that Rotha was drawn to the avowed integrity of Sam Rainsy. His family had supported Rainsy since he became Finance Minister, and Rotha began campaigning for the Sam Rainsy Party as a teenager in high school. During one of our lunchtime conversations, Rotha breathlessly told me that when Rainsy was Finance Minister he narrowly escaped machine-gun fire from illegal loggers whom he confronted after racing down the Mekong in a boat.[3] It was this willingness to sacrifice his own wellbeing for that of Cambodia's that made Rainsy, and not either Prime Minister, Cambodia's most popular politician when the first-ever opinion poll was conducted in 1994.[4]

Bookish in appearance, with Harry Potter–style glasses and an effete demeanour, Rainsy was born of the ruling class. His father was Deputy Prime Minister in the 1950s and his grandfather was President of the Royal Council of Cambodia before that. His family fell from grace in 1959, however, when his father fled Cambodia to escape execution for planning an opposition movement against Sihanouk, the then ruler of Cambodia. Afterwards, Rainsy's mother spent one year imprisoned in a cramped, dark cell and some family friends were killed. Rainsy and his four siblings were forced to live with their aunt in a wooden hut on the banks of the Mekong, deprived of all property and belongings. In 1965, Rainsy and his family were driven by police to the Vietnamese border and forced out of Cambodia at gunpoint.

Finding asylum in France, Rainsy was sixteen when his family arrived in Paris. Already fluent in French, due to France's colonial legacy in Cambodia, Rainsy completed high school and gained entrance to a prestigious university.

Supported by his devoted mother and older siblings, who worked long hours for a minimum wage, he studied economics at university, believing it would prepare him to help his impoverished homeland. He became a successful investment banker, and went onto establish his own company in the 1980s. By this point, Rainsy had married a fellow investment banker who was also a Cambodian exile, and through his wife's family he reconciled with King Sihanouk because, 'my family's story is just a drop of blood in the ocean into which Cambodian people have been plunged'. He pledged to help Sihanouk rid Cambodia of its 'Vietnamese occupiers' and lobbied countries at the UN to recognise Sihanouk and the Khmer Rouge as Cambodia's legitimate representatives rather than Hun Sen's government. Although both Rainsy and Sihanouk hated the Khmer Rouge and had had friends or relatives die at their hands, Vietnam, which had controlled Cambodia for parts of the nineteenth century, was their greater evil.

Rainsy was Sihanouk's aide during the Paris Peace Agreement negotiations that ended the civil war, returning to Cambodia after the Agreement was signed in October 1991. His mother wanted him to stay out of politics, scared of losing him like his father, and his teenage daughter also begged him to stay in France. But Rainsy felt the pull of Cambodia too strongly.[5]

Rainsy's regal mix of righteousness and destiny withstood the grenade attack of 1997, and a further one the following year, after he attempted to uncover election fraud. The Sam Rainsy Party, founded in 1995 (under the name Khmer Nation Party), won seats in the National Assembly as Rainsy became the champion of the dispossessed. With human rights defender Chea Vichea, he jointly established the Free Trade Union of Workers, which mobilised tens of thousands of garment workers in his support, infuriating the CPP. In a still-unsolved murder, Vichea was gunned down while buying a newspaper in 2004. Sam Rainsy accused the CPP of assassination and claimed that he was on a list of five people they wanted to kill. Hun Sen sarcastically offered Rainsy a tank to protect himself.[6]

A tank could not protect Rainsy from defamation charges for these accusations, but his parliamentary immunity did. Then, in February 2005, Cambodia's National Assembly held a closed session, barred foreign diplomatic observers and voted to remove Rainsy's parliamentary immunity. That night, Rainsy flew to France using his French passport, knowing that the CPP-controlled courts would find him guilty. He was later tried in absentia and sentenced to eighteen months in prison.[7]

In a rare expression of contrition, and with foreign governments brokering his return, Sam Rainsy wrote to Hun Sen, recanting his accusation and offering to be less outspoken in future. Hun Sen accepted his apology and a pardon was arranged.[8] Yet Rainsy failed to temper his attacks, accusing Cambodia's Foreign Minister of leading a Khmer Rouge prison and alleging that Hun Sen had let Vietnam encroach on Cambodian territory. The Cambodian courts found him guilty of defamation, racial incitement and destroying Cambodian border posts with Vietnam (after he encouraged supporters to rip one up).[9] By 2009, Rainsy was back on a plane to France, where he lived alone while his wife remained a National Assembly member in Cambodia.

With their leader in exile, the Sam Rainsy Party performed poorly in the 2012 commune elections. It ran closer to a competition for second place with the Human Rights Party than challenging Hun Sen's CPP.

The leader of the Human Rights Party was Kem Sokha, a shorter and squarer man than Rainsy. Sokha's face is leathery, and his mouth generally downturned, causing my quick-witted colleague Kannitha to admit, 'If I look at his face, I don't like him at all. Look at his face, cannot win my trust. But I like his opinion, I like the way he speaks. I like his words. [They are] from the human rights perspective. I like the way he says things. For example, "As the driver, if you drive very well, the passenger will not be scared or express fear. If you drive well, smooth, passengers will be calm, happy. If the passenger always complain, maybe the way we drive, maybe something wrong." Simple talk, so that illiterate people can understand.'[10]

Sokha was previously a member of FUNCINPEC but was disgusted at its corruption and resigned to establish the Cambodian Centre for Human Rights. In 2005, Kem Sokha organised people to write their anonymous opinions about government abuse of human rights, which would then be erected on banners in the middle of Phnom Penh.[11] Police confiscated the banners and Sokha was found guilty of incitement and defamation. The government openly talked about arresting Sokha in the media and a warrant was issued days before they moved to arrest him, hoping a scared Sokha would leave Cambodia of his own accord. Defiantly, Sokha chose to stay. He was in jail for weeks and the experience, counter to what the CPP hoped, only strengthened his resolve. Realising that he could survive jail, the threat of imprisonment lost its terror, making it more difficult for the CPP to control Sokha, as it would try to do again years later.

Despite both having pushed for greater democracy and human rights since the 1990s, there had been friction between Rainsy and Sokha over the years. It was not a surprise that when Sokha decided to re-enter politics he set up his own party, rather than join Rainsy's. Equally unsurprising was his failure to wrestle support from the CPP; instead, support for the CPP grew during this time.

Soon after the 2012 local commune elections that had dispirited my colleague Kannitha so much, Rainsy and Sokha held a two-day conference in the Philippines. When they looked at each other, their own failure stared at them in the face. They realised that fighting each other would consign Cambodia to Hun Sen for a lifetime and they must join together to oppose him. In the depths of despair, the Cambodian National Rescue Party was born.

A few months before the National Assembly elections in July 2013, my Khmer language teacher taught me some words and phrases related to politics, such as 'political party', 'election', 'vote' and the names of the Cambodian People's Party and Cambodian National Rescue Party. Without giving any reason, he also taught me words that on reflection revealed what he expected to happen: 'demonstration', 'strike' and 'riot'. I doubted how often I would use these words: while I knew an election was coming, it didn't feel as though anybody was speaking about it. And maybe they weren't, but my language teacher knew that they would be.

A few weeks later, I was in a car with Cambodian friends going to enjoy a day beside the Mekong. We planned to graze on snacks, play cards and watch the women in the group paint each other's nails. I sat in the car listening to friends yak away. I tried to follow the conversation but couldn't keep up, so my attention drifted. I pressed my head against the window and gazed at streets full of mobile phone shops and fruit sellers.

Then I heard a phrase I knew: 'political party'. And then the name of the new opposition party, the Cambodian National Rescue Party. My heart filled with a desire to hug my language teacher. I wanted to start asking questions but realised that my friends may stop talking about politics if they knew I understood what they were saying. Even though we were in a car with closed windows travelling at sixty kilometres an hour, my fellow passengers would still feel inhibited. I kept my head pressed against the window, now listened intently as my friends talked excitedly about Rainsy and Sokha joining together.

As we sped out of Phnom Penh, I saw the same CPP sign that dotted every road throughout Cambodia. It showed the holy trinity of Hun Sen and two other CPP leaders looking out over the country they ruled.

The deification of Hun Sen had been achieved through his physical presence in the life of every village, his face on signs and his name on schools. Like his emblems of development, Hun Sen's authority was apparently concrete. But concrete is made of sand, and the sands of Cambodia were shifting.

CHAPTER 5
SHIFTING CURRENTS

Cambodia's annual Water Festival marks when the heavy rains of the wet seasons quintuple the size of the Tonlé Sap basin, forcing the flow of the Tonlé Sap river back towards Phnom Penh, where it meets the Mekong. Colourfully painted dragon boats with more than fifty rowers line up to race each other, cheered on by thousands on the riverbanks. The government cancelled this festival in 2013, ostensibly due to extreme flooding, but the CPP also found itself in a race, one where the confluence of new technology and demographic change meant that it was rowing against the current.

At the 1998 election, more than 90 per cent of the voting population had been alive when the Khmer Rouge's regime collapsed in 1979. At the next national election in 2003, just over three-quarters had been. The proportion continued to fall so that by the 2013 election, most of the voting population had been born after 1979 and were only young, if born at all, during the civil war of the 1980s.[1] Their political memory was of UNTAC and the promise of a democratic Cambodia, not of war, refugee camps and famine. Hun Sen prided himself for knowing reality but the reality that he knew, of gratitude for rice and a strong spoon, was not the reality of the new millennium.

The reality of the new millennium was what could be seen on social media, which included gleaming shopping centres in Singapore and skyscrapers in Kuala Lumpur, as well as government corruption in Cambodia. The proportion of Cambodians with access to the internet had exploded from 1 per cent in 2010 to 12 per cent just two years later, as smartphones became more common, supported by expanding mobile telephone networks.[2] By 2013 a million Cambodians had Facebook accounts,[3] and it was through Facebook that Rotha first saw videos of young people on motorbikes, shouting for change. He showed his wife but she was not interested in joining the rallies, being less politically active than her husband. Rotha began showing her videos of villagers being thrown off their land, scarred hills where ancient forests once stood and government officials flaunting their wealth that had been stolen from the nation. Rotha's passion was infectious, and a few days later the young couple were standing outside the National Assembly shouting for change with CNRP stickers on their faces.

About 1000 people had arrived to campaign for the CNRP, including Rotha's colleague Soveacha and Soveacha's wife. The sun would still be up for another hour as they set off to electrify the streets of Phnom Penh. They drove past the Kandal Market, near where I had first heard the shouts for change with Neary, and continued around the city's busy markets, avoiding some of the main roads where authorities had banned them from driving. They were able to pass near Hun Sen's opulent mansion, though, and their shouts grew louder as they did.

As they drove down residential streets, people came onto the pavement to wave and roar, *'Doe, min doe? Doe!'* (Change or no change? Change!) When Rotha and his wife were driving home after the moto parade, with stickers and flags still on display, other drivers beeped their horns and passengers held up seven fingers, the number of the CNRP on the ballot list, to show their support.

Rotha and his wife rushed to tell his wife's mother and sister about their daring. Both promised to keep it a secret from Rotha's father-in-law, a committed CPP supporter. Despite being a married father in his thirties, Soveacha felt he had to keep his escapade a secret from his mother. He said this was to spare her the worry of the family being labelled opposition supporters, but it was also to avoid his mother ordering him to stop attending the rallies, an instruction he would feel obliged to obey, so strong is parental control in Cambodia.

A few days later, Rotha and Soveacha were back outside the National Assembly with an even bigger crowd. Their wives were there too, as was Soveacha's six-year-old daughter, sitting proudly in between her mother and father on their moto. This was just a few days before the election and the large moto parade moved slowly through the city. Driving up Monivong Boulevard, which bisects Phnom Penh from south to north, Rotha saw popular political commentator Kem Ley standing at a roundabout, smiling as he watched thousands of people rally for change. After touring the city, the campaigners arrived at Freedom Park in central Phnom Penh, where a band sang about the great Khmer nation of the past and lamented the lost lands of lower Cambodia, which were now part of Vietnam.

I could see the effervescence of Rotha and Soveacha every time they came into work before campaigning. Their anticipation would build during the day as the clock ticked towards 5.00pm, the time when they could rush out of the door to re-join the rebels in the evening. Rotha was usually the last to leave the office, but in July 2013 there were greater things at play.

Nothing was greater than the prospect of Sam Rainsy returning to Cambodia before the election, despite the near certainty of arrest. Rotha hoped that the CNRP would do well without Rainsy, but with him in the country, he believed they could win. Rainsy wouldn't be able to win from inside a prison, though, and our lunchtime conversations were full of speculation about whether he would be brave enough to return or smart enough to stay away. There was only one man who could release Rainsy from the straitjacket that Hun Sen's police and courts had tied him in: Cambodia's King.

King Sihanouk had abdicated in 2004 at the age of eighty-one due to ailing health and embitterment at his waning influence over Hun Sen.[4] One of his sons, Sihamoni, replaced him. Sihamoni had lived most of his life outside Cambodia, having undertaken his schooling in Czechoslovakia during the 1960s. He studied classical dance and music during his university degree in Prague and became a professor of classical dance in Paris during the 1980s. He was born with his father's love of the arts but not with the same desire to rule. Sihamoni never sought to involve himself in Cambodia's power struggles and was content living in Paris as the Cambodian Ambassador to UNESCO until his father's abdication. It was Sihamoni's apolitical nature that Sihanouk said made him a perfect successor.[5]

Sihamoni had been King for nine years by 2013 but had been a mostly silent presence, living apart from Cambodian society. He ate alone, meditated alone, listened to music alone, prayed alone and even cycled within the walls of the palace alone. He was a dancer who no longer danced.[6] The government's Minister of the Royal Palace dictated what he did and who he saw, which amounted to presiding over Buddhist religious ceremonies and meeting tycoons who had paid tributes to Hun Sen.[7]

It should not have surprised Sam Rainsy that his letter to King Sihamoni requesting a pardon went unanswered – the King may never even have seen it. The Cambodian National Rescue Party lobbied the United States, the European Union and the UN to pressure the CPP to allow his return, but Rainsy could not even enter Cambodia through Thailand due to Hun Sen's close relationship with that government.[8]

Sam Rainsy had braved bullets and grenades in his twenty-year quest to oust Hun Sen and decided that it was now time to risk jail. Three weeks before the election, Rainsy declared on Facebook that he would return to Cambodia before the election 'to sacrifice my life for the sake of the nation': 'I dare to rescue the nation from destruction.' Rainsy said that his return would 'test' whether the elections were free and fair, but he was actually testing Hun Sen. If Rainsy returned, Sen would have to decide whether to arrest him and risk a rise of sympathetic support for the CNRP or do nothing and risk Rainsy inspiring even more to follow him.[9]

Hun Sen's official title is garnished with honorifics. It translates as Lord Prime Minister and Supreme Military Commander, and his authority is partly based on a widespread belief among the population that he controls all within Cambodia's borders. Rainsy had called Sen a 'coward' for not letting him stand in the upcoming election; if he lost control of Rainsy's return, Sen's sheen of invincibility would be tarnished. Seeking to protect Sen, CPP officials asked Rainsy to write to Sen seeking a compromise. Unlike previously, however, Rainsy refused to apologise and offered no deal in exchange for a pardon.[10]

Sen decided that he had to act and requested King Sihamoni to grant a pardon 'in the spirit of national reconciliation, national unity and to make sure the national election process is conducted under the principle of democracy with freedom and pluralism'.[11] Hun Sen's letter, signed on the day that his father died, was read out on national television news channels, most of which are owned by Sen's family or CPP colleagues. It was important that people saw Sen was choosing to allow Rainsy to return, and indeed a narrative was spread that his conciliation was sparked by his father's passing. A few days later, King Sihamoni granted the pardon and Sam Rainsy was boarding a plane for Phnom Penh.

Rotha did not go to the airport when Rainsy was touching down as his duty to work took precedence – surely something Rainsy would approve of – so he could only watch on Facebook what others were witnessing in real life.

One man there at the airport holding his hands out for Rainsy was Chamroeun, a married father of two who had only recently decided to step out of the shadows. 'Before, in my life, when I start to realise about politics, I never support the ruling party. Only in 2013 that I got involved like that,' Chamroeun told me.

'What changed in you at that time?' I asked.

'I was, you know, kind of scared. The first time, I never expect myself to be so brave like that. In the procession, riding my own motorbike.' Chamroeun's smile widened and he leaned forward. 'You know what took me there? Because I saw a lot of people, big crowd, like a critical mass, where people who are scared, who are hesitating, just go without thinking about their family, without thinking about what are the consequences. If somebody see you, "Okay, I don't care about that." Many people, so we just go. Actually, I was still afraid, but only like 10 per cent to 20 percent, but my courage is 80 per cent and it just took me there. The whole campaign, everywhere, every day. Every day, we only thinking about this. The happiest thing was to go out every day with the young people. I think the young people took the old people like me with them ... We just look at the video on Facebook and say, "Wow! *Very* interesting."'

Chamroeun worked for the government in the 1990s, training teachers before transferring to the Ministry of Foreign Affairs in pursuit of his dream to become a diplomat. It turned out to be a pipe dream, though: 'If you don't make corruption, you will not survive. I could not get along that way. I had to quit. I *had* to quit.' Chamroeun left to work for an organisation that works closely with government to improve health and education services and, wary of repercussions for his career and family, suppressed his frustration with the government for years. His emphatic nodding as he watched the protests online with me signalled an agreement with himself that it was time to be true. 'I went to shout for change with my colleague. We took off our office clothes and wore simple clothes,' said Chamroeun, that day in a brown checked shirt, conjuring images of Clark Kent transforming into Superman in a phone box. 'We went to Freedom Park to shout, and I even spent my money to buy food for people who cannot afford it. Not from any connection to the party, you know. It's like ... from just my excitement, my real feeling. We just contribute a small amount of money together and give to the opposition. One person go to the rally, to give to the opposition, without putting [all of] our names [down as donors].'

'Did your family know?' I asked.

Chamroeun clasped his hands on the table in front of him and looked straight at me. 'My wife knew and my child even asked me not to go. She is only six and she heard people talking about danger.'

'And your parents ...?' Thankfully, Chamroeun knew the question I hesitated to ask in a country where anybody in their sixties or seventies had survived the Khmer Rouge and the civil war.

'Still alive. I told them. They just say, "Don't go!" Then, "Be careful." But they also enjoy watching the videos I showed them on my phone after coming back. But they still say something like, "Be careful, be careful. Something might happen."'

There was a lightness in Chamroeun's voice, as if his parents' advice no longer carried much weight. How could it when he saw their excitement in watching his videos? He sensed that they too were rediscovering the dreams of their youth.[12]

At the centre of those dreams was Sam Rainsy, who stepped off a plane onto Cambodian soil for the first time in nearly four years, knelt down on his hands and knees, and kissed the tarmac. July is in Cambodia's wet season, but the clouds were light, fluffy and white. Rainsy was hoisted onto the back of a 4x4 pick-up and clasped hands with Kem Sokha. They raised their hands high above their heads, with a huge Cambodian flag waving behind them. Chamroeun saw each hold up seven fingers, signifying the CNRP's number on the ballot. It prompted Chamroeun, and the tens of thousands around him, to chant *'lake pil'* (number seven) over and over. Rainsy announced that he was back 'with the people with whom I share my blood': 'Today we start our journey together. I came here to save our nation with you, my brothers, sisters, nieces and nephews.'[13]

The motorcade, with people hanging off it and others clamouring to hold onto it, crawled through the streets that had been momentarily reclaimed by the city's poor and trampled upon. Women wearing brightly coloured Angry Birds pyjamas – a common fashion choice for market sellers due to their airiness – cheered and waved. Behind them, piled up against shop fronts, were bicycles cast aside by people who had joined the march of the oppressed. Rainsy and Sokha bowed towards their supporters, pressing the palms of their hands together to express respect and service. Chamroeun felt a sense of euphoria among the crowd, hailing the return of Cambodia's saviour.

Three children, old enough only to recognise hope and joy rather than the reasons for them, ran ahead of the motorcade hoping to be gifted a wave back in return, while others filmed on their phones what their eyes struggled to believe. Some climbed onto their motos, up lampposts or onto balconies so they could behold Sam Rainsy. A Cambodian National Rescue Party official declared that the CNRP would end corruption and people roared in hope of what might become.

It was only when watching video footage later that I noticed the traffic lights had still been operating, flashing from red to green and back again.

They may as well have been disco illuminations on a day when rules were forgotten. Rainsy and his motorcade crawled past government buildings on the Russian Boulevard as two policemen stood idle and confused, powerless. The only thing the CPP could do was to order all TV and radio stations to omit that Sam Rainsy had returned in their coverage of that day's news.

Sam Rainsy had been in exile when the youth started asking their compatriots whether they wanted change or no change. Rainsy decided to borrow this mantra. It was the first time that Rainsy had, in person, in Cambodia, asked Cambodians, 'Change, no change?' and his hesitation was reminiscent of the young people I had heard on their motos. The resounding response may have made him realise that the movement had grown beyond himself.

I asked Chamroeun how important he thought it was that Sam Rainsy had returned. 'I think it is very important ... he is a symbol of opposition against the government. The people who are educated, they really admire him, his courage. He used to be Finance Minister in the coalition government and he did something good for the country. He was brave. He faced danger. He went on a boat to arrest the illegal smuggler and the illegal smuggler is connected to the CPP so only [Rainsy] dares to do that. He first got the reputation then and people looked at him. So, when Rainsy comes into this situation, he is very admired. People in the city understand this and really support him. Even some government [officials] have some admiration, but they cannot say anything.'

For my colleague Kannitha, Rainsy's actions show that he has the nation's interest in his heart.[14] Soveacha believes that Mister Rainsy, as he calls him in English, 'always thinks about the people, the tuk-tuk drivers, the moto-taxis, the factory workers'. Seeing him back in Cambodia led Soveacha and his wife, and even his parents-in-law, wearied from decades of war, to believe there could be 'a big change in Cambodia': 'We thought that CNRP would win the election. We saw a million people go to the airport to accompany [Rainsy] back to the city. I remember that all the media, CPP-controlled, did not cover this. Nothing on TV about it. They did not mention. This information spread around the people via Facebook. All the government people say not one million go to meet him, just a thousand, two thousand. They try to change the real information.'[15]

It took five hours for Rainsy to travel the ten kilometres from the airport to Phnom Penh's Freedom Park, and by the time he arrived the colours of the sky had begun to change with dusk. The soft blues and pinks always induced mellowness within me, but the thousands at Freedom Park were vibrant as Rainsy took to the stage. Their voices chanted *'song-kruh-cheeit'* (rescue the nation), with their fists pumping in time with the rhythm.

When Rainsy began to speak, the crowd settled to a hush. 'We live in the dark, but we need the sunlight to shine. Do you want change? We need to change from losing our land to holding onto it, forever. Do you want change? We need to protect our national treasures. We need to protect our forests from destruction so that we can appreciate them forever.'

CNRP officials, standing beside Rainsy on stage, could see the crowd's adulation and looked at each other, hardly believing what they were witnessing as the applause rose with Rainsy's oration and flags danced in the sky.

'I am back now. I am here with you. Let me hold your hand, put my hand on your shoulder, and together we will break down the walls. I [will] save the nation with you. We are working together to save our nation.'[16]

The party continued into the night and speeches gave way to pumping, raucous music. Hands were held high and a man stood on his moto waving a giant CNRP flag with its logo of a sun rising against a blue background. A group of women in their fifties wearing pyjamas stood behind me; a woman in front of me held her baby. The music was by young people, but the spirit had drawn people of all ages.

A group of youths filled the stage and began to lead a traditional dance. People's bodies swayed rhythmically in tune to the softer music. The baby was looking at me over her mother's shoulder, unperturbed by the drama. She let out a yawn and closed her eyes.

∞

Sam Rainsy set off on an immediate tour of the country and was greeted by flocks of people wherever he went. In Svay Rieng, he was welcomed by thousands of flag-waving CNRP supporters who heard him accuse Vietnam of stealing Cambodian land: 'Many *Yuon* have come. They move their border posts close into our territory,' he said, using a slang for Vietnamese people that is often derogatory. 'I pity Khmers very much. They have lost their farmland, because *Yuon* are always coming in, and the authorities do not protect their fellow Khmers at all, but protect the invading *Yuon*. Now they have brought *Yuon* to vote for Hun Sen, so Khmers should vote for Sam Rainsy to protect our territory.'[17]

Cambodia has had a volatile relationship with its much larger neighbour to the east for many centuries. The Angkor Empire covered a territory far beyond Cambodia's current borders, but as it waned, Vietnam expanded into the Mekong Delta region, then Cambodia's territory, and gained complete control of it towards the end of the eighteenth century. Powerless between rising Thailand and encroaching Vietnam, Cambodia became a protectorate of Vietnam, which ruled it cruelly at times. Tributes had to be paid, the Vietnamese language was imposed, and the Cambodian King had to visit a Vietnamese pagoda every month and bow to his masters. Incidents of Vietnamese brutality became folklore.[18]

The Vietnamese defeat of the Khmer Rouge in 1979 did little to change Cambodian perceptions. David Chandler, one of the foremost historians on Cambodia, suggests that the 350,000 people who fled Cambodia for the refugee camps on the Thai border were not escaping the retreating Khmer Rouge but the incoming Vietnamese, even though they brought food, aid and security.[19]

Rithisak grew up in the refugee camps of the 1980s, and a few years ago made a tearful pilgrimage back to where his camp once stood. Brooding on his time in the camps, Rithisak recalled when 'Vietnamese soldiers were everywhere in Cambodia', children learnt Vietnamese and portraits of Ho Chi Minh were hung in classrooms.[20] He still burns with anger at Vietnam's controversial K5 Plan to clear forests, dig trenches, plant landmines and build 700 kilometres of fences near the Thai border as a front during the civil war: 'They conscripted people from the villages to fight. Any male in the family. If you don't join, they will shoot you. A lot, a lot of people were killed by Ko Pram [K5] plan. After Khmer Rouge killed their own people, Ko Pram killed people. And nobody talk about it. They talk only Khmer Rouge but not Ko Pram. A lot of mines. People step on a mine and they come back, only the bones. Bones on a tray. "Hello ma'am, this is your son; this is your husband."'

He, and many Cambodians, believe their country was under the heel of Vietnam during the 1980s, pointing to the decade-long imprisonment of Cambodia's first Prime Minister after the Khmer Rouge because he dared to disagree with his Vietnamese advisers. For Rithisak, the occupation never really ended: 'They just change their clothes from military ... maybe marry Khmer girls and make family. Hundreds of thousands of families now.'[21]

Rotha told me that Vietnam was one of the most important issues for the 2013 election because Cambodians 'are afraid of Vietnam, the people and border issue. Afraid that government officials are Vietnamese people who speak Khmer very well. We cannot identify who are Khmer or who are Vietnamese. We are afraid of becoming like Laos, controlled by Vietnam.'[22]

Leap had a senior role at an international organisation in Cambodia, and he believed the CNRP knew how to manipulate the well of resentment towards Vietnam for political ends: 'The opposition do not talk about budget allocation. No, they talk about land, natural resources and corruption. They do not want to talk about [school] enrolment, about budget allocation. "Want to talk about that? [Go] work for an NGO."'[23]

Addressing 20,000 supporters in Siem Reap, Rainsy charged: 'We are full. We have been eating Vietnamese sour soup for thirty years. This time we need to eat a traditional Khmer soup.' Pointing to land concessions given to Vietnamese companies and alleged illegal immigrants from Vietnam, he declared: 'We have to kick the Vietnamese out and collect our property back.'[24] At another rally, Rainsy warned, 'More and more *Yuon* come to grab our land and catch our fish. *Yuon* log our trees and take our jobs. *Yuon* take advantage of the Khmer because the current authorities protect *Yuon*.'[25] He even warned that Cambodia was at risk of becoming a 'province under control of Vietnam' and that 'if we don't rescue our nation, four or five years more is too late. Cambodia will be full of Vietnamese, we will become slaves of Vietnam.'[26]

A movement that had begun with a few young people yelping for change in a corner of Phnom Penh had leapt into towns throughout Cambodia as Rainsy toured the country. Watching via Facebook on his smartphone, my friend Sophal thought Rainsy looked like a hero born again. He was certainly being treated like a god.

Uncharacteristically tall for a Cambodian and strikingly handsome, with large, dark eyes, chiselled cheekbones and broad shoulders, Sophal was in his late twenties. Just days before the election, Sophal was on a bus from Kep, a tranquil, coastal village known for its crab market, to Phnom Penh when his journey intersected with a CNRP rally. Bus drivers usually motor at reckless speeds in order to make a return journey the same day, but this time the driver began to slow. The excited passengers pleaded for him to stop so that they could temporarily join the revolution.

Sophal had grown up in a hut that flooded for months of the year. His family's poverty that meant he was not seen as good enough by his girlfriend's family. He had struggled as a moto-taxi driver. Unshackling himself from the binds of his social position, Sophal thrust himself into the swell.

When we spoke, the memories of that day still made his heart beat quicker. He gazed beyond me as he remembered being swept along in the tide as people cheered and held up seven fingers, believing a brighter future was within grasp: 'We were so excited. The dream was going to come true.'[27]

Soveacha, conversing in stuttering English because he wanted to practice with me, found eloquence when earnestly asking me to understand that it felt like 'an important moment for Cambodia'. Ever since that first night with Neary on the street corner, I felt that I understood the importance of the moment, but not its driving essence. I was not alone. Rotha pondered, 'We saw other people go, and we followed them but without really knowing the objective of the moment.'

My spell checker tells me that 'the objective of the moment' is grammatically incorrect. My spell checker understands rules but lacks humanity. It was moments, such as seeing young people shout for change or the intersection of a rally and a busload of enthusiastic passengers, that propelled people like Sophal, Chamroeun, Rotha and Soveacha to act in ways that they had never done. The emotion coursing through Cambodia could not be explained by the prospect of one politician being replaced by another, nor with the CNRP's promise of higher wages. People believed their whole nation was on the cusp of change.

I have known Rotha and Soveacha for years. I was a guest at Rotha's wedding, where we danced and drank stout that turned his cheeks rosy-red, although I did not stay the whole night. I, and other Cambodian friends, had to go to another wedding, a fancier one with more expensive food and whisky instead of beer. Rotha was our close friend but there were other rules to follow.

'Rotha, do you think a rich person and a poor person have the same level of respect in Cambodia?' I asked.

'Noooooo.' Rotha chuckled at the ridiculousness of my question.

Soveacha's face was stern when he explained that Cambodia was 'unfair' because 'the rich man wins, and the poor ...' He paused, trying to find the right words, before going on to describe a litany of sufferings where the rich 'take the territory, the home, from the poor person. They always look down on the poor people.' I asked Soveacha, who has worked as a guard and whose wife works night shifts in Phnom Penh's casino, if he felt that people look down on him. He nodded and replied softly: 'Yes.'

'Do you think it will ever change?'

Soveacha was not looking at me when he disconsolately conceded: 'Not easy to change. Unless we have another party who wins the election.'

Cambodia's ancient Angkor Empire had a strict social hierarchy of three levels: peasantry, officialdom and royalty. Families remained in their strata for generation after generation.[28] Ou Ritthy, a friend who previously lived in India, explained that a social hierarchy, although not quite as strict as the Indian caste system, remained in Cambodia today. He said that at the bottom were the 'Cintri people'. Cintri is the waste-management company that collects all rubbish in Phnom Penh. Many of its workers will be seen walking at night, in sandals or barefoot, pulling a three-metre cart on two wheels from their shacks at the city's edges into Phnom Penh's centre. Some will be children; others will be carrying children. These are the Cintri people, defined by their grubby company polo shirt. In Phnom Penh, they are creatures of the night, foraging in dark corners after everybody has finished their fun.

Just above Cintri people are tuk-tuk and moto-taxi drivers, alongside garment factory workers. Chanthy was the moto-taxi driver who stood outside my apartment waiting for customers every day. Moto-taxi drivers, like tuk-tuk drivers, would sometimes only get two or three passengers a day, barely covering the cost of rice for lunch. That corner had been his for fifteen years. Each day he hung out with the security guards and tuk-tuk drivers or exchanged the odd word of broken English with ex-patriots. In all that time, he never had a conversation with the wealthy Cambodian family who lived below me and affectionately fed me on occasion. He may have nodded when they passed, said hello, or even helped to open the gate when they were returning home with bags laden from the market, but they never spoke. He was just a moto-taxi driver.

Along with an idealistic youth and an educated middle class, the CNRP had become an alliance of people who had been cast aside, belittled or treated unjustly. This had become their moment to talk, and their objective was not just to change the government; they wanted to change society.

CHAPTER 6
ELECTION EVE

I was sitting on my balcony late on a Sunday afternoon watching the streetscape below. Sam Rainsy had returned two days previously and the election was racing towards us. I heard a commotion rolling towards me and the familiar call of 'Change, no change? Change!' coming down the street. The CNRP were on the march.

A cacophony of tuk-tuks and motos crawled up the narrow street, their drivers waving flags and cheering as they went. A shiny Toyota Lexus 4x4 approached the intersection from the left and waited as the stream trickled by. Another one approached from the road beneath me, before deciding to do a U-turn and drive away. Tuk-tuk drivers and security guards stood at the roadside watching the campaigners until one of them got a CNRP flag and started waving it, egged on by his cheering friends.

The following day I was turning onto Sihanouk Boulevard, one of Phnom Penh's main arteries, which has three lanes going either way, separated by a long park forty metres wide that houses a statue of the late King Sihanouk. At one end, near where the grenade went off at Sam Rainsy's rally in 1997, a crowd of around 100 young people waved CPP flags and cheered as people went past. Despite the wide pavements, they spilled onto the road, creating a bottleneck. Sitting on my bicycle, the two walls of CPP youths towered over me with their arms and flags arched high, forming what felt like a tunnel. Coming out the other side, I noticed that most of the drivers were staring straight ahead resolutely, as if unable to turn their heads.

The tenor of each major party's campaign was different, partly due to the motivations of those taking part. The CPP had many thousands of people joining their campaigns, but they were being paid $1 to $7 per day to be there,[1] while garment factory workers, already bare to the bone, were giving money to the CNRP, and tuk-tuk drivers held buckets for people to throw notes into as they passed.

The CPP could pay supporters due to a vast slurry of cash that came from public servants. Anybody employed by the government – be it a teacher, doctor or bureaucrat – was encouraged to become a CPP member, which involved a monthly membership fee. Some public service jobs were impossible to get without being one and those who refused to join found themselves outcasts, denied promotion. This was the reason the CPP had five million members, more than half of Cambodia's adult population. The CPP paid these public servants to join campaigns throughout the country, offering government vehicles for travel and government buildings to host rallies and meetings.[2] Assisted by local Commune Councillors, these supporters would organise village-wide meetings or go door-to-door giving out sarongs, MSG and rice. Ritthy, my friend who had studied in India and told me about the Cintri people, showed me photos of the CPP-emblazoned bowls that his parents had been given. He laughed when explaining that his mother was so honest that after accepting the bowls, she said she would not be able to sleep if she did not vote CPP.[3] A minister gave away $25 to $125 to pregnant women, older people and poor families in Svay Rieng. It is estimated the CPP spent $15 million on gifts during the campaign.[4]

He who gives can also take away, and Hun Sen threatened that a major land-titling scheme would not continue if the CPP lost the election. Few records of property survived the Khmer Rouge regime, meaning that most Cambodians lacked the paperwork to show they owned the land they lived on. This made it easy to throw people from the homes they had lived in for years. In response to public outcry, Hun Sen had established a mass land-titling scheme that, despite being conducted by untrained students and plagued by allegations of corruption, had provided documented ownership for many families, but many more were left hoping their turn would come after the election.[5]

'To those whose lands have not been measured and those who have not been given land titles, I would like to inform you that the youths can return to work only if the CPP wins the election,' Hun Sen said. 'If you want the youths to come back, there is only one choice for you: to vote for the CPP.'[6]

The words of Hun Sen reached into every Cambodian's home through television channels and newspapers owned by his associates. The CNRP may have been flying high on social media, but the mainstream media belonged to Hun Sen. Of Cambodia's nine television stations, two were owned by Hun Sen's daughter, four by Hun Sen's personal advisers, and another partly by the Ministry of Defence.[7] Ou Ritthy, working for an election-monitoring organisation called COMFREL (Committee for Free and Fair Elections in Cambodia), monitored hours of television leading up to the election and found that 80 per cent of political coverage focused on the CPP, with only the little-watched national broadcaster providing any balance. Television stations also glorified the CPP during news broadcasts by showcasing the party's leaders opening health centres, schools and roads. In contrast, the CNRP found it difficult to stick their posters up anywhere.[8] Similarly, half of Cambodia's main newspapers were aligned to the CPP. Hun Sen's daughter owned one, and a CPP Senator owned another.[9] The CNRP had relied on spreading its message via radio, which thrives in rural Cambodia. But just three days before the election, the country's most popular radio station warned that 'if the CNRP win the election and forms government, all investment will leave Cambodia': 'After three months of CNRP government, armed forces will be deployed to rule the whole country, leading to a breakdown of diplomatic relations and new bloodshed, like under the Khmer Rouge.'[10]

Hesitating voters may also have been swayed by the fact that the Cambodian military were strong supporters of the CPP – its leaders were all members of the CPP Standing Committee.[11] Hun Sen's son was Vice-Chairman of the Joint General Staff and in the lead-up to the election toured the country calling on soldiers and citizens to vote for the CPP, as did the Chairman of the Staff. The armed force's Supreme Commander told voters not to be fooled by CNRP propaganda and to vote for the CPP. An army general led a 40,000-strong procession of soldiers through the town of Sisophon to show support for the CPP, which hosts one of the largest barracks in the country and has an entrance guarded by two huge billboards of a smiling Hun Sen and his wife.[12]

On the night of Sam Rainsy's return, somebody shot a bullet through the window of the CNRP office. The streets were tense and soldiers were deployed in the main parts of Phnom Penh for a whole month before the election, standing on busy street corners with army fatigues, black boots and guns. There were 122 cases of political violence investigated during the campaign, including threats of death, arrest and eviction. CNRP members were nearly always the victims.[13] Hun Sen sowed fear to halt the growth of support for Rainsy, warning that 'for sure, civil war will erupt if they win the election': 'He has not yet won power, yet he announced that members of the ruling government will be brought to trial [for crimes committed when Khmer Rouge members]. Problems will happen like during Pol Pot's regime. Nobody will be waiting to be arrested.'[14]

Hun Sen warned of impending war multiple times in the lead-up to the election, and as it drew closer, he sought to strike fear into the hearts of Cambodians: 'I would like people to rethink things clearly. The change of a political party or a prime minister is not normal. If you are angry with your commune chief or deputy commune chief and will not re-elect Hun Sen and the CPP, it will lead to chaos across the nation. If you choose the wrong lawmakers and prime minister, it will cause national destruction.'[15] Of Rainsy, he said, 'If you accuse the neighbouring country of invasion, war within the country and with neighbouring countries would be inevitable.'[16]

Hun Sen hoped to paralyse the population by invoking the trauma of the past, but the youthful daring of hope had intoxicated too many. Kannitha told me that when she rebuffed a moto-taxi driver's question about the election by saying she was not interested in politics, he exclaimed, 'Oh, sister! Now it is okay, not afraid to talk about politics.'[17]

On the final afternoon of campaigning, I stood on one side of the six-lane Monivong Boulevard. The road stretches for seven kilometres from the River Bassac in Phnom Penh's south, through the city until it turns and crosses the River Sap in the north. Thousands of CNRP supporters paraded by in tuk-tuks and on motorbikes. People waved at me as they drove past, and some slowed to high-five with a group of young Cambodians beside me. There were families on motos, groups of friends riding side-by-side; tuk-tuks overflowing with people. One tuk-tuk was full of orange-robed monks, defying orders to stay neutral politically. Even those in the parade were awestruck: a father driving a moto, with one daughter sitting in front of him and another wearing a CNRP cap behind him, pulled over to look back as the crowd rolled past.

At that time, garment workers would be transported to and from factories in the back of open-topped dumper trucks. They would stand together like cattle, nose to nose, shielding themselves from the sun. But on this day, the same women in the same trucks wore white CNRP shirts with number 7 stickers on their cheeks, smiling and waving as they sang the CNRP songs that had reverberated throughout Cambodia for the last week or so. It was a political rally but it felt more like Carnival in Rio de Janeiro or a pride march in San Francisco. It was what I imagine the streets would be like if my country ever won the football World Cup. The extraordinary flourishing of fraternity, of finding that there are millions who have been secretly holding the same dream as you and are now riding with you to achieve it, was intoxicating.

The sense of fraternity even extended to a small group of FUNCINPEC supporters who had come down the other, empty, side of Monivong Boulevard. Some CNRP supporters, ignorant of FUNCINPEC's future duplicity, leaned over the barrier to shake hands with them, united in believing that change was coming to Cambodia.

I watched the procession for about five minutes and the same steady wave of CNRP supporters kept coming. I could not see the start or the end of it. CNRP rallies often attracted between 10,000 and 40,000 people in major cities like Phnom Penh, Siem Reap and Battambang, but this was the biggest I had seen.[18] Bewitched, I got on my bike and moved with the crowd to Freedom Park.

I arrived there about 5.00pm, as the sun was beginning its descent from a sky peppered with light, powdery clouds. I was standing at the back, 100 metres from the stage, with a sea of people before me. Just behind me, a well-built, handsome young man wearing shades, jeans and a white t-shirt stood barefoot on his moto, looking like a Cambodian James Dean, waving a Cambodian flag high in the sky. Next to me, a woman in her early thirties sat on her black Honda Dream 125 with a bright blue number 7 sticker on her left cheek. Turning to face me, her hat pulled down to her eyes, she smiled and held up seven fingers, showing how she would vote in two days' time.

CHAPTER 7

GHOSTS AND NOBODIES

Months ahead of the election, Cambodia's National Election Committee (NEC) and independent election observers found that nearly 1 million eligible citizens, some of whom had voted previously, were not on the voting list despite believing they were registered.[1] Meanwhile, there were so many deceased individuals listed and other voters listed multiple times that there were more than 9.5 million people registered to vote even though there weren't that many Cambodians of voting age.[2]

It is tempting to blame such errors on malevolent corruption by Hun Sen's appointees on the National Election Committee, fitting the narrative that all happens by his design. But one should not underestimate the scope for mistakes in a country where systems are based on paper and pen and administered by people with little formal education. Indicating that the errors may, at least partly, have been due to poor administration practices is that one of Kem Sokha's daughters appeared on the voter registration list twice – hardly a successful ploy to diminish the CNRP vote.[3]

I was in Siem Reap, a tourist town in northwestern Cambodia, on election day and spent the morning cycling around the town's polling stations, many in the grounds of schools, to see if predictions of people not being able to vote would prove true. At the first polling station I stopped outside, I saw people craning their necks to scan the lists of names on papers pinned to the wall. I was tense, fearing that I would witness an explosion of indignation when voters couldn't find their names, but instead, people searched for a few minutes, nodded to themselves and turned to join the correct line. One man in his early forties leaving the polling station after voting saw me standing with my bicycle, trying to be discreet. He walked over and motioned for me to take a photo. He held his right forefinger, stained in purple ink, out in front of him as proof that he had voted.

The few polling centres I cycled past were peaceful and the town's atmosphere felt calm. Travelling down a side road, slightly out of town, I came across a vacant concrete building on which there was the rare sight of graffiti, written in yellow. In English, it said 'I want kiss you.' I wanted to kiss Cambodia that day too.

I had lunch with a friend, who looked at my photo of the man with his finger and then showed me his finger, which was clean apart from purple traces in his fingernail. COMFREL, the leading independent election monitor, had raised alarms before the election that the ink could be washed away, making it possible for people to vote twice,[4] but my friend seemed quite happy not to have a purple finger for the rest of the week.

The serenity I was enjoying in Siem Reap was in stark contrast to the emotion in Phnom Penh's impoverished Stung Meanchey area. Locals, thousands of who had lined the streets to welcome Sam Rainsy's return ten days earlier, were seething that their names were not on the voting list, meaning they could not vote. They complained to a National Election Committee staff member, who pretended to faint to avoid the confrontation and then retreated into a locked room, further inciting the growing crowd.

The military police arrived to rescue the staff member from the school. The swollen crowd vastly outnumbered the 100 police officers, though, and seized on this moment to vent their anger at the injustice. They pelted police with rocks; the officers abandoned two pick-up trucks in their hasty escape. A group of scrawny young men began rocking one, flipping it onto its back, chanting anti-government and anti-Vietnamese slogans. One man climbed on top while others kicked and beat the car with sticks.[5]

Such violence was rare across Cambodia but Stung Meanchey was not an isolated incident. Transparency International Cambodia, who had observers stationed at hundreds of polling stations, had to evacuate their staff from another polling station in Phnom Penh because 'angry mobs' unable to vote were seeking to vent their frustration, and another polling station in Kandal province was forced to close early.[6] Outrage at not being able to vote was intensified by rumours that Vietnamese residents had temporary registration papers allowing them to vote despite not being Cambodian nationals. Social media was alive with comments like '*Khmer can't vote* – Yuon *can*', and there were rumours that the CPP were bussing Vietnamese citizens in from across the border.[7]

The Stung Meanchey mob turned on one man who looked Vietnamese, beating him severely. As the afternoon wore on, the crowd set the two police pick-up trucks ablaze, blowing up the petrol tanks. Plumes of smoke rose into the darkening sky.[8]

Ou Ritthy, whose mother voted CPP because she had received bowls from them, was working in COMFREL's office on election day. He was busily updating Facebook and Twitter with news of turnout and voting irregularities when he looked up from his laptop to see an old classmate rushing in. Ritthy's friend had challenged a man who, having washed the ink off his finger, tried to vote at two different polling stations, but it was Ritthy's old classmate who local authorities tried to arrest. Sprinting away, Ritthy's friend had jumped on his motorbike to drive the 60 kilometres to COMFREL's office in Phnom Penh.

'He was not even registered as an observer, but at that time, everybody played the role [informally], you know,' Ritthy recalled. Ritthy's old classmate gave a quick comment to the press and was spirited off to a safe house.

Suspicion of CPP fraud was firing on social media in tandem with speculation that the CNRP had gained many votes. Chamroeun was excited, and nervous: 'We did not go anywhere, we just want to follow the result. When everybody understands that the CNRP gain more votes, the streets started to get quiet. People probably remember the past, the bitter past: when there is a change of regime, something happen. You know, the petrol station was closed at that time. It started to be a strained environment. The country was tense.'

After lunch, I had cycled off to visit the ancient temples of Angkor Wat, hidden among the towering forest near Siem Reap. It was dark, just before 7.00pm, when I returned to my guesthouse. I was grimy from cycling all day and eager for a shower, but I paused as I walked through the reception. The young guesthouse owner was slouched in front of the television, muttering to himself. A manicured presenter was reading results from individual polling stations at random, meaning it was hard to determine how each party was doing overall. The results reported also seemed to be coming from small, rural villages, where the CPP had gathered a majority of votes, rather than the towns and cities, where the CNRP were expected to do well.

Like everybody else in the country, Chamroeun was watching the results on television. He had not long returned home after waiting to hear the final tally at his local polling station and was excited to know how other parts of Cambodia had voted. But he watched in dismay: 'I was very frustrated. You know, immediately after they close the poll, people start to listen to find out the results. People are so eager to know the result. It was not known until some time in the evening. And it was not interesting. They announce the results from a very remote area, not significant. I, and others too, begin to suspect why they did that. The opposition must gain the vote. That's why the delay.'

Large numbers of police and military were out in force across the country, especially in Phnom Penh, where they were on many street corners.[9] Rolls of barbed wire blocked some main roads, like those near the Independence Monument and Hun Sen's compound. Troops were posted to monitor the CNRP headquarters.[10] Memories of CPP and FUNCINPEC battling in the streets were vivid as people hurried to their homes. Ritthy had never seen Phnom Penh so quiet as he drove home after work; he only saw a few people filling up containers with petrol and emptying the ATMs of cash.[11] People closed their doors, huddled around radios, televisions or a smartphone, and waited.

Sam Rainsy had been riding a wave since his return and he was desperate for that momentum to continue. In early evening, he issued a statement declaring victory, claiming that he had information from foreign diplomatic missions indicating the CNRP had won a clear majority, with seventy-six seats.[12] His claim was quickly repeated on Facebook.[13] But in a press conference an hour later, Rainsy made no declaration, preferring only 'to thank all Cambodian people … regardless of their political affiliation … for their dignified participation in this election, for their contribution to make democracy move forward.'[14]

People were sure the CNRP had done well, but the tempering of Rainsy's usual belligerence cast doubt on whether they had done well enough. The country waited for the answer, knowing that it wouldn't come from the mannequin on television monotonously reciting numbers from far-off villages. It could only come from one man, but he wasn't ready to speak. Instead, he turned the power off and plunged the capital into darkness.

CHAPTER 8

DROP BY DROP, THE BUCKET FILLS

The electricity was cut in Phnom Penh for only about twenty minutes, but it was time enough for people to fear what the darkness may bring. It was also time for the CPP to finalise their counting. At 7.30pm, the CPP Minister of Information announced that the CPP had won sixty-eight seats and the CNRP had won fifty-five seats, but the mood was subdued. There was no victory speech by Hun Sen; there was no party for CPP staff; there was no triumphant rally of his supporters. There was silence. The streets remained empty except for Hun Sen's foot soldiers. Everyone else locked their front doors and remained inside.

The following morning, Rainsy and Sokha held a press conference rejecting the result, claiming that the list of voters was riddled with errors. They alleged that 15 per cent of eligible adults were not listed while 200,000 people were listed twice, plus there were 1 million ghost names. With only 300,000 votes separating the CPP and the CNRP, the CNRP believed these irregularities could have made the difference.

Rainsy declared that they were 'not seeking to bargain with the government': 'What we want is to render justice to the Cambodian people so their will is not reversed.'[1] Rainsy doubted that the CPP-dominated National Election Committee (NEC) would adequately investigate the complaints, and the Cambodian Constitutional Council was presided over by a permanent member of the CPP steering committee, so he called on the UN to complete a joint investigation within a month.[2]

The next day, Rainsy repeated his claim of victory, declaring that based on calculations by activists at polling stations, the CNRP had won at least sixty-three seats. He predicted massive nationwide demonstrations if the government did not establish an independent committee into the election result.[3] Kem Sokha went further when addressing crowds of CNRP supporters, suggesting that at 5.00pm on election day, the ballot counting showed the CNRP had won seventy-six seats but somehow the results were 'turned upside down'. The CPP declaration was a 'trick to cheat us'.[4] The NEC denied these accusations, saying that there was no large-scale wrongdoing and that it would resolve any complaints. They rejected any need for UN involvement.[5]

Barbed wire and barricades remained on the streets throughout Phnom Penh, most visibly around the silent house of Hun Sen, from whom nothing had been heard. A common view was that the CPP had only won because of intimidation, the giving of money and gifts, voter list irregularity and a biased NEC. Hun Sen's authority was damaged, and there were rumours that he had left the country, with the CPP central committee divided over whether he should remain as leader.[6]

Of the hundreds of thousands of people who had returned to their home province to vote, one in ten chose not to come back to Phnom Penh for fear that violence could erupt. Production at garment factories slowed due to staff absences, and some businesses, including the lunchtime restaurant near my work run by Vietnamese-Cambodians, remained closed, the iron shutters rolled down.[7]

Chamroeun told me that Hun Sen's silence had heightened the tension even further since election day: 'The Prime Minister, during the previous elections, he usually came out to talk about the result. This time he was quiet. The atmosphere was really tense. I think people worry so much. They think that something bad will happen. Some go to withdraw money from the bank, buy food and store at home. The atmosphere invades people's minds.'

In the weeks that followed, Phnom Penh remained locked down, with anti-riot police, soldiers and barricades restricting access to main roads and markets. Armoured vehicles were occasionally seen on the streets, and the Cambodian army chose this time to hold military exercises near the capital. In a chilling echo of the 1997 attack, a defunct hand grenade was found near a pagoda where Sam Rainsy was giving a speech, and several explosive devices were found in Freedom Park, the National Assembly and Wat Phnom.[8]

In a strange juxtaposition, some Cambodians felt a greater sense of freedom amid the tension. Having lunch at the corner restaurant three days after the election, a female colleague talked loudly about the unprecedented support for the CNRP, the government's possible fixing of the results and what Hun Sen would do next. I looked around and then looked at her; she saw my alarm and jovially said that it was okay because now everybody knew other people were thinking the same.

This new emboldened citizenry encouraged the CNRP to continue rejecting the election result and refuse to take their seats in the National Assembly, in the hope of preventing it from being established and forcing another election. Initially, Hun Sen appeared willing to negotiate with the CNRP, but he quickly defaulted to a familiar defiant tone: 'We don't need to beg another political party to attend the Assembly ... we only need 63 members [of the National Assembly] to approve a law and appoint a government.'[9] Independent lawyers countered that while sixty-three Assembly members or more can approve a new government, at least 120 members are required to approve the formation of a new Assembly.[10]

Two weeks after the election, the NEC released provisional results that matched what the CPP had announced on election night. The CNRP rejected these, prompting the government to deploy armoured personnel carriers and soldiers in Phnom Penh ahead of possible protests.[11]

Rainsy and Sokha decided to delay demonstrations, preferring to lodge official complaints with the NEC. They argued that the voter list was so flawed that the NEC should hold elections again in nine whole provinces and in parts of five other provinces. The CNRP also requested the NEC check the results or recount votes at hundreds of other polling stations where they alleged correct counting procedures had not been followed or results may have been recorded inaccurately.[12]

The NEC rejected all but four of the complaints, citing insufficient evidence and alleging that CNRP party agents had already approved results submitted from polling stations. The NEC did, along with CNRP and independent representatives, review documents from a selection of polling stations in four provinces and judged there to be no irregularities that would make a difference to results. No recount was done, however, even in the province of Kandal, where just 167 votes separated the CPP and CNRP.[13]

The CNRP appealed the NEC's decision to Cambodia's Constitutional Council. It verified that there were no discrepancies in forty-one polling stations and declined to investigate 434 other polling stations identified by the CNRP. Apart from a finding that soldiers should not have been sent to a polling station in Siem Reap, all of the CNRP's claims were dismissed.[14]

Having exhausted all legal and procedural avenues in the month following the election, the CNRP called for mass demonstrations in six towns throughout Cambodia. Crowds of up to 40,000 people returned to Phnom Penh's Freedom Park. Rotha said it became like a village: 'People came from different parts of Cambodia. They build tents there. When I go to Freedom

Park, it was full, crowded. My colleagues would give money and we would buy food for them [the protestors]. There were many people holding signs up – *Where is my vote?*

For Rotha, the objective of the moment had become clear. 'We wanted another vote, another election,' he told me. The CNRP had a new slogan reverberating throughout the country: 'Hun Sen, *ouey choh chenh tow!*' (Hun Sen, step down, go!)

I walked to Freedom Park, which was mostly paved. The searing heat of the sun bounced back at me from the concrete, so I found some shade sitting with six women, all neighbours, under one of the small trees that frame the edges of the park. The youngest woman in the group was in her mid-twenties and fluent in English from working with foreigners in the aid sector. One of her neighbours could also speak some English due to her engagement with foreigners in a different sector, one involving late-night bars and karaoke.

Two much older women in the group were small, wrinkled and smiling brightly, wearing CNRP t-shirts and stickers on their cheeks. They had lived through civil war and the Khmer Rouge in the 1970s, Vietnamese occupation in the 1980s and the deadly squabbles of the 1990s. It would have been easy for them to accept that the Cambodia of 2013 was better than before and good enough for now, but they didn't. They were protesting because they believed that something better was possible.

We huddled in the patch of shade, watching people flow into the park, marching with banners written in Khmer and English that asked: 'Where is my vote?' Some held placards up; many had CNRP stickers plastered on their faces or were sporting CNRP t-shirts and caps. Others carried large Cambodian flags, waving them high above their heads and calling the masses to follow.

While there were tens of thousands of people, it was a smaller crowd than that which had lined the streets to celebrate Rainsy's return. It didn't have the surging emotion of the pre-election rallies either, and I wondered if the CNRP had lost impetus by waiting too long to protest the results. There was no sense that these protests, six weeks after the election, would force the CPP to reconsider sharing power.

The tone of the protests had also changed from before the election. Hope had been replaced by anger. On the first day of these protests, there were small clashes between police and protestors who had upturned barricades. Later that night, a group of people unable to get home because of police roadblocks began to throw stones at police, who replied by firing warning shots, exploding tear gas and baton charging the protestors. In the chaos, one man died after being shot in the head by police. He was returning home after attending a protest and wore a bandana that said, 'We demand justice.'[15] Many protestors who had come to Phnom Penh from rural provinces hunkered down and spent the night sleeping on the concrete slabs of Freedom Park.

King Sihamoni hosted negotiations between Hun Sen and Sam Rainsy, but they reached no agreement, so Rainsy attempted to persuade other senior CPP officials to support his proposal that the CPP could retain control of government if the CNRP had control of the National Assembly. The CPP were united in their refusal, though, offering CNRP the Vice-Presidency of the Assembly and chair of nearly half the Assembly committees instead.[16]

The women under the tree in Freedom Park asked me what my country and the international community would do to help the people of Cambodia. I floundered, searching for words to explain how international sympathy and inaction can be twins. Surveys found that Cambodians had as much trust in the 'international community' as they did in the Buddhist orders of monks, and much greater trust than for government institutions and courts.[17] The women, almost pleadingly, queried why the UN would not come back to bring peace and democracy to Cambodia, like the UNTAC had done in 1993. That miraculous time had instilled a faith in the power of the international community that would only bring disappointment now.

By 1993, the communist world had dissolved and a new world order, headed by a lone American superpower, was forming. Concomitant with a belief that democracy had vanquished communism, Western democracies felt a duty to create liberal democracies in other countries. In Cambodia's case, this obligation was fuelled by the guilt of indirectly supporting the Khmer Rouge during the 1980s and forcing economic embargoes on Cambodia.

The world had changed a lot in twenty years. The belief that every country would eventually become a liberal democracy had been replaced by a fear that the world would become engulfed in a clash of civilisations. America was enmeshed in Iraq and Afghanistan, and a war was flaming in Syria. Even if America cared, its power had diminished.

In 1993, a broken Russia and an impoverished China meant that the United States could sway the UN Security Council, which must approve all major UN actions or declarations. By 2013, Russia had regained sufficient strength to invade Georgia without sanction and China was rising to become a global superpower. Russia and China were now aligned to block American action in the UN.

Despite these changes, Sam Rainsy devoted himself to building relationships with US Congressmen and using his connections in Europe to encourage foreign governments to act. His lobbying had some success, with two US Senators calling for a freeze on US aid to Cambodia and one Congressman condemning Hun Sen as a 'corrupt, vicious human being', concluding that it was 'time for Hun Sen to go'.[18] These words did not translate into sanctions though, and the American government appeared keen to encourage negotiations. A spokesperson for the US Deputy Secretary of State, who met Rainsy after the election, admitted that there were 'serious election irregularities' but called only for 'a credible and transparent review of the election'.[19] The EU issued a similar statement, proposing swift, fair investigations. Neither the EU nor the United States took up Sam Rainsy's call for a UN-led investigation, never mind pushing for a re-election or for Hun Sen to step down.[20]

Western governments knew that their power to influence events within Cambodia was limited by Hun Sen's dominance of government bureaucracies and the weight of China's support for him. Hun Sen was no longer servile to Western donors and brushed off threats to cut aid: 'This won't affect the government. Don't talk so much. If you want to cut, just cut it.' Referring to military aid from America, Hun Sen continued, 'Last time they cut our aid, they were going to give us 100 old trucks. The Chinese saw this and gave us 257 trucks.'[21]

Hun Sen pressed King Sihamoni to convene a National Assembly based on the results of the NEC. The King ignored requests from the CNRP to delay the Assembly's formation, citing a constitutional interpretation that an Assembly must be convened within sixty days of an election. The King advised the CNRP to attend the Assembly's opening, but the CNRP preferred to hold a Buddhist ceremony at Angkor Wat instead.[22]

King Sihamoni, as is custom, invited foreign ambassadors to attend the opening of the Assembly, and they, operating in Cambodia with the consent of the King, dutifully attended. The US Ambassador stressed his attendance was not an endorsement of any election outcome, and, along with the EU, called on the two parties to negotiate the CNRP's participation in the Assembly.[23]

The CPP had a further boost when independent election monitors, usually critical of the government, concluded that the results announced by the NEC generally matched their records and that the CNRP had provided no evidence to support their claims of winning more seats than the CPP.[24] Stationed at just over 60 per cent of polling stations, election monitors observed only 11,000 people arriving at a polling station but being unable to vote.[25] One of the lead monitors, Pen Raksa from Transparency International Cambodia, told me he could not understand why Rainsy announced that he had won, except as a political tactic: 'He is a politician, and this is what they do.'

Raksa was sitting beside Kem Sokha's daughter, herself a senior CNRP politician, during a meeting after the election. 'Oh, she was very unhappy with me and Transparency International. She did not like our report. I explained that I work from evidence, from quantitative facts. I said to her, "Show me the evidence!" I could not understand the CNRP after the election.'[26] Raksa acknowledged that the CNRP had legitimate complaints regarding the counting of votes but considered these relatively small-scale. Even if they had been corrected, the CNRP may have picked up another seat, but the CPP would still have won a majority.

Election observers may have accepted that the results were accurate, but they did not judge the election to be free or fair, stridently criticising the conduct of the election and the campaigning period before it. The body responsible for running the election is the NEC, which many Cambodians believed was doing a poor job.[27] Its members were appointed by the CPP Minister of Interior, approved by the Council of Ministers headed by Hun Sen and authorised by the CPP-controlled National Assembly. CPP control of the NEC means that officials involved in running polling stations and counting ballots are usually members of the CPP. Furthermore, the Commune Councils organise the registration of voters, and 97 per cent of Councils were controlled by the CPP in 2013.[28]

Less than 300,000 votes separated the CPP and the CNRP in the official results, but a staggering 1 million eligible people were not on the voter list and unable to vote. This included 36,000 people who had been inappropriately deleted shortly before the election.[29] In a few communes, the number of people registered to vote inexplicably fell by 50 per cent compared to the year before, and the CNRP went on to receive a much lower share of the vote in those areas.[30]

Commune Councils also have the power to register people who may not have the required identification. There were 750,000 people registered this way in the year before the election, including 150,000 in the hotly contested Prey Veng province alone – equal to 20 per cent of all voters there. The ink that could be washed away could, in theory, allow people to vote twice: once with their real identification and once with their letter from the Commune Council. Sceptics believed that the NEC and Commune Councils were deliberately working to enable CPP supporters to vote twice,[31] although no evidence was found of this happening on a significant scale.

It was for all of these reasons, plus the CPP's domination of the media, use of public servants in campaigning and close relationship with the military, that Transparency International Cambodia advised that even though the counting was accurate, they could 'not express with confidence that the outcome of the election reflects the will of the Cambodian people'.[32] Yet while election observers may have doubted that the CPP victory reflected the will of the people, they had little evidence that there was a predominant desire for the CNRP to form government.

Chamroeun, like many CNRP supporters, did not expect the CNRP to win or even for the result to be so close. He describes himself as an 'agent for change' but his decades of experience in government and social development has taught him that change can be glacial rather than volcanic. I asked him what he thought would have happened if the CNRP had won the election: 'There could be some kind of rocky transition, not smooth. The way the ruling party has built the system, it does not allow the smooth transition. They did not prepare civil servants to accept the new government. The rocky transition could take some time to happen ... The young people did not think too much about a rocky transition. They just thought that it would be smooth. My observation: I thought there could be some difficulty. The ruling party could come back quickly. The young generation did not think like this.' This difference in thinking meant Chamroeun was taken aback by the demonstrations that followed the result: 'After the election, I did not expect them to demonstrate at that time ... I was kind of surprised that the opposition still have a lot of support even after the election.'

'So you did not join the demonstrations?' I asked.

'I was satisfied with the result!' Chamroeun was incredulous that others may be dissatisfied. 'Because I, personally, did not want the CNRP to take immediate control of government. They don't have, you know, capital, political capital. They have to build their base support to win the next election. That's what I expected. When I see the campaign, the protests, I did not denounce it but I was surprised that they did that. They still not satisfied with this result? They want more?! I still support those who protest, but ...'[33]

For Chamroeun, the CNRP had fought a better fight than they could have hoped for. In the drama, people had begun to dream that sudden change was possible. Chamroeun looked around and saw the overwhelming military, economic, media and bureaucratic might that Hun Sen still controlled. Change was not at the corner but rather five years away, down a long road that led to the next election. Chamroeun said that many wanted the CNRP to follow a Buddhist proverb that teaches *'tork, tork, penh bompong'* (drop by drop, the bucket slowly fills). 'Even though they voted for change, they see reality,' he told me, and this reality involved continuing to live under Hun Sen. The government was not playing at keeping power; it was deadly serious about it.

CHAPTER 9
VENG SRENG STREET

I met Kunthea and Channa, both garment factory workers, at Channa's home in the western outskirts of Phnom Penh. The apartment is on the third floor of a new concrete block yet to be finished. It has a small bathroom and one large room, approximately three metres by five, in which Channa, her husband and two children cook, eat and sleep. The room had been prepared for my arrival, with furniture pushed to the sides so that there was enough space for us to sit on the tiled floor. All of the clothes hung on a rack next to a child's red bicycle. There were photos of Channa's two children on the wall and of Sihanouk's funeral, but no photos of King Sihamoni or of Hun Sen and his wife, as is common. Kunthea, Channa and I, plus my interpreter, each sat with a cushion under us for comfort. A plate of watermelon and pineapple rested in the middle. Channa's husband, a friend of mine, stood in one corner, hovering on the edge of the conversation.

Channa and Kunthea were seventeen and twenty years old respectively when they left their rural villages to find work in Phnom Penh. Their families were reluctant to let them go but desperate for money.

'It took one year of persuasion before the family agreed,' Kunthea began, in a surprisingly husky voice for a slim woman in her mid-thirties. 'At first, they thought that it was not good. Not good for a lady, their daughter, to go far away from family. But I feel confident that I can look after myself. The family thinks that we might be cheated and sold. Scared of me being trafficked. They also thought I could have difficulties crossing the road.' I smiled: such was the rhythm of rural life in the 1990s that moto traffic was as feared as the trafficking of humans.

'Even though poor, they thought it was better to stay together in the village,' Kunthea continued, '[but] I knew that I could send money back to them. There are no factories in rural areas. Later on, we saw someone else from the same village go to Phnom Penh and get a job. So they agreed to let me go.'

'What did you feel when you arrived in Phnom Penh? What was it like?'

'It was very different!' Kunthea responded immediately. 'I didn't know anybody. Didn't have family members here. I had never lived away from parents and family. I tried to bring food and other things from the province and I only had a very small amount of money. I dared not spend the money as I feared I couldn't find a job. So I ate ten eggs for ten days. One egg per day.'

Kunthea had moved to Phnom Penh in 1998. 'When I arrived, it was full. No jobs. I had to wait another two months, and even then, it was only me that got a job, not my sister. I paid $70 to an agent to help facilitate. The first month, I got $28. The next month, at the end, my sister got a job. Then we had some money left to send to the family.'

The pace that Kunthea spoke at explained her hoarseness. Throughout our conversation, my interpreter would often plead with her to take a breath so that he could interject. Kunthea would apologise immediately and fall momentarily silent, before picking up the same pace as soon as the interpreter had finished translating her answer.

There were only 19,000 other garment factory workers in Cambodia when Channa made her journey to Phnom Penh in 1995. By the time Kunthea arrived three years later, the industry had quadrupled.[1] Every week for the next decade, a thousand more daughters packed a bag, wiped away tears and said goodbye to their family. They would pay somebody to find a job, work fifty hours a week for $80, sleep huddled on a floor in a single room with three others, and send as much back home as they could. This was not their dream, but it was the reality for the more than 500,000 Cambodians working in garment, textile or footwear factories in 2013.[2] I asked if either had joined a trade union to campaign for better conditions.

'At first,' Kunthea explained, 'there were no unions. A few months later, Sam Rainsy came in and then Chea Vichea appeared. They started to form unions. We decided to join when they became available. We realised that there was no problem to join a union and the union would help us. Prevent us being pressured by owners.' Chea Vichea was the man who co-founded the Free Trade Union of Workers with Sam Rainsy, and it quickly attracted members and support. 'At first, when there was an announcement about Chea Vichea's union being set up, there was a man who came in and asked, "Who dare to be vice-chair of a union in the factory?" Nobody did as they were scared and thought they may be fired. Later on, I said that if nobody volunteers, I would do it, but I could not read and write well, so there should be a secretary. Anyway, I became deputy and persuaded my cousin to become a member too.

'Before unions, if, for example, we have to take fifteen minutes or thirty minutes to leave early, the time that you work that day is cut. But later, the union asks that we can take leave for up to three days. I know because I learn a lot and know the law. Because of Chea Vichea, the workers can have better conditions.'

Unsurprisingly, given her admiration of Rainsy for helping to start trade unions, Kunthea became a devoted supporter of the CNRP. In December 2013, when the CNRP began to hold daily protests they said would continue until a re-election was promised,[3] she was one of 20,000 people who walked, rode on motos or got a lift in a tuk-tuk to Freedom Park on the first day, and the day after that, and the day after that. 'We wanted to say that we didn't trust the election result,' she explained to me. 'The important thing is that at that time, while counting the ballots, they know Sam Rainsy and Kem Sokha won the election. The electricity was disconnected. Fifteen minutes later, Hun Sen won the election instead. At that time, the leaders [Rainsy and Sokha] spoke, convincing us that it was possible. The leaders say that we follow the law of Cambodia and we should not feel afraid. Protestors believe and trust this.'[4]

For the first few days, the numbers of protestors remained steady at 20,000, smaller than the crowd who had protested in September. Ou Ritthy, the young man who had volunteered with COMFREL, explained this was partly because it was the wrong time of year to protest. He had grown up in a rural village in Pursat province, wedged between Thailand and the Tonlé Sap basin in Cambodia's west. As a boy, he would rise at 5.00am to tend the family's chickens and cows. With his younger brother, he would catch small fish in the paddy fields, shoot birds with his slingshot and, during harvest, scythe, gather and mill rice by hand. His greatest challenge was trying to keep the massive bull from mounting cows all the time. His father was a primary-school director, so he made sure that Ritthy attended school in the afternoon, and Ritthy's aptitude meant he was one of the few from his village to attend the far-away high school. One of his four younger brothers took his place on the farm as he left to live with a family near the school, where he bought food and cooked for himself. Ritthy was meant to return home as a teacher but, at the last moment, he sold his place to the next candidate in line and set off for university in Phnom Penh. His fretful mother was reassured when Ritthy found space to stay at Wat Ounalom, but she didn't know that many of the teenaged monks were drinking, gambling on the football World Cup and, once, peering over a wall to see a fellow monk frolic with a young woman.[5]

Ritthy's family still live in the same village he grew up in, and when he returns home he notices that life has remained largely unchanged from when he was a boy. Roads are better and more places have electricity, but Cambodia is still a nation of farmers, where each family has a small plot of land near their house. Dilapidated or wholly absent irrigation means that for most there is only one harvest a year, beginning in December after the last drops of the wet season, from which to make a year's living. Just as Rainsy was calling for daily protests, entire villages were assisting each other to harvest rice before the rains returned.[6]

'I met a lady who came from Prey Veng,' Ritthy recalled. 'And to stay there [Freedom Park], she would stay in Kien Svay [20 kilometres from Phnom Penh] with a relative, a moto-taxi driver. They would buy corn, boil it and then sell it. I asked her if she was a seller. She said, "No, I'm a protestor, but this is how I survive."'[7]

Sunday 22 December was the eighth day of consecutive protest and the biggest yet. Sunday is the only day factory workers get off, and at least 30,000 people marched down Monivong Boulevard, turned along Mao Tse Toung Boulevard, went up and around Phnom Penh's Olympic Stadium, and turned east along Charles de Gaulle Boulevard before returning to their base, Freedom Park. While walking along Monivong Boulevard, Rainsy and Sokha halted the protestors as they neared Hun Sen's house and invited some to explain why they wanted Hun Sen to step down.[8]

One garment factory worker climbed up onto a pick-up truck, grasped the loudspeaker and reminded her comrades about the three young female garment workers shot by the Governor of Bavet: 'Our workers were shot by authorities ... We asked the Prime Minister to find justice for us, but he does not care. Therefore, we need Hun Sen to step down!' Another factory worker said Hun Sen should step down if he could not provide a minimum wage of $160 a month. Rainsy and Sokha threatened that if the CPP did not organise another re-election, protests would continue.[9]

Immediately after the election, the government had announced a review of the $80 per month minimum wage. Then, just two days after the factory worker stood 500 metres from Hun Sen's house demanding $160 per month, the Ministry of Labour announced that they would increase it to $95 only, before increasing it incrementally to $160 over five years.[10] On 25 December, a meaningless day in the Cambodian calendar, half a million workers filed into factories across Cambodia to hear the news that the government valued their slaving away in sweltering conditions at less than $4 a day.

Workers from 240 factories went on strike, rushing to join the CNRP's daily protests at Freedom Park. Seven of the biggest unions wrote to the Garment Manufacturers Alliance of Cambodia (GMAC) and the Ministry of Labour advising that if their demands were not met within a week, workers from every factory would join the strike. GMAC, representing factory owners, advised factories to consider closing to avoid violent protests at their gates.[11]

The twenty-ninth of December was a day that some hoped would prove to be a turning point in Cambodian history as unprecedented numbers of people turned out to protest, willing to be identified as an opponent of the CPP.[12] *The New York Times* estimated that it was tens of thousands; *Al Jazeera* claimed hundreds of thousands. It felt like half of Phnom Penh as the streets crammed. Onlookers hanging out of apartment windows could barely see an inch of tarmac as the roads were a sea of people sitting atop tuk-tuks or in trucks singing CNRP songs and waving flags. Others held signs demanding Hun Sen step down. One of the signs said in English, 'People no need Hun Sen'.[13]

Rainsy, with Sokha at his right side, stood in the back of a white pickup, waving, bowing, cheering and possibly wondering whether this moment, twenty years after being ousted as Minister of Finance, was the heralding of his eventual triumph. Dressed in a white shirt, Rainsy called Hun Sen's government illegal, warning that the protests could no longer be ignored, and gave the government a week to consider the CNRP's demands.[14]

The CPP responded within days by declaring they would increase the minimum wage to $100 per month as a final offer and warned unions to halt the strikes immediately or face recriminations. They also began legal action against Rong Chhun, one of the most admired union leaders.[15]

Veng Sreng Street begins just beyond Stung Meanchey's market when coming from the centre of Phnom Penh. From the headquarters of Phnom Penh's military police, it stretches for seven kilometres until it merges with the national road that takes you to coastal Sihanoukville. Factories dot the roadside, slotted between phone shops, food markets, shoe sellers and car mechanics. The biggest factories, though, are set back from the road. Nearly halfway along Veng Sreng Street sits the entrance to Canadia Industrial Park, which covers 100 hectares and houses nearly fifty factories.

Just before 7.00am, every Monday to Saturday, tens of thousands of women, and the odd man, arrive by moto, in tuk-tuks and pressed against one another in open-top dumper trucks. Some workers wear patterned cotton pyjamas, to keep cool in the sweltering heat; others wear tight-fitting jeans. Most will have socks on with their sandals, and all will have tops that cover them to their neck, which is as much to do with the desire for white skin as traditional notions of female modesty. Identity lanyards dangle like proprietary necklaces and tiffins carrying rice are in hand as women hurry to their places. At 6:59am, the bustling cacophony of Veng Sreng Street vanishes behind giant doors as the working day begins. For many, it won't end until 6pm.

The second day of January 2014 was different, though. Most workers did not take their places at 7.00am, staying outside the factory, on strike, playing music, singing and eating.

Moeun Tola led the Community Legal Education Centre, which provided legal support to garment workers during the strikes and in the aftermath, when union leaders and strikers were commonly arrested. He was holding a press conference about why workers wanted a minimum wage of $160 now, not in five years, when he heard about trouble at Yakjin factory near Veng Sreng Street; the factory's owner had used his connections to call in military police to arrest union leaders and break up protests.

Arriving at Yakjin factory, the barrel-chested Tola tried to engage some soldiers. 'I talk to soldiers, try to hear the soldiers. Ask them how much they earn and can you survive on your salary? Then I get a phone call, more people arrested at Veng Sreng, and people ask me what to do.' Events were turning quicker than Tola could keep up with; three of his colleagues who had gone to Preah Vihear, Cambodia's second Angkor Wat, had also just been arrested. Tola sent lawyers on the nine-hour drive to mountainous Preah Vihear while he rushed over to Veng Sreng Street.

When Tola got there, he took off his spectacles, not believing his eyes. Tyre barricades burned on the street, Molotov cocktails were being hurled through the air and the police went to war on their own people. Tola and a human rights worker called Soeng Sen Karuna saw drunk, young men vent a fierce rage. Tola said it was the only time he had ever suffered 'brain freeze'. His speech slowed when recounting what happened, as if the sense of being overwhelmed was returning. 'Every time we have problems, we approach the UN office. But that time UN people rush to ask me for help and what to do. And then I think, *oh my god, who should I go to for assistance?*

Who can I ask for help?' All Tola could do was to ask them to let him think for a moment.

Talking to protestors, Tola heard that they had been protesting peacefully when a truck carrying twelve young men arrived and smashed their music speakers and microphones, and then another group of young men arrived saying that they should fight back and began to burn tyres. Tola believes that both groups of young men were plain-clothed soldiers or government-hired gangs, whose role was to provide justification for a police crackdown.[16] Karuna also half-suspected that the drunk young men he witnessed throwing rocks and petrol bombs were not factory workers but government plants.[17]

Kunthea was there too. I asked how many people were out demonstrating that day and she told me, 'Everybody! Thousands! Thousands! Many people.' Kunthea's view, from among the ranks of protestors, was different, though. She said it was male workers who were throwing stones and making petrol bombs from the one-litre glass bottles that petrol is sold in, while she and other female workers stood behind the front ranks shouting at the police. Kunthea believes it was the arrival of the military police that prompted this violence: 'Normally, the police come and just stand there. This time ... the police came wearing helmets, masks, armour. With guns.'[18] This seemed to inflame rather than intimidate the protestors, with some believing that the full-face masks were hiding Vietnamese soldiers.[19] Hun Sen had recently made an official visit to Vietnam, delivering a speech in fluent Vietnamese, and some protestors thought that Sen, still 'Vietnam's puppet', had sought blessing or instruction for the ensuing crackdown.[20]

Soeng Sen Karuna has been working for Cambodian human rights organisations since 2004, but his interest in human rights began in 1993 when, as a young man, he attended a two-week training course organised by UNTAC. The certificate he gained is still on display at his home. Jovial and portly, Karuna seems to value human life for the enjoyment it can bring as much as any philosophy of individual liberty. It is a wonder that such a convivial man can so often find himself caught in situations of violence. Just two months earlier, in November 2013, Karuna had tried to quell a protest that became a riot in which police shot eight people, killing one innocent bystander. A man huddling next to Karuna was shot in the torso and paralysed for life.[21]

Somebody once told Karuna that it is better to stand behind police lines during a riot, as you are less likely to be shot at. Arriving at Veng Sreng

Street, he followed this sage advice, watching protestors throw rocks from the other side of police lines. It wasn't long, however, before he felt a stone strike the back of his head. Rubbing the emerging bump, Karuna turned around to see who had thrown it, but the street lay empty behind him.[22]

Kunthea left Veng Sreng Street at 7.00pm, not long after darkness had fallen, and Tola rushed off just before 8.00pm to deal with the arrest of colleagues in Preah Vihear province. Sensing more trouble, he texted other staff asking them to be at Veng Sreng Street in the morning because he was sure that the factory workers would be even angrier after the crackdown.[23] Karuna was still there trying to calm tensions at midnight, when police fired shots at protestors, breaking through barricades of burning tyres to clear the area.

Karuna was back on Veng Sreng Street at sunrise, as was Kunthea, and the mood was already soaked in anger. Workers burned a guard's motorbike and dragged Canadia Industrial Park's huge metal gate onto the road, drenching it in gasoline and setting it ablaze not far from where burning tyres blocked the road.[24]

The first squads of military police appeared about 9.00am and were greeted by a hail of stones. The military police, armed with machine guns and smoke grenades, were not there to control the protest but to shut it down. The Phnom Penh Governor had reportedly said that he, the National Police Chief and National Military Police Commander had met and decided that as they had not been able to 'blow the smoke away', they 'had to put out the fire'.[25]

Kunthea said the police warned the protestors they would start firing if the crowd did not disperse. 'Then they started to shoot and one worker fell down and died. Other workers feel very angry, so they want to go back. I saw the worker fall ... the workers want to take the boy to the clinic nearby but the police stopped them. I tried to ask permission from the police but the police would not agree. I began to cry and the police said that if I showed this feeling before he had been shot then maybe nothing would have happened.'[26]

Kunthea backed away from the police. She asked protestors to stop throwing rocks, but they kept hurling volley after volley. The police kept shooting into the crowd and the workers turned and fled, pursued by the police. Kunthea said the protestors 'were like chickens they [the police] were trying to shoot'. There are crowded apartment blocks down an alley beside the Canadia factories; some protestors ran into them and up the stairs, chased by the police. Onlookers closed their doors in fear of stray bullets, which left the protestors caught with nowhere to go. They were dragged back down the stairs and beaten in the street.

Now standing with the protestors opposite police lines, Karuna was trying to film and take photos, holding the camera above his head while ducking behind a barricade so that only his hand was showing. He heard the bullets whizz by and saw two people get shot, one in the body and one in the shoulder. He could not believe they found strength to continue throwing stones despite such injuries. The stones would arc for only a few metres before falling to the ground. Karuna thought to himself that if the protestors had guns, they could have battled for the whole of Phnom Penh, such was their commitment.[27]

Tola spoke to military police who said that their orders were to crack down. Their warnings simply told *non-protestors* to leave the area, they said. For Tola, this was a sign that they wanted the protestors to remain and be fired upon,[28] and police also ignored Karuna's appeals for them to stop shooting and use water cannons, tear gas or rubber bullets instead.

Tuk-tuks were ferrying bloodied people to pagodas and hospitals as Veng Sreng became the site of a pitched battle of rubble, fires and chaos. A critically injured protestor was carried to the doorstep of a clinic 200 metres from the eye of the storm. Two staff came out to check on him but did not want to treat him or other injured protestors for fear of aiding opponents to the government. Protestors, furious at this, looted the clinic, burning mattresses and smashing equipment.[29]

By high noon even more military police arrived in trucks to clear the streets and round up remaining protestors, ending the rebellion. In the aftermath, it was established that four protestors, all factory workers, had been killed and twenty-five suffered bullet wounds, while others were beaten badly.[30] A sixteen-year-old boy, a worker in one of the factories, had been shot and was lying unconscious on the ground. He was from Svay Rieng, the same province as Kunthea and the three young women shot by the Governor of Bavet. Karuna saw the boy being taken away by authorities, but nothing was seen of him again. The family pleaded with Karuna to find their son. They found some flesh and bone on the street, which was sent to the United Kingdom for DNA testing, but it wasn't him. It was somebody else's son or daughter.

'In Cambodia, always waiting. Waiting, waiting, waiting.' Kunthea's energy was wilting. 'We have to wait to hear what happened to that boy from Svay Rieng. Waiting.'[31]

CHAPTER 10

THE THIRD HAND

The day after the events at Veng Sreng, Rotha made his way to Freedom Park once more. Among the protestors, he saw his uncle, who was an activist back in their home province. His uncle was waiting for the tsunami that he knew would follow the violence at Veng Sreng Street: 'I asked him if he was afraid. He said he is not afraid. "If I die, I cannot change this." *He volunteers to die? Oh*, I thought, *this is something very strong.*' Rotha was unsure if he should be in awe of his uncle or worried for his sanity.[1]

Kunthea was also at Freedom Park that morning, before returning home, like many others did, for lunch and to escape the burning midday sun. It was about 1.00pm when Kunthea got a phone call telling her that military police had stormed Freedom Park to break up the protest. Kunthea sped back on her moto, arriving to see military police shooting guns into the air. Hundreds of police, even more than were at Veng Sreng Street, were in full riot gear, wading into Freedom Park. Rainsy, Sokha and the trade union leaders had been summoned to court for allegedly inciting the protests at Veng Sreng Street, leaving the protestors bereft of leadership. Faced with such overwhelming force, the protestors did not want to suffer the same fate as some of those at Veng Sreng Street the day before. People scrambled to get their things together and hurried away as the police hit those not moving quickly enough. Kunthea took videos of what she witnessed and put them on Facebook. Shortly afterwards, a friend told her to delete them, close her account and throw the SIM card away.[2]

The government entombed Freedom Park in a ring of steel boards metres high. Police arrested Rong Chhun and six other trade union leaders for causing intentional damage under aggravated circumstances, even though they were not at Veng Sreng Street during the protest.[3]

The resolve of the movement broke. The CNRP still refused to join the National Assembly, but negotiations with the CPP began. Small protests involving hundreds of people still infrequently occurred at the edge of Freedom Park, but the angry chants calling for Hun Sen to step down had fallen quiet.

⸎

After monitoring the election, Ritthy continued to act as an independent observer of the protests and strikes that followed. He worked with a young female photographer who threw herself into the action. 'Every morning, she came to my home and said "Let's go!"' Ritthy shook his head at her energy. 'I asked bodyguards of Sokha and Rainsy if I could stand on the roof of the car and take photos. I was not good, I was wobbly. The two bodyguards hold my legs above my ankles to hold me up, lift me up.' Ritthy laughed, his shoulders shaking, at the memory. 'Back then I was fifty-two kilograms, so slim and fast – now I'm sixty-four!'[4]

Ritthy missed the protests at Veng Sreng Street as no moto-taxi was willing to take him near the area, but he was there the morning after and could not believe the number of bullet casings littering the road.[5] '[It] looked like a place of war. Still burning. Tank is still there. Electricity wires were cut, hanging.'

I asked him if he had ever seen anything like it before, and he shook his head. 'Not in real life ... A nightmare.'[6]

Six months later, nearly one whole year after the election, Ritthy was monitoring a protest that the CNRP had called for at the edge of Freedom Park. The day before, the Ministry of the Interior had warned that people would be beaten if they demonstrated because the right to protest had been suspended.[7] A few hundred people, led by three senior CNRP officials, gathered at the edge of Freedom Park on the morning of 15 July 2014. They were quickly confronted by security guards and military police. As the protestors unfurled a banner that read 'Free the Freedom Park', security guards, who had forged a reputation for violence when dispersing protestors, tore it down and began to hit protestors with their batons. A woman, protesting because she had been forced from her land, was whacked on the head; Ritthy leapt in between her and the guard to stop her being hit again. The guards used their shields to squeeze the protestors into a huddle.[8] Some protestors broke free and, according to Ritthy, picked up sticks from the ground and began to defend themselves. 'Somebody was beaten by some stick and then they see sticks. Then, you defend yourself. You're fighting already.'

The protestors, so long the victims of overwhelming force and brutality, saw the outnumbered security guards regrouping and decided to attack them first. One guard was beaten viciously on the ground to the point of unconsciousness. Other protestors intervened to stop the beating of security guards, but another guard was already being stripped from his uniform, which was then set on fire.[9]

Video footage shows that at least some protestors used their flagpoles, feet and fists to beat the security guards. Ritthy, however, is suspicious of how the protestors came to be armed. 'At that time, somebody dropped sticks along the way. I don't know who. The Third Hand. And then moto-taxi and tuk-tuk [drivers] got angry and picked up the sticks that had been dropped and beat the security guards. Beat them seriously. But who drop the stick? Nobody knows, but all blame to opposition. They fall into the trap that they play. They are the victims. It was well planned. Well designed. Then they start accusing the opposition.'[10]

Thirty-nine security guards were injured, some seriously. At least six protestors were also injured. CNRP officials who had attended the protests, some of whom were close confidantes of Rainsy and Sokha, were arrested and imprisoned immediately.

One week later, with several CNRP officials facing thirty years in jail on charges of insurrection, Hun Sen, Sam Rainsy and Kem Sokha met. Five hours later, they emerged onto the steps of the Senate and announced that the CNRP would take their seats in the National Assembly as part of a deal nearly identical to that Hun Sen had offered just after the election: the CPP would hold power based on the election result; Kem Sokha would become Deputy President of the National Assembly; CNRP members would chair half of the largely powerless National Assembly committees; the National Election Committee would be completely reformed; and the CNRP would be granted licences to set up their own radio and television stations. The CNRP members who had been held in prison since the protest were promptly released on bail, with the possibility of future conviction if antagonism flared again.[11]

The CNRP's main goal in boycotting the National Assembly was to de-legitimise the government, forcing it into an early re-election. But the agreement with the CPP only specified that the next election would be held at a time to be agreed, possibly just five months earlier than the expected July 2018 date.[12]

Rainsy told his supporters that 'the only appropriate choice was to end the political crisis, and to end the tense situation'.[13] He explained that his new rationale was to prioritise reforming the National Election Committee and the voter list. 'The rest,' he confidently predicted, 'can happen in a matter of time.'¹⁴

CHAPTER 11

A CULTURE OF DIALOGUE

Those with the most time can often be the people most impatient for change, and so it was that some of the CNRP's young, fervent supporters did not agree it should make a deal with Hun Sen's CPP.

Rotha and Soveacha, who had devoted their time and belief to the CNRP, felt that it could have pursued other options. 'They could do protest with other democratic countries because the government is not legal,' Rotha stressed. 'If we keep going, no one will support this kind of government, a one-party government. This is not right for the Cambodian constitution. Sam Rainsy, Kem Sokha said they would not join, but at the last minute, they join.'[1] Soveacha, recalling the photo of Rainsy and Hun Sen standing on the steps of the Senate together smiling and shaking hands, laughed at Sokha's inability to hide his own view of the agreement. Sokha stood two metres behind Rainsy, slightly to the side, with a face like thunder.

Chamroeun, nearly two decades older than Rotha and Soveacha, thought that the CNRP made the right decision to take their seats in the Assembly: 'It was tense. I feel they did the right thing and I support the decision. There is no better way. Cannot boycott forever, but I think a lot of people don't agree with that. Especially those who support another faction within the CNRP. They just want a quick change, a quick win.' He continued, 'Those who follow Kem Sokha, they listen to his speech. "There is never change without sacrifice" – it's almost that he describes something like people power. Revolution. People who follow him take that direction. It could be a dangerous thing if they want to face with the ruling CPP at that time. They [the CPP] might use their iron fist to suppress.'[2]

Chamroeun believed that Sen, Rainsy and Sokha would cooperate in the interests of the country: 'When Sam Rainsy, when Kem Sokha, went to meet Hun Sen in the National Assembly ... they talk nicely,' Chamroeun explained. 'I trust them 90 per cent that Cambodia would move in the right direction. Some people were talking about a coalition government between Sam Rainsy and Hun Sen ... that this might be a good time for Cambodia to move together and forget the bitter past. A culture of dialogue so that we avoid bloodshed, revenge. So I believe 90 per cent it would be smooth and only 10 per cent that there would be a problem. I believe that Sam Rainsy might take a chance to build a network by working in a coalition government. He could build more network, favour to him.'

I asked Chamroeun if he had envisaged a situation where Hun Sen was Prime Minister and Rainsy was Finance Minister. He interjected, 'Or deputy Prime Minister!' I nodded. 'And do you believe that over the five years [before the next election], there could be a transition of power? Foundations laid for a transition?'

Chamroeun sighed. 'I think that was the best way. I did not see any better way to ... Ignore the ruling party who control the country for so long? Just get them away? They would not let you do that. The only way is to work together. But not exploit or try to shake hands and kick the opponent with your leg. If you try that, then you still have the same problems of the past. I think Sam Rainsy was smart enough to avoid that. I notice the words Prime Minister Hun Sen express to Rainsy in *Songkran* (Khmer New Year) celebrations in Siem Reap in 2015. They went together. Hun Sen openly said, "I never seen any other opposition leader like Sam Rainsy. And now Sam Rainsy come to join with me. So Cambodia will have a smooth direction now." He said that! At that time, I was so excited. He said that to Sam Rainsy!'[3]

Sam Rainsy returned Hun Sen's praise, believing that as they were both 'getting older' they were 'readjusting our goals in life'. Hun Sen had become 'sincere' in his desire to create a better Cambodia 'to leave to the next generation'.[4] Sen and Rainsy heralded a 'culture of dialogue', changing the history of politics in Cambodia.

In the ancient kingdom of Angkor, there was only one ruler and no need for dialogue. During occupation by Thailand, Vietnam and then France, Cambodians were largely excluded from political dialogue. After independence, Sihanouk executed those guilty of critical dialogue, showing their deaths to silent audiences in cinemas. He, in turn, was toppled by a military coup whose only dialogue with the subsequent Khmer Rouge was through guns and bombs. The Khmer Rouge took Cambodia back to year zero when people slaved rather than spoke, and dialogue was rare during the ensuing civil war of the 1980s. The coalition government of the 1990s communicated using tanks and one side's tongue was literally ripped out. Since then, dialogue has occurred within the CPP's Central Committee or via Sam Rainsy's megaphone, often from abroad. When talking with Chamroeun one day, I told him about a husband and wife, one of whom supported the CPP and the other a CNRP supporter. He was flabbergasted. He could not comprehend how they could live together and support different sides.

Sophal, the handsome young man who jumped off a bus to join a CNRP rally, and Kimsorn, the CPP group leader who whisked away a *krama* to show me his new television, had lived close to each other for many years, although their relationship was distant, the two separated by a political divide. Despite his hesitation, Sophal agreed to interpret for me whenever I met with Kimsorn. During my first meeting with Kimsorn, Sophal faithfully interpreted everything Kimsorn said, although I could sense that he found it strange to be speaking words of praise for Hun Sen and the CPP. Leaving Kimsorn's house, however, the earnest Sophal admitted that he was glad to have interpreted because, never having asked Kimsorn, he had learned a little about why Kimsorn supported the CPP.

For a culture of dialogue to exist there must be a willingness to listen, including an acceptance that the other person's view may have some validity. Without it, we turn our backs on each other, decrying the idiocy, evilness or corruptness of the other camp. Silence creates a Grand Canyon of denial and conflict; *I am right and you are wrong and we cannot talk until you submit to that.*

One evening, I was sitting with Leap, the senior official at an international organisation, and two other friends in the Red Cow restaurant. A lively place at the end of an alleyway, it serves cheap beer and grilled beef that you dip in tasty *prahok*, a kind of liquified fermented fish paste. One can hear the clinking of glasses and the regular exclamation of *'jul muy'* (cheers), which happens every time a man goes to take a hearty swig.

We began talking about the culture of dialogue. I asked them how the phrase 'agree to disagree', a phrase they knew in English, would be translated into Khmer. Leap tried, venturing an attempt that he knew would not work even before finishing, and paused, shaking his head and declaring, 'Even the [concept] does not make sense in Khmer – agree to disagree.' Another muttered something but could not offer anything better than Leap's suggestion. Bamboozled, the three agreed that it was an impossible idea to express in

Khmer and that you would end up saying that you agreed with something you disagreed with.

Ritthy, the observer of the protests, joined us an hour later. After he ordered a beer, we smirked and put the challenge to him. He closed his eyes, opened his mouth and began an attempt, then paused and finally gave up. 'We never say this! No. It does not make sense – why you agree with someone that you disagree with?' Ritthy asked.

'The problem is English,' concluded Leap amid whoops of laughter.

After we clinked our glasses and gulped our beer, Leap gave further insight into the cultural difference: 'In Khmer, some people, if they don't agree with you, they may not like you. The culture can be like this. In English, you have the phrase "I don't mind." But in Khmer, I would mind if I don't agree. In English, I don't agree but I don't mind. But in Khmer, if I don't agree, I mind. Revenge.'[5] The other Cambodians nodded and Leap continued, explaining that there are political ramifications of this culture. 'At the top level, there is no "I hear your argument, I respect your argument but I disagree with your argument." Our Assembly, there is no idea of debate. It is not like that.' Leap said that the example set by leaders makes it impossible for those lower down to talk, even if they want to: 'There are two parties. Us and them. You are one or the other.'[6]

While completing a degree in India, Ritthy was amazed at the constant chatter about politics in cafés. The debates intrigued Ritthy, who had grown up remembering the battles of 1997, and he realised that in Cambodia, 'there are lots of people who have degrees, but we still have a problem tolerating different ideas'. When Ritthy returned to Cambodia, he established Politikoffee, an informal weekly group that he hopes will cultivate a space for dialogue among young people, who come to drink coffee, hear guest speakers and discuss politics. 'If we can get young people doing this now and, by chance, they become a leader, there is more chance agreeing to disagree will happen.'[7]

We began talking about words like 'consensus' and 'dialogue', and Ritthy advised that while *'chluh k'nea'* is used when translating 'to argue', it actually means something closer to conflict. More befuddlement and laughter followed our failed attempts at a more accurate translation, noting that in English an argument need not be a negative concept as one can construct an argument to explain the logic of one's opinion, eliciting understanding and dialogue. In Cambodia, it seemed there is no word for an argument without conflict.

The migration of new concepts into Cambodia became clear to me when I would sit in meetings and Cambodians would pepper the discussion with the odd English word. My colleagues would explain that as there was no equivalent Khmer word, it was easier to use the English word rather than a stream of Khmer words to approximate it. Thoughts and beliefs can exist even if we do not have the words to express them, but thoughts and beliefs more frequently communicated, that we hear around us every day, can become dominant currents in society, shaping our opinions and behaviour. Agree to disagree; to argue without conflict: concepts that are apparently absent from the Khmer language and of which some would never have heard.

Hun Sen and Sam Rainsy agreed that to build a culture of dialogue, personal relationships would have to be developed. As two rivals that had spent thirty years opposing each other, they had rarely spent time together. In an effort to initiate such closeness, the families of Hun Sen and Sam Rainsy gathered together for a private dinner in one of Phnom Penh's most expensive hotels. Eating in the ballroom around a huge round table, they mingled, posed for group photographs and even took selfies. One taken by Hun Sen with Sam Rainsy shows that even political leaders have the qualities of the most embarrassing dads.

A priority for the new relationship between the CPP and the CNRP was to pass laws amending the National Election Committee's constitution. It was agreed that the parties would each appoint four members to the NEC and then they would agree on a neutral ninth member. The CNRP made two interesting choices. One was to appoint Rong Chhun, the firebrand President of the Cambodian Confederation of Unions and the Cambodian Independent Teachers' Association, who had been arrested after the protests at Veng Sreng Street, and the other was to appoint the Prosecutor General to the Supreme Court, and therefore an employee of the government, Hing Thirith.

In 2004, Hing Thirith had famously dismissed the case against the alleged killers of Chea Vichea, the trade union leader, calling the arrest illegal (the pair were later cleared). Previously, he had shocked people by signing an arrest warrant for one of Hun Sen's nephews after two people had been shot following a traffic accident.[8] Thirith's punishment for these actions was being sent to work as a municipal judge in Cambodia's most far-flung province of Stung Treng.[9] The CNRP may have thought these were examples of his willingness to oppose the CPP, but as they were to find out in years to come, they actually displayed his devotion to the letter of the law, regardless of that law's provenance.

Rong Chhun and Chea Vichea had been like brothers. Chhun had been a high-profile factory trade union leader for nearly two decades despite working as a high-school maths teacher. Teachers, as they are public servants, are not allowed to form a union in Cambodia, so Rong Chhun established a Teachers' Association. A colleague of mine had once been a student of Rong Chhun's and spoke warmly of his skills as a teacher and his dedication to his students, which included never charging students fees for attending classes, like many teachers do to supplement their low wage.

Teachers in Rong Chhun's Association pledge not to take bribes from students or charge fees and the Association campaigns heavily against corruption in the education system, which often makes its members outcasts in their own schools. However, even teachers who are not members hand out Rong Chhun's mobile number to colleagues who have suffered unjust treatment. Even if not an Association member, Chhun will press their case with the Ministry of Education or work with lawyers to inform them of their rights.[10]

Rong Chhun was an inspiring teacher, but it had been a long time since he was allowed to teach in a school. Rather, he spent a short time in prison along with Kem Sokha in 2005 when facing a charge of defamation against Hun Sen. Notoriously vocal, Rong Chhun knew that if he joined the National Election Committee, he could no longer be an independent critic.

Rong Chhun spoke to friends and eventually surmised that if the NEC had acted independently, the CNRP would have won the 2013 election, which would have led to 'big changes for teachers and garment factory workers'. He hoped that by joining the NEC he could 'protect the interests of the people'.[11] On the day of his confirmation, Rong Chhun announced he was 'sharpening his spurs' to challenge any barriers to a free and fair election.[12]

The original nomination for the ninth, neutral position was the French Ambassador's wife who had brought Sihanouk and Hun Sen together in the 1980s and had returned to Cambodia as president of a human rights organisation, but she declined, stating that the NEC's independence was not guaranteed under the new laws. Hang Puthea, the Executive Director of NICFEC, which was a leading member of the group of charities who monitored elections, was surprised, and possibly flattered, to be asked to be the neutral member instead, telling me, 'I didn't think that I could come to this place [the NEC].'[13]

The group of election monitors praised his appointment and the reform of the NEC but criticised other election laws made at the same time. New laws could lead to heavy fines for charities that were judged to have 'insulted' a political party during an election campaign period. They also objected to a shortening of the official campaign period, during which government officials had to remain neutral. Their greatest fear, however, was of a law that allowed the dissolution of a political party because of an offence committed by one its leaders.[14] With little public consultation, the new laws had passed when both CPP and CNRP members voted for them in the National Assembly.

Meanwhile, the newly formed NEC set out to develop an accurate voter register. The old system relied on handwritten records and a national database that used an outdated code for typing Khmer, which has the longest alphabet in the world, that was incompatible with provincial electronic records.[15] A whole new computer system was developed with financial and technical support from Japan and the EU and records were digitised. The records included photographs of each voter to prevent duplicate entries.

Progress was quick. Rong Chhun told me that 'members had different political minds but we focus on the work'.[16] The neutral appointee, Hang Puthea, told me that decisions among the nine members were made by consensus. If there were a 'hot issue', they would put it aside and go back to it when all else had been agreed. With pride, he said, 'In some countries, they bang shoes to make their point. Here, we discuss.'[17]

CHAPTER 12
DIALOGUE UNRAVELS

If the election campaign was a honeymoon period for the CNRP's marriage of two parties, its aftermath dragged Kem Sokha and Sam Rainsy into the bickering of daily life. They had to compromise so they could negotiate with Hun Sen.

Conspicuously absent from Hun Sen and Sam Rainsy's family dinner was the third member of the dialogue: Kem Sokha. The CRNP's success was based on the equal partnership of Sam Rainsy and Kem Sokha, and some feared that Sokha would not be content outside the inner circle. 'If Sam Rainsy and Hun Sen work well together, he might feel the odd one out,' Chamroeun speculated. 'He might lose his position if Sam Rainsy joins with Hun Sen. That's why his daughter, his supporters, try to oppose that.'

Chamroeun felt that Hun Sen did not have the same bond of trust with Sokha that he had begun to build with Rainsy: 'Some people in the CNRP make the PM unhappy. Make the PM start to believe that they could not work with this opposition. Sam Rainsy could not separate himself from Kem Sokha because the young people really want these two people together for change. Sam Rainsy wanted to work together with Hun Sen, but he could not go away from Kem Sokha. He had to speak to Kem Sokha as well. That make Hun Sen not trust him. Mistrust. It was then that Hun Sen made life difficult for Sam Rainsy. From that point.'[1]

Hun Sen believed that Sam Rainsy was failing to control the anti-Vietnamese campaigns of his party members, and in June 2015, CNRP politicians led a heated rally at the Vietnamese border that ended in brawls.[2] Weeks later, the CNRP organised an even larger rally at the border, bussing activists in from elsewhere, to protest that Cambodia was losing land to Vietnam, affecting farmers in the area. Two leading organisers of this second rally were among the eleven CNRP officials who had been released on bail as part of the agreement between the CPP and the CNRP, and the courts quickly re-arrested all eleven. Exactly one year after the agreement between the CPP and the CNRP, the eleven CNRP officials were convicted for their 2014 protest, which had turned violent, and sentenced to jail. The two who led the recent rally at the Vietnamese border were given twenty years.[3] Upon hearing the news, Sam Rainsy chose to continue his visit to France, where he planned to fundraise for the CNRP's television station and rally international condemnation of the sentencing.[4] The day after landing, challenged by a French newspaper on why he didn't cancel his trip, Rainsy compounded the growing discord in an unintentionally ruinous interview.

Rainsy was keen to downplay the impact the sentences would have on the CNRP and CPP's working relationship, saying the events were 'transient phenomena that do not call into question the culture of dialogue'. The culture of dialogue was a long-term process that would create a 'lasting vision of a democratic Cambodia'. He even ventured that '20-year sentences never last long' in Cambodia and that the 'judicial posturing' was a 'storm' that would 'pass'. While 'thunder is thundering again', he stressed that 'the trend is improving'.

Relaxed in his French apartment, Rainsy explained that his patience came from confidence that Hun Sen wanted change, putting this down to 'the effect of age, of the realization that his reign is coming to an end'. He confided that Hun Sen is 'obsessed with [avoiding] the same fate as Gaddafi' and 'fears a witch hunt' if the CNRP formed government. Perhaps enjoying demonstrating that he had become a confidant of Hun Sen, Rainsy declared that he and Sen were 'preparing the ground for the future' to ensure that 'the transition is smooth'. The transition that Sen hoped for apparently focused on his children, the three sons who he had promoted to high positions in the military, national intelligence and the National Assembly. Rainsy, stripping away Hun Sen's strongman impregnability, disclosed that Hun Sen 'told me verbatim: "I am nothing, [my] children are everything to me."'[5]

The notion of protecting face is part of Cambodian culture just as it has been since ancient times throughout Asia. In China, the concept of *mien-tzu* was first recorded in the fourth century BC and is described as a measure of prestige bestowed by others in your society. This form of prestige is gained through attaining high-status positions, wealth and social ties to prominent people. You may also acquire prestige (*yao mien-tzu*) by building things for the common people, like schools or hospitals, just as Hun Sen has done.[6] People can move up the social hierarchy by gaining prestige and others must adapt how they show respect to you (or give face). The Cambodian language has indicators of this hierarchy, such as the words used to address certain people or the height you hold your hands when greeting them traditionally, with a *sampeah*. Except for the King, Hun Sen was undoubtedly at the top of Cambodia's social hierarchy, and Rainsy's casual sharing of Sen's intimate fears challenged his status, betraying a weakness that could be preyed upon by internal competitors who had previously vied for his favour.

Then Rainsy went further by putting his family on an equal standing to Hun Sen's: 'He knows his children will not be able to lead the country with an iron fist like him,' Rainsy told the French journalist. 'He would like his children to pursue a political career in a democratic setting.' This was why 'Hun Sen wants his children to know mine, to learn to talk to each other, to work together'.[7]

A narrative of Hun Sen needing Sam Rainsy was not one that Sen could accept. Speaking at a bland public forum on industrial development policy, Sen went off-script, unleashing his anger. 'Do my children go from Cambodia to meet his children in Switzerland or America, or do his children come from America, from Switzerland, to meet [mine] in Cambodia? In spite of the relationship between our families, he is trying to get one over on me politically. [How] can I keep calm?! Can I let [Sam Rainsy] gain?! I am very regretful that given everything [we] have tried to build, he has acted dishonestly.'[8]

I asked Hang Puthea about the culture of dialogue and he sighed, admitting that 'Cambodia has been in situation of war' since 1970. He credited Hun Sen for establishing a culture of dialogue to engage the CRNP 'not just once, twice'. Puthea has known the Rainsy family for decades, and remembers giving a silver box to Rainsy's daughter when she was small, but he could not understand why Rainsy acted as he did. 'It's not polite when Rainsy say that. Hun Sen invite families to have dinner ... After this dinner, Rainsy go to France and say that we have dinner because Hun Sen will lose power so he has invited my family to help take care of his family, sons and daughters. Hun Sen could not accept this interpretation. This is impolite. This is not part of the dialogue. After this, they make divorce. Starts from individual issue and goes from there.'[9]

Dav Ansan has been an adviser to the National Assembly's President and is currently Executive Director of Cambodia's Development Center and an Under-Secretary of State in the Ministry of Industry, Science and Technology. He also works closely with Hun Sen's youngest son, Hun Many, who is a member of the National Assembly. I asked him what he thought of Hang Puthea's interpretation. 'I am thinking about whether I should share with you,' Ansan teased, already knowing that he would. 'We amend the law to make His Excellency Sam Rainsy to be equal to the Prime Minister and say whatever he wants [in parliament] to be constructive.[10] They had dinner together, the families. My boss was there. The son of the Prime Minister. It was a sweet time.' He added this wistfully before returning to a more official tone. 'I concur with the idea of Dr Puthea. I do not understand why His Excellency Sam Rainsy did that.'[11]

When your 'face' or status is threatened in a public conflict, you protect it with a display of dominance.[12] Backing down means disgrace and defeat. In Cambodia, parents will separate fighting children but will rarely ask them to apologise,[13] and Dav Ansan once told me that older people would never say sorry as these were 'difficult words to get out'.[14]

The concern over 'face' and the desire to show dominance are combined in the Cambodian concept of *kum*, which translates as holding a grudge and exacting disproportionate revenge so that you take 'a head for an eye'.[15] Haing S. Ngor, who won an Oscar for his role in *The Killing Fields* (1984), wrote:

> *Kum* is a Cambodian word for a particularly Cambodian mentality of revenge – to be precise, a long-standing grudge leading to revenge much more damaging than the original injury. If I hit you with my fist and you wait five years and then shoot me in the back one dark night, that is *kum* ... Cambodians know all about *kum*.[16]

In a boxing analogy given by one Cambodian, if you knock your opponent down, you do not just stand there waiting for him to get up, you kick him until he is unconscious.[17] Hun Sen felt Rainsy's interview was a punch to his gut.

Ansan said that Hun Sen wanted Rainsy to play a role of constructively criticising ministries to help improve government, because Sen 'becomes weaker' if he continually criticises his ministries.[18] This was one of the reasons why, according to Ansan, Hun Sen had forgiven Sam Rainsy's previous slanders: 'Actually he [Rainsy] apologised to Prime Minister Hun Sen several times for his own rhetoric. Insulting him as a dictator. Selling land to Vietnamese. His wife having an affair with the Vietnamese leader. Elder son not his real son.'[19] Ansan believes that Hun Sen put these barbs to the side for the sake of Cambodia's future and that Sen's past shows he can be conciliatory: 'During the fighting with Khmer Rouge, the Khmer Rouge was very clear. Whenever they have chance, they had a list of who they would kill – including Prime Minister Hun Sen. But when he saw the chance to integrate the Khmer Rouge in 1998, he bring in everyone to work in government. The senior military of Khmer Rouge were clear that they would kill him. Now, whenever they meet, they make joke, 'Twenty years ago, you should have shot me …' He can still work with those kind of people, so why not Sam Rainsy? Why not Kem Sokha?'[20]

Speaking of Rainsy, Hun Sen said, 'I cannot smile at you when you shake my hand and step on my toes.'[21] He proclaimed that seven CNRP lawmakers should be arrested for the 2014 protests, in addition to those just sentenced: 'I do not make threats, but when the court summonses you, please go. If you don't go, be careful, for the [court] sentences in absentia, which means you give up the right to defend yourself.' The CNRP protests at the Vietnamese border accusing Sen of giving up land to Vietnam further angered him: 'Using [CNRP members] to insult and incite. What is that?' he fumed. He called for the arrest of a CNRP Senator for posting a mistaken version of the Cambodian–Vietnamese border treaty. Despite having parliamentary immunity, the Senator was jailed three days later.[22]

Shortly after that, two other CNRP Senators were dragged out of their cars as they were leaving the Senate. Set upon by a gang of plain-clothed soldiers, they were punched and kicked, then stomped on as they lay on the ground trying to protect themselves.[23] Police looked on without interfering. Both Senators suffered broken bones. Despite twenty men being present during the attack and at least ten actively involved in the beating, only three were questioned, charged and convicted. All three were senior members of the Prime Minister's elite Bodyguard Unit who had voluntarily come forward.[24] Released after five months in jail, two were immediately promoted to colonel and one became a general.[25]

The Prime Minister's Bodyguard Unit headquarters organised a protest the same day as the beating of the Senators, with military leaders bussing soldiers and villagers in to call for the dismissal of Kem Sokha as Vice-President of the National Assembly. Several hundred protestors went to Sokha's house and threw stones and bottles. His wife, huddled inside, phoned the authorities for help but no police or security aided her.[26] A few days later, CPP members voted to remove Sokha as Vice-President of the National Assembly, despite Cambodia's Constitution only allowing for removal due to death or resignation.[27]

Addressing Cambodians living in South Korea, Rainsy called Hun Sen a dictator and warned that the recent victory of Aung San Suu Kyi in Myanmar had 'created panic' in Cambodia.[28] Hun Sen responded by calling Sam Rainsy the son of a traitor, reminding the public that Rainsy's father was a close aide of Sihanouk but was exiled after allegedly plotting a coup, and organised for Rainsy to be ejected from Parliament, without constitutional basis, stripping him of immunity.[29] A warrant was issued to arrest Rainsy for prior defamation and incitement charges that were not covered by the King's pardon of 2013.[30] Fearing violence if Rainsy returned, CNRP leaders advised him to stay abroad, hoping to calm the Prime Minister and revoke the arrest warrant.[31] But Sen's sense of *kum* dictated this would never happen, forcing Rainsy to return to his apartment in Paris, likely never to set foot in Cambodia again.

It is possible that Hun Sen's wrath was driven not just by a loss of face, but also by a frustrated sense of betrayal over what he believed to be within his grasp. 'I see the feelings of the Prime Minister to have Sam Rainsy be on board,' said Ansan ruefully. 'He [Sen] decides to move his own party, especially those who have a conservative mind. He wants to move because he also wants to move the country for his people. The government understand that a lot of things need to be done for the people and we need a smarter opposition to contribute to move together.' He paused. 'Finally, that opportunity is missed. I hope that you have a chance to ask him [Rainsy] yourself: why did he need to do that?'

There are other Cambodians, such as Ou Ritthy, who disagree with Ansan's and Puthea's assessment that it was Rainsy who caused the rupture. Ritthy believes that Hun Sen was never truly committed to a culture of dialogue between equals. When he looks at the photo of Hun Sen smiling with Rainsy on the steps of the Senate in 2014, he does not see the dawn of Cambodia's culture of dialogue, but the first day of the CPP's new plan: 'Immediately when they had the agreement 22 July 2014, they start arranging everything.'

PART II
2015–2017

'Don't use an egg to hit a stone.'
កុំយកពងមាន់ទៅដល់នឹងថ្ម

Cambodian proverb

By the end of 2015, Hun Sen had spent more than thirty years as prime minister of Cambodia, and most Cambodians had lived their whole life only ever knowing him as their leader. In that time, Reagan, Bush Snr, Clinton and Bush Jnr had come and gone, and Obama was approaching the end of his second term. Gorbachev's glasnost had given way to Yeltsin's Russia, where oligarchs gorged, before a shirtless Putin rode in on horseback promising a resurgent bear. Europe opened the Iron Curtain when the Berlin Wall crumbled, then Balkanised with Milošević, expanded with Chirac, formed a single currency with Kohl, crashed economically with Blair and Brown, and gaped at a brewing Brexit. The Middle East watched as Iraqis and Iranians murdered each other for years, defended Kuwait in the first Gulf War, came close to peace when Arafat and Rabin shook hands, burned in chaos when Hussein fell and ISIS rose, scraped the sky with construction in Dubai and was lit up by revolutions in Egypt, Libya and Syria. China sent tanks into Tiananmen, promised Hong Kong a one-country-two-system model, ended peasant communism, welcomed Coca-Cola and the World Trade Organization, suffered SARS, manufactured for the world, hosted the Olympics and became a global superpower.

Cambodia? Cambodia had Hun Sen.

How can one man control a country for so long? Cambodia's story is of a small nation twisted by geopolitics; of brutal reality crushing the illusions of hope; and of the people, the Cambodian people, who till the soil, bury the past, dream of the future and die waiting for it. There is nothing inevitable about democracy – this is how it can be stopped.

CHAPTER 13

A GAME OF CHESS

I had come to meet Doung Virorth, the Vice-Chairman of the Civil Society Alliance Forum, which, while officially independent, has offices in the imposing Council of Ministers building next to the Peace Building that houses the Office of the Prime Minister. Indeed, it was Hun Sen who established the Forum in 2016, appointing a CPP Secretary of State to be its chairman.

Before joining the Civil Society Forum, Virorth worked for the UN Development Programme, completed postgraduate studies in peacebuilding at an Australian university and spent eight years at the Cambodian Development Institute. During those times, Virorth would often facilitate meetings between government and charities, noticing 'those that work on human rights, democracy – sensitive issues – they have problems cooperating with government'. He believes that charities working in these 'sensitive' areas were 'too quick to take to the street and protest' rather than engaging first, 'so from that point of view, there should be one mechanism to facilitate and coordinate links to government and policymaking. That is the point of the Civil Society Forum.'

Virorth denied accusations that the Forum aims to co-opt charities into a system that the government can control,[1] but was open about the government's displeasure at charities that speak out. 'Some are going in the way of partnership, but some are going in a different direction. We have some information about that. Some evidence that shows they are not working to promote wellbeing of the people but trying to create some problems by using empowerment.'[2]

Kunthea, the husky-voiced garment worker, had earlier told me the story of how she persuaded her cousin to join a union. 'I said to him that when we are born, we have the right. But when asked what rights we have, we don't know. I told my cousin that we have to be able to protect our rights.'[3]

It was this kind of empowerment that charities had been promoting ever since UNTAC, and it clashed with a political leadership forged during communism.

Virorth advised that civil society grew in the 1990s because the government 'was very open and gave freedom'.[4] Due to a pliant National Assembly that rubber-stamped government edicts,[5] charities had become the main voice holding government to account, criticising corruption, abuse of human rights, disregard of the poor and sale of Cambodia's riches. The CPP suspected charities were being directed by their Western donors and decided it was time to end their freedom.[6] Virorth said the government 'learnt' from China, Russia and even America, who all exert some 'control' over what charities can do. 'Sometimes [charities] create problems … so we need to create policies and laws. So LANGO was accepted.'

'LANGO' is the controversial *Law on Associations and Non-Governmental Organisations*. At the time of the law's passing in 2015, Cambodia had an estimated 5000 charities providing literacy classes and food support, delivering health education and vocational training, running schools, building irrigation, setting up social enterprises, protecting forests, defending people in courts or supporting claims against land dispossession. All those charities had to apply for registration or be considered illegal. When applying, charities must have a letter from their Commune Chief, normally a CPP member, stating their office's address and bank account details, with biographies and photographs of each founding member. Government oversight continues after registration, with each charity having to provide annual activity and financial reports, as well as any documents relating to planned projects. The government can de-register organisations, forcing closure, if they believe a charity to be acting in ways that 'endanger the security, stability and public order, or jeopardize the national security, culture, tradition, and custom of Cambodian national society'. All charities must be strictly neutral in relation to political parties, and can be closed if they 'jeopardise national unity'.[7]

Cheang Sokha is the leathery, crinkly-eyed leader of the Youth Resource Development Program (YRDP). He was looking comfortable in jeans and a loose Hawaiian shirt when we met at his office. On the day that the National Assembly approved the law, Sokha took fifty youngsters to join protests, one of many acts that has not endeared him to the government. After becoming YRDP's Executive Director, he asked the Ministry of Interior to change the charity's registration details, but the Ministry rejected their paperwork three times. 'Everything is technically correct, but politically? A problem,' sighed Sokha.

'Do they want you to stop being director?' I asked.

'I already resign! This is one of the reasons. To ensure YRDP still exists.'

It took Sokha months to find another person willing to become Executive Director. We were talking in YRDP's radio studio, where they broadcast programs hosted by young people. The soundproofed walls were adorned by the slogan *Break the Silence*. 'We want young people to be active citizens,' explained Sokha. 'Want to help them have critical thinking and scientific reason. Education system just trains people to repeat what the teacher says. After in-house training, young people go to stay in the places that we are talking about.'

YRDP takes groups of young people, often students, to stay with indigenous people living in the forests that Chut Wutty tried to protect, or with farmers who have lost their land to mining developments. '[We] want them to see the effects of development. Of government development,' Sokha said. 'Speak to the local people. Stay two or three nights. Then they come back with what they have learnt and talk about it on the radio station. They want to inform more people. Fill the gap between what the media report, which is controlled by the government, and the reality.'[8]

Sokha explained that the new law paved the way for additional regulations to restrict activity, including requiring charities to give authorities three days' notice before conducting field activities.[9] 'We cancelled one [trip] to Svay Rieng. The district chief agreed to have an event at the local pagoda ... but the Provincial Governor ...'. Charities counted that police had broken up sixty meetings without legal basis in twelve months between 2016 and 2017.[10]

I asked Sokha what reason the ministry had given to reject their registration paperwork. 'They asked about [a] change [in] the board in 1997 or '98. At the time, a board member was President of ADHOC.'

The Cambodian Human Rights and Development Association is known by its French acronym, ADHOC. It is the organisation that Karuna, the man hit on the head with a stone at Veng Sreng, works for. ADHOC was Cambodia's first human rights organisations, founded in 1991. In 2013 alone, it supported 6500 families in legal disputes over land concessions.[11] Police would often target ADHOC meetings, taking photos and noting personal details of those attending, and once broke up an evening meeting with the claim that meetings weren't allowed after dark. As people like Karuna and Sokha told me, providing project reports to government is like giving the accused notice of your efforts to expose them. One charity reported that the government wanted verbatim minutes of board meetings.[12] A month after the law was passed, an ADHOC coordinator was one of seventeen people arrested – community activists, a journalist, a doctor. Days before, three activists had been jailed for working with fishermen to protest sand dredging. When weekly 'Black Monday' protests began after human rights workers were jailed, police quickly arrested twenty-one activists, sentencing one to six months in jail. Other charity leaders fled Cambodia, fearing more arrests.[13]

I asked Virorth if he thought the law restricted the activities of charities. 'It just says that if you change your leadership, your location or bank account, report it to the ministry. It is not restriction. It is a framework. For human rights [organisations], they may see it as restriction. One priority is maintaining peace and stability for economic growth, so whatever you do, you should do to enhance this.'[14]

The Cambodian Constitution states that freedoms to form associations and groups will be recognised and respected,[15] but when I asked if the government really had tried to engage with civil society, Viroth responded, 'If the government doesn't acknowledge the role, the government may not allow it to operate, in a simple way.'

The Cambodian Constitution also guarantees the right to form trade unions. In the 1990s, the influence of UNTAC and Western countries, whose aid was rebuilding the country, meant that Cambodia signed up to all of the main International Labour Organization conventions, including the right to organise and collective bargaining. The CPP could not break international conventions to stop the emergence of trade unions without risking their ability to export goods tax-free to the EU, its biggest market, and America. Instead, the CPP supported the proliferation of unions so that there are now more unions than there are factories, successfully dividing the union movement.

Pich worked for an international organisation that has promoted labour rights in Cambodia for many years. He explained that factory owners will often collaborate with a floor supervisor to create a union for staff that is friendly to the owners. This can lead to a factory having multiple unions, making it difficult for workers to negotiate collectively.[16] And each trade union is only allowed to operate within one factory. For workers in different factories to campaign together, their different unions must form a federation, which can then partner with other federations to form larger confederations, like a series of Babushka dolls. The owner-friendly unions have joined together successfully so that of one of Cambodia's largest union confederations is led by a government-employed adviser to the Ministry of Labour, who once said: 'My union is Hun Sen's union. All my union members will vote for Hun Sen.'[17] Speaking of this union leader, Pich warned, '[He] can do rain and storm for the labour movement.'[18] Closely aligned with the CPP, union leaders in this confederation act as CPP campaign leaders within factories during elections.

It is rare that owners blatantly prevent workers from joining certain unions,[19] but Pich revealed their more subtle methods. For instance, the factory administrator may give a union membership form along with a contract to a new employee, who may be illiterate and doesn't know what she is signing. Some factories skip that step and automatically enrol new workers in the owner-friendly union. Other staff are tempted to join because of better treatment from managers, such as the granting of overtime.[20]

A factory worker can only be a member of one trade union at a time, and once a member of a CPP-aligned union, it can be difficult to change allegiance. Factory managers may accuse workers of stealing clothes or not renew their fixed-term contract.[21] A young leader of a CPP-aligned union planned to move to an independent one. Driving home one night, police stopped him without cause, lifted the seat of his motorbike and found nine small packets of pills he knew nothing about. He was sentenced to ten months in jail.[22]

Kunthea realised that the union in her factory was not independent so decided to submit a request to the Ministry of Labour asking for permission to set up a new union. 'I started working with a factory near here and the supervisor – sometimes his words are difficult to accept. After a few days, I want to stop working there. In the factory, there is an existing union but it is quite different from others. Normally, the membership fee is 2000 riels (50 cents). But this one is only 1000 riels per month. I start to study about the union. It is the union that is pro-owner of the factory.'[23] I asked her what the managers did in response to her Ministry of Labour request. 'At first, they say that I should not start a union because if I start it, I would be fired, and if I was fired, I would have to go back my village. No job in any factory. They checked how long I had worked there for. If I was in probation, they would have sacked me, but I had been there four months.'[24]

Fortunately, Kunthea has a permanent contract and could not be easily dismissed. The factory managers spread rumours she would use membership fees to buy gold, and when that failed, they offered Kunthea a supervisor role with a salary four times her normal one. Kunthea could not be swayed, though. 'I know because I learn a lot and know the law. Because of Chea Vichea, the workers can have better conditions. Whenever supervisor uses bad words to workers, I call them for a meeting. You can complain but not use bad words.'

Workers in other factories have faced even greater challenges trying to establish unions: forty-five were sacked at one factory for their attempt, and sixty at another factory were sacked for being trade union activists.[25] One worker recounted how the factory owner called him to a meeting just after he was elected president of a new union. '[They] asked me whether I wanted to set up a union. I got scared and said I didn't. They called me again for a meeting the next day and another man was in the room. He introduced himself as an officer from the Ministry of Interior. He asked me how much money I wanted to leave the factory. I didn't accept the money. The next day, the factory manager called me, the vice-president and the secretary [of the union] and told us our performance was not good and we were being dismissed.'[26] Union leaders are also the first to face punishment for strikes: after the violence at Veng Sreng Street, over 100 union leaders were sacked from factories throughout Cambodia. These factories supplied Adidas, Calvin Klein and Armani, among others.[27]

Kunthea remained working at her factory, and within two years had attracted 400 workers to join her union. 'More members join the factory union because when they start, they have to thumbprint [a thumbprint acts as a signature in Cambodia] to join. But some leave to join us because people are looking at the union and see the kind of benefits and how successful we are at advocating and protecting their interests and benefits. We convince them to understand.'

Kunthea started her union just before the CPP passed the new *Law on Trade Unions* in 2016, which sought to neutralise the CNRP's base of support. Similar to the law for charities, the law for trade unions requires unions to register with the Ministry of Labor and Vocational Training before they begin to operate. The process for trade unions is even more convoluted and can only begin when at least ten workers agree to form a union. The minutes of the foundational meeting have to be submitted, as do the trade union's bank details, statutes and administrative regulations. Names and details of leaders responsible for the union's administration must also be provided.[28] Three weeks after passing the law, the government issued a decree requiring the family details of union leaders, too, which Pich said made people 'scared'.[29]

As an illustration of the bureaucracy, Pich passed me sheet after sheet of paper, showing me all the documents that I would have to complete to start a union. 'If you organise at a factory that employ 5000 workers and 3000 agree, they need three original attendance lists. You imagine? You need to bring the list to register the union. Imagine. 3000 people? Then three times! Imagine the amounts of paper.'

'You need to photocopy the list three times?' I asked.

'No, original. Original!' Pich's voice was strained. 'Very stupid, you know.'

'So the worker must sign three times?'

'Yes! The worker must sign three times. See here?' Pich showed me the wording of the law. 'They don't put original here, but in practice they demand the original. And see here?' I was scrambling with more paper, this time an annex to the law. 'They say three copies, but when you go to register, they demand three originals. When you conduct, you have only one original. Then, they say you need three. Then what happen? You have to go back and get 3000 people back again. Time, money, administration. Not easy.'

Pich handed me yet more paper. 'They have a union by-law template. You need to follow it. Every provision. You just change the name. You don't have the right to draw your own by-law. It really violates the ILO (International Labour Organization) convention.'

'You don't have the right to make your own rules?'

'No! The union has to have the same by-laws [as other unions]. Just change the name. Because this is the template, and you have to follow this. Very strange. When they put thirteen chapters, you need to have thirteen chapters. If you want twelve, or maybe sixteen, you cannot. When you register, not only by-law, they have a template for administrative rules and you have to follow that too. If you don't follow that, you fail.' Pich showed me that if a person put a full stop at the end of each bullet point, the application would be denied: 'They say, "No, don't do that. Just do one full stop." If you don't put space, they say, you need space. They will pull your application back. By law, you just need to read and write Khmer, but when it comes to registration, even if you have a doctor degree [PhD], you feel faint!'

I thought back to Kunthea. The first time she led a union, she had to ask for a secretary who could read and write to help her. Struggling to comprehend the minutiae of control, I gamely ventured that since there were lots of unions, many people must have managed a way to complete all the documents. Pich demurred. 'It is different for pro-government union, independent union and opposition union. It is different for each. There are 700 new unions, but when we check, most are pro-government unions. There are two different standards applied for different trade unions. You see here the template, the biography of the leader? You have to fill all of the information. You have to attach with the employment card number, but if the factory doesn't have an employment card, even if you have more than ten workers, you don't have the right to form a union ... Then, if you have an employment card but your workplace not a member of the NSSF [National Social Security Fund], sorry, you cannot register.'

Even if workers manage to form a union, its right to negotiate on behalf of its members are limited by the *Law on Trade Unions*. Only the union with Most Representative Status can negotiate improved working and employment conditions with the owner. A union must have a membership of at least 30 per cent of all workers in that factory to obtain Most Representative Status. Other unions in that factory can only speak to managers if an existing rule has been broken.

Kunthea's union has 400 members in a factory with 2000 workers. In her factory, it is the pro-owner union that has Most Representative Status and can negotiate pay, overtime rates, number of holidays and lunch allowances. The multitude of unions makes it difficult for any union to achieve Most Representative Status within a factory. Pich told me one factory had ten unions in it. Unions would need to pledge their support to another union for any single union to get over 30 per cent, which is rare, as the proliferation of unions leads to competition rather than collaboration.

The *Law on Trade Unions* only allows for unions with Most Representative Status to take complaints to Cambodia's Arbitration Council. In 2015, the year before the law was passed, 338 complaints were filed with the Council; in 2017, the number had tumbled to fifty.[30] The law dictates that if workers want to strike, they need to have a secret ballot of all workers in the factory at which more than 50 per cent of workers are present. Then, more than 50 per cent of those present need to vote in favour before a strike can begin. Pich told me that it is difficult to organise such a vote: 'When they do this in the factory, they are not allowed. And when they do this outside the factory, the authorities not allow. So they need to find a place. Where?! If five or six people gather, they come and say, "What are you doing here?" So how about even more people who want to decide on the strike issue? It will be a problem, you know. Plus, the employer can get a court injunction, forcing the strikers back to work within forty-eight hours or their strike becomes illegal.'

Trade unions, like charities, have to give three days' notice of any planned activity, which gives factory owners enough time to persuade restaurants or hotels to cancel bookings for trade union meetings.[31] In one case, a factory security guard locked sixty workers in a room to prevent them from participating in a vote.[32] In the years before the *Law on Trade Unions*, there had always been over 100 strikes a year, peaking at 147 in 2013. The year after the law was implemented, there were thirty-two.[33] The law also restricts what workers can do when holding a strike, making it illegal to 'congest or block the entrance' or 'close off public roads'.[34]

Pich had taken me into an overwhelming bureaucratic labyrinth. I tilted my head back, exhaling deeply. Pich was perched on the edge of his plastic seat, leaning forward. His naturally pursed mouth twisted with a trace of a smile. There was more.

To be a trade union leader, you must not have been convicted of a misdemeanour or a felony. The Cambodian penal code includes articles on defamation that are vaguely worded and open to wide interpretation by Cambodia's notoriously pliant judges. Hun Sen once won a defamation case against an opposition politician because she accused him of defamation, which in itself the court judged to be defamatory. The opposition politician was fined $4000.[35]

Trade union leaders are also liable to be charged with incitement, which has a wide definition: expressing dissatisfaction and criticism that *could* incite others to disturb social security qualifies.[36] The Ministry of Environment once accused NASA of incitement because they published satellite images that showed deforestation in Cambodia.[37]

The Cambodian Labour Confederation is one of the largest confederations of independent unions, and in the three years following Veng Sreng, forty-six of their union leaders faced ninety charges, including defamation and incitement. Officials from other unions were also arrested, often at the request of the factory owners. Police arrested two union leaders, despite admitting the protest was legal, because the company said it was affecting their business.[38] At another factory, three union leaders were arrested for incitement even though the police chief admitted that the strike had been peaceful. He said the company had complained about declining production.[39]

The CPP did not see trade unions as independent; they saw them as part of the opposition, especially after unions allied with the CNRP for mass protests about the minimum wage. After the violence at Veng Sreng Street, Rong Chhun had charges hanging over him for inciting violence even while he became a National Election Committee member. Ath Thorn, President of the Cambodian Labour Confederation, was also charged for his alleged involvement, along with four other union leaders.[40] Another union leader, Vorn Pov, was held in jail for four months.[41] Pov and twenty-two protestors were hidden in a jail for five days before family and lawyers were told where they were.[42]

Pich told me that trade union leaders would often get anonymous phone calls threatening them, and some even received messages from Hun Sen.

'From the Prime Minister?' I asked incredulously. 'How?'

'Phone or message, directly. He has everyone's phone number.'

The Prime Minister had everyone's phone number because in December 2015 the CPP passed a law that required all telecommunication companies to provide service data if requested to by the government. The same law also enabled the government to secretly record or intercept any email, SMS or telephone call without judicial permission. The right to privacy was effectively removed and any communication that 'may affect public order or national security' was prohibited.[43] To enforce the new laws, the government set up telecommunication inspection teams to monitor what was being said, and by whom. The fear that Hun Sen had an ear in every conversation had returned.

CHAPTER 14
HERE IS MY SON

If it was charities that highlighted the issues and unions that provided the masses, it was the youth that ignited support for the CNRP. The CPP had established the Union of Youth Federations in Cambodia in 2012, officially naming it the successor to the Hun Sen–led United Youth Association for National Salvation of Kampuchea, which was set up in Vietnam in 1978 to oppose the Khmer Rouge. To save another acronym, I will call the Union of Youth Federations in Cambodia what everyone in Cambodia does: Hun Many's organisation. Hun Many – a CPP member of the National Assembly and the prematurely balding youngest son of Hun Sen – is its President.

Dav Ansan, the senior CPP official who wanted me to ask Rainsy why he gave his ruinous interview, is a central committee member of Hun Many's organisation. He estimated that there are 120,000 active members, with some young people joining for one-off projects too. I asked Ansan, who was born in the early 1980s (the definition of youth is rather elastic in Hun Many's organisation, as Hun Many himself was born in 1982) what he thought of young Cambodians.

'I see their lifestyle is quite different from older generation. First, young people don't value seniority as much. If the idea is reasonable, that is the basis. But for older people, seniority is important. Older people say, "I see the sunlight first" or "I have eaten more salt than you have eaten rice."'

Ansan has already had a varied career. A qualified lawyer, he has a Master's degree from the Royal Academy of Cambodia and studied development economics at the prestigious Williams College in America on a scholarship from the World Bank. He has also worked for charities, the French Embassy and the Khmer Rouge Tribunal, and is the current Executive Director of the Cambodian Development Centre.

'I personally went on strike against corruption and burned car tyres,' he told me. 'During my second or third year at law school, I volunteered for an NGO that worked for advocacy for local people – democracy, voting rights. Later on, I got to work with the government. When I work with NGO, I see the government as a bad guy – the authority. When I work for the government, they also good people and want to deliver. They also have goodwill to change the country, to be better. At that point I realise that oh, my generation, this is good for them to get an education about their rights, but at some point they forget that they also have an obligation and responsibility as the future of the country. They only want to claim their right and not the responsibility of the good citizen of the country. The UYFC is a mechanism.'

Before meeting Ansan, I looked at a photo so I could recognise him. He had square-jawed face bearing a smirk, and his arms were crossed over a puffed-out chest. The man in person was quite different. He was hesitant, thoughtful and open, and physically smaller, in his simple polo shirt, than he looked in his picture.

'Personally, I believe to be able to move the country faster, each individual needs to strike a balance between rights and responsibilities. Social change begins with the individual, so UYFC works with the young people, gives them a platform to help them perform. My observation is that when they are free individuals, they talk and complain. "Why not this? Why not that?" But when given some responsibility, I see some different behaviour. When asked to be a group leader, I observe autocracy in their minds as well. When individual: "Why don't you use democracy? Government leader is dictator." But when doing it themselves, they want work done, so skip voting. Just "Do this. Do that."'

I met two provincial leaders for Hun Many's organisation, both of whom were selected to join because of their senior roles in provincial offices of the Ministry of Education, Youth and Sport. I asked them if they saw changes in the young people who participated in Hun Many's organisation.

'Yes, we do,' both said, nodding rapidly before one continued. 'They build teamwork and gain new experience. Can raise cultural awareness. Twenty years ago, because of war, social disorder, killing, youth did not pay attention to social [issues]. Now that we establish education system and youth federation, plus support from government and many NGOs, we can get the attention of youth. We find that youth increase participation in social work, like educating people about throwing rubbish away. Plus, we can get them to be involved in monitoring things like Grade 12 exams to reduce corruption. The idea of establishing UYFC is to promote participation to develop society.'[1]

The provincial leaders stressed that the UYFC is apolitical, despite its obvious links to the CPP, and more concerned with promoting clean environments, the value of education, participation in sport and knowledge of traditional art and culture than with politics. Its first big activity was to organise a festival at Angkor Wat for Khmer New Year, the Angkor Sankranta.

An important holiday when everybody returns to their homelands, Khmer New Year celebrations had previously only occurred in homes with family. Pagodas may have had some music, and gleeful children in Battambang will throw water and flour over each other (or passing cyclists, as I experienced one year), but otherwise there were no large-scale events. The Angkor Sankranta attracted tens of thousands of Cambodians to Siem Reap for celebrations involving classical dancing and theatre, Cambodian kickboxing, buffalo racing and even a selfie competition, as well as more than 2000 young Cambodians hopping and swaying in style, gaining a world record for the largest Madison line dance. That same year, Hun Many's organisation also built the world's largest sticky rice cake (four tonnes) and followed that up with the longest dragon boat (87 metres). After that they made the world's longest krama. Cambodians pointed to these triumphs as proof that the country had progressed from needing the UN to beating the rest of the world.

In their province, they had provided more than 100 scholarships to local universities and offered forty scholarships to Chinese universities. I asked if they had criteria to select young people for scholarships. Their answer was prompt. 'The student must go through selection process through district authority. And they have to be [an] active [member] of UYFC.'

When I met a group of about fifteen young people who had travelled to see the effects of deforestation and mining with the Youth Resource Development Program, I asked them if any of them had joined Hun Many's organisation. The group, hitherto nervous, rippled with sniggers at such a suggestion, even though a few of them came from CPP-supporting families. When the titters dissipated, one young male student quietly stunned everybody by admitting that he had. Reth had arrived late, which meant he was sitting at the far end of the table near the door, and we all turned to look at him. He explained that one of his friends was already a member and part of a team that would visit an orphanage to give food to children staying there. One day, the friend invited Reth, whose mother has a local CPP position, to join them. 'It was called Kitchen for Kids ... near Tuol Sleng [the site of the Khmer Rouge genocide museum in Phnom Penh]. We would give rice, Khmer noodles, bread. They are happy and we are happy when we see that they are happy coming to play.'

Reth's friends then asked him to join them on trips to villages near Phnom Penh.

'It was two villages in Kandal. For promoting people to go to vote [in the 2017 Commune Election].'

'When you went to Kandal, did you go to a meeting, or to people's houses, to explain?' I asked.

'Normally, the Village Chief would organise, assisted by the Commune Chief too. So lots of people come. The youth group would provide information about voting and encourage people to go to vote and to vote for CPP. Because the organisation is linked to CPP.'

'Would there be a meeting with food and gifts?'

'Usually would have MSG, sarong, some money, food. Show people how to tick the box. Show where CPP is on the list – "Don't be confused!"'

'What did you expect to happen? Was it like you expected?'

'Not too different. I knew what it would be like. Knew that it would be about CPP and promoting CPP. I know that CPP is not good, but I was interested to go and see what it was like.'

'Did you find it interesting? Did you enjoy it?'

'It's interesting to learn, but not so satisfying. Not happy. It's about CPP and voting for CPP. It's not really good to do like that.'

'Did your friends ask you to go a third time?'

'Yes, but I didn't go.'

'Your friends, why are they still involved?'

'Some people are passionate about supporting CPP, and they keep going. Some people go because they want to show off. Take selfie with important people. Looking for any good opportunity in case they get to know good people. They can make links.'[2]

Being active in Hun Many's organisation, as is required to apply for certain scholarships, was also a gateway into the CPP. I spoke to another student, Kimchhay, who explained that as the son of a senior government official he would be able to join, but others would not be welcome: 'To do with them [Hun Many's organisation], you have to be privileged ... Like —'

'It's not open to all young people?' I offered.

'Open, but practically ... I cannot say for all people. To join that organisation, it will bring prestige to young people so then we got more opportunities, especially in the government. So, yeah. They are very selective. It is not very much meritocratic. There is some [of this], but ...'[3]

Another young man, the son of a provincial education director, had been invited to join but declined. He told me that people 'wear the blue shirt of the UYFC to get benefits': 'If you wear it, then you will not be stopped by the police if you are not wearing a moto helmet, for instance.'[4] A university lecturer told me he had never heard of somebody with no connection to the CPP joining Hun Many's organisation.[5]

Ansan got involved in Hun Many's organisation because he saw a chance to help develop Cambodia's youth, but Ou Ritthy, the young man who worked at COMFREL and set up Politikoffee, was disparaging of its objectives. 'What do they do? Make the world's biggest *krama*?!'[6] Ritthy was scathing of how the CPP viewed young people's development. 'You can't say, "I believe in youth – here is my son!"'[7] I have friends who are materialistic. It is those people who are attracted to Hun Many's organisation. I then ask why are they now so politically interested: "Before you hate me for talking politics, now you seem to be more interested than me – you seem to be more Christian than the Pope!" So many people like that. These people – for them, their political participation is not based on vision, it is based on material interest.'

Ritthy feels some pity for these deluded, selfish climbers who will find 'there are people who cannot move above the ceiling': 'You need to support the elite above the ceiling, but you cannot go above. You are not involved in the greater purpose or plan. You are just serving them.'[8]

A senior government official close to Hun Many's organisation told me that Hun Many never intended the Union of Youth Federations of Cambodia to become a gateway to power for the sons and daughters of governors and senior CPP leaders, even if that is what it has become.[9] Cambodia is a society built on patronage. In its simplest form, people get jobs because of who they know and children get into university because of who their parents are. Hun Many's organisation was, deliberately or not, drawing young people into this system of patronage that the CPP controls so deeply many people feel you cannot live without it.

CHAPTER 15

KHNORNG

Sotheavy was astounded. 'You've never heard of *khnorng*?' She looked at me sideways, an eyebrow arched. Clearly disappointed in me, she explained, while sipping her red wine, that *khnorng* is the word for 'back' but is also used to mean 'backing', as in support. Sotheavy tried her best to explain how important it is to have *khnorng* and that how much you have depends on who your *khnorng* is.

Sotheavy and I were sitting next to the open window of a second-floor bar in the Western city she now lives in. Suddenly, out of the warm evening air, we heard a drunk man shouting aggressively at two women on the street below. We, along with other people in the bar, peered over the ledge to see what was happening. 'Oi!' shouted a man in his early thirties sitting at the table next to us. 'Leave them alone! Stop that or I'll call the police.'

Sotheavy stared at me, her huge brown eyes wide open. 'See?! You couldn't do that in Cambodia. You couldn't just shout at somebody like that. What if he had *khnorng*? Or bigger *khnorng* than you? You can't just phone the police, either. They won't do anything. Not unless you have *khnorng*.'

I nodded, beginning to have a feeling for what the rule of law means in daily life.

'Let's say you are in a car crash,' continued Sotheavy. 'You have to work out who the other person's backer is. Then you can work out if you have more *khnorng* than they do. Your *khnorng* may mediate with the other person's *khnorng*.'

I asked Sotheavy how you know if a person has *khnorng* when you first meet them.

'It is in the way they carry themselves. Like, when they walk into a place. If I see some guys in a café not looking at the waitress when ordering, or dismissing her, I know they are connected.'

The Cambodian phrase for connections to powerful people is *ksae thom*, which literally means 'big string'. You have *khnorng* (backing) if you have *ksae thom* (connections to important people). The reason that the men in Sotheavy's imaginary café walk around as if they own the place is because they probably do. Or they know the person who does. These strings, or relationships, form a network, and if you are outside this network then you are vulnerable, as Sotheavy went on to describe. 'If you're not connected, local authorities or police will test you to see what connections you have. They may try to get money out of you or make things difficult. If you're not connected, then people know that they can "fish" in your area.' 'Fishing' is slang for extortion.

Sotheavy's father diligently built up his *khnorng* after returning from the Thai refugee camps in 1993, meaning Sotheavy comes from a networked family. One day at university, where Sotheavy was student president, she was riding pillion on her friend's old, worn-out moto. Her friend confessed that she was surprised Sotheavy would be friends with her because her family was poor. Sotheavy was shaken. She had never thought about friendship being dictated by status but, looking around, she knew it to be true. Years later, Sotheavy's friend came to her with a problem. Sotheavy told her father that her friend would call him for help and he must give it. Her father agreed and provided *khnorng* for Sotheavy's friend, resolving the situation. Her friend is now connected to the network and so has a little *khnorng*.

Sotheavy has a loving but difficult relationship with her father, mostly caused by Sotheavy's unwillingness to do as he says. When she was eighteen, her aunt told her that she might notice a man observing her. She confronted her father, asking if he was setting her up with a potential suitor and refusing to be married off. They had had many disagreements before, but this was the biggest. It ended with her dad taking her motorbike keys away and cutting her off from the family. Their mutual stubbornness subsided as love for each other brought them back, but Sotheavy still struggles to ask him for help. She needed a Cambodian police check to get a residential visa for a Western country and government officials were holding out for a sizeable bribe. Her brother, an enterprising businessman who, when stopped by police, merely passes his phone so they can speak to one of his backers before carrying on, was having no luck and told Sotheavy that she needed to speak to their dad. Her father got it the next day.

Before the 2013 election, Sotheavy's father got her a CPP card, saying it was for her 'protection'. She was not even in Cambodia at the time. 'It seemed like, if it came to it and he had to prove which side he was on, the card would protect his family,' Sotheavy reflected.

Protection comes from being connected to the CPP. It is the man at the top, Hun Sen, who pulls the strings and controls that network. Sotheavy said that there were people who didn't want to support the CPP, but to maintain their lifestyle, they must maintain the network. Her brother has become rich importing goods, providing regular gifts to customs officials, as well as being there when they needed help. There is no welfare state to look after you or police to protect you. There is the network, the CPP and Hun Sen.

Sotheavy has asked her brother to join her living abroad, but he would not cope. She knows of other connected young Cambodians who have tried to live in countries like America, France or Australia, but they struggle to adjust to the different set of rules and the absence of their *khnorng*.[1]

We left the bar after another glass and went to a small Thai restaurant nearby. I smiled as Sotheavy's meal arrived and she picked up her chopsticks to eat. The shape of chopsticks, wide at the top and narrow at the bottom, means that the two pointed ends cannot meet cleanly, making it more difficult to pick up the thinnest slivers of food. Every day, billions of people in Asia use them like this, and have done for over 5000 years. In all that time it is only Sotheavy who I have seen turn the chopsticks upside down and use the fat ends as pincers. She cannot see why you wouldn't. Her father wanted the best education for her, so Sotheavy says he cannot blame her for interrogating some traditions, even if it means she can never return home.

Maly had recently returned to Cambodia from studying abroad when I met her for the first time. Walking into a café in Phnom Penh, I knew that Maly had to be the diminutive woman in red wedged heels, tight jeans, a loosely fitting red jumper and lipstick. Only a Cambodian who had lived in Australia for two years would dare dress like that.

Maly is the second youngest of nine children and her family struggled when she was growing up. It was not that Maly's blacksmith father earned less than most other fathers; it's just that there were more mouths to feed.[2] In Maly's community, it was rare for children to finish school because parents didn't see the point of investing in education when good jobs still went to those with connections rather than qualifications. It was even less common if you were a girl. Why would parents send daughters to school or university when they were going to get married anyway?

Maly had always wanted to go to university though, envisioning a different future for herself than that of the women in her community, who typically became stay-at-home mothers. With her English teacher's encouragement,

Maly sat the entrance exam for the Institute of Foreign Languages and passed with flying colours. None of her brothers had gone to university, but her parents said they would find the money because she deserved this chance for having always strived so hard. Maly, aware of the pressure she was putting her family under, began teaching English privately to help out.

Every day of her first year, Maly's parents would ask if she was managing to keep up with the lecturer, anxious that they would have to pay for her to repeat a semester. They only relaxed, and fully realised their daughter's talents, when she came second in the class. The respite was short-lived, though. In Maly's third year, her father became seriously ill, and the family had to find money to pay for medical treatment as well as Maly's university fees. Maly took on more private tutoring and a second job to help.

Her father lived long enough to see her graduate and begin teaching at a prestigious Cambodian university, which is where Maly first experienced the negative effects of *khnorng*. She was popular among students, who talked to one another about admiring her cleverness, and colleagues came to value her opinion as well. Despite this, she was repeatedly passed over for promotion in favour of colleagues with connections. 'It really pissed me off,' she said, using strong language rarely spoken by Cambodian females in public. Maly felt that nepotism was blocking her ability to advance and so help the people of her country.

For four years while studying and working at university, Maly 'drip-fed' her mother the idea of going to Australia on a scholarship to complete a Master's degree. Her mother threw up reasons why it wouldn't work: Maly wouldn't be able to look after herself; she couldn't cook or clean; she would never come back; it was dangerous. Then one day without apparent reason, Maly's mother said she could go.

Maly had left a big family to live in Australia alone. A sister called to ask how she was doing and Maly replied that she had so much to do it felt like there were only twelve hours in the day. Her sister laughed, replying that this was because at home she had had three older sisters doing everything for her.

Assuaging her mother's worries, Maly did learn to cook and clean. But she would eat by herself three times a day. She said it is difficult for someone to comprehend true loneliness until they experience hearing only the scraping of their own fork on the plate: 'Without realising, tears would fall onto my cheek. I live by myself in the whole world.'[3] Maly told me that even today she still missed her 'dearest friends, my kangaroos': 'They visit me every morning – every time I open my curtains.'[4]

Maly was offered the chance to do a PhD but wanted to return home to her family, at least for a while. Maly could have worked in government but didn't want to be part of 'a system that corrupts you'. Maly explained that you have to 'kiss up and kick down ... I could not do that.'[5]

More and more Cambodians are earning scholarships to study abroad in China, Japan, Australia, America or Europe, learning new ways of living. The vast majority return home, eager to use their experience to help Cambodia, only to find obstacles in their way. Sreyleak was a midwife in Cambodia and was awarded a scholarship to study a Master of Public Health abroad. When she got back, she had been removed from the civil service despite having been granted leave.

'Why do you think they deleted you?' I asked.

'The chief always make argument with me.' Sreyleak explained that the medical chief would only give patients half the medicine they needed, keeping the other half for his clinic. Sreyleak could not stand by and watch this happen: 'For me, one is one; two is two. I argue with him. Because it's my nature since I was young. If something I don't like, I don't like. You are wrong, I say you are wrong.'[6]

When Sreyleak left to study abroad, it was her first time out of Cambodia and she had to make a life while leaving her husband and baby son back there for the first few months. She believed the sacrifice would be worth it because a Master of Public Health would make it easier to find a good job and support her family, but it took her four 'terrible' months to find a job after returning to Phnom Penh. Discarded from a public health system chronically short of skilled staff, she found a job in a private hospital and trained midwives as a volunteer on her day off. Her boss only works afternoons because he also has a job in a government ministry. She does not blame him, though. 'Actually, he is very kind to me. He understands about me a lot. But just like you need to have *khnorng*, so he join the Party.'

Sreyleak could have had an easier path but she turned down an offer to work at the Vital bottled water company owned by Hun Sen's daughter. 'Now, most of the scholars who came back from abroad and who finish the scholarship like me, they all went to join CPP. Most of them went there [to Vital] and they got salary $1500 [per month]. Just go there and count the number. Count the bottle. In stock, out of stock. The knowledge that they study abroad, they don't use it at all. It's useless. Useless. I feel very shameful. The guy, he's like the chief of our alumni, he tried to approach me. "If you want to get just like easy job, you just do that. Go and join the Party."'

'So you have to join the Party before you get a job?'

'And do everything for the Party ... Once you enter the Party, you cannot move around. The first time, you follow. Then, later on, you lead the work ... and try to attract members. Contribute money every month to support the mission of the Party. For me, I say no. I don't want to sell myself. I feel like the knowledge that I get from studying, I should share this and use for my country. Now the only way that I can share my knowledge is through Cambodian Midwives' Association. The thing is that I have to take the day off from work to [volunteer].'

'If you joined the CPP, would it be easy to get a job?'

'It's really easy. I could get a high position in the Ministry of Health.'

Sreyleak may be sure that one plus one is two, but she also knows how to make it three. Sreyleak's husband is a car mechanic with his own garage. I asked if it was difficult to set this up. 'Okay, I tell you. If you need to build a roof, need to pay Ministry of Land. But I don't have to pay. I tell you honestly ... at that time, my uncle was in a high-ranking position. I call him and he tell everyone that it is his business. Otherwise, I could not. I didn't want to do it, but ...'

Sreyleak's family know that she is vehemently opposed to the CPP but her uncle has an obvious soft spot for her, as well as a sense of familial duty. '[He said], "You have any problem, call me. No one can touch you." You know, even my car, we have name of the ministry [on the dashboard] and when the police see this, they dare not touch. I think that if I go and the traffic light is red, I just show the card and he let me go. I never do this. Just the one time, when I have no choice, I used my uncle.'

That one time became multiple times after the garage was established because government officials and police demanded that their cars be fixed at a specially discounted rate, 'fishing' to see if she had *khnorng*. 'My husband said, "No, it is below my costs." He just call me to negotiate [with them]. I tell them, "We also family of the CPP," this and that. They agree to pay an appropriate price. My husband says it is hard, we have first come, first served. But "No," they said, "I need you to do this."'

Sreyleak may have refused to join the CPP, but as a mother trying to support her husband and two sons – one a plump newborn and the other a hyperactive toddler – she knew, and resented, that she could never evade the Party's reach.

CHAPTER 16
A SLAVE TO ONE SIDE

I was slurping Vietnamese pho alongside Chhay, my former colleague who survived the Khmer Rouge because of his strong spoon, when he told me a story from his office. 'Last week, one of the directors promote one and make another jealous. The other staff say, "He is new! Just come here to work but I work here long time. Thirty years and don't get the promotion!" And then the boss say, "Because he always go with me [campaigning] and support the Party ... he's given priority." He say publicly, like that! ... I always support the CPP but I don't like this. Because I want all qualified people, even from different parties, they can talk, work here. Then the boss can treat everyone fairly.'[1]

The law allows civil servants, including doctors, teachers and police, to join any political party, but they are prohibited from working in the interests of that party in their role.[2] Yet *khnorng* is in their culture, as Chhay explained: 'At the national level, a minister may be responsible for [the province of] Kompong Speu. So, each department under his supervision has to follow him to Kompong Speu. Do campaigning, every weekend.' Responsibility descends in a pyramid. A minister can be responsible for a whole province; his deputies are then responsible for districts within that province; their subordinates are responsible for communes within those districts; and individual staff are assigned to villages within those communes. When he worked in government, Chhay would organise meetings for community members, using contributions from civil servants' salaries. 'Sometime I have to find schedule, this weekend or this week, I have to go to commune. I have to strengthen three communes sometimes.'

'People will come to the meeting and get something?' I asked.

'Sarong, t-shirt, MSG. Minister ... he find some resources. Computers, some kind of book, printing, [something] useful for students.'

'And the money to pay for sarongs, MSG?'

'From those people! At the ministry!' Chhay's voice rose.

'From their salaries?' I asked, just to confirm what everybody in Cambodia already knows.

'I used to contribute! I, I, myself. I used to! I still remember every weekend, planning event for the pagoda, because you want to attract the monk and the monk continues to attract the community, so you have to offer money to be put on the wall. Even my name. There. On the wall!' Chhay laughed that somewhere out in the middle of Cambodia, there were pagodas that bore his name on a brick because of his 'donation'.

'People in the Ministry, how much would they have to pay a month?' I asked.

'Sometimes you pay $10, $20. For me, this is long work. I contribute $100 to [my boss]. Little bit, little bit at a time.'

Chhay paid $100, a small fortune at the turn of the century and more than normal, because he worked on an internationally funded project, meaning there was more cash to be earned. Another friend who works in government told me that provincial office staff in a Battambang department are paying $20 per month.[3] Chhay explained that leaders allow or even encourage corruption so their subordinates can earn extra money, which enables the flow of money upwards.

After the internationally funded project, Chhay left for a full-time job outside of government but remained a civil servant, working a few hours a week. Before the 2013 election, Chhay was called to a meeting with other staff in his department, during which they were told how much the CPP had done for the country. At the end of the meeting, the boss held a bag out for them to put money in as they left the room. As he had another job as well as his government job, Chhay had to give even more to the CPP than others. 'That's why, if the government try to work but using politics, it's not good. It's not transparency. Not democracy … They link to politics always. I don't like, I don't like. In the workplace, you can talk politics whenever at the weekend, but don't involve people here. Don't announce the strategy here.'

Like other civil servants, teachers are expected to give part of their salary to the CPP. Until 2015, teachers' salaries were paid in cash, which meant that cash would go from the provincial treasury to the provincial education department, to the district offices where school directors would take the cash back to teachers at the school. This method was used to distribute school budgets, too; without a network of banks, there was no other way.

As bundles of cash passed through various hands, a little would go missing each time, meaning that when teachers received their salary, deductions for the CPP had already been made. Now, salaries are paid into the bank, meaning teachers have to give cash back every month. Vanna, a teacher at a school near Phnom Penh, told me that his school director is sometimes asked to donate extra money to the CPP, prompting the director to ask teachers to contribute $1 or $2. 'Everyone has to pay. You have to pay, you have no choice.'[4] Some school directors and teachers are also given leave to campaign for the CPP and sometimes host meetings at schools with commune leaders so students can hear about the CPP's success.[5]

Phirun works as a senior civil servant. Over chicken fried rice one lunchtime, he told me that while you might support one party politically outside the workplace, 'you have to provide service to all the parties that have seats in the National Assembly'. Despite this, Phirun believed CNRP parliamentarians were prejudiced against him and his colleagues, believing they were biased towards the CPP. 'I said, "We are here, neutral." You can ask them: if they request us to do something, we never say no, we always help.'[6]

Phirun would insist on picking me up or driving me to the airport whenever I was travelling abroad, arriving five minutes early and waiting patiently as I stuffed clothes into a rucksack. No matter the time of day, he would always be there. So I could easily imagine him affronted that the CNRP would think he wouldn't fulfil his duties as a civil servant. Attempting to show how he found the behaviour of CNRP politicians perplexing, he talked about a series of meetings abroad he attended with a group of CPP and CNRP politicians. The group included a CNRP senator whose actions confounded Phirun to the point of incomprehension. 'I don't know how your culture works, but here, in this country, when they have free time, they stick to their own group. When there is a meeting, they join together. I think maybe not so different in your country. So, outside the meeting, they go to their own group – CPP, CNRP. The CNRP MP, the one of two who was beaten: even during the break time, even our private time, he was walking with our group, the CPP. He is an MP! So sometimes, we don't feel comfortable discussing things privately. And he was there all the time! Why doesn't he stick to his group?! You know, even when we go to have our private lunch or dinner. Why? Why?'

'Was he trying to be friendly?' I offered.

'I don't know. He didn't say. He was just ... among our MPs. He just smiled. He didn't say anything serious. He just showed his presence. To get some information? There is no way to get some information. They know. How can, among the CPP circle, there be one CNRP? Even in a private dinner. So why? What is he doing?'

Phirun paused, recognising that he had called the CPP 'our MPs' and admitted that he always ate with the CPP group. 'Sometimes, we tend to be biased to this side [CPP] a little bit. Because we need to survive.'

A year or so previously, in a quiet moment when walking together, Phirun had told me that people at work did not like his demeanour because he always tried his best. Phirun said that maybe things would be different in the future and that people like him would be appreciated, rather than those who had strong *khnorng*,[7] but for now his children, who he has dreams for, depend on his survival in a system that rewards taking sides. 'If you are neutral, you have no chance of promotion,' he confided. 'You have no chance of success. Because if you are neutral, the CPP will think, *Oh, maybe you belong to CNRP*. And the CNRP will think you are CPP. See? So if you are neutral, you have no connection at all. No support. This person is free all the time – the CPP is afraid to use this person, the CNRP is afraid to use this person. You have knowledge, but no opportunity. So you have to be affiliated with one or the other.'[8]

Chamroeun, the father who changed clothes like Superman in a phone box to ride with young CNRP supporters, worked in government for many years before resigning because he could no longer stand the endemic corruption. I asked what it would be like for civil servants who did not join the CPP or go campaigning. 'Very difficult for them, if they don't do that they will be discriminated against, left out, won't be promoted, not get benefit. It is really difficult for them. Dilemma, if they don't support the ruling party, they cannot stay in the government. A difficult situation for them … You will never change the system; the system will change you.'[9]

Even if political loyalties are weak, cultural expectations and the role of *khnorng* strengthen them. 'This patronage system is intertwined in Cambodian culture like Buddhism,' Chamroeun advised. 'When you're the boss, you like to call your subordinates "grandchildren" (*kone chao*). You treat your colleagues below you as grandchildren. It means that you have to listen to your parent. Also, you protect your parents, would do anything to protect them. It is really difficult to remove this patronage system. If you want to remove that way of working, it is very hard when people have the same mindset. Even nowadays, in the ministry, the government, they have this kind of system.'

The role of *khnorng* means that civil servants' jobs are dependent on connections to leaders in power, so civil servants become heavily invested in maintaining the CPP in government. This ensures that Cambodia's institutions, as one charity leader told me, are enfeebled: 'We are a weak state. The autonomy of the administration and independence of the judicial system are not yet functioning. So a weak system. We cannot even enforce the traffic law properly! Only Hun Sen is strong. Just the individual, not the state.'[10]

Chamroeun explained that this system persists because those within it accrue so much personal benefit. 'Some people, people in the government, they feel by keeping this system they will benefit their family. The current system cannot hold them accountable. For instance, they go to work, but they don't work professionally. They just go for two to three hours and they go to find second job. Even in the ministry, they try to make a lot of bad deeds, like corruption, not benefit the public interest. That's what they still do. They are still happy with this situation and want it to prevail. They still get the benefit. Even if maybe it is bad in the long run.'

Senior civil servants, like Phirun, know that gaining or keeping a job does not just depend on your skills and qualifications. For decades, the leaders have been members of the CPP and therefore connection to them requires you to be in the CPP too. The more active you are, the stronger your connection can be. I was told me about a civil servant who has a relatively senior role in a ministry. Every weekend for three to six months before an election, he will deliver gifts at the villages he is responsible for. If he doesn't do this, his job would be in a 'critical condition'.[11]

This lack of choice led Yeang Sothearin, a journalist who would later be imprisoned, to reflect that in Cambodia, 'There are so many good people – just a few that are bad. It doesn't mean that all public servants or court officers are bad. Somehow, the system makes those people unable to move or to adjust themselves to do good.'[12]

Chut Wutty was not killed by people who hated him or even necessarily by people who wanted to be arresting him. Moments before his death, one of the soldiers shouted at Wutty, 'We are both slaves! We are both the same.' Wutty, the lone ranger in his cowboy hat, retorted, 'I am a slave to who?'[13] It was Wutty's refusal to join the winning side that cost him his life.

CHAPTER 17
RULE OF LAW

It was only two months after the new Telecommunication Bill, which allowed covert surveillance of telephone calls, came into effect that a series of recorded telephone calls were posted on the Facebook account of Khom Chandraty, commonly known as Srey Mom. Srey Mom was a 24-year-old hairdresser, and the recordings were purported to be intimate conversations between her and Kem Sokha, Vice-President of the CNRP.

Srey Mom said she knew nothing of the recordings and that her Facebook account had been hacked. She also denied that it was her voice in the recordings or that she was having an affair with the much older and married Sokha, whose hair she did cut.[1] Police became involved when a high-profile woman being talked about in the recordings complained that Srey Mom and Kem Sokha had defamed her. Without explanation, the case was passed to the Counter-Terrorism Unit, who questioned Srey Mom for hours about her relationship with Kem Sokha and pondered whether she could be charged with prostitution, because the man in the recording can be heard promising to buy gifts for the woman.[2]

The hairdresser, the youngest of four children from a rural village, suddenly found herself at the centre of a storm that she didn't see coming.[3] Alone amid the turmoil, Srey Mom went to ADHOC, the human rights organisation, for help.

ADHOC has a policy of never turning anyone away, but Srey Mom's case posed a challenge. With Rainsy out of the country, the future of the CNRP seemed to rest on Kem Sokha as its de-facto leader. The furore was only growing as the government's Anti-Corruption Unit began investigating Kem Sokha, inquiring how he could afford to offer expensive gifts.

Nay Vanda works for ADHOC and was there to meet Srey Mom when she arrived, desperate for support: 'When Srey Mom came to us for help, I discuss with my wife, I say that I am at a dilemma. If we do not help her, then it means the CNRP would vanish from the surface of the earth and all the hope of the people would vanish as well. But if we help her? It's a danger. We face prison or death. It's a very, very big case. High-profile. Not many NGOs would like to interfere or get involved. She and her family had no hope. The life of the CNRP is at stake.

'We decided to take the risk ... I think that we need to show the people that we are not too coward, that we are daring when we do our job. We need to show the people not to run away, not to be afraid of imprisonment, not to be afraid of death.'[4]

ADHOC met with Srey Mom a few times, providing legal advice and $204 for food, accommodation and fares to visit her family.[5] After denying the affair and prostitution to the Counter-Terrorism investigators, Srey Mom was called for questioning by Phnom Penh's top prosecutor, who alleged that she had lied to investigators and that, despite taking no oath during those proceedings, could be charged with perjury.

Immediately after the questioning, the prosecutor announced that Srey Mom had admitted that the recordings of her and Kem Sokha were real and that the two were indeed having an affair. Three days later, Srey Mom released a letter alleging that Nay Vanda and other ADHOC staff tried to bribe her with $204. She said they promised her asylum abroad if she denied having an affair with Kem Sokha.[6] Nay Vanda kept his composure. 'When she changed her answer and put the guilt on us, I was not surprised. My wife woke me up at 3.00am to say, "Srey Mom written a letter and put a blame on you" and I said to her to "Go to sleep. I know already about these things." I also need to take sleep. I know what will happen.'[7]

A few days later, Hun Sen gave a speech, during which he talked about the taped conversations and ADHOC's alleged bribery of Srey Mom. Nay Vanda's colleague Ny Sokha realised immediately that the authorities would come for them. 'At that time, some embassies asked us if they could assist us. We said we feel fear but cannot run away. We did not do anything wrong so it's better that we should challenge to find justice.'[8]

Vanda, Sokha and three others were summoned by the Anti-Corruption Unit to discuss the bribery charges. Vanda said they wanted to go to their questioning 'confidently, still smiling': 'We needed to show the government that we stick to our own beliefs. We stick to our own dignity. The government cannot use fear or threats or imprisonment to bar us from doing the right job.'

They were interviewed separately under what Vanda called a 'modern way of torture' – the air-conditioning was turned right up. Vanda said the questions were 'like spears that can come in a hundred ways': 'If you go one way, another one will hit you. It comes to us, comes to Kem Sokha, but mostly comes to the ADHOC President. If we put the blame on the ADHOC President or Kem Sokha, we can be free. I refuse to put the blame on others.'

At the end of the first day, the four men and one woman from ADHOC, including Vanda, were released and asked to come back the next morning. In the evening of the second day, they were all taken to meet a senior figure in the Anti-Corruption Unit in a room that had a long dining table full of food. This official had earlier threatened Vanda with five years' imprisonment for refusing to answer questions but now he seemed to be trying to make them relax. Vanda asked to be excused so he could go to the toilet, as did one of his colleagues. 'We go with guards. We return. It has finished. All of the food has gone. They realise they will not get us to talk. Then, they arrest us.'

The five were kept in permanently lit rooms for three nights without being able to make a phone call but were never questioned again. Then they were moved to Prey Sar, a prison ten kilometres from Phnom Penh. 'We arrive at 7.00pm and a lot of prisoners come to the windows. They come all together and they shout, "Bring them to our room." They support us. They see us on TV and hear the radio. They know us.

'[The guards] put us all in separate rooms. I was upstairs and my colleagues were downstairs. My room had thirty-four people, and was four metres by five metres.

'Before I come to the room, they ask me to stand outside and they go in and ask the people, "Any CNRP activists in here?" "No!" The guards tell them to treat me okay, a special prisoner. But inside, I meet three or four activists. I meet the government informer. Every room has an informer. He didn't tell me, but you know I used to work for government for many years. I used to be a ghost, so I can see ghosts myself.'

Vanda had been Deputy Governor of a district in the beautiful, quiet coastal province of Kampot, next to Sihanoukville. He moved to become an English professor at the Institute of Foreign Languages in Phnom Penh, before joining ADHOC in 2008.

'The room is too crowded ... people sleep on the hammock above the heads. I sleep on a concrete bench. Rest of people on the floor. They are on top of each other, in front and beside the toilet. The first night I cannot sleep the whole night. Sitting there and watching, it was like an alien place. People sleeping like a bird hanging and some sleeping like a worm. I sleep like a dead person in a coffin.'

Many of the other people in the cell had been sentenced to twenty years or more. The contingent included people convicted of murder. Their thoughtfulness surprised Vanda that first night. 'I had no money. And I had not eaten so I need dinner. The prisoners are very kind. They say, "You want noodle?" and I say yes. They say, "One or two packets?" I say, "Two would be good." They say okay and one climbs up the wall and shouts to the other room, "Two packets of instant noodles!" And I think, *What is happening?* They have a shoe tied to a string and they throw the shoe and then it comes back with two packets of noodles in it. You can get anything from up to five rooms away as it passes from one to the other.'

Despite their kindness, Vanda found it difficult to connect with the other prisoners. 'I'm totally different from them. It's hard for them to know how to be with me. Like putting a cow in the pig shed. Different. It's hard to explain.'

Prosecutors called Kem Sokha for questioning as a witness to the alleged crime of ADHOC bribery but he refused to go, arguing he did not have to because of parliamentary immunity. Armed police went to CNRP headquarters to arrest him for failing to appear in court, but he was protected by CNRP staff and guards.

Sokha hunkered down in the headquarters for the next few months, never leaving, always surrounded by a vigil of CNRP supporters who took turns to guard him. The court tried Sokha for failing to appear as a witness and sentenced him to five months in jail,[9] but he remained in CNRP headquarters, enjoying significant international support, with ambassadors going to meet him and posing for photographs. After six months of confinement in his office, Sokha wrote to Hun Sen, asking him to request that the King grant a pardon. Hun Sen agreed and King Sihamoni promptly quashed Kem Sokha's conviction.[10]

The ADHOC 5, as they became known, remained in jail, though. Seven months after their arrest, the court said it was still collecting evidence and so continued to hold them in pre-trial detention. In reality, nothing was happening. Srey Mom had disappeared, into a new life set up for her somewhere secret, and the ADHOC 5 were never pulled from their cells for questioning.

'Before, I feel confident that I would not stay long in the place,' Vanda admitted. 'In the prison, the biggest fear I can feel in the prisoners is the desperation. They would lose something sooner or later. Firstly, they would lose the family and that is what they fear the most. Family is the foundation of life. In the prison, there are some reasons naturally and some artificially created by the guards and government to separate you from your family. Not only physically, but also spiritually and mentally. They do this to me.' Vanda became solemn. 'Your wife would come to visit and then they would tell her that they will call you to come. They will pretend to call and then say that they cannot find me. Or that I'm having a bath. Or that I'm busy talking to other people. So that after one hour, she is still waiting in a bad place and now she is thinking why is she sitting there waiting for an arrogant person. And one day my wife says that she could not come to visit me any longer. It is too difficult.'

Vanda cut off contact with CNRP activists held in the overcrowded, insect-infested jail. 'I would speak to them and then one hour later, they would stop the water. Ten times I speak to the CNRP people and ten times they stop the water. I think okay, I cannot keep talking. So to them, I said, "Brother, maybe we should stop shaking hands. Every time I shake your hand, they do not let me go." I knew that would be the end and I had no hope. I used to teach English to the prisoners and then say no more. Then I said to my friends in the cell that I will stop listening to the radio. They said, "Please, sir, no, it is very important to you. You must listen to it."'

The radio often played Sinn Sisamouth, who had begun composing and singing in the 1930s. Favoured by the Royal Family, he performed at state receptions and appeared on national radio. The first program on Cambodian television was one of his songs. With a smooth, crooning voice, Sisamouth brought Western rock and pop to Cambodia's fledgling music scene, adapting hits such as The Beatles' 'Hey Jude' into Cambodian. Over a 35-year career, Sisamouth wrote hundreds of songs, performing Latin jazz, cha-cha, agogo and even psychedelic rock effortlessly as Cambodia swayed to his beat. Many Cambodians, even younger ones, think of the 1960s as Cambodia's golden period, and when they do, it is Sisamouth's voice they hear. The Khmer Rouge was never going to tolerate his poetry and, like most artists, he was dead within a few months of their rule. When the Khmer Rouge fell, Sisamouth's voice rose again, and even today, more than forty years since his death, people of all ages name him as their favourite singer.

One day, the man lying next to Vanda began playing one of Sisamouth's melancholic songs on his Walkman. It was named 'Twenty Years in Prison', causing Vanda to weep. 'When I wept, people get surprised. They call to the guy sleeping next to me and say, "Why play the sad song?" They want to beat him up. He says, "No, no, I want him to sleep better, try to soothe him."

They say, "No, the sad song make him cry. Look! Stop that song. Play it again and we will beat you up, okay?"'

Vanda smiled as he remembered the care these 'criminals' had shown for him. Inspired, Vanda began to write his own songs. 'I would sing about the conditions of jail. They would sing too. The lyrics of the tune were happy, but the meaning is very sad. One day, they cut water and cut electricity. Electricity is okay; you can be creative. You can get a plastic bag and put it into the big cover of the fan and it makes a bigger fan. But without water, you cannot do anything.

'They asked me to sing a song but I choose the best singer, who sung my song. The guards feel pity because of the song and the water starts to flow. They [cellmates] check the water and it is clean water. "Why don't you sing a second song?!" I sing a second song and two more containers come. We get three and then they ask me to sing another song!'

Vanda has heard that his former inmates still sing his song in memory of him.

After 427 days in jail, a guard came to the cell and said, 'Vanda, please get dressed. You are free to go.'

Vanda did not believe him. 'I said, "No. Please, no kidding." He said it a second time. And I said, "Please, no, I am reading. Don't interrupt me. You are kidding again."' He got annoyed and frustrated with me and he opened the door 180 degrees – and they normally never open it that much. It can be dangerous. But the big iron door was wide open and he stood there and said, "Now, do you believe me?" And I thought, *Now is time to get out!*'

All five were released on the same day, but under conditions of bail. They would still face trial. Nonetheless, when they arrived at ADHOC's office, there was a big party with family, friends and members of the communities they had defended throughout the years.[11] Ny Sokha, one of the ADHOC 5, remembered feeling that even court officials seemed happy they were being released: 'The court officer, even though they decide to detain us, they feel disappointed with the decision. We clearly realise that our detention is not really the decision of the court but orders of the leaders. We heard in the past, but it was difficult to believe, that it is not the court who makes the decisions. The courts just follow the decision of the leaders. When we have this problem, we understand its truth. When we were released finally, we feel that the court officers also feel happy. So it means that while we were in the prison, the court's officer is waiting for the green light from the leader to release us.'

In his fifties, and certainly thinner than the huggable Vanda, Sokha's health had been faltering, but in jail he was mostly concerned with the health of his newborn son, who he had yet to meet. Sokha's youngest child has a hole in his heart and required specialist treatment only available at a children's hospital six hours away. 'When I was in prison, he could not go. When my wife gave birth, it was very difficult for her.'

Both Vanda and Sokha talked about how tough it was for their families while they were inside, with Vanda saying that his wife was 'also staying in a hell'. 'Like she was staying in the most isolated island. Not many relatives would talk to her. Neighbours would not. Even her mother. Before they put me in jail, they do a good preparation to make my family and in-law family cut ties. Her sister's husband, a top-ranking police officer. So they divide the family. Even my mum-in-law was taken away. She [Vanda's wife] was put in isolation from all the family. Luckily, I have friends.'

Vanda's wife was intimidated by people following her moto and a 'gangster and drug dealer' moved in beside his family. At night, people threw sticks at the house. Vanda's family had been intimidated before – a bag of snakes was put outside their house one night – but this time Vanda knew it was different and moved their two children to different schools.

Sokha's eldest child gave up school completely to help care for the family. While Sokha was in jail, colleagues would visit his daughter, often finding her in tears. 'At my house, many visitors. Even some people from embassies. Even Special Representative of UN in Cambodia visit my house. These visits make my family feel proud. She feels proud of my work. I give my thanks to friends who support my family, even with the money to help my wife give birth. And my children at school – paid for by other people. All this support, it encourages us.'

The ADHOC 5 were eventually found guilty of bribing a witness and given five-year suspended sentences. They were warned that they could return to jail if they were too active in cases against the government.[12] Vanda moved to an administrative role, conceding, 'I am not like Vanda as before.'

I asked Sokha if he thought twice about returning to ADHOC. 'We do not take the easy option to make things smooth for ourselves or family,' he said. 'We do not take that opportunity because we want to help people. I tell young people who come to work for ADHOC, if you want to be rich, have a nice house, nice car, et cetera, don't come to work here. I have enough to eat but not more than that. To be able to do the job, we have to prioritise the country and the issues of the people above our own lives and above our families. There is a saying that you cannot hit a stone with an egg and some people say, "Why put yourself at risk for something like that?"'

In Cambodia, the stones are those people who hold power, with lots of *khnorng*, and the peasants are the eggs, easily scrambled. Sitting in prison, Sokha was initially angry, feeling the injustice of a government that can decide 'black is white and white is black'. Alone in a room of thirty, he was left searching for answers he knew would never come: 'If I committed something wrong, I would not suffer, as it would be fair. But this is unfair. My work is to help society. Why they arrest me?'[13]

Sokha thought about the country his newborn son would grow up in and decided he would give him a nickname related to what had been promised by UNTAC in 1993. Pleasant-sounding with a gentle rhythm, he named his boy Nytoroth, which means 'rule of law'.

CHAPTER 18

THE MAN IN THE WHITE SHIRT WITH A BLACK HEART

In July 2016, amid the throes of Kem Sokha being holed up in the CNRP headquarters and the ADHOC 5 in jail, Global Witness published a report showing that Hun Sen's family owned or were registered directors of more than 100 companies, spanning hospitality, tourism, construction, real estate, mining and telecommunications. Global Witness contended that some of these companies may have been avoiding taxes or profiting at the expense of the state. Three of his children partly owned Cambodia's second-biggest electricity provider, which had lucrative contracts with the Ministry of Energy. Hun Sen, Global Witness alleged, had misused his power to become a billionaire in a country emaciated by poverty.[1]

At the time, Kem Ley was Cambodia's most prominent social and political commentator. He appeared on *Radio Free Asia* to discuss the report's findings. Handsome, broad-shouldered Sophal, my friend too poor to be accepted by his girlfriend's family, explained Ley's popularity to me: 'He was not afraid to talk and speak out, and he was able to say things. Ordinary people could not say it. He was very well educated and spoke slowly. He would explain so that everybody could understand. He came from a poor family. He told people about his background. I really like him. He speaks like a song. Like Sinn Sisamouth. That same charm. That softness.'[2]

Kou Sina had worked with Kem Ley on a HIV project years earlier. She recalled that he was a 'kind, open, gentle man, and very clever' and 'a good leader who was encouraging'. He was always at ease, she remembered. 'One time, he was giving a presentation and he had used an old figure ... the government representatives criticised him. He just smiled and said that he would do more investigation to correct it.'[3]

Kem Ley had helped to establish a new party, the Grassroots Democratic Party, in August 2015, after the CPP and the CNRP failed to forge political dialogue. But he never intended to lead it. He removed himself to remain neutral, unaligned to any party.

A few weeks before the Global Witness report, Kem Ley embarked on a project to spend 100 nights with families in villages throughout Cambodia, bringing people together from all sides of the village to talk as one. During his travels, Kem Ley began to write a tragi-comedy about a political leader called 'The Man in the White Shirt with a Black Heart'. Every few days, he would post a short chapter on Facebook that was liked, shared and commented on by thousands. He criticised the government's 'black' imprisonment of the ADHOC 5 and then posted a fable, which he announced would be the first of ninety-nine.

These fables used light-hearted imaginings and characters with strange names to skewer the CPP's system of government. In one, a gardener is praised for watering the flowers while the sun is shining. It starts to rain heavily, so the gardener stops watering, prompting the owner to shout: 'Why haven't you continued to water the flowers?' The servant says, 'It's raining, boss!' The boss scolds him: 'If you're afraid of getting wet, why not bring an umbrella to cover you as you water the garden?' The fearful gardener returned to watering the garden in the rain.[4] His eleventh fable tells the story of a high-ranking official named Uncle Villas who challenges villagers who are hungry and deeply in debt to remember, 'We're building schools, roads, hospitals, bridges and so on. We have this much, what more could we want?'

Despite the criticism of his government, Hun Sen wanted to meet with Kem Ley. Ou Ritthy, the young man who established Politikoffee after coming back from India, was friends with Kem Ley and revealed that a close associate of Hun Sen had approached Ley to organise a meeting between the two.[5] While seeking Ritthy's advice on meeting Hun Sen, Ley showed Ritthy some of his unpublished fables. 'I read one by one and asked whose ideas they were. He said this guy, that guy and one guy, including a general. I was so happy that I pay for all food and drink. First time! He keep telling me all of the story.'

It was not unusual for people to buy the smiling Kem Ley food; often when going to pay for his morning noodle soup, the seller would tell him that somebody had already paid for him. Sometimes it was a government employee who did so because they admired him for speaking 'what they want to speak', Ritthy told me.[6]

Ritthy and Ley talked for hours about their plans to bring older and younger leaders together to discuss the past and what Cambodia's future could be.⁷ Finally, it was time for Ritthy to bid farewell – he had to pack for the Netherlands, where he was due to study on a scholarship. The same day Ritthy left, Ley appeared on *Radio Free Asia* talking about the Global Witness report. It had been published three days before.

For half an hour, Kem Ley criticised Hun Sen's conflict of interest and called for a clear separation between business and politics. He said that, on occasion, the corruption was so significant that 'ordinary ministers cannot make decisions', only the Prime Minister.⁸ Kem Ley urged further investigation by charities and Transparency International because the Anti-Corruption Unit that reports directly to Hun Sen 'dare not investigate'.⁹

Without giving names, Kem Ley also criticised 'children of high-ranking officials' for dealing drugs. This could be taken as a reference to Hun Sen's nephew Hun To. In its report, Global Witness advised that Hun To had been connected by an Australian newspaper to the trafficking of $1 billion worth of heroin into Australia – allegations he denied – and claimed that the Australian government's plans to arrest and question him in Melbourne were derailed when the Australian Foreign Ministry denied him a visa on the basis that his arrest could cause a 'diplomatic incident'.¹⁰

The radio host, Yeang Sothearin, knew that the content was politically sensitive, but he and Kem Ley had discussed sensitive topics before; this program seemed no different. During the talkback section, one CPP supporter rang in to criticise Sothearin for only featuring government detractors on air. Ley responded that it would be good if CPP-supporting channels invited critics on their programs. After the show, the two friends shook hands and bid farewell, as radio staff congratulated them on the segment.¹¹

Two days later, Kem Ley was where he could be found most mornings – drinking his coffee in the Star Mart café of the Caltex petrol station at the corner of Monivong and Mao Tse Tung Boulevards in Phnom Penh. A former soldier entered, walked up to Kem Ley and shot him in the head, killing the married father of four instantly. Ley, wearing simple grey tracksuit pants and a red polo shirt, fell to the floor as blood oozed over the tiles.

Ritthy was in Bangkok, preparing for the Netherlands with other scholarship students, when Kem Ley was killed. A fellow Cambodian student came over to him during an induction session and said, 'Very sad, brother. Kem Ley was shot.' Ritthy left the room and stumbled back to his hostel. It had a hairdresser nearby, and soon he ventured out to it. 'Thailand, it is the same,' he said. 'Haircut when somebody die.' Ritthy took his glasses off and put them beside the mirror, and then had his head shaved completely. People passing him in the street would glance, knowing that something terrible had befallen him. George Soros's Open Society Foundation, which sponsored Ritthy's scholarship, asked if they could arrange asylum for him, but he declined.[12]

Sothearin was at his brother's home in Sihanoukville for a religious ceremony when a friend called to say Kem Ley had been shot. Sothearin asked a colleague to go to the Star Mart café, where Sothearin had often met Ley, and fifteen minutes later got another call. The phone fell from Sothearin's numb hand. 'I had no feeling at all. Nothing. It was so shock to me. I could not believe it. Not believe it! It was too fast. Too fast. We just talk to each other and then … yeah …'[13]

Sothearin got in a car for Phnom Penh, with his brother accompanying him for safety. 'Because we don't know. We don't know. Two days after the discussion, he was shot, and what going to happen to me?' Back in Phnom Penh, Sothearin felt even more uneasy and left to stay with his parents in the Mekong Delta region of Southern Vietnam, or what Cambodians call *Kampuchea Krom* (Lower Cambodia) from when it was part of their kingdom.

Not long after Kem Ley's death, Sothearin started to receive phone calls from a woman who refused to give her name. At first Sothearin thought her advice was friendly, but then he realised her intentions. 'She told me not to, you know, say something, or to say all the facts. I say, "Why? Why? I am a journalist. I cannot write anything that is not the truth. I have to write the truth." She say, "I know that you are a journalist, professional, but you should think about yourself, especially also your family, your children. You know, they are still young." Then I start to realise, *oh, it is not a kind offer, this is a threat.* She said, "You are okay but, you know, your children, they still children. Pity them. What happened if you lose a finger, a small finger, one of your finger?'

⚬

Tes Putheara grew up in the house opposite Kem Ley's, and his eldest daughter shared the same birthday as Ley. Lifelong friends, the two fathers joked that their children would end up marrying each other. When Putheara read Kem Ley's fables and the story of the man with a black heart, he asked him, 'Who do you think you are? Do you think you are a writer? Storyteller? As well as a researcher?' Ley responded that he was like *samlor kor ko*, a traditional Cambodian soup that mixes lots of ingredients.[14]

Putheara, like Ritthy, thinks that Ley believed he could be arrested but did not expect to be killed. Putheara feared for him nevertheless: 'I warned him that he might be dead by an accident ... this is Cambodia and people can expect bad things.' Ley laughed it away, joking, 'Don't worry, my father passed away when he was forty and now I am fifty. Don't worry.'[15]

Two years after Kem Ley's death, I found a fidgeting Putheara at the café where Ley was killed, desperately trying to make sense of it all: 'I want to know the situation. I want to know how people react. I want to see how it changes here. Also, I want to know the person who is the eyewitness who saw him here and saw him gunned down.'

Putheara has asked the staff and other regulars if they were there at the time Ley was killed, but he has never found anybody who can explain what happened. He certainly doesn't believe the official version that Ley, who he said never borrowed money, was killed because of a loan he couldn't pay back.

After shooting Ley, the killer walked out of the petrol station and jogged down the road. Video footage shows a policeman on a motorbike speaking to him before the man runs on for another few hundred metres and crosses the road to meet the same policeman, who has driven ahead. Another policeman joins them and puts the killer on the back of the motorbike, and the three drive away from chasing onlookers. No handcuffs were ever put on the shooter.[16]

When the police arrested him, the man gave his name as Chuob Samlab, which means 'meet to kill', and said that Ley had borrowed $3000 from him and never paid him back.[17] Within a few days, Phorn Bopha, one of the two journalists with Chut Wutty when he died, tracked down Chuob Samlab's friends and family.

The man's real name is Oeuth Ang, and he hailed from a small village in rural Siem Reap, hundreds of kilometres from Phnom Penh. His friends and relatives said he was a gambler who had just sold his motorbike to pay a debt. They doubted that he would have $3000 to lend anyone, never mind a famous social commentator they didn't believe he had ever met. Two weeks before the assassination, Oeuth Ang left his village, telling people he was going to Phnom Penh to work as a soldier again, earning a substantial $300 per month. The next time they saw him was on television announcing he was called 'meet to kill'. Oeuth Ang's mother does not believe her son could have acted alone: 'There must have been someone behind my child's back.'[18]

Many believe that Kem Ley was killed because of his interview with *Radio Free Asia*, but neither Ritthy nor Putheara think this; others have said worse and never been harmed. One person told me that a senior CPP official suspected Kem Ley of being the Global Witness report's anonymous author, and maybe it was for this greater crime that his murder was ordered.[19]

The Global Witness report was published three days before Kem Ley's death, but Oeuth Ang had been recruited two weeks earlier. The fables were cutting, but Ritthy dismissed them as the reason for the murder.[20] He believes that answers may lie with the mysterious general who had given ideas for the fables. Ley never told Ritthy who the man was, only that he was a four-star general he had met a few times and who had introduced him to other government people. When Ley and Ritthy met just before his death, Ley spoke about the General and how the military was the base of the CPP's power.[21] 'Unlike others who just analyse the issue from outside, he go inside,' Ritthy said. 'He go and make relationship with generals. Stay with them, eat with them, listen. Especially, he is good at listening. Listen to the story of the generals. The General keep telling him, sympathise with the situation. Live in the forest. You know, Cambodians, we don't ask questions. We tell. We don't ask. Kem Ley, he has a style with people. Asks questions to get inside. It's not just listen and report. That is why he is so good. He can convert, can change people.'[22]

Ritthy believes that people in the CPP feared the influence Ley could have on this general and his army colleagues, and that his murder was an outcome of the CPP's plan to regain total control. 'Assassination is not unintentional. It is part of the plan. Control, eliminate. It is a long-term plan that is implemented slowly. Unfortunately, it was him.'[23]

Putheara sees Kem Ley's killing in the same way. 'They want to scare the country. They want to kill one person and kill everyone in the country.'[24]

The day before he died, Kem Ley published his nineteenth fable. A group of savage animals – lions, tigers and cobras – found a corner of their garden abundant with food. Despite that corner having enough riches to feed all the animals of the garden, the savage animals kept it for themselves, scaring the good-natured animals away. Eventually, the good-natured animals held a meeting and one said, 'Brothers and sisters, so many of us have been killed. The fact that we don't dare stand up and don't join together means that all the good food is still controlled by the savage animals ... and always will be.' Kem Ley's final words were that it did not have to be this way.[25]

Kem Ley's body was laid out in a pagoda before the funeral. At lunchtimes Putheara would go to the pagoda, where he would buy Ley a coffee and tell him he worried about Ley's eighty-year-old mother, who had gone 'quiet', and Ley's pregnant wife and four children, who had fled to Thailand, fearing for their lives. Putheara would rue to Ley that it was only he who could make people stand up, that even those who were scared listened to him.

Channa, the garment worker I met with Kunthea, also went to visit Ley's body at the pagoda. 'I was interested in him so I wanted to go to see him,' she said. 'He was an educated man. He was saying the right things about the situation in Cambodia. I didn't have a smartphone but I could hear him speak through the radio and I wanted to see his face. I asked friends to show me on their smartphone. He looked like a kind man. When he was killed, I felt so sorry. I questioned why an educated man like him would be killed. I worried about his family and their security. It is good that they have left.'

The day after he died, Channa got a moto-taxi to the pagoda where there was an hour-long queue of people lining up to see the body. Channa spent a day and a half's salary just paying the moto-taxi driver to take her there and back, and it would have cost more without a sympathetic discount from the driver. Channa's husband, hitherto a spectator to our conversation, began chuckling with surprise; this was the first he had heard of her going to see Ley's body. I looked at Channa, who gave me a sideways glance and allowed a smile to dimple her cheeks before she continued.[26] 'He was an educated man who was loyal and honest. He was not scared of speaking the truth, despite the possible difficulties. There is nobody like Chea Vichea and Kem Ley now. And maybe in the future, people like them won't appear because it's the same government still and …' Channa trailed off. Her face curled into a scowl, the dimples now absent.

The authorities did not want Kem Ley's funeral to be in Phnom Penh, so it was to be held at his mother's house, 90 kilometres away. The funeral procession began at the pagoda in Phnom Penh, leaving at 7.00am. Thousands converged at the pagoda. People had stuck photos of Ley to the front of their motos and truckloads of people bore banners saying *Forever in our hearts*. Others played recordings of Ley on speakers as they crawled through Phnom Penh. Soon, there were tens of thousands of people in the procession, with even more lining the streets.[27]

As the body passed by, rows of onlookers, Channa among them, gave a *sampeah* – bowing and pressing their palms together. Some were even kneeling and prostrating on the ground beside lotus flowers. By 12.30pm, the sun now blazing, the procession had only travelled fifteen kilometres.[28]

The government did not close roads for the funeral procession. Instead, they attempted to block one road with two trucks, and closed petrol stations so people couldn't refill.[29] Angry with the government's tactics, people ferried bottles of petrol from stations further away.[30]

Ritthy was not able to come back from the Netherlands for the funeral and spent the day 'thinking about what I did with him'.[31] Putheara drove down to his family home ahead of the procession, arriving at noon, five hours before the body did. Even then, he had to park kilometres away from his house because the area was already full of cars and motorbikes. Another close neighbour made three giant pots of Khmer noodles, enough to feed 100. He spoke to people who had travelled in minivans from across Cambodia, even from provinces nine hours away. They told him they had come because it was the last chance to see 'the heart of the Cambodian people'.

Sothearin returned from southern Vietnam to report on the procession, wanting to pay respects to a friend and mentor. 'It's hard for me to find someone like him ... even though some criticise him ... even those people attack him, he keep smiling, keep smiling. Like he is happy. I still want to cry when I speak about him and when I recall what I see about him. For me, he is not just my source, he is my hero and my model. I should learn from the way that he controlled his feelings.'

Sothearin was surprised to see so many people at the funeral. There were a similar number of attendees at King Father Sihanouk's funeral four years earlier, which was a public holiday. Sothearin believed Ley would continue to be an inspiration for Cambodians in death, as he was in life: 'I feel like, you know, his death also teach the youth one thing – we shouldn't be afraid. Why be afraid when we do good thing and we die, many people join us like this? It leaves an honour instead. And we should die like him, like that. That is the lesson that I see.'[32]

CHAPTER 19

THE RISE OF ROZETH

Hun Sen, having seen the crowds that gathered for Kem Ley's funeral, was not going to risk Sam Rainsy returning to Cambodia, especially not with Commune Council elections due within a year. Private polling for the CPP, completed two months after the funeral, found that more people intended to vote for the CNRP than the CPP, especially if Rainsy was still the CNRP leader.[1] The next month, Hun Sen ordered all government agencies to prevent Rainsy from re-entering the country, confiscated his properties and froze his assets in lieu of damages owed for a defamation conviction.[2]

In February 2017, Hun Sen proposed amendments to the *Law on Political Parties* that would ban people convicted of crimes from leading a party and allow the disbanding of a political party if it was deemed a threat to national security or unity. He declared: 'We shall ban not just a few people, but we shall get rid of the whole slate.' With a slew of convictions against him, Rainsy resigned as President from the party he had founded.[3]

As Vice-President, Kem Sokha became the CNRP's new leader. New vice-presidents were appointed, and the changes were submitted for registration with the Ministry of Interior. The Ministry refused to accept the changes, though, saying that the CNRP had not followed its own internal processes for electing leaders. Simultaneously, the CPP tried to ban the CNRP from using its new slogan, 'Change the commune chief which serves the party with the commune chief which serves the people.' The Defence Minister called it a threat to national security and the Prime Minister said it was 'incitement' and thus against the law. The CPP then declared that the word 'change' and the phrase 'Hun Sen step down', favourites from the 2013 campaign, were also illegal.[4]

As the Commune Council elections neared, the Interior Ministry still refused to register Kem Sokha as the CNRP's new leader, leaving Sam Rainsy as the official president, which would render the CNRP ineligible to stand in the election. With no other option, the CNRP acceded to the CPP's demands to stop using its slogans, and in return the Ministry of Interior recognised Kem Sokha as the new leader of the CNRP.[5]

As usual before an election, Hun Sen warned that an opposition victory would inevitably lead to war, without explaining why: 'I still insist that war will happen if the Cambodian People's Party isn't in power'. People would 'see how fragile this peace is', he said. For Hun Sen, the election was a simple question about 'whether you choose to live in peace time or ... civil war'. He warned people not to protest a CPP election victory, threatening to 'close the doors and beat the dogs' if any group did so. His Minister of Defence said he would 'smash the teeth' of anybody protesting the result, cautioning, 'To ask for change or stepping down, it will not happen anymore.'[6]

Shoring up the army's support, the government promoted 700 soldiers to the rank of general and promoted another 450 people to senior ranks. With stars falling on epaulets like confetti, Cambodia's Ministry of Defence could no longer say how many generals Cambodia's small army had, but they numbered at least 3000.[7]

Hun Sen was asked what would happen, hypothetically, if the CNRP won the election and took control of government. He replied with a question: 'How can this happen if the troops are in my hand?' Staggering even the strongest of his critics, he laid bare what he was prepared to do to keep power. 'To ensure peace and to continue development, the only option is that the CPP must win elections at all stages ... To ensure the lives of millions of people, we are willing to eliminate 100 or 200 people because we have seen bitter past experience.'[8]

Sen did not stop at targeting Rainsy, or even Sokha; CNRP officials at the local level would begin to feel his wrath.

Sin Rozeth was only twenty-six years old when she was elected Deputy Commune Chief of O'Char Commune in Battambang. This was in 2012, when the Sam Rainsy Party was desperately looking for candidates, before the opposition parties merged to create the CNRP. Existing councillors had been induced to defect to the CPP, some just days before the election, and other members hesitated to become a target of government pressure. Rozeth had grown up living with her mother in the Battambang town office of the Sam Rainsy Party, where her mother worked as a cook and cleaner. With nobody else volunteering, Rozeth put her hand up.

At that time, Rozeth did not live in O'Char and was not well known by villagers, and her relative anonymity wasn't helped when her campaign banners were torn down by the CPP. On election day, the Sam Rainsy Party struggled in O'Char commune, as it did elsewhere, winning fewer seats than before. Rozeth got one of them, though, and became the Sam Rainsy Party's leader in O'Char. Despite her victory, she sensed that her party had lost the hope of the people. '[For] some reason, once people become disappointed, kind of hopeless, their perspective on politicians becomes the same.'[9]

Lacking higher education, Rozeth tried to learn from the CPP councillors she served with, but 'every time, they walk away. If I am in the [commune] office, they would walk out. If I went out to join the conversation, they walked away. I sat alone in the office, as the other two Sam Rainsy Party councillors were never there.' She was the only women among the men. 'When I attend the meeting, I would raise an issue about what was happening in the commune, but they treated it as nonsense. Nobody listened. I would try to talk to the district or provincial level, but nobody would do anything because the Commune Chief is [from] their party. As a deputy commune councillor for almost five years, I never received any reports about funding, budgets, activities.'

Ostracised, Rozeth decided to keep herself busy getting to know the people of O'Char. Seeing their impoverished conditions, she felt that 'nobody was supporting these poor people'. Rozeth encountered many 'intimidated and scared of politics. They may know that I am from the opposition party ... they wouldn't want to talk.' She slowly earned their trust by challenging the commune's corrupt practices, such as demanding bribes to issue birth certificates. Having failed to form relationships with CPP councillors, Rozeth began to challenge them openly. 'I would film things and share what was happening. People could then be shamed into acting.'

Rozeth stared intently at my interpreter's lips each time he spoke, as if willing herself to understand his English translation. A petite woman, she sat erect when listening with her hands clasped on the table, like a student waiting to be tested, but she made small, quick gesticulations when speaking. She spoke like a steam train leaving the platform, getting quicker and louder as she gathered momentum. I realised that after twenty-five minutes, I had asked only two questions. My interpreter would endeavour to translate a monologue and immediately after he finished, she would say 'and ...' and the train would leave the station again.

There is a video of Rozeth campaigning for the CNRP during the 2013 National Assembly election. She is standing on a roadside with a loudspeaker haranguing thin air as motorbikes whizz by. Nobody stops and few turn their heads, but Rozeth keeps talking. There is no pause for breath or stumbling over words. Clearly and confidently, Rozeth tells anybody within earshot why they should vote CNRP.

The CNRP did well in the 2013 national election, but Rozeth knew that the 2017 local elections would be different. 'For the National Assembly, when they have an election, people think that it is a chance to change the national leadership, which is very important. But at the local elections, they have a lot of sentimental relationships with local councillors. They know they do corruption, but they think it's fine. It is usual. And they know the people. They [the CPP] have concrete foundation at the commune level. Some commune councillors have a lot of relations with local people and some will have a very close relationship, like used to work with them or relatives. Even if they are corrupt, they are very close to them. People will look at the sun [the CNRP's logo], but I have to let the villagers know about me and how I will lead them.'

Rozeth began to build relationships with young people in the lead-up to the 2017 local elections. 'Normally, I am meant to wait to be told what to do by the national party, but I have to be smart and think what I can do … The first time I go house to house, sometimes I would speak to children, but parents would not come to speak because they are afraid. The second time, there would be more young people and then the third time, parents came with young people. I would speak to young people about birth certificates. If they didn't have one, I said that if they spoke to their parents, I can help their parents get them a birth certificate. They may then go to speak to their parents.'

Birth certificates are essential for registering to vote, establishing a business or even attending school. More and more families started going to Rozeth for help, realising that she would make sure they weren't charged improperly by commune officials for requesting a birth certificate. She also began using Facebook to raise funds for her impoverished community from Cambodians at home and abroad.

Rozeth started to feel that she was breaking down people's cynicism with politicians and saw her opportunity to call for change. 'I explained about the support that I can give if I become leader, but they have to choose to change … I did something opposed to the norm by not giving gifts. I would say to people that they should compare the politicians who give gifts and those who don't. I explained that if we have a clean commune council, the people can get services without being charged and it will be done faster. This will help them live in a better way.'

More and more people began to attend her meetings, attracting the attention of local authorities. 'When I have a meeting, the police would be there and people would be afraid so they would go home. But when they went home, they would think that Cambodian society is now not good because they saw government spies and police. They did not like that they were being intimidated. They did not think this is how it should be. I did not argue with police officers or the Commune Chief – when they are there, we just go back to our homes and people reflected on this. They can see. The next day, I go back to the same place.'

Rozeth has become used to intimidation, having received three serious death threats via Facebook. 'The first time, I could identify the [account] owner. I filed a complaint to the police but the owner said that somebody hacked his account because he didn't log out when in an internet shop. The second time, not sure who. It was because me and Soy Chamroeun [CNRP youth leader] intervened in a Treasury matter. The third time, I file a complaint. The case just sits. No action.'

Rozeth has kept the threats secret from her elderly mother, who suffers from high blood pressure. While being unsettled by them, she knows it comes with the territory: 'Being an opposition party member, I accept this way.' Rozeth refused to change her approach. 'Sometimes, I had to visit people at night, but going at night showed that I was willing to take care of people. When I heard villagers had issues, I could not ignore it. I had to take action. We serve the people who are in need, and if we don't serve them, and we flee from supporting them, the people hate us.'

Rozeth became admired throughout Cambodia, despite only being a local politician. At the 2017 commune election, nearly two-thirds of people voted CNRP in O'Char commune, making Sin Rozeth their new Commune Chief. The people of O'Char had found their champion, rather than their patron.

Rozeth paused to take a breath and there was a moment of silence. Her dark hair was tied back and she had little beads of moisture on her brow – unusual, as most Cambodians appear immune to the sweltering stickiness. I asked her how she felt when she heard that she had become the chief, and her eyes widened with her smile. 'Excited! It was what I wished for, hoped for. It became true. All the observers walk to the party office full of energy. They had worked all day but they were not tired ... I had to compete. There are ten communes in the city and my commune got the highest vote. So I had strong feelings. Old men in the party would sometimes say that I may think I am smart but I would see what happened in the election. They doubted. That result proved I had good communication and relationships with people. It proved I did it right.'

CHAPTER 20
A TRANSFER OF POWER

The reformed National Election Commission, established after the deal between the CPP and the CNRP in 2014, was still in place with the same ruling committee members for the 2017 Commune Council election. They had transformed the system so that there was an accurate list of registered voters, which included 1 million new voters.[1] They also dictated that each polling station must post the results on the wall for all to see and the NEC would publish results for each commune. Rong Chhun, the former union leader who said he was 'sharpening his spurs' when joining the NEC, said that the changes were what the CNRP had hoped for when they decided to make the 2014 deal, vindicating his decision to join.[2]

Hang Puthea, a fellow NEC member, called 2017 'the good election' when discussing it with me. Transparency International stated that overall, 'voting went smoothly with little to no intimidation ... and polling officials followed proper procedures'. The biggest independent monitor of the election, COMFREL, praised 'significant' improvements in the registration of voters and said the management of voting and counting on Election Day had 'improved considerably'.[3]

In the UK's 2019 election, 68 per cent of registered voters actually voted, while Japan struggled to get 56 per cent turning out in 2021. The choice between Trump and Biden brought 71 per cent of registered American voters out,[4] but this still lagged behind the astounding 90 per cent of registered Cambodian voters who participated in the 2017 local election.[5]

Cambodians had waited four years for this moment, since the disputed 2013 election, which many felt robbed them of the government the country wanted. People waited outside after voting, not wanting to go home. Some sat in the shade near polling booths sharing predictions, while others paced around nervously, pulling on a cigarette. When polls closed and the counting began, people all over the country asked officials to open the doors so they could see and hear the counting of every vote.

I asked a COMFREL staff member and Karuna, the human rights worker hit on the head by a stone at Veng Sreng Street, whether they thought the election was free and fair. They immediately responded with an enthusiastic 'Yes, yes!' before remembering their default opposition to the CPP and adding 'well, nearly – not quite'.[6]

Chamroeun, who changed clothes like Superman to join CNRP rallies, agreed that this was Cambodia's best election yet, but explained why he did not consider it fully free and fair: 'If we talk about free and fair, in the Cambodian standard it was as good as it's been. But if we compared to a developed country, it is not. The pre-election is not free. The ruling party has civil servants who campaign every weekend. They use their work to persuade the voter. The opposition have nothing like that. It is not fair. But for Cambodia, who moved from communist or dictator, this is much better. The opposition can campaign.'

The CPP certainly had vast resources – tens of millions of dollars and access to government-owned buildings and cars for campaigning. They were the only party that could buy television airtime, and news coverage was overwhelmingly, and positively, focused on the CPP. What little coverage there was of the CNRP was mostly negative.[7] While most people could freely participate in the election, Sam Rainsy was still in exile and was not even allowed to broadcast a Facebook video to supporters in Cambodia. Other senior CNRP leaders remained in jail.[8]

The CNRP may have been muted, but people were still willing to stand as candidates for them, and the public felt free to express their opinions on who they would vote for. This led Chamroeun to judge that Hun Sen had failed: 'They tried to intimidate. To use political intimidation, violence, the killing of Kem Ley, in order to make people scared. But they couldn't do that. And the results showed clearly in the commune election.'[9]

Sophal, Rotha and Kunthea all described the booth where people voted as 'the secret place'.[10] The CPP may have taken control of trade unions, charities and civil servants, but the sanctity of the polling booth remained. People still believed that they could vote and nobody would know who they voted for.

When the doors to schools and commune halls were opened and crowds hushed each other to hear the counting, Cambodians felt that they were arriving at the future they had been promised twenty-five years earlier, when UNTAC arrived in their bruised country. This was an election they could believe in and, when the counting finished, nobody would doubt the accuracy of its result. Four years after the power was cut and the country plunged into darkness, people were back huddled around radios, televisions or smartphones listening to a robotic mannequin recite the results from around the country. And the result was the same: 3.5 million people had voted for the CPP and 3 million had voted for the CNRP. The votes for all other parties were insignificant. The CPP had won Cambodia's freest and fairest election.

I asked many people who did not support the CPP why people would vote for them. Each time, I was given one of four reasons, all tinged with condescension. First, they said that old people stuck in the past would vote for the CPP because it had defeated the Khmer Rouge decades ago. Second, people are scared of returning to the wars of the 1970s and 1980s – since the CPP had brought order and stability, it was better to stick with them and ignore their faults. Third, Cambodia still had many uneducated and illiterate people, especially in rural areas, who were too easily impressed by infrastructure, such as new pagodas and schools. The outside world was unknown to them, so they could only compare present-day Cambodia to its forlorn past, not its potential future. Plus, they did not fully understand democracy, so they just voted for whoever the CPP-appointed village chief told them to.

The last explanation, and the most scathing one, was that people voted for the CPP because it served their own interests. These people were corrupt and part of the system that stole from the nation for individual benefit. They could be civil servants who received a salary but never worked, or businessmen with lucrative government contracts getting massive kickbacks. It could even be the local police chief who had been promoted because of his CPP connections, or the rural housewife who was given a sarong, rice and MSG by her CPP commune councillors.

In each explanation, the CPP voter lacked a certain virtue. The old people were trapped by the past; others scared too easily or were too stupid to know what was best for them, or they were selfish and greedy. CNRP supporters could not concede that there may be legitimate reasons to vote for the CPP, or indeed, that overthrowing the Khmer Rouge, bringing ongoing peace and stability, and taking Cambodia from year zero to become a lower-middle-income country are remarkable achievements of the CPP.

Ritthy and Chamroeun offered an additional perspective, talking about personal connections to CPP councillors who may have served the commune well over the years, approved a voter's application to open a business or helped the local school install a toilet. He – it was nearly always a he – may even have graced a voter's daughter's wedding, giving generously.[11] The community voted for him, rather than the party, as Chamroeun explained: 'Sometimes, people think the commune election, they could not change much ... and they still have loyalty to the commune councillor because they see the opposition councillor and they see he has no capacity, not qualified. So, people look at that. They like the opposition but they vote CPP. They know the person, they have a connection and, with a local election, it doesn't matter if they vote for the ruling party. That's why the opposition could not win the majority even though they gain significantly. People still loyal to the people they know.'[12]

Sotheavy, my friend who explained *khnorng* to me, had been discussing politics with her younger brother, a successful businessman connected to the CPP. During their conversation, he asked her how she knew the CNRP politicians would do a better job. She was stumped. She didn't know, and for the first time questioned whether they would.[13]

The CPP had won the 2017 Commune Council elections, but it was viewed as a defeat because the CPP had lost control of hundreds of councils. Before the election, the CPP ran 97 per cent of all councils. Afterwards, the CNRP controlled nearly one-third of them,[14] meaning CPP council chiefs were having to hand power over to their CNRP opponents. Governing would be a new experience for the campaigning CNRP politicians, and for Rozeth this was a time of nervous anticipation. 'I couldn't sleep after knowing the result. I was so excited, but my main question was whether I could perform the task or not. I don't stop working, I keep going house to house even after the result. I made a schedule to go to each village to thank them for voting for me.'[15]

I asked her what the first council meeting was like. 'The first commune meeting is to set up the rules and regulations. They begin to argue with me. The ruling party, they join the meeting but they don't join the meeting. They join to argue. In the first meeting, we could not find chairs to sit on. They took them away to their Party's office ... then they ask why we have no table and chairs. For me, I knew how many tables and chairs there were. I was also aware that those people used smartphones to record my voice and catch me saying something that they could post on Facebook. So I would always try to negotiate with them in a soft way. Try not to be tricked by them. I don't blame people for taking the table and chairs and just say that at the next meeting we will have table and chairs, but at this meeting, we need to form the regulations.'

Rozeth took to her smartphone and raised money to buy desks, chairs, a computer and a printer for the office. She tried to make it a friendly work environment, giving everybody a desk with their name and position on it, but many never came to actually work. 'When they came, they just tried to fight and argue or find mistakes.'

Commune chiefs have responsibilities to work with school directors, the police and officers of education and health. I asked Rozeth if these organs of the state respected her as chief. 'They treated me the same way [as before]. Just ignored me. Would not invite me to school openings. They would invite somebody from the provincial authorities. I never got any information from higher government authorities. If there was a visit from government leaders, they should contact me, but they never did. They followed party lines.'

There wasn't just an intertwining between party and state – the CPP had swallowed the state whole. Across the country, elected CNRP officials were being cut out, excluded from the business of government. Rozeth was exasperated. 'I never received any budgets or funds when I was chief. Instead of receiving a budget from the commune, I raised money to do things. I had to pay for the electricity for the commune office using my own money. If I didn't pay, they were going to cut it off.'

Rozeth wrote to district and provincial officials, but instead of receiving assistance, she incurred the wrath of the Battambang Provincial Governor for not charging villagers fees for services, such as registering births and marriages. 'Maybe I was the only one to face this in Cambodia... I serve the villagers from my heart so I didn't charge them a fee, but the government asked me to pay the missing fees and to start charging. I was given four warnings for this. I had just started and they should have shown me what to do but they didn't. For the first month, helping the villagers with forms, the fee was 400,000 riels ($100), so I had to pay that from my own money. The Commune Clerk acted as a spy for the ruling party. He would feed information back about what I was doing. Despite the warnings, I still did not charge fees to any villagers.'

In Rozeth's first four months as Commune Council Chief, she issued 400 birth certificates and, astounding everybody, won a court ruling that returned land to the commune which had been illegally seized by a senior provincial policeman. She turned it into a preschool. 'Nobody would expect me to do the administrative job because I had never done it. Even people from the same party, they never expect me to do this job. For some people, they believe that until you have high knowledge, you cannot do the job. I have no higher education but I have a very strong will, and I want to serve the people. Although I am not good at computers, I try to contact NGO staff, CPP people, to help me type documents. Finally, I manage to do it. I could do it all according to my will. If you have only high knowledge and no will, then you cannot do the job either.'

In nearby Siem Reap, the country's youngest commune council chief, 26-year-old Chen Sokngeng, was also encountering obstacles. Sokngeng had won Sala Kamreuk commune on the outskirts of Siem Reap town, trouncing the long-standing CPP chief with twice as many votes. Like Rozeth, Sokngeng had struggled internally to be accepted as a candidate because he was young and lacked experience. The CNRP had tiers, and he was near the bottom. He continually pressed that age is not the only measure of experience; passion is just as important. Eventually, the CNRP leadership relented and selected him as a candidate.

His parents would have preferred he continue working as a doctor, but they did not try to dissuade him, instead giving him money for t-shirts and banners. Donations also flowed from Cambodians abroad, meaning he could hire a car with a loudspeaker to help him campaign.[16] When the CNRP won the commune, many people came to celebrate. 'Normally,' Sokngeng said, 'the CPP win and have a big dance. The CNRP won and didn't dance. Didn't want to gloat.' He told his supporters and fellow CNRP councillors to 'respect the minority': 'They have been voted by the people too.'

When all the councillors arrived at the office for the first time after the election, they may have noticed the flowers Sokngeng had planted at the door and that the leaky roof was being fixed, as he sought to create 'a good place for people to come to see us'. Sitting at the head of the table, Sokngeng welcomed everybody: 'In the office, we are not CPP or CNRP. We just serve the people. No parties. No corruption in here.'

Sokngeng hoped to 'get rid of the culture of grudge and revenge',[17] but instead the outgoing CPP Commune Chief locked the door to the chief's office, refusing to give Sokngeng the key. He only relented after a barrage of media and online criticism.[18]

Locals in Sokngeng's commune had been complaining about the stench from sewage and stagnant water since before the election. Facing similar budgetary problems to Rozeth, Sokngeng asked people to contribute to a new sewage system with culverts. He raised $20,000 as he quickly built trust among locals and wealthier Cambodians living abroad. Like Rozeth, he also ended 'under-the-table fees' to process documents for citizens, signing them within two hours, rather than taking a week or more.[19]

It was a challenge for Sokngeng to learn all the rules and regulations fast. He could sense the CPP councillors hoping he would fail, but he didn't. His popularity rose as he built relationships with village chiefs and raised money for schools from Cambodians abroad. CPP councillors began to work with 'open hearts', allowing them to discuss possible actions together.[20] Even the police, he said, began to listen to him as he began to grow into his role. His parents, living in a different commune, had strangers congratulating them on their son as his reputation spread.[21]

Nationally, Sokngeng felt the 5000 CNRP councillors were showing their strength and providing good services for the people. They were proving that an alternative government was possible, answering the question Sotheavy's brother had asked.

CHAPTER 21

TO CATCH A TIGER

I was speaking with a close friend in August 2017, right after the commune elections. CNRP councillors had only just finished arranging their desks and finding the right height for their chairs, but my friend was apprehensive. He warned me that in Cambodia, a tiger is at its most dangerous when cornered.

In the preceding two years, Hun Sen had banished and beaten CNRP leaders, passed laws to restrict charities and trade unions, deepened control of the civil service and the military, and imprisoned human rights and CNRP activists. But he was still not in control of his country. The spark that was lit when Sam Rainsy touched down at Phnom Penh airport in 2013 was burning stronger than ever before.

The CPP had lost the chief in hundreds of commune councils, and with it the power to 'go to peoples' houses and control them', as one government employee put it.[1] The party worried that this could affect their chances in the 2018 national elections, and CPP polling confirmed that people were more likely to vote for the CNRP in national elections than they were in commune elections. The polling predicted that the CPP was nine percentage points behind the CNRP, even if Sam Rainsy remained abroad and Kem Sokha continued to lead the CNRP. Pollsters found that the CPP could only match the CNRP's popularity if neither Kem Sokha nor Sam Rainsy were leading the CNRP, and respondents said they were even more likely to vote for the CNRP if the CPP limited their ability to campaign.[2]

Government repression in Cambodia had gone unnoticed internationally because of the hellish infernos burning in other countries. Cambodia of the 1990s was nothing compared to Rwanda, Liberia or the Balkans. The anarchy of Afghanistan, Iraq and Somalia consumed the world in the new millennium, and Cambodia's protests were incomparable to the raging wars in Libya and Syria in the 2010s.

Hun Sen saw what happened to leaders in the Arab Spring. Gaddafi, who was celebrating a year as Chairperson of the African Union in 2010, was dead by 2011, executed by Libyan opposition forces just months after protests began. Egypt's Mubarak was imprisoned for life while Tunisia's Ben Ali was forced into exile. Bashar al-Assad was retaining control of Syria but was killing half the country to do so.

Titthara, Chut Wutty's journalist friend, told me that in Cambodia, 'when someone loses power, they go to jail. So they don't want to lose their power. This is the problem for Asian countries, not just Cambodia. They see Malaysia. That is an example for Hun Sen. He will not do like that because of the landslide, the landslide in Malaysia. So, he will prepare the grassroots ...'[3]

In 2018, the defeated Malaysian Prime Minister, Najib Razak, was stopped trying to leave the country and prosecuted for abuse of power and massive corruption. In Thailand, Hun Sen's old ally Thaksin Shinawatra was ousted as Prime Minister, sentenced to jail and now lives in exile. Hun Sen could also look back in Cambodian history to see the sorry fate that befalls the losers of power.

Hang Puthea from the National Election Committee told me that Cambodia lacks the political understanding required for democracy. 'It is different from the democracy in the US. The number of voters in favour of Trump was fewer than that of Hillary, but he was allowed to run the office. They have true political understanding ... Cambodia does not have political understanding yet. Any party that wins the election will be troubled.'[4]

Phirun, the civil servant perplexed by a CNRP politician wanting to dine with CPP ones, paraphrased a Latin saying: in Cambodia, 'if you want peace, then you have to be ready to go to war.' He explained that CPP leaders had 'gone through so many important things in life' and feared some form of retribution if they ever lost power. Phirun looked at me solemnly. 'So, without winning the election, they think they will die. This is Cambodian culture.'

Phirun said that the years of relative peace proved the CPP's magnanimity: 'If the CPP wins, everybody – ruling party, opposition party, everybody – can survive. Until now, you can see. Other people win, we are not sure. Will they tolerate [criticism]? Will they forget the past? This one important thing. If the CPP wins, the country is at peace, everybody can live harmoniously.'[5]

Before the election, Hun Sen was enraged by a CNRP supporter's comment on Facebook that called for the destruction of the Hun family.[6]

Returning to this just after the election, Hun Sen told hundreds of villagers at an event to mark his escape to Vietnam that the CNRP was attempting to 'destroy the Hun family'. He asked his three sons, one the Commander of the Royal Cambodian Army, another the Deputy Chief of Intelligence and the third a member of parliament, to stand behind him as he accused the CNRP of fomenting war. 'Your tongue is creating war,' charged Hun Sen, who was dressed in a green military uniform, medals hanging from his chest. 'As long as your tongue and your writing insult me, I say that Cambodia is still at war … the army is ready to crack down on any movement to overthrow and undermine the country.' Hun Sen counselled people to 'prepare your coffins' if they continued to 'make insults and threats to kill'. Repeating his pre-election pledge, he declared, 'To protect the peace for millions of people, if necessary, 100 or 200 must be eliminated.'[7]

Hun Sen's warnings of a second Cambodian colour revolution, after the horrific Red Khmer one, had already begun before the 2017 commune election, when he addressed 5000 military and police at the headquarters of his bodyguard unit: 'The armed forces must be loyal to the government and prevent any act of colour revolution.'[8] Days later, his Minister of Defence told graduating cadets that the CNRP's 'attempt to create a colour revolution was putting society in turmoil', and one of his top generals said the army was determined to prevent a colour revolution because 'the army belongs to the Cambodia People's Party'. Aware he was breaking rules of impartiality, the general said he was speaking 'frankly' when he told the public 'every solider … belongs to the CPP because [Hun Sen] is the feeder, caretaker, commander and leader of the army'.[9]

Two weeks later, a 25-year-old student was arrested and charged with incitement for asking people via Facebook who would 'dare to make a colour revolution with me?' The young man was sentenced to eighteen months in jail.[10] When the ADHOC 5 were arrested, protestors called for people to wear black t-shirts to show their opposition. Its leaders were quickly arrested and the government released a video, which they promoted heavily, warning that an attempted colour revolution would lead to civil war, as in Syria.[11]

Having established a narrative of conspiracy, the CPP then began to name the conspirators.[12] It published a chart purporting to show how the United States had instigated previous colour revolutions and named its International Republican Institute and National Democratic Institute as crucial actors in these.[13] The Deputy National Police Commissioner accused sixty unnamed charities of trying to topple the government by aiding the CNRP and dubbed the garment factory protests at Veng Sreng Street an attempted colour revolution.[14]

Immediately after the 2017 commune election, Hun Sen accused COMFREL and other charities of being a 'base' for a colour revolution.[15] A CPP spokesperson said the government had proof that *The Phnom Penh Post*, *Radio Free Asia* and *The Cambodia Daily* – the most popular media without connections to the CPP – had foreign agents in them advocating for colour revolution.[16]

With the 2018 national election less than one year away, Hun Sen was preparing himself for 'a last battle'. A senior official in an international organsiation told me that he believes Hun Sen, understanding the international condemnation that his actions would bring, thought, 'Now I will close my eyes to that side. I want to make sure to control this table and when I feel confident that I control this table, this table belong to me for the next five years, then I will start to come back [to the international community].'[17] The tiger would defend his mountain at all costs.

CHAPTER 22
RADIO SILENCE

Before moving to Cambodia, I had expected to miss my routine of reading a newspaper in the morning, especially on a Sunday. I had only been there a few days when I picked up *The Cambodia Daily*, published in English, whose motto heralded 'All the news without fear or favor'.

An American publisher, wanting to repay the debt for America's saturation bombing of Cambodia during the war in Vietnam, established the newspaper in 1993, operating out of a hotel room with two computers. Foreign journalists were hired to train novices, including a pagoda boy and two moto-taxi drivers, and *The Daily* became Cambodia's school of journalism, transforming how news was reported. One of its twenty-year veterans reflected: 'The news that we focused on [in a former job] was just what happened –the government inaugurating a school or a bridge. But when I came to *The Daily* it was very different – we were focused on hard news and in-depth investigations. We wrote professionally, we wrote accurately and we verified our facts.'[1] Each issue was full of journalists traversing the country to find the truth.

Phorn Bopha was the young journalist who was with Chut Wutty when he was shot, and also investigated the man who shot Kem Ley. She moved with her family to Phnom Penh the same year that *The Cambodia Daily* was established. She had always loved reading – unusual in a largely illiterate society – and particularly loved the works of Krom Ngoy, the Khmer poet from the early twentieth century Hun Sen also declares himself a fan of.[2]

Bopha realised that she wanted to become a journalist in her teens but kept this quiet as she knew that people would find the idea 'peculiar'. She was inspired by one journalist who always got *The Daily*'s front page, and feisty Bopha told herself that one day she would be good enough to 'kick this guy out'.

Growing up, Bopha was told to return home immediately after school, so when she started at *The Daily*, she didn't know the places people were talking about or where she was being sent to cover a story. The man she was going to 'kick out' turned out to be a mentor as he guided her through those first few months. Every night, Bopha would cut out the English versions of her articles, which had been edited by a foreign journalist, and place them beside her Khmer version in a big book so that she could study and learn.

When her mentor left on a scholarship to study in America, the 24-year-old Bopha was promoted to be an assignment editor. I asked how her older, mostly male colleagues reacted when she told them what stories to follow. 'I think they hated me!' she replied, laughing. 'I really do. But now I think it's okay. Woman? Young? In that position? Oh my god. Regardless of the big boss you have behind you ... you gotta be strong.'

'You felt vulnerable sometimes?'

'I cried a few times. Sometimes, it's really hard. I think, *Fuck, man, I want to quit!* But I can't leave because if I quit, what am I going to do? I want to write. I like writing.' Bopha's impish body tensed. Foreign journalists at *The Daily* have talked about the zeal with which their Cambodian counterparts believed in their mission to expose corruption, and Bopha was the epitome of this.[3]

'I was obsessed with work. I would leave home at 7.00am and I would come home at 10.00 or 11.00 at night.' At one point, her sister said to her, 'Who do you think you are? Like, you are coming [home] at like 11 o'clock. What is going on with you?' Bopha just shrugged her bony shoulders, knowing her sister wouldn't understand. 'Every time you are looking for the news – looking for contacts, calling people, typing the story – you don't have to time to check your phone. One time, I looked at my phone and I had twelve missed calls. My mum had called me, my sister had called me. One I pick up and they are like, "What are you doing? Who do you think you are?" I am like, "I am *sorreee*."'

In 2012, Cambodia hosted ASEAN (Association of Southeast Asian Nations) and Bopha attended the press conference. "Hun Sen, I asked him a question, and he's like, "Oh, you know, you have to be careful asking that question. You know that story you write about ..." and I thought, *What the fuuuck?*' Bopha had slid down in her seat, hoping she could disappear. 'And then I thought, *Okay, I'm a journalist. I have to be ready for that.*'

This was also the year that Bopha went on the tragic assignment with Chut Wutty. She only went because she had come back from enforced leave early. A few weeks previously, Bopha had interviewed a man who she would only refer to as 'one of the family to the top'. She went to his house and asked him about rumours that he smuggled drugs: 'He's like, "No, man, look at me. Look at my house, my business. I'm a nice man."' Bopha went ahead and published the story and the next day received multiple text messages and phone calls: 'I was so scared ... Before me, *The Daily* publish stories about him, but they never put a byline. But for me it's already too late because I met him, I was there at his house. So I put my name. And then my boss was like, "Shit, Bopha, you cannot stay here! You have to get out of the city. You have to get into the provinces for a bit, at least for a week."'

Bopha spent all of two days in the serene, sleepy town of Kampot, watching the flotilla of small boats make their way down the river at sunset to fish in the ocean. Upon arriving back in the office, Bopha's editor told her to go home, but another journalist wanted Bopha to accompany her on that ill-fated trip with Chut Wutty. 'I was like, "Oh, why not? I love Koh Kong. It's beautiful."' In the car on the way to the forest, Bopha was relaxed, sitting in the back reading *Life of Pi*, happy to be on a story again.

Lying on the ground after Wutty had been shot, Bopha was sure she would be next: 'I was thinking, *Oh my god, I feel bad for my parents*. I did not make them happy. I was thinking, like, *This is it, man ... I wanted to make change for the better. This is what I deserve.* When these things happen, the first thing you think of is your parents. I'm thinking, *I am sorry that I was not good. I was a not a good girl. I was stubborn and I never listened to you.*'[4]

I asked Bopha if she had ever told her parents what she was thinking as she lay waiting to be killed.

'Actually, I haven't. I have not told them that.'

'Do you think you will?'

'I think I will, but when we talk about this, it's kind of emotional. Especially for my mum. I remember that day. My youngest brother, he loves me, he start crying, and before I came back home, he told the family that he would go to Koh Kong to get me back.' Bopha laughed at being saved from the army and police by her little brother. 'The funny thing is that after the thing happened, my boss came to pick me up from Koh Kong. I asked him, "Please don't let this get on the news otherwise my parents will know and they're not going to let me do this job anymore," and he's like, "Ah, don't worry, no, no."' Bopha laughed at her own naïvety. 'Then I realise, *Shit, why do I get so many messages?* I click and it said like 120 something. I'm like, *Holy shit, I'm sure my parents know about this.*'

Bopha had recurring nightmares about the shooting for a month afterwards. 'I wasn't even sure if it was just a dream or even a memory, you know?

Was it real? Scary, real crazy shit. And I did not talk about it for a long time. When I went home, my sister start asking me questions. I started to choke up and was like … I didn't say anything, I would just walk away. So they get the sense, *Oh, don't ask her*.'

'Did you ever meet his family?'

'No … I wanted to but I was, like, scared. But I felt bad when they had his funeral. I did not go. I was scared shitless of everything. That partner [the fellow journalist] who went to that trip with me, she came back and the next day she went *fssshhhhheeeewww*,' said Bopha, imitating a plane taking off. 'She left the country.'

We talked more about that incident, the shooting of the garment workers at Bavet and the shooting of the young girl in Kratie during a land clearance, all happening within a few months of each other. 'I don't understand why they just keep shooting people, you know?' Bopha squinted behind her large, round glasses, unable to see the logic. 'It's life. Even like with a dog, you don't shoot a dog because it's life. Even the small cockroach. You not going to shoot the cockroach, right? The cockroach is going to die in front of you. It's painful. How could you watch an insect or animal die? It's just sad. Fuck, man.'

Bopha is usually moving, even when sitting. She will lean forward when talking and curl up when listening. Her eyes will dilate in surprise and narrow when concentrating. Our moment of contemplation lasted a second only before she blurted out, 'I swear a lot! I'm sorry.'

I couldn't help but laugh, wondering if she had read my mind. Her profanity was not something I had ever heard from a Cambodian woman before, and very few men either.

'I don't drink, I don't smoke, right? I don't go partying, I don't go to bars. I like reading. If I go to a bar, I think, *oh, crazy*. And I only drink coffee. First, when I start swearing, there was much tension within me. I need to do something, right? I did not have a boyfriend and did not have a social life. I sacrifice my time to work, right? So I needed something, a means to release my stress. So swearing is the only way I could … I allow myself to do that.'

By the time of the Commune elections in 2017, Bopha had left Cambodia to work for ABC News in America. She was still in America when, just after the 2017 Commune elections, the Cambodian government decided that *The Cambodia Daily* owed $6.3 million in taxes and was told to pay it in one month or 'pack up and go'.[5]

'I was crying. Actually, I was trying to contact other people. Email. Contact anybody in the US to try to get help, to stop it from happening.

But I could not stop it from happening. It's the place where I worked for six years. Where I learned basic journalism, you know, the foundation of journalism.' Bopha paused. 'The place where I kind of understood and learnt my potential, that I could do much more. Really sad.'

The Daily had been run on a shoestring, and the owners, the daughter and son-in-law of the paper's founder, had no way of paying the staggering sum. The staff doubted whether it would matter even if they did. When it closed, newspapers around the world ran obituaries, often written by one of their staff journalists who had spent their formative years in the chaotic press room of *The Cambodia Daily*. Half the Cambodian journalists at the paper when it closed wouldn't work in journalism again, their devotion to the truth rendering them unemployable.[6] One who reported on land and environmental issues for twenty years scraped a living by raising fighting cocks.[7] Another was charged with incitement and received asylum abroad.[8] Cambodians mourned the trailblazing newspaper that began during UNTAC, reported from the scene of Sam Rainsy's grenade, covered the battle between Hun Sen and Ranariddh's FUNCINPEC, was with Chut Wutty when he was shot in the forest, and photographed Kem Sokha's arrest. Even Phirun, the loyal civil servant who said it was impossible to be neutral, was a 'fan'. Like so many others, he could only mutter, 'It is sad that it shut down, yeah …' as though it was inevitable *The Daily* could not survive Cambodia.[9]

When *The Daily* closed, the Editor-in-Chief of the award-winning and even more widely read *Phnom Penh Post* dismissed the possibility that his paper would be next.[10] Only weeks later, Cambodia's tax department declared that *The Phnom Penh Post* owed $3.9 million in unpaid taxes.[11]

The Post's Australian owner felt he had no choice. He sold the paper to a Malaysian public relations executive, and the tax bill was settled as part of the deal. *The Post*'s journalists were furious, and wrote a front-page article alleging that the new owner had distant links to the CPP.[12] The new owner's lawyer had much closer links, however, having worked with one of Hun Sen's sons, as well as with Hun Sen's lawyer.[13] The new owner's lawyer instructed the story must be taken down.

Journalists resigned rather than recant the story, and the Editor-in-Chief was sacked for letting it be published, prompting more resignations in protest.[14] Two months later, the company's registration details were changed, and the lawyer replaced the Malaysian public relations executive as *The Post*'s sole company director, also becoming the Chief Executive and Publisher.[15]

One week after *The Cambodia Daily* was hit with its fatal tax bill, the government alleged that *Radio Free Asia* and the equally popular *Voice of America* were also guilty of tax violations and did not have proper media licenses. *Radio Free Asia* and *Voice of America* did not have their own stations so leased time from dozens of local stations to air their programs. In the days after the allegations against *Radio Free Asia* and *Voice of America*, both funded by American agencies, the government closed twenty-one radio stations for broadcasting too many of their programs. Other stations were warned to focus on entertainment.[16]

Quickly, no station would lease time to *Radio Free Asia* and *Voice of America*, meaning they could publish online only. Farmers in the fields of Kampong Cham, tuk-tuk drivers on the roads of Siem Reap, students hanging out in Battambang, and sellers in the markets of mountainous Mondulkiri all sat in silence. The buzz of Cambodia had been replaced by the noise of vastly resourced government-owned media such as Nice TV.

One week after *The Cambodia Daily* closed, the staff of *Radio Free Asia*'s Cambodia office gathered with tears in their eyes to be told that they were closing, too.[17] They had been working in Cambodia for twenty years and their journalists had previously been threatened, jailed or forced to leave the country, but this pressure was 'unprecedented', according to senior management.[18]

The pressure was coming because Hun Sen called it 'a radio against the government'.[19] It had riled government by using antagonistic phrases, as Huy Vannak, President of the Union of Journalist Federations of Cambodia (UJFC), explained: 'They keep using the words "Hun Sen regime", "Phnom Penh regime". But if you understand Khmer culture, that's too much. The words, the language, the tone. It's not journalism that provide information, they provide piece of opinion. And their own agenda ... They don't work on balance.'

Vannak had previously worked as a journalist for *Radio Free Asia*, before completing a Master's degree in America, and he felt that the station had fallen from the principles it once held and was full of 'hate' against the CPP. 'Before, we produced a mixed program, but now it's a platform for politics. Before, we have agriculture, we have education, we have science, we have law. And the idea for our talk show is to provide solution to the issues, not make a judgement ... Their style has changed ... They don't uphold the profession.'[20]

Vannak may have been disappointed by the lack of impartiality shown by *Radio Free Asia* but, as well as being President of the UJFC, he is also a

Secretary of State in Cambodia's Interior Ministry. In his early forties, with a coiffured side-parting, he is one of the young reformers given prominence after the CPP's near defeat in 2013. Vannak talked about how he admired Singapore and hoped Cambodia would follow its model, prompting me to ask if it concerned him that Singapore at that time was rated by Reporters Without Borders to have less press freedom than Cambodia.[21] His reply was instant: 'I say this over and over before. To me, it doesn't mean I don't care, but what I care about is quality. What I care about the most, whatever, wherever, with anyone, it's about quality. Quality. Freedom is just complementing. Freedom, yes, but if the way you speak is stupid ...'

Sothearin, the *Radio Free Asia* journalist who hosted the program with Kem Ley, had told me that Cambodian journalists practise self-censorship because they don't want to be cut off from government information, plus the paper may lose advertisers, and their families want them to stay out of danger.[22] Vannak disagreed, advising that their behaviour was evidence of 'self-awareness', rather than the 'Western concept of censorship'. 'I think that is a wrong perception of a different culture. In Cambodia, it's self-awareness ... Everyone has self-awareness here, you know, follow the code of ethics, what is right and what is wrong ... You see, our culture is a more respectful culture – we are Buddhists, we listen to teachers, we listen to monks, and listen to fathers and parents.'[23]

Vannak had grown up in a poor, rural farming family, living in a pagoda for three years so he could attend high school, which was far from his home. His first journalism job was at *Radio Free Asia* before a scholarship to America set him on the path to lead news departments and become one of Cambodia's most famous television anchors. I asked Vannak, who was sitting with me at a five-metre-long table in the UJFC headquarters, surrounded by photos of himself with dignitaries such as Hun Sen, what he felt when he saw *Radio Free Asia* close. Misunderstanding me, he replied, 'I think that's a misinterpretation. They just closed down. Closed themselves.'[24]

Radio Free Asia did close, but Sothearin explained there were powerful circumstances surrounding that decision: 'We saw the relationship with *The Cambodia Daily* and yes, local [stations] closed down. Targeted. It will be us. So, we, we, you know, we decide – we force, actually, we force ourselves. It was a sad day, and the last show that we did, you know, all of us in the studio ... we miss the office ... we have no job yet. It is like we are in the middle of nowhere. We don't know what happened, what will happen. Where are we going to get a job? For where we go? So, um, we are stunned. Stunned.'[25]

There were rumours at the time that *Radio Free Asia* staff may try to keep working to provide information back to their office in America,[26] or even that they may return to air, but Sothearin was pessimistic: 'I know that the situation is not so good for us ... I decided to quit, I say sorry to my boss, I have to quit at this time. I went to Lower Cambodia for one month in order to show the government I stop.'

About two weeks after getting back from visiting his parents in southern Vietnam, or *Kampuchea Krom* as Sothearin calls it, he received a phone call from Uon Chhin, a former colleague. Police had been searching a hotel and found a room that Chhin had set up with filming and recording equipment: 'I am afraid that the police might arrest him. Police might seize his property. So I go there to be a witness. After they found out that we used to work together at RFA, they know my name. They know who I am ... they arrest both of us.'

The police arrested Chhin and Sothearin without telling them what the charge was. Four days later, an investigating judge charged them with espionage and working for a foreign power, on the grounds that *Radio Free Asia* is funded by an independent agency of the US government. The police also charged Chhin with pornography after allegedly finding homemade videos on his computer.[27] Vannak said that he twice offered to mediate and resolve the situation – provide them with some *khnorng* – but Chhin and Sothearin refused his support, saying they had done nothing wrong so shouldn't need it, and were transferred to Prey Sar, the same prison that had held the ADHOC 5.

Given a prison uniform and a shaved head, Sothearin remembers being introduced to his cellmates: 'Some very friendly, good to us. They come sit with us, say, "I support you. You should not be here."'

'Some of them used to listen to RFA?' I asked.

'Yeah, yeah. A guy who had been in jail three or four times in three years, the first time he saw me, he said, "I know you, brother, I know you. I listen to you when I was outside."'

'The prison guards, what were they like to you?'

'Some talk secret to me. They say, like, "You should not be here. In the prison, there is a lot of injustice." One man whispered to me, "Take care of your health, take care of your health. Don't think too much." And he took my photo. So we still have people with us, even though we are in hell.'[28]

The cells were stinking hot and the twenty-five prisoners had to do everything in that one place – wash, eat, go to the toilet. Chhin and Sothearin had rashes and scabies, and for Chhin the anxiety was never-ending.[29]

Sothearin is married with two children, who were ten and eight when he went to jail. Sothearin didn't want his children to worry, so he told them he was at university. When they came to visit, his daughter asked why some wore orange clothes and others wore blue. 'I said blue colour for BA and orange colour for Master's and PhD. And you know what my daughter says outside? "Oh, my father is a very nice student because wherever he go, people always follow him." Because in the prison, they always follow you. All the time.'

His children eventually discovered the truth. Understandably, they struggled while their father was in jail, beginning to do poorly at school. Sothearin said that his son 'lost warmth, lost trust in life'.[30] His wife found it 'very, very, extra hard'. Karuna, the jovial ADHOC worker, called his wife: 'At that time, my wife, she, you know, she was very weak. But Mr Karuna tried to explain about our value. He told my wife that our case was different to that of other people so she should be proud of her husband. So my wife, my wife said that she get stronger and stronger, and she still praises Mr Karuna for his advice.'

Sothearin himself was strengthened by support from Titthara, the journalist friend of Chut Wutty, who was leading a campaign to free him. However, Sothearin knew that he wouldn't be released before the 2018 national election – and that was eight months away.[31]

CHAPTER 23

CHHOB

After only just winning the Commune elections while Rainsy was in exile, the CPP sought to limit his influence even further. The government had already banned people with convictions from holding leadership positions in a political party, but new amendments meant that political parties could be suspended or dissolved for even using the 'voice messages, images, written documents or activities of a person convicted of felony or misdemeanour'.[1]

Parties were also banned from 'openly or tacitly agreeing or conspiring' with convicted individuals and those whose actions could 'affect the security of the state' or create 'incitement that would lead to national disintegration'.[2] The Ministry of Interior could suspend, indefinitely, any party it believed to be guilty of breaking these laws and recommend Cambodia's Supreme Court dissolve that party and ban people from political activity for five years.[3] Cambodia's quiet King Sihamoni did not object but went abroad with his mother for medical check-ups, leaving it to the CPP Senate President to sign the amendments in his absence.[4]

Since 2013, the ubiquitous billboards of Hun Sen and the CPP had been joined by thousands of CNRP posters showing Kem Sokha and Sam Rainsy standing together, hands clasped triumphantly above their heads. Within a couple of weeks of the new law, the image of Sam Rainsy had been torn from every one of these posters so that Kem Sokha was left standing alone, grasping thin air.[5]

In 2015, when Hun Sen gave his furious response to Rainsy's French newspaper interview that ended the culture of dialogue, he also mentioned a recording of Kem Sokha speaking to Cambodians living in Australia.[6] The recording was of a speech given in 2013, during which Sokha said, 'I don't just do what I feel. I have experts, university professors in Washington, Montreal, Canada hired by Americans in order to advise on the strategy to change the leaders.'[7] Now, in September 2017, Hun Sen was ready to use that video to kill the opposition. Just before midnight, over 100 armed police broke through the fence surrounding Kem Sokha's house, held his bodyguards at gunpoint and entered the bedroom where Sokha and his wife lay.[8] One of his lawyers at the time, Sam Sokong, told me that the police could not tell Sokha what they were arresting him for. 'He asked the police to show the warrant. And then the police only say that they cannot show him.'[9] Instead, the police asked if he wanted to call Hun Sen, presumably to resign from the CNRP, but he shook his head.[10] Sokha was whisked to a prison 200 kilometres away without his lawyers being told for two days.[11]

The next day, Hun Sen, referring to the video, said, 'the treason of colluding with foreigners to betray the nation requires [us] to make an immediate arrest'. It hardly seemed to be an immediate arrest given Sen had known about the video for over two years, but nevertheless, a government spokesperson announced that Sokha had been caught 'red-handed', meaning his parliamentary immunity was annulled. A CNRP spokesperson asked, 'How can it be a red-handed crime since His Excellency Kem Sokha was asleep like a log? This is ridiculous.'[12]

Sam Sokong and a team of lawyers visited Sokha in jail. 'He feel so sad ... so sad. He feel angry also. Because he said that he did not commit any crime. He said the video, as proof of evidence, was not enough. He said it is a political issue. He told me the ruling party want him to resign from the presidency of the CNRP or they want to break him, cause a break between him and Sam Rainsy. But Kem Sokha still did not want to break. He did not want to resign.'[13]

The government began publicising a second video, also from 2013, which showed Sam Rainsy calling on soldiers to disobey orders and support the CNRP.[14] CPP-aligned news agencies published numerous stories alleging that Kem Sokha's daughter was a CIA spy colluding with US Embassy staff, local charities and journalists to topple the government.[15] The Cambodian Youth Party filed a complaint against the CNRP for attempting a colour revolution. The previously moribund FUNCINPEC roused itself to make a similar complaint, saying that the crimes of Kem Sokha could not be separated from the CNRP as a whole. The Ministry of Interior promptly requested that Cambodia's Supreme Court dissolve the CNRP, and threats of arrest caused an exodus of CNRP leaders, including vice-presidents.[16]

Hun Sen had painted a picture of a situation similar to the American-engineered coup against Sihanouk in 1970, which ended Cambodia's halcyon period and precipitated the rise of the Khmer Rouge. 'The Americans used to do it with Lon Nol [the military leader who overthrew Sihanouk],' said Hun Sen, 'and now the American[s] do this with Kem Sokha.'[17] Hun Sen warned CNRP commune councillors and parliamentarians that they should defect to the CPP immediately and would keep their jobs if the CNRP was dissolved, but most chose to believe that the CNRP was too big to be dismantled.[18]

Hang Puthea, the neutral member of the NEC, interprets Sokha's speech in the video as 'admitting that he collaborates with a foreign country', which means 'he is in a foreign group that aims to seize power in Cambodia'. He said Sokha worked with the Americans to 'have a revolution' and that Sokha's problems became the CNRP's because he refused to resign: 'Maybe he wants to play a role as a hero. You know, Rainsy is cleverer than him. When the court tried to convict Rainsy, he resigned from the party. When the problem come to Sokha, he did not resign. Activist members go to him and ask him to resign. He said, "No, no." This is their [the CNRP's] internal problem. We could not control this.'[19]

The few CNRP leaders remaining in the country hesitated to organise protests, hoping that the international community could 'find a solution'. Cowed, CNRP officials agreed to police demands that they take down banners calling for Sokha's release.[20]

Under laws of the time, if the CNRP was dissolved, all seats would pass to the CPP, as it was the only other party in Parliament, which Hun Sen knew would look bad internationally. The CPP quickly passed amendments so that CNRP seats could be distributed to other parties who competed in the last election,[21] maintaining the pretence of Cambodia as a multi-party democracy. Significantly, at the local level, where events are less evident to the international community, the CPP passed amendments meaning that if the CNRP was dissolved, the CPP would have 99.5 per cent of all councillors.[22]

Despite the extensive machinations, many people did not believe that the CNRP would be dissolved. On the day of the Supreme Court hearing, Karuna, the jovial ADHOC worker, was standing outside with 100 other observers and journalists. The heavy police presence kept the large group scattered so that there were never more than five people close together. In huddles, they debated what would happen. For most, including Karuna, the CNRP, with more than 3 million votes and 5000 commune councillors, seemed so big that 'the CPP wouldn't dare to dissolve' it. Some even thought there could be an opening for reconciliation.[23]

While Karuna stood debating, a UN car pulled up at the entrance gates and motioned for him to jump in so that he could get inside the court. Crammed into the room with eighty other people, including ambassadors and UN staff, Karuna was wedged between a fellow human rights activist and a Reuters journalist.[24] There was a hushed silence as the prosecutor read the charges against the CNRP. Six lawyers then showed the video of Kem Sokha speaking and played multiple radio clips of Sokha and Rainsy as the lawyers hammered home their accusation of treason. 'I feel worried,' Karuna said. 'I think that this is special for this case. I have never seen like this. Some video they show again and again. I look to embassy people and they cannot ... and the journalists are worried too.'[25]

One of the government's lawyers repeated comments made by Donald Trump, who said America would *no longer* attempt to overthrow governments, saying this was proof of historic interference. A second lawyer buttressed that argument by identifying multiple meetings between CNRP officials and US State Department officials and members of Congress.[26] The lawyers alleged that the protests after the 2013 election were evidence of an attempted 'lotus revolution' by the CNRP to overthrow the government.[27]

There were no defence lawyers to object or rebut. 'He [Kem Sokha] thought that if he give the lawyer to defend this case, it mean that we want to be involved in the legal issues,' Sokong explained. 'He knows that it is a political issue, not a legal issue. If we become involved with the legal issue, we cannot win. We could not win because the court is not independent. The court wait to get order from the ruling party. Mr Kem Sokha decide not to send his lawyer to defend this case.'[28]

The nine Supreme Court judges rose from their bench and retired to deliberate. Nobody expected a lengthy deliberation, so everyone remained in the courtroom. Karuna debated what the result would be with those sitting either side. One believed the CNRP would be dissolved, the other didn't. Karuna was undecided, bewildered by what he had witnessed but still believing that it was impossible to dissolve a party half of Cambodia had voted for.

At 5.00pm, after about ninety minutes of deliberation, the judges returned. The lead judge, a member of the CPP Permanent Committee, spoke for less than five minutes. Holding the typed judgement up in two hands so the bottom of the paper touched the bench, he read the words monotonously, never looking up. Upon finishing, he stood up and strode out of the courtroom.[29]

The verdict was greeted with complete silence. There was no intake of breath or gasp of shock. There wasn't even applause from CPP supporters. Nobody said anything and nobody wanted to make eye contact. Karuna didn't even speak to those he was sitting beside. He just wanted to get out of there. He burst out in a rush of disbelief and confusion, desperate for air. A policeman standing in front of him asked for the verdict and Karuna replied with one word: 'Dissolved.' 'Chhob?!' the policeman exclaimed incredulously. Karuna could only nod, confirming that the last four years of Cambodian hope had come to an end. 'I heard my lips,' recalled Karuna, 'but I did not believe it.'

Karuna saw the same UN car that had brought him in and opened the back door, but it was already full. He tried to hurry away from the court, but his leg – which had deep bruising from a motorbike accident the day before – was too sore. Hobbling back to ADHOC's office, all he could mumble to himself was, 'I thought they would never do this. Oh, my.'[30]

Sam Sokong read the full judgement, about forty or fifty pages, which he said was like a 'copy from the complainant. They copy from the Ministry of Interior.' The primary piece of evidence was Kem Sokha's alleged treason, which had still not been tried in court.

The night of the CNRP's dissolution, Sam Sokong went to meet Kem Sokha in prison and talk with CNRP leaders, who were unsurprised. 'They say that they know the result before the Supreme Court decide because they thought that this is a political case, not a legal case.'[31]

After the Supreme Court dissolved the CNRP, the National Election Committee, the body that had modelled the culture of dialogue and organised Cambodia's 'best election', was responsible for re-assigning their seats to other parties within seven days. Rong Chhun, one of the four NEC members appointed by the CNRP, refused because he felt obliged to 'respect the will of the people'. Two other CNRP-appointed NEC members stood with him and all three resigned. If they could persuade two other members to resign, the NEC would not have enough members to pass decisions to reassign seats.

The eyes of Cambodia were on Hang Puthea, previously a high-profile campaigner for free and fair elections, and Hing Thirith, the judge who famously enraged the CPP for freeing the framed killers of union leader Chea Vichea. I asked Puthea if he was feeling the pressure. He was indignant at the CNRP, which he thought expected him to follow Rong Chhun in resigning: 'Really, we come from different sides – ruling, opposition and …

me alone. I am not under CPP or CNRP. I am the person that did not ask CPP or CNRP to join NEC. So please let me make decisions by myself. The law makes us neutral. Why, when I am neutral, do I have to follow CNRP or CPP? I play my role by the law. I don't want to follow CPP or CNRP.'[32]

I asked Puthea what he thought of his three colleagues who objected to the CNRP's dissolution and chose to resign. 'They resigned because of a political issue. They have a relationship with Rainsy and they play game. He wants to destroy NEC.'

Puthea, to the dismay of people he had worked with for twenty years to create free and fair elections, chose to stay and reassign the CNRP's seats, prompting angry Cambodians to circulate images on social media depicting him wearing a Vietnamese army cap.[33] Thirith, a former Supreme Court judge himself, told me it was 'easy' for him to continue working at the NEC and he had 'no problem' with reassigning the CNRP's seats. He did not feel it was his role to intervene in politics and 'the Supreme Court and the complainant are responsible [for the CNRP's dissolution]. We only follow the laws.'[34]

Rong Chhun knew that his resignation would not stop CNRP's seats being given to parties few people had voted for. Nevertheless, Chhun believed that he, as a NEC member, did have a role to play in upholding democracy and setting an example for the Cambodian people. 'Impossible for us to sit there. We disagreed because the will of the three million people had been violated and their votes had been dispersed to other parties who took seats that belonged to the CNRP after people had voted for them. These parties took seats without having received votes. Have to respect the will of the people. We wanted to be clear to the people that not everyone in Cambodia who has a job with air-con, a good car, a salary, driver and bodyguard, we never leave. Wanted to show that there are people willing to do that.'

I asked Chhun if resigning was a difficult decision and he thought back to all the other choices that had led him to this point.

'I could have continued to teach maths and do extra classes to earn more money, as I was a popular teacher. It would have been a much easier life if I had chosen to participate and work with the Ministry. I could have had a high position and even been a His Excellency, working high up. I had the chance when at the National Election Committee to switch to the CPP and be given a high position. However, my will does not allow me to do so. I cannot open my eyes to see teachers and workers living in difficult circumstances and look for a comfortable place for myself.'[35]

CHAPTER 24
CLEARING THE TABLE

Sin Rozeth was working in the Battambang Commune Office when her phone started buzzing with Facebook notifications about the CNRP's dissolution. She wondered how long she would have left as Commune Chief. She calculated that if she worked quickly, and the police didn't come for a week or even ten days, she could process the 200 birth certificates that were still requiring paperwork. The night her party was disbanded, Rozeth worked even longer than normal, finishing at 9.00pm.

The next morning, Rozeth was up early and back in the office to plough through the forms. She did not expect it when municipal authorities arrived to remove her and her official stamp, finding it 'incredible', even 'unbelievable' that the CNRP would be dissolved one day and she would be gone the next. Government rarely acted so quickly in Cambodia.

'They bring people so that they could arrest me if I did something,' said Rozeth, but she refused to be intimidated. 'When they appoint me as commune leader, I have a document from the Ministry of Interior, so when they remove me, they should have something too. When I asked this, nobody answered. There was silence.'

The gaggle of men phoned their leaders to ask about official documents but there was nothing. 'They could only respond that the court dissolved the party,' said Rozeth, shaking her head. 'I asked them to let me complete another 200 birth certificates for the families before I leave ... they did not allow me to. I didn't argue anymore. I just thought about the villagers and when they come to get birth certificates, if I had signed them, they would not be accepted. It would not be taken as official.'

Rozeth's voice had never faltered as we spoke but her eyes had begun to fill with tears. They sat on her eyelashes, waiting to fall. She did not wipe them away as she continued, 'Those who came to take the stamp away, they did it because of the instructions they received from their leader. Some of them had tears in their eyes.'

In that moment of crushing injustice, Rozeth still believed in the power of dignity. 'When they dissolve the party ... I don't treat them as an enemy. I treat them as fellows, but they come to rob me of the position. I wanted to show them a good model of working. Usually, they take the table and chairs for their party, but I did not do that. I hand over everything – the computer, the printer. Everything. Within the four months I raised money to buy office furniture, and I hand it all over. My goal is to tell them that when we leave the office, the furniture is to serve the people. It is not ours. I want to teach them; their mindsets are different. Even old chairs, they take.'

The only thing that Rozeth took was a painting that villagers had given her as a present, and she hung it near the entrance to her noodle restaurant. Rithisak, my friend who grew up in the refugee camps on the Thai border, was with me this time I spoke to Rozeth, and as we went to leave, the three of us stood looking at this large painting depicting Rozeth and a family examining flooding around the family's house. Rozeth had changed that family's life, and the lives of many others in that village, by raising money to build culverts that would carry the heavy rains away. In return, she incurred the wrath of the CPP provincial authorities, who sent her an official warning that she could not build such things without planning permission.[1]

Rithisak and I nodded and thanked Rozeth for her time. We both knew that we needed a moment before hailing a tuk-tuk or moto taxi. After fifty metres of walking in silence, I turned to Rithisak, a hulking, surly, gruff man with a low voice but who nobody ever asks to speak up, and asked him what he thought of the woman he had wanted to meet for months. 'Look at me!' Rithisak exclaimed. 'People are scared to even post on Facebook. Yet, she ... she even stands up. When she talked about them coming for the stamp, I had wet eyes.' We fell back into silence, thinking about Rozeth as we walked in the dark, dodging potholes and barking dogs.

I thought of my late grandfather, who used to sit beside the fire in his living room, smoking cigarettes or a pipe, drinking whisky and talking long into the night with whoever sat opposite him. A small, wiry Glaswegian, he had once been asked to stand as a candidate for a political party but declined. He was more interested in the questions of humankind than the squabble of party politics. When I was planted in that chair opposite him, he would ask me about the philosophies I was studying at university, a privilege he had never enjoyed.

A recurring question, which he never resolved for himself, was about the qualities we should look for in a leader. He would often ask me whether I thought it would be better to have a leader who was intelligent, knowledgeable and astute but lacked integrity, honesty and morality, or to have a politician who was just, selfless and trustworthy but lacked acumen, education and shrewdness. I never imagined I would find the answer while sitting in a noodle restaurant in Cambodia, but I had.

CHAPTER 25
FLATTENED

The day before the Supreme Court abolished the CNRP, the army and police undertook a massive, coordinated operation across Cambodia. Multiple checkpoints were erected on roads leading to Phnom Penh, and military police patrolled towns to prevent people driving towards the capital. Some CNRP officials were asked by authorities to sign statements promising not to visit Phnom Penh on the day of the court hearing.[1]

At 7.00pm the night before the hearing, thirty-five armed soldiers surrounded the offices of Cheang Sokha's Youth Resource Development Program, which is opposite the Minster of Defence's giant villa. The female guard, who suffers from a heart condition, frantically called Sokha to say that soldiers were arriving. He calmed the guard down and told her to let the soldiers see that there was nobody hiding in the office waiting to protest at court the following day.[2] Squads of thirty to forty soldiers also visited ADHOC, COMFREL and other human rights organisations.[3]

Given the devotion of the CNRP's millions of supporters, I was surprised that there were no demonstrations on the day of the hearing or after the ruling. Many Cambodians were too, a few urging me to find out why. Bunroeun, an ageing CNRP commune councillor I knew in Banteay Meanchey, could not understand why Rainsy was reticent. 'Why don't we file a complaint to the Cambodian court and the international court? We win fifty-five seats. This number is not few. Fifty-five seats is equal to over three million people. Why are we withdrawn so easily?'[4]

Bunroeun understood that being abroad allowed Rainsy to lobby for international support, but he wanted Rainsy to return and 'show that he is strong and committed to Cambodian people'.[5] Sam Rainsy, who would have been silenced through harsh imprisonment or possible death, never moved to return.[6]

Chea Chiv was the CNRP's leader in Battambang province and said that on the day of the Supreme Court hearing, major roads were locked down and full of police. They feared mass protests, but Chiv explained none were planned because of division within the CNRP: 'At the sub-national level and provincial level, they want to protest. But the national level, they don't want to. That's why the sub-national level can't do anything. The political situation was growing hotter and hotter. If we want to do something that the national level does not allow, they could be arrested or put in jail.'[7]

Sokngeng, the 26-year-old Commune chief, said that the CNRP leaders did not want to confront the CPP, a tactic he seemed to agree with, in case it erupted into a flaring conflict with people hurt or killed.[8] Bunroeun, the ageing CNRP councillor, was told by his friends not to fight back and to calm down: 'Even though I am angry, I cannot stand up ... there is so much pressure, and so much broken heart among people ... but CNRP supporters must be flexible. Cannot go against the flow, must go with it. If you are strong against, then you may be killed or put in prison. And if you are killed, who can serve the country? So you must be flexible.'[9]

Rong Chhun was generally taciturn when speaking with me. He could understand English but preferred to use an interpreter, perhaps to give himself more time to prepare responses. Always wary, he mostly looked straight ahead and out the door when speaking, only turning to face me towards the end of his answers.

'The leadership stand for non-violence,' Chhun confirmed, 'and they have a good stance, but they need more activity. If we ask about the activists in the provinces, they are not afraid. But they are waiting for their leaders to show up and lead the protest. When are they willing to come to the country? That is what they are waiting for. It appears that CNRP activists are braver than their leaders. But we do not include Kem Sokha in this. He has great devotion.'[10]

I was having lunch with Vanna, my teacher friend, at a vegetarian restaurant near the Russian Market in Phnom Penh. I put it to him that there were one million people who came out for Kem Ley's funeral, and millions who voted for the CNRP, but when the CNRP was dissolved, there was nothing. 'Do you not know why?' Vanna asked.

'No!' I replied, laughing because it was obvious that I didn't and was desperate to.

'They know very well what would happen. They [the CPP] were prepared. Soldiers were ready on the streets. We have experience of this. Like in 1997.'

I stopped laughing. I have never experienced civil war, the Khmer Rouge, tank battles outside my home or grenades going off in crowds. 'The people killed after 2013,' he continued, 'people remember these.'[11]

To dispel any lingering thoughts of rebellion, Hun Sen warned that he would not tolerate protests like those of 2013–14. 'You [protestors] are lucky because I didn't see the video clip back then,' Sen said. 'If I had seen it at that point, I would have ordered the killing of all of you in just a few hours. I would not have allowed you to protest. I view that as a moment of life or death, because you declared war.'[12] To set an example, the head of a student federation was summoned for incitement after he called for peaceful demonstrations. He quickly fled the country.[13]

The pressure on Sokngeng, one of the best-known and most popular commune chiefs, was tightening. He said his CPP counterparts showed no remorse for his removal as chief because they 'were just happy to get their jobs back', although some came to show tinges of regret later.[14] Local people were unhappy but hesitated to complain, daring only to comment that they noticed there was a new chief when they visited the office.[15] Hun Sen wanted to 'break the legs of the CNRP at the local level' by pressuring former CNRP people to defect to the CPP and ordered CPP members to 'do this work ... day and night, mobilising any forces necessary'.[16]

Before the CNRP's dissolution, the large, round-shouldered Chea Chiv had been offered the lucrative position of Deputy Provincial Governor if he defected to the CPP, but he refused: 'I do not get involved in politics to gain position like that. It is to help people.' After the dissolution, Chiv was one of the 118 individuals banned from political activity, which he found out by reading the news on Facebook: 'There was no administrative letter to instruct me of the decision. Nobody ever got any documents.' Chiv's smile fell from his face. 'I feel that the ruling party ... they crossed the line of democracy.'[17]

Former CNRP commune councillors were often called for questioning by police. One of Chea Chiv's colleagues was accused of murder. Police and soldiers visited others at home after dark, intimidating families. One former commune councillor was charged with incitement for calling the CPP 'stupid' two years previously. With no party to support them, they were left defenceless, at the mercy of what ADHOC's Vanda called 'a giant willing to eat its young'. Some CNRP councillors defected, feeling they had no choice but to take the side of the giant.[18]

Scared and hoping to weather a storm, at least 200 CNRP officials, many of whom had received threats or subpoenas, sought asylum with the

UN's High Commission for Refugees in Thailand. Sokngeng was one of them, hoping that it would be temporary and he could 'come back and serve people again'.[19]

The older CNRP politicians found it difficult living in a strange place, unable to speak Thai and not knowing what to do with themselves. Many didn't have passports or official refugee status so feared going outside in case they were picked up by police and deported back to Cambodia. The UNHCR provided housing but nothing else, and most people had little money. One day, when somebody made soup for sixty people, everybody raced to slurp without pause.[20]

Sokngeng missed his commune in Siem Reap, which is named after a famous defeat of an invading Thai army. *Siem* refers to Siam, the old name for Thailand, and *reap* means to prepare, or in this context, to flatten. In Siem Reap and in towns and villages throughout the country, it was the CNRP that was now flattened. Obliterated.

CHAPTER 26

WHAT THE WEST FAILS TO SEE

The first meal I ever had in Cambodia was *samlor machou yuon*, a sweet-and-sour Vietnamese soup. *Yuon* is the slang word for Vietnamese people that Rainsy often used in negative contexts. From abroad, Rainsy had continued to stoke anger towards Vietnam for Cambodia's woes, saying in 2016 that Cambodia was in 'the claws of *Yuon*' and that 'the problem in Cambodia is not a problem between Khmer and Khmer; it's a problem between Khmer and *Yuon*'.[1]

Rithisak, my hulking friend who grew up in a refugee camp in the 1980s, often plays five-a-side football against a team of Vietnamese-Cambodians who still speak Vietnamese, have Vietnamese *and* Cambodian names and call themselves Hanoi FC. Despite Rithisak believing that the 1980s was a time of Vietnamese occupation rather than liberation and that there are still too many Vietnamese companies and immigrants in Cambodia today, he goes to one of Hanoi FC's players to get his football trainers fixed when the soles peel off, as the repairman gives him a discount. Warily, Rithisak agreed to take me to meet him at his pavement stall one day.

The repairman – whose family have lived in Cambodia since 1984 – and his vocal friend sitting nearby were glad that Sam Rainsy was in exile, because it meant 'fewer problems' for them. The repairman tried to ignore it when Rainsy used the word *Yuon* but said 'it affected me seriously', as CNRP supporters had shouted at him and he encountered daily rudeness. He thought the CNRP had been using Vietnam as 'some excuse' and hoped Rainsy wouldn't come back, although he did think it would be better for Cambodia if there was an opposition party to compete in elections.[2]

The CNRP's focus on Vietnamese immigration and disputing the border had disappointed Ansan, who works with Hun Sen's son, Hun Many, in his youth organisation: 'There are a lot of problems, challenges, that the opposition can criticise in a constructive way to show the public they are a new, smart opposition, but all they talk about is territory.'[3]

Vannak, the former *Radio Free Asia* journalist who joined the CPP and became President of the Union of Journalist Federations of Cambodia, was not just disappointed by the CNRP but feared that they could cause Cambodia's downfall if they were ever in government: 'You cannot make war or resist against our neighbouring country. Cannot. I mean, if you talk, if you are a leader of a country, you need balance ... That's stupid policy, stupid, if you fight Vietnam.'[4]

The CPP argued that Western countries, human right organisations and media like *Radio Free Asia* deliberately ignored the 'populist', 'irresponsible' and 'racist' side of Rainsy,[5] while the same media covered Hun Sen unfairly, accusing him of 'deriding democracy' when he had actually criticised Western countries for using democracy and human rights as pretences for going to war.[6] With the CNRP increasing in popularity just before an election, the CPP said they were 'faced with a dilemma: the choice between the implementation of a pure and perfect democracy imposed by the 1991 Paris Agreements and the gradual quest for improving the well-being of its citizens.'[7]

The Paris Agreements signed by the warring Cambodian factions were brokered by countries including France, Indonesia, Australia and America, and stated that the future Cambodian constitution would protect human rights and follow a system of liberal, pluralist democracy.[8] The CPP now said this 'perfect democracy' conflicted with their national goal of economic development, which was 'the top priority'. It asserted that 'compared to political rights, there are more urgent human rights', listing rights to food, housing, health, education and employment. Given the devastation after the Khmer Rouge and lack of a democratic tradition, the CPP pleaded that in just twenty-five years, 'What more could Cambodia have done? How more democratic can it be?'[9]

Kosal, a senior director in a government ministry who had studied and worked in America, told me that foreigners who criticise the Cambodian government fail to understand the challenges it has faced. When taking power in 1975, the Khmer Rouge declared Cambodia to be at year zero on the path towards a new apogee of society. The tragedy was that it took Cambodia closer to the Dark Ages than it did the twenty-first century. 'At the time, there was no other way around having incompetent managers,' said Kosal. 'We were lucky enough to have people at work to propel the country forward. There was nobody else. People were still frightened, tormented, traumatised. People just wanted to live. People had small houses. Five families in one house. I pull the partition, I see my aunt, my cousins ...'[10]

After the Khmer Rouge, there were few teachers or doctors because they had all been killed. There was little food because the soil had been scorched by bombs, mines and war. Families had been ripped apart, with parents disappeared and children at opposite ends of the country. Cambodia was at death's door, struggling back to life. There have been decades of aid since but that doesn't change a feeling, sowed by sanctions and famine, that caused Kosal to ruminate, 'We've been sort of abandoned. The world has abandoned us in some way.'[11]

Phirun, the loyal civil servant, once told me of a meeting he had with UK government officials: 'I remember one thing. The UK delegation said, "Cambodia has human rights violation problems, land grabbing, corruption ..." and the leader of my delegation said, "What you said is partly true. If you talk about human rights, let me ask you, during the Khmer Rouge regime they kill Cambodian people, so why did you not talk about human rights at that time? We didn't see you at the UN – where were you?" They go silent. They have nothing to reply.'[12]

After the CNRP's dissolution, the United States announced that it would reduce aid to Cambodia, and five US Senators introduced a bill to halt debt relief and freeze assets belonging to Cambodian officials in America.[13] Hun Sen dismissed the moves: 'I wholeheartedly welcome the US to cut off its aid to the National Election Commission – I really welcome that. You talk about democracy, yet you will cut aid to the National Election Commission. You have not just failed to defeat me, but you have also involved yourself in killing democracy in Cambodia.'[14]

Indeed, Hun Sen did not care if the United States 'cut off all aid to Cambodia entirely', which he said would result in the death of charities like ADHOC: 'Go ahead and kill your own offspring ... those who die first will be the NGOs that are plotting against us.' Seeing these charities as agents of the US, Hun Sen said that they 'will be audited soon' and that those found to be 'spending money in Cambodia to destroy us ... will not be spared.'[15]

The European Union was more difficult to dismiss because it is Cambodia's biggest export market, allowing all goods, except arms, into the EU without tariffs as a part of a free trade agreement known as Everything But Arms (EBA). Garment manufacturers from China, Taiwan and South Korea set up factories in Cambodia not only because of abundant cheap labour but because they can avoid tariffs that they would have to pay if exporting from their own country.

The month after the CNRP was dissolved, the EU Parliament called for a review of the trade agreement and possible temporary suspension, as well as asking for assets in the EU belonging to Cambodian government officials to be frozen.[16] Hun Sen said he would not be a 'dog that acts just for a bone or a piece of meat', even if withdrawal of the agreement would cost garment manufacturers $676 million in annual tariffs and push them to consider taking their factories and jobs elsewhere.[17]

Sam Rainsy hoped that if the EU withdrew the free trade agreement with Cambodia, economic problems would cause a popular revolt, leading to the end of the CPP government. Phirun, the loyal civil servant, thought this a despicable tactic, as he vented to me over grilled fish and shredded mango one day: 'The question of [Rainsy] asking the international community to stop assistance to Cambodia: how many famous leaders in the world do like that? He claims he is highly educated. He claims he has a patriotic love of his country. Does a patriotic person ask for stopping financial assistance to his own people? Never. If he is highly educated, there are many other options he can do … You can find other ways to get the support of the people … Because he is an important person, what he says across the world, people will listen. At least it impacts the decisions of his Western friends, and the same language, the same tactic has been used many, many, many times … Now, we can see the impact. They start to consider the suspension of the EBA for Cambodia. And they see this as a good thing! Success! Success for them … but is this really success for the whole country? I would choose a different path. I wouldn't ever do anything that would put the burden on my people. If you stop the EBA, of course we cannot wait to die. We have to find other options. We go to China – and then they blame us for going to China!'[18]

As Phirun noted, it would be garment workers like Channa and Kunthea who would suffer if the EU withdrew its free trade agreement, so I asked them what they thought about Sam Rainsy calling for this to happen. Channa hadn't heard too much about it because she had stopped listening to online broadcasts of *Radio Free Asia* or *Voice of America*, fearing that her neighbours may hear her listening to them. Kunthea, given her role in the trade union, had heard more about it, and had weighed up what it could mean: 'It may harm, and it may help, the future of Cambodia. To me, I think it is a good thing more than bad thing.'

A few days later, Channa heard an announcement over the loudspeaker in her factory. A manager called for workers to leave their station and give their thumbprint to a petition asking the EU to maintain the free trade agreement. Channa didn't move. She looked at colleagues beside her. They didn't move either. Only some new workers trudged off to sign it.[19]

For months, EU leaders pondered the EU Parliament's call for a review of Cambodia's trade agreement. Just one month before the 2018 election, the EU announced that it would send staff to gather information. The EU delegation met Pich, the man who had over three hours explained the trade unions to me; the EU gave him sixty minutes. Pich recognised that the suspension of the trade agreement would have 'big consequences' for workers but believed it would be a price worth paying: 'If we want to change the country, people need to suffer for a period of time ... People suffer for a short period of time is better than people suffering for a long time.'[20]

The EU was in no rush to take action, though, advising it would take eighteen months to make its decision. Meanwhile, the US Senate bill to halt debt relief and freeze assets gathered dust for over a year without going anywhere.[21]

It was now the turn of Bunroeun, the ageing CNRP councillor, to feel abandoned by the international community. He asked me why it did not come to help the Cambodian people: 'Even though the CNRP leader is abroad and speaks about what is happening ... no action. I feel so hopeless and disappointed. Before the CNRP dismissal, I thought that international countries or the EU are powerful, but now it seems they have no power. The Cambodian people carry the pressure, feeling disappointed and carrying a lot of difficulties. A lot of difficult emotions.'

'Do you feel let down?' I asked.

'Yes. Yes! For example, the USA is one of the most powerful countries in the world. This country must take action, but now it seems that they have no power over this government. It seems that they are just a normal country. For the economy, no problem in Cambodia for people to survive. But people need democracy. I feel really disappointed with the USA and the UN. We only need international support for democracy – the economy we can do ourselves but need help with democracy. Why doesn't America care about people, when many people cry a lot? If they take action, sure they can change things ... like UNTAC in the 1990s when countries come to help and bring democracy.'[22]

The UN was hit by a barrage of questions and calls for action. I took a wearied Leap, a senior official in an international organisation, out for grilled beef that we dipped in *prahok*, fermented fish paste, while the waitress brought us bottles of Angkor beer. Leap said critics showed a 'lack of understanding about what the UN is'.[23] The UN has a Secretary-General with 40,000 staff and agencies like the Office of the United Nations High Commissioner for Human Rights, but it cannot force sovereign countries to do anything. The United Nations can only act with the agreement of its member countries, and as Leap pointed out, 'China is a member. Cambodia is a member. So, the UN cannot do what the US or EU can do.'[24]

The UN is based on the principle that all countries are sovereign, meaning that the UN should not interfere in the domestic issues of a country, but the UN also has a role to uphold human rights and challenge violations within countries.[25] Leap advised that some countries tend towards insisting on respect for sovereignty regardless of human rights, while others demand respect for human rights regardless of sovereignty. This disagreement, he said, causes 'issues within the UN family', plus there are member countries wary of drawing attention to their own human rights records. 'People interpret [sovereignty] differently. Then [Hun Sen] says it is an internal matter. What are countries going to do? It's not the 1980s, [Cambodia] is different. I think officially the UN try to encourage, say some things. But it's not easy. We know it's not easy ... In the past, I know the top leaders were exchanging messages ... it's a big institution, sometimes difficult to get something to be agreed.'[26]

Leap emphasised that the UN's Charter is 'all important', as it describes the purpose and scope of the United Nations. He pointed out that the word 'democracy' appears nowhere in it, meaning it becomes something that the UN can merely 'encourage'.[27] Only the UN Security Council could pass a resolution to approve intervention or global sanctions on Cambodia, but the Security Council did not even discuss the CNRP's dissolution. 'The Council discusses matters, subjects, that matter to the world, global humanity, issues that affect the core, permanent members of the Council. It has its own way ... the UN has no mandate to come in. It has not been called in. The UN can only pray for its norms, standards and principles to be respected. Very difficult.'[28]

Cambodia's turn away from democracy only merited a few words at a UN media briefing, perhaps because, as one person described it, the use of violence was 'minimal, just in a few places'. Leap paraphrased what he thought many in the UN were thinking: 'The situation in Cambodia is not terrible, but it's not good. The economy is growing, it is quite good. There are businesses and there is investment. People have access to education, higher education and there are health services. You compare it to other countries, and maybe there are a few problems in different parts of the country, but not across the whole country …'

Leap called Hun Sen 'a smart man' who is willing to accept international criticism because 'now he has control and then later he can release [the pressure on opponents] a little'.²⁹

At the time of UNTAC in 1993, America was the world's dominant superpower and Cambodia's biggest aid donor. By 2017, China had become the largest investor in Cambodia and Hun Sen had forged a close diplomatic relationship with China's government. An intransigent Hun Sen was confident enough in China's backing to rebuff UN criticism about the CNRP's impending absence from the 2018 election, saying that Cambodia did not 'need the U.N. Secretary General to acknowledge its election is legitimate'.³⁰ Just twenty-five years previously, Cambodia needed the UN to administer the country; now the UN was being dismissed as inconsequential.

The seeds of China's patronage lie in its quest to control the South China Sea, through which a third of all global maritime traffic passes as goods are transported from Asia towards Africa and Europe. It is also the path for the vast majority of energy imported by Asian countries. China imports more oil than any other country, and 80 per cent of it is shipped through the South China Sea. As well as oil being shipped across the South China Sea, titanic quantities of it lie beneath the seabed, possibly 130 billion barrels, which would make it the second-largest reserve in the world after Saudi Arabia. There is also gas buried in the seabed; trillions of cubic feet waiting to be tapped. But to be tapped by whom?

The South China Sea is littered with tiny specks of uninhabited rocky islands and coral reefs, all of which are surrounded by multiple countries that have nearby coastlines. Both the Philippines and China claim the Scarborough Shoal, and both Vietnam and China claim the Paracel Islands. The most hotly contested are the Spratly Islands: tiny Brunei claims part of one reef; Malaysia claims three islands; and the Philippines claim eight of the islands. Vietnam and Taiwan claim all of them, as does China. Citing history, China lays claim to virtually the whole sea, all the way from its own coast down to Singapore and Malaysia, 1200 miles away.³¹

In 2012, Cambodia hosted the annual meeting of foreign ministers from the ten countries of the Association of Southeast Asia Nations (ASEAN). During this meeting, Vietnam and the Philippines pushed for ASEAN to issue a statement about China's presence in the South China Sea, particularly its incursion into Vietnam's Exclusive Economic Zone as delineated by the UN Convention on the Law of the Sea. The meeting, chaired by the Cambodian foreign minister, became heated when he declared that ASEAN should not get involved; rather, individual countries should solve the issue with China bilaterally, which is what China wanted. For the first time in ASEAN's history, the foreign ministers failed to issue a joint statement because the Cambodian foreign minister rejected a draft approved by most other foreign ministers.[32]

Enraged, other ASEAN countries believed that China had heavily influenced Cambodia, especially after the Chinese foreign minister thanked Cambodia for supporting China's 'core interests'.[33] An ASEAN member even alleged that Cambodia had inappropriately shared a first draft of the joint statement with China, who then told Cambodia what to object to.[34]

The leaders of the ASEAN countries met shortly afterwards, with China attending as a guest. Across Phnom Penh's wide boulevards, the government had replaced tourism banners proclaiming Cambodia to be 'The Kingdom of Wonder' with ones that declared, 'Long live the bonds of friendship, solidarity and cooperation between the Kingdom of Cambodia and China!'[35] Chinese flags lined the streets. There was no recognition of any other country from ASEAN or otherwise.

During his closing speech as host, Hun Sen announced that ASEAN had agreed that countries should negotiate with China individually. The Prime Minister of the Philippines interjected, denying there had been any such agreement. It also became apparent that Cambodia had not formally requested China to begin talks on a Code of Conduct for resolving the dispute even though it had been agreed that Cambodia, as chair, would do so. Instead, China declined talks, quoting the Cambodian statement that advised ASEAN would not get involved.[36] In desperation, one ASEAN foreign minister asked, 'Why are we ignoring these gross violations instead of identifying them so that we can deal with them?'[37]

The answer to his question lies in Western aid no longer being the salvation of Cambodia. Since UNTAC, Western countries had given Cambodia approximately $500 million every year in grants and cheap loans.[38] Global agencies led by Western countries, such as the World Bank, had been lending hundreds of millions of dollars as well. In 2011, however, the World Bank withheld funds because the Cambodian government was complicit in selling a lake and adjacent land to a developer, who filled the lake in and kicked people out of their homes. Protests erupted and residents were jailed.[39]

Hun Sen had always bridled at what he believed to be patronising admonishments from Western countries about how the Cambodian government mismanaged aid. Every two years, Hun Sen had to attend a conference during which he would listen to the urgings of donor countries while placating them with pledges of imminent reform.[40] By 2012, the year of the ASEAN summit, China's aid had risen to $595 million and Hun Sen felt confident enough to cancel the forum. He has never held one since.[41] In 2013, Chinese investment in Cambodia jumped to a mammoth $3 billion, without the environmental and social requirements that accompanies aid from the West.

Cambodia has developed to a point where it now looks for trading opportunities to increase wealth rather than seek succour for survival. America does very little trade with Cambodia, neither importing nor exporting many goods. The EU is a significant importer because it allows clothes to be imported from Cambodia without tariffs, but China is Cambodia's biggest partner, responsible for about one-quarter of all Cambodia's trade, most of which takes the form of investment in Cambodia.[42] In 2017, the year of the CNRP's dissolution, China invested $600 million in the country, and a further $800 million in 2018, adding to the billions previously invested in power stations, agri-business, mining fields and a new airport for Phnom Penh.[43]

Cambodia has become a strategic priority for China because of the location of its deep-sea port in Sihanoukville. Ninety per cent of commercial goods that go from one continent to another are transported by sea,[44] so for China, as the world's biggest exporter, reliable shipping routes are like vessels to the heart. China has built or operates over forty ports in thirty-four countries under its Belt and Road Initiative, creating a 'string of pearls'[45] from China to Cambodia and then onto Myanmar, Bangladesh, Sri Lanka, Pakistan and Djibouti, before arriving in Europe with a port in Greece. China has agreed to invest billions to expand Cambodia's Sihanoukville port, create a special economic zone that will become home to 300 Chinese companies and take 99-year leases on more than 50,000 hectares in national parks to create mega tourist resorts.[46]

Sihanoukville, a once sleepy seaside place whose beach was lined with shacks holding bars and restaurants, has become a raucous, dizzying boomtown. The influx of Chinese construction workers to build ports, roads and resorts has caused an eruption of eighty towering, glaring casinos to keep the thousands of them entertained.[47] The town has been ripped open and cement poured into it for new apartment blocks, karaoke complexes and hotels in a manic construction race. Cambodian property owners have moved Cambodian tenants out and leased houses to Chinese people at five times the price. Other Cambodians have sold land, having seen the value multiply ten-fold, and become millionaires overnight.[48] Asked why the government was pursuing such high levels of Chinese investment despite Cambodian anger at their favourite coastal town becoming a 'mini Macau', an official replied, 'The government gave the Europeans and Americans fifteen years to develop here and all they brought was backpackers and marijuana.'[49]

Within a week of the CNRP being abolished, the Cambodian Foreign Minister met his Chinese counterpart, who reiterated China's support for the Cambodian government's actions. Quickly afterwards, China and Cambodia held a high-level summit pledging to expand cooperation between the two countries with further Chinese investment and military support. The Chinese Premier announced that 'our similar historical experience and common struggles have brought our peoples firmly together. A friend in need is a friend indeed.'[50]

America was not Cambodia's friend. When Obama visited in 2012, Hun Sen's meeting with him was strained and they posed awkwardly for photos, unsure how close to stand to each other.[51] Hun Sen has previously said: '[Americans] don't understand the Cambodian way of thinking. I study a lot of American history but I don't understand America. If I try to understand Cambodia in the Western way, it's wrong.'[52] In this, Sen was echoing a Cambodian prime minister from the early 1970s who said that Cambodian politics 'may be a little hard for Westerners to understand' as 'it is not strictly logical, it is more like a complex piece of Angkor sculpture that unfolds slowly to the viewer'.[53] Today, Cambodia is still a country of intrigue, mystery and even wonder, so I asked Phirun what it is that foreigners fail to see.

'For many years, a long, long time, the opposition, they have the intellectuals from abroad, from overseas. At the time, after the Khmer Rouge genocidal regime, we didn't have many intellectuals. They were killed, they died. So these new intellectuals, they have high education, they come from overseas, they have connections with outside world, much broader. After we were liberated, we were stuck with no development of human resources but at the same time, the party outside the government, they have been lobbying the Western world, most of the world. The CPP at the time, the ruling party, we didn't have the language. The world just hears one side of the story.

So, believe me, when you hear one side of the story, first time, it is okay. Second time, third time, a hundred times, whether or not true, you believe it.

'Each country has its own reality, its own culture. Like you mentioned, different cultures. You cannot apply democracy in UK here in Cambodia. We have to adapt. We have to accept the differences. It doesn't mean democracy in UK is very good and then applied here you have the same. It takes time. Democracy is a new concept in this country. Also, you may consider, we experience the darkest period of our history, making a huge impact on the mentality of people in the country. It takes time. You see change happening. Yes, change happening. You can see for yourself already.'[54]

When Hun Sen first became Prime Minister, he was the youthful reformer in contrast to the old guard of Chea Sim. Praised for appointing people with qualifications rather than old friends, he led the liberalisation of the economy away from communism.[55] Dav Ansan believed Hun Sen is still a reformer at heart, pointing to the American education Sen chose for his children as evidence that he embraces new, even foreign ways of thinking.[56] Both Ansan and Kosal stressed that change, the CNRP's watchword, was what Hun Sen wanted too, and Phirun advised that Sen had previously shown great willingness to prioritise this: 'The Prime Minister is not that selfish. As long as you do not threaten him, you can work with him. Harmoniously. Example: 2013 election. The CNRP won fifty-five seats and the rest is CPP. Immediately, knowing the result, you know what my Prime Minister offer? He knows the CNRP is gaining more and more popularity. Immediately, he appear on TV. He make an announcement, he make an offer. In my opinion, he make a big compromise. He said, "Okay, we at the National Assembly, we have ten commissions. CNRP will chair five commissions, CPP will chair five commissions, and the first Vice-President of National Assembly will be for CNRP." Immediately he offer that. It means that he recognise the strength of the CNRP and he want to work better for the whole. The benefit of the whole country.'[57]

Listening to Phirun, I remembered Ansan telling me how Hun Sen had successfully cooperated with former Khmer Rouge leaders to end the civil war of the 1980s and then again to end their guerrilla resistance of the 1990s, even though they had been sworn enemies for decades.

'But CNRP was happily acting arrogantly,' Phirun continued. 'They wanted more. They wanted President of the National Assembly. But this is not possible ... this is Cambodia, you cannot make change overnight. So, after the election, they have nationwide protests. Months and months and months. The Prime Minister just keep silent, allow them to. Months and months. Nationwide protests. But he has the limit, you know. Enough. And then when the time came, he said no more protest. And they have the protest for one year. Lobby the internationals. He allow for one year! Enough is enough. If you are leader of the country, you cannot let this continue. There needs to be a ban. This is Cambodia, not Europe. So, no more protests. And then, the final result they got? They receive the original offer.'[58]

Phirun paused, waiting for a sign that I understood.

'The five commissions, the deputy —'

Phirun tapped my hand resting on the table. 'This is the original offer. So, what is the meaning of one year's struggle? One year! They spend time, they spend money, they spend human resources and you get the same result. If you accepted the first offer, you would have accepted it with dignity. So you think they have good vision or not? See, I want you to know that the Prime Minister is not *that* selfish. Willing to offer. Willing for national reconciliation.

'So what has the West failed to see? Ha ha. The compromise of the Cambodian government. They know their strengths and their weaknesses. They are willing for national reconciliation as well. But as long as you are the vice-president, not the president. This is what I think.'[59]

PART III
2018

'One mountain cannot have two tigers.'
ភ្នំមួយមិនអាចមានខ្លាពីរ

Cambodian proverb

CHAPTER 27

CLEAN FINGERS

Two weeks after the CNRP had been dissolved in November 2017, Rainsy announced, from France, that he would return to Cambodia to re-establish the CNRP and win the 2018 national election.[1] He appealed to soldiers to put their guns away if ordered to shoot protestors, promising that he would 'eliminate the corrupt powerful and high-ranking generals' and 'take the wealth of those generals to share with the soldiers'. Hun Sen called this a 'declaration of war' and said that Rainsy, like his father, was now a traitor to the country.[2] That same month, Rainsy was found guilty in absentia of defamation for accusing Hun Sen of bribery and ordered to pay $1 million in damages.[3]

In January 2018, when Rainsy was expected back in Cambodia, he went to Texas instead and announced to Cambodians living there that he would create a new Cambodian National Rescue Movement, of which he would be president. The movement, supported by former CNRP officials now in exile, would campaign internationally for the release of Kem Sokha and reinstatement of the CNRP in time for the election in July 2018.[4]

Intriguingly, Kem Sokha, still languishing in jail, announced through his lawyer that he did not support the Cambodian National Rescue Movement. Rainsy had apparently not communicated with Sokha about the new movement at all and speculation of divisions grew.[5]

For years, there had been rumours that while Rainsy and Sokha had united to form the CNRP, their respective supporters from the old Sam Rainsy and Human Rights parties remained divided.[6] Journalists noted that those who had signed up to the movement led by Rainsy were mostly from the old Sam Rainsy Party, while those from Kem Sokha's Human Rights Party wanted to continue under the banner of the CNRP, which Sokha still led.[7] The comradeship of 2013 was crumbling.

Rainsy planned to pressure Hun Sen into reinstating the CNRP through protests and a mass boycott of companies with ties to Sen's family. The first target was Vital, the bottled water company owned by Hun Sen's daughter, which Sreyleak told me offered returning graduates a job if they joined the CPP.[8] Rainsy urged Cambodians to stop buying this popular brand, but without CNRP officials organising activities within Cambodia, the boycott spluttered and had the effect of a trickle rather than a wave.

Three months before the national election, Rainsy realised that Hun Sen would not be pressured into allowing the CNRP to participate, so he called for all CNRP supporters to boycott the election instead. Rainsy announced that if people did not vote, it would be a 'joke of an election' that other countries would not recognise, causing Hun Sen to 'lose legitimacy', making it impossible for him 'to lead the country anymore'.[9] Rainsy published leaflets online calling for a boycott and asked his supporters in Cambodia to print and share them.

Cambodians have the right not to vote, but there is a law that makes it illegal to 'prevent eligible voters from going to cast their ballots' or cause 'confusion resulting in the loss of trust in the election'.[10] The National Election Committee argued that asking people not to vote violated these laws and said legal action would be taken against anybody who printed the leaflets or shared them online.[11]

Rong Chhun, who resigned from the NEC in protest at the CNRP's dissolution, adamantly disputed that calling for a boycott was preventing people from voting and creating confusion. He believed the NEC was misinterpreting the rules and that it was the CNRP's absence causing a loss of trust in the election.

Chhun's former colleague at the NEC, Hang Puthea, disagreed and found an hour for me to explain why, despite being interrupted by phone calls and people coming into his office. Sitting on a deep leather couch, one arm outstretched across the top, Puthea was proud about the accurate voter registration list the NEC had organised and optimistic for a well-run election. His only irritation was the campaign for a boycott. 'Yes, this is the political issue. But people who live in this country should follow this country's law. People living abroad should follow that country's law. The law makes sure that, after five years, people can go to vote. But the former head of the opposition party, they play the game that don't want people to go to vote.'

Puthea spoke of Cambodia being a 'victim' beset by decades of civil war as it was caught in a geopolitical battle between communism and democracy in the early 1970s. 'When these theories come into this country, the country splits into two teams. The power of China and the power of USA – they use Cambodia as a place for their own disputes. When UNTAC come, we have to learn how to fight by idea, not by gun. We have to learn how to manage the country by voting. When Rainsy tells people not to vote, he doesn't play a democracy role, but the other role. Sam Rainsy does not allow people to vote. If the election does not have CNRP, then he tries to say it is not a true election. But we should look to the law. The law does not say that the election must have CPP or CNRP, et cetera.'[12] Puthea reminded me that it wasn't even legal for the NEC to register the CNRP for the election as the courts had ruled it must be dissolved.

The NEC complained that the promotion of a boycott was creating public disorder – a criminal offence – and asked the government to intervene, which it duly did. The government declared that it was illegal to call for a boycott, naming it a 'rebellion'. Businesses were warned they would be punished if they printed the leaflets Sam Rainsy had produced.[13]

Following the government's lead, one provincial governor ordered police to take action against anyone calling for a boycott, and some local authorities threatened to fine people who didn't vote and withhold government services such as providing birth or death certificates. The Deputy Commander of the National Police called for all CPP members to monitor their communities and send reports to him of anyone advocating for a boycott. Despite this pressure, some people still promoted the boycott online. Police went to the homes of those they could track down, and even to the homes of their relatives, to serve warnings of punishment.[14]

Shortly before the election, the round-shouldered Chea Chiv invited neighbours and friends to his wooden home for a Buddhist ceremony, including a feast of Khmer noodles and curry. Chiv often hosted Buddhist ceremonies in his small village, especially at Khmer New Year, when old people and Buddha statues are showered with water and gifts.[15] Unsurprisingly, given he had been the CNRP's leader in Battambang province, most of the sixty people at Chiv's house were CNRP supporters. During the afternoon, Chiv suggested that they all gather for a photograph. As they lined up in front of his house, huddling together hip to hip, Chiv had an idea: why don't they all hold up their right forefinger? In 2013, when I was watching people stream out of the polling booths, a man strode towards me and held up his right forefinger, covered in ink. He had voted and he was proud. Five years later, people were now holding up a clean finger, untainted by ink, as a sign of defiance.

'There was no instruction, it was just an idea,' said the tall, forty-something Chiv. 'That is not inciting people not to vote. It is just my right to express. After they took the photo, I posted it on Facebook and said, "Our fingers are clean." That's all I did.'

Chiv's Facebook post was actually a bit longer, saying 'My finger is truly clean, my finger must be clean if have no CNRP',[16] but it still did not appear to be evidence of preventing people from voting. Nevertheless, Chiv's local commune council, now full of CPP councillors, made a legal complaint about the photo.

Chiv was interviewed by his local Commune Election Committee, who decided that the photo merely warranted agreement from Chiv that he wouldn't do it again. According to Chiv, all agreed that the complaint would be withdrawn – except that it wasn't. Chiv believes that a minister pushed for the complaint to be upheld and the NEC fined Chiv $5000, five times the annual income of an average Cambodian. Two of his friends were fined $2500 each.[17]

Chiv was not alone in posting photos of a clean finger. People joined the 'Clean Fingers' campaign all over Cambodia. At the other end of the country, in Kampot, five former CNRP members were fined $2500 each for the same crime. Their lawyer, Sam Sokong, who had also defended Chea Chiv in his case, said that many former CNRP members in six other provinces had faced complaints but avoided fines when they promised not to continue supporting the boycott.[18]

Two months before the election, Sophal took me to meet Kimsorn, the CPP group leader who had whisked a *krama* away to reveal a colour television. Kimsorn was fully confident that the election would go well for the CPP: 'We have prepared from the bottom ... have already destroyed the opposition. The election will happen normally.'[19] He went over to a table, on which sat piles of CPP Family Books and CPP membership cards, proudly bringing some back to show me.

To record the number of inhabitants, each Commune Council gives out family books for households to complete. These books serve as an official record of dates of birth, gender and family relationships. After the CPP nearly lost the 2017 Commune Council elections, they instituted a new type of family book, the CPP Family Book. The CPP has over five million members, but only 3.5 million people voted for it during those Commune Council elections. The CPP's new slogan was 'One member, one vote for the CPP'.[20] Each commune was now divided into sections and each section assigned a leader, like Kimsorn, who would interview every person in every household. Those who agreed to join the CPP would have their photo and details entered into that household's CPP Family Book.[21] Looking at the books Kimsorn collected, I saw details of names, dates of birth, gender and jobs, and even that one person spoke French.

Kimsorn also had a list of registered voters in his commune, which he said the CPP had received from the NEC. Sophal was aghast. After we left Kimsorn, he could not stop talking about how his photo and details, which he had supplied to the NEC, were now in the hands of the CPP. 'Unbelievable! They make a net to catch a fish!'[22]

It is in the CPP Family Book that the power of the CPP lives. The detail in it gives the impression, as Sophal repeated many times, that the CPP 'know everything'. Section leaders, like Kimsorn, were meant to meet frequently with CPP families and report if there were any 'changes of their political feeling or disappointment'.[23] The CPP banked on minimising any change in political feeling by doling out $12.50 three times a year to CPP families.[24] A dejected Sophal commented, 'They buy hearts.'

Kimsorn knows of some who planned not to vote, but this was 'no problem'. People in other communes reported greater pressure to sign up as a member of the CPP. One village chief demanded CPP members drink blessed holy water while promising to vote CPP, while others admitted to demanding CPP members swear upon their lives that they would vote CPP. One voter was told by his village chief that photos were recorded in the CPP Family Book so that cameras in the polling stations could match their faces and record how they voted.[25]

After meeting Kimsorn, Sophal and I went for lunch with a friend of Sophal's and began talking about the upcoming election. The outdoor restaurant was a series of individual huts spaced apart from each other, perfect for private conversations, but even with most huts empty Sophal made us turn the fan on to create noise while we were talking. After the waitress came with food and drinks, Sophal asked us to stop calling Rainsy and Sokha by their names in case somebody overheard us – even though the chance of waitresses or other guests understanding English was slim. Rainsy was christened 'the one in France' and Sokha 'the one in jail' as our conversation continued with us leaning closer to each other.

Both Sophal and his friend had voted CNRP in 2013 and were adamant that they would boycott the 2018 election. When I asked how many they thought would boycott, both firmly agreed 'A lot. Forty per cent or more!'[26]

Pen Raksa of Transparency International thought the same.[27] Titthara, the journalist friend of Chut Wutty, thought that if the turnout dropped below 50 per cent, the CPP would have difficulties being accepted as a legitimate government.[28] In contrast to 2013, the CPP knew it could only win by getting as many people to vote as possible.

CHAPTER 28

CHARM OFFENSIVE

Sophea works for the government in Phnom Penh, where she lives with her parents, some siblings, her husband and their toddler son. She is small, probably not more than five foot, and wears thin, rectangular glasses, in marked contrast to the large round ones that have become fashionable among young people hoping to appear sophisticated. Forty years ago, the Khmer Rouge would have killed anybody wearing glasses for being bourgeois.

The ministry that Sophea works in was assigned by the CPP to campaign in a province in Cambodia's northwest, near the Tonlé Sap basin. For nine months before the election, Sophea would spend her weekends in a small village 250 kilometres from her home in Phnom Penh persuading people to vote.[1] This village had one of the lowest votes for the CPP at the 2013 election. When she first arrived, the Village Chief, a public servant paid $50 per month for official duties, informed her about each villager. 'Normally, we classify black, brown and white,' she told me. 'Those who belong to CPP are white, black is totally no, no change. Brown is maybe. Sometimes they register as our member but their mind is still not sure. They join for benefit ... I think this is what the ruling party is afraid of. Sometimes, their mouth says yes but we don't know.'

'You visit the homes of the brown and white?' I asked.

'Yes, sometimes. We collect data. But the Village Chief is the main person for persuasion. Some of us, we don't have the skill for that. But what we do is to support the Village Chief to collect the data ... tell the villagers that you will get benefit of this or that if you support our party.'

'Does the Village Chief ask villagers what they would like?'

'During the nine months, one village got a new road ... Sometimes we [support] for better transport.'

One government official I know characterised the CPP's campaigning in 2013 as going to communes 'in big cars, they show off, and on the way back they go to karaoke', only serving to turn people away from them. The CPP had learnt from those mistakes and embedded campaign teams in communes, living alongside villagers. In the final few weeks before the election, Sophea was stationed in the village permanently, only returning to Phnom Penh a day or two a week. She and her team organised doctors to visit the remote villages, a highly valued service, and nightly entertainment, such as music, dancing and film screenings, including of the Khmer-language thriller *First They Killed My Father* (2017), directed by Angelina Jolie. Sophea, always in a CPP polo shirt, established a bond with the villagers which went beyond a political transaction. 'The first time [there], I was a bit tired,' she said – understandable given she was working, campaigning, raising a toddler and trying to be selected by the government for a scholarship abroad. 'But later, once we had been going for a while, I feel the same as my team – I miss the villagers.'

Many villagers came to the nightly entertainment, which Sophea put down to the influence of the Village Chief: 'My Village Chief is nice to everybody. I observe this. Those who support others, she still nice. She is still nice to me. We don't talk about politics.'

This was Sophea's hint that she did not support the CPP, although she still 'felt the achievement' when she saw the result for her commune; the CPP had won over 90 per cent, with nearly everyone voting. I asked Sophea if her role made her more supportive of the CPP. 'Not much. It is just the job. It is a voluntary job, but if you don't do that you would be classified —' Sophea didn't finish explaining that her own name would be coloured brown or black otherwise. 'During my interview, my boss asks if I will accept working for the ruling party. Before entering the place, you have to accept that you are working for the ruling party and know what you will have to do.'

Sophea may not have believed in the CPP, but she believed in doing a good job, saying that she and her team 'really try our best' to ensure her village didn't finish last again. She also acted out of loyalty to her boss, who she admires: 'I still believe my boss is good and knowledgeable. I think he is busy so I try to help him ... I don't think all who support the ruling party are the same mind as the Prime Minister.'

Sophea's boss, who has a PhD from a European university, was one of the highly educated young technocrats brought in by Hun Sen following the 2013 election to initiate reform and improve public services. Another technocrat given new responsibility was Kosal, the man who had talked to me of Cambodia feeling abandoned by the world during the Khmer

Rouge regime. A baby when the Khmer Rouge ruled, he, like many of the other young technocrats, grew up in a very different world to Hun Sen: 'I remember before 1995, when I was a student at high school, there was separation between male and female. Taboo, holding hands, kissing. When walking, there is like a line between boys and girls that you cannot cross.' Kosal was grinning widely, as if recalling the times he snuck across the line. 'In 1995, I went to live in a Latin country. Quite a shift. A liberation from a closed, conservative culture to a more open, very expressive, I would say modern way ... In Latin culture, people kiss when greet each other. I was at high school, the ladies walk into the class and they start kissing the boys in the class. I was like, "Whoa, what is wrong? What is she doing? Does she like me? She is kissing him too!" Once it sinks in, I like it. I like it.'[2] Kosal's eyes twinkled.

Kosal later moved to the United States, where he found himself in a strange land again. 'Different culture when speaking to the teacher. Here you don't look at the teacher when you are speaking to them, you don't meet eyes with them. In the US, it is rude if you don't look at the person when you are talking to them. They say, "What? Am I not good enough? What is wrong? You can't look at me?!" But here it is different. It is like a challenge, but more importantly, it is respect. There, it is like an insult if you don't look at their eyes.'

Kosal and I were tucking into breakfast before he had to go to work, and Kosal was eating as fast as he was talking. 'In our culture, we beat around the bush rather than ask directly. "What is wrong?" they said to me. "What are you trying to say?" So, I start again and they said, "Why didn't you just say that?"' Kosal laughed at the confusion he lived in for many years. 'In the US, it was difficult for me. Here, you get very clear instructions. There is a rule and a prescription to follow. There, "Here is your assignment. You have two weeks. Go and do it." Very different. There, I was asking what does the teacher want and the teacher would say, "Go do whatever you want."' Kosal would be left scratching his head.

Everything was new and different to him in the United States. Even the fact that people asked the teacher questions 'shocked' Kosal: 'Here, we never challenge the teacher ... even if the teacher was wrong, we say the teacher was right. It took some time, three to four years, to adapt to the culture ... I was curious, asked questions and people found it funny. Some people didn't like Asian people, for instance. Some people would ask, "Why are you here? Go back home. You are a Jap, go home." I would explain: "I am not Japanese,

I am Cambodian.'" Kosal's protest would be met with 'I don't care, go back home.'

I asked Kosal if the United States was what he thought it would be.

'Honestly, much, much better. I think how my parents came through the Khmer Rouge. To that, America is magical. Miracle. I only lived six months in Khmer Rouge. Growing up, nothing. Barely have any toys. I notice my kids, at home, how much options they have. They have environment to go out, play together. When growing up, I have nothing. Good and bad [though]. Could go fishing, catch cricket. More like a raw, natural way. No video game back then. Catch fighting fish with my childhood friend. Fly kites. Play soccer. Basic, natural things. Interactive. Nowadays, lot of iPads. Even my own [kids]. To see flying kites, you have to go out of the city.'

Kosal continued living in the United States after completing his Master's degree, working for a charity, but his father became ill back in Cambodia. His mother, who he spoke to every week, counselled him to return: '"In the US, you are nothing. There are so many resources. To Cambodia, you could be important. You could play your part. We need resources."'

Kosal decided to come home, but quickly realised that he had become 'Americanised': 'In the US, when you go out and eat ... people share the bill. That was one of the first weird things. But I found it nice. If you go out as a big group, you order and pay for your share. I find it very nice. At first, when my friends [in Cambodia] call me, I was hesitant. You can just invite that one, and then somebody else comes – crap, I have to pay for them too. When I come back home, I invite my friends for lunch. I then pay for my share. They all ask what am I doing? I say, "I am paying for what I have eaten." They say, "You invited us, though." I say, "Yes, I invited you. I eat and now I am paying for what I ate." So that's one thing ... Sometimes for my group of friends, I invite them, they make a joke: "Remember to bring your money, guys."'

Years after returning, Kosal still feels adrift. 'There is a crack that I have fallen between. I don't have close friends here. I don't have close friends there. To be good friends, you need a good foundation – trust. Trust take time. Can't trust overnight. When I move there at seventeen, I have to start all over again. Building that trust and circle, takes time. By time I know how it works, I realise I have to go back. Twelve years. Over here, I have to start from scratch. People my own age, they have their own friends, family.'

Kosal started working in government after returning to Cambodia, but his boss did not like him. Kosal was 'too straightforward' and lacked 'the art of communication', which in Cambodia means making your point without causing offence. 'I talk like this. I talk honestly, directly. Some people think I am being hurtful.' Offended colleagues would say to him, 'If I am wrong, you can tell me in a different way. Don't have to subject me to embarrassment.' Kosal would respond with mock incomprehension. 'But if you are wrong, how can I say it in a different way?'

Kosal did not feel that he could 'value add' in his first government role so requested a move to another department, where his new boss had a PhD from Australia. 'We get along well. We talk about the social fabric, popular issues. We realise we can talk about frustrations, our feelings. Things have changed, but not fast enough.'

Kosal still sees the corrosive influence of *khnorng* holding his country back: 'I think in the US, there is fairness ... You cannot go through the back door. Here, it is different, it is worse. In business, you have to sort of – not quite bribe, but similar. They expect an envelope every month to keep the relationship. Like in the old days of China, a group of gangsters that controls a neighbourhood ... Protection. Protection money. It's hidden, but it is still there.'

Kosal understands that in the past, Cambodia's destruction meant that they were 'lucky' to have anybody in government at all. People were still 'frightened, tormented'. Now, Kosal thinks, 'it's sad, very sad' that some government officials are more concerned with their wealth than with building a country for their grandchildren: 'I don't know. Do they think "I will be dead so I don't care what my kids have to go through"? I don't know, I don't get it ... If I leave a legacy, I want a system that works.'

Kosal was given a chance to create that legacy in 2013 when he was promoted to work closely with one of the reforming ministers who had been handpicked by Hun Sen. Kosal sees himself as a 'moderate' who believes there is 'always good and bad in any decision' and his job is to balance them. Despite this, Kosal is firmly, and voluntarily, embedded within the CPP. He believes they have rapidly grown the economy and improved services.

At the 2017 Commune Council election, Kosal was responsible for a commune that he knew would be desperately close. His colleagues left their own commune to help his campaign. On election day, Kosal counted the votes coming in from the different polling stations, eyes wide, palms sweating. The CPP won by a few votes.[3] For the 2018 election, Kosal was moved to a different commune. Rural and about two hours from Phnom Penh, he spent most of June and July there, while still trying to do his day job. Kosal's colleagues joked that they did not recognise him in sandals, with messy hair and skin darkened from being out in the sun. His wife and children saw little of him. 'I had to win. I had to win, you know. I had to go meet people.' Kosal felt he had to make the villagers feel 'like family'.

'Was there resistance at first? Was it difficult to win them over?' I asked.

'Well, we were lucky. The court dissolve the opposition!' Kosal's support for the CPP does not cover his eyes completely. Kosal's commune had a CNRP Commune Chief who refused to join the CPP when the CNRP was dissolved. Kosal said he was a lot like Rozeth, the young, female Commune Chief in Battambang: 'He is strong, talks a lot. I like him. I do. I do. Because he's so committed. Manages things. Does things. People love him.'

'Does his best for the people,' I ventured.

'He does! He does! Well, he did. Not now …'

Reflecting on why the deposed chief did not switch to the CPP, Kosal said, 'I do not blame him because I realise that our party has a flaw … I still respect the guy … He was honest. He was helpful. He tried to be a good Commune Chief. He tried to do his best … this is a good guy for the people.' Kosal tried to get the CNRP Commune Chief reinstated but couldn't find a way.

'Right now, you know, I spend a lot of time helping the commune. Because the new [chief], the new …'

'Is not so good?'

'Worse.'

By this point, one of Kosal's friends, also a senior CPP official, had joined us and was laughing at Kosal's half-joking description of the new Commune Chief. Her surprise turned to astonishment when Kosal explained what he did after failing to get the former chief reinstated. 'Now, he become staff. Seriously.'

'How?' I asked.

'Contract staff.'

Kosal's friend was gobsmacked.

'But what does he do?' I enquired.

'He does little bits.'

'Really?' Kosal's friend almost shrieked.

'Really, really, really, really. I like him because he's a good guy! And he's done so much … I think I want to him, I help him,' Kosal protested.

Kosal also helped the former chief's assistant and gave a job to a daughter of a CNRP supporter so she could get work experience in Phnom Penh.

She was one of the few who finished high school in a commune where many drop out after primary school to work in the fields. Kosal talked to families about the importance of education, and how with it, the child can get a good job and look after the health of the whole family.[4] He also helped many students prepare for the high-school graduation exam.

Khemera is another young technocrat who joined a ministry after the 2013 election. Like Kosal, he was educated in America, completing a Master's and a PhD, and became so close to the family he stayed with that his 'American parents' came to Cambodia for his wedding. They then had to console a lonely, tearful Khemera back in America because the United States refused his new wife a visa. Khemera and his wife were apart for three years before he could return to Cambodia and work for the UN.

After the 2013 election, the government offered Khemera a job, which made him think about where he could make the biggest contribution. His family and his wife's were split about whether he should take it, some urging that the pay cut was too great. Khemera, however, had grown frustrated at the UN; his foreign boss quashed his opinions and ignored the Cambodian context when advocating international perspectives. After days of deliberation, he and his wife gathered the families to tell them he was taking the job. 'I went to the US for study because the government supported me to get there ... I feel a moral [duty] to return the favour and to influence lives of many others.'[5]

When Khemera arrived on his first day, he was shown to his office, which turned out to be the same one his late father had occupied decades before. Immediately, he knew he was where he should be. I asked him what he feels when he hears the United States, a country he still feels connected to, vehemently criticise the government he works in. 'I respect their criticism, some of it is true. Cambodia has a long way to go to make changes. But at the same time, not all of the words from the USA government is ... I think they need more time to understand Cambodia. But the government has to be more proactive to accept that criticism and make changes, because some of what they say is for the better. It should listen and patiently think what could be truth. Some at the ministry say, "No, the CNRP are bad." No, they are not all bad. Some things they say are stupid, but not all. Some of what he [Rainsy] says is true. Sam Rainsy is an economist. He is not stupid. But he has a different way of viewing the world. I can see what he and Kem Sokha are trying to say. Even though I don't agree, I can see. But for Rainsy, the sad thing is that he criticises without recognising what the government are trying to do. That is the unfortunate thing. Nobody is perfect. He does not recognise the good things.'

Khemera had always been a 'big supporter' of the CPP and looked forward to being active in its campaign. When he first went to the commune he was assigned to, he asked the new Commune Chief and Village Chiefs to take him to meet people. In going from house to house, they sometimes skipped a house, prompting Khemera to ask what was wrong with those houses. 'And [one], she let it slip. "That is the CNRP house." We said, "Okay! Let's go there." That's where we wanted to go.'[6]

The CPP hadn't gone door-to-door in that commune for twenty years. Khemera criticised his predecessors for 'not even seeing the community members' and was determined that he would live and sleep among the villagers, forming bonds by singing old songs together in the evening.

Khemera held meetings in all the different villages to hear what people needed, and talked with the recently deposed Commune Chief, who Khemera called 'a super-duper CNRP driving force'. It was when sitting down with him, asking lots of questions, that Khemera began to understand the community's situation. The former chief talked about the importance of irrigation for farming, but the new chief was uninterested in this. So Khemera asked the former chief to show him around, and together they took a boat and walked kilometres to inspect the damaged canals. Khemera gathered the resources, and repairs began the next day.[7]

Khemera said the impact on the villagers was 'striking'. They commented with surprise and gratitude that Khemera's group did it before the election. Previously, new developments and support for villages arrived only if a majority voted CPP; those villages that did not vote CPP would be ignored.

Khemera is senior enough in government to have the title of His Excellency, but he pretended not to be an excellency so he could speak to villagers more easily. Years earlier, I had heard villagers complain that CPP officials disrespected them with a desultory *sampeah*, loosely interlocking their fingers at chest height and rocking their wrists to mimic the act of bowing. People like Kosal and Khemera had transformed how CPP officials were viewed, serving the population with sensitivity and dedication, just like hundreds of other CPP campaigning teams throughout the country. For Kosal, it was more than campaigning to win an election: 'I have to be there so the people have hope.'[8]

Hun Sen had chosen to remain above the affray of campaigning during Cambodia's first few elections, but 2013 changed everything. A ruler's authority and a populace's fear of change would not keep Sen in power forever. He needed to become something he had not always been: popular.

It was not enough to be popular among old people in rural villages. Sen needed to win over the swathe of garment factory workers who had previously marched to his house, hollering for him to stand down. After the near defeat at the 2017 Commune Council election, Hun Sen decided to meet thousands of factory workers every Wednesday. In the year to the 2018 election, he made fifty-one visits to factories, addressing 700,000 workers.[9] Workers who attended received cash and the day off, and television news programs showed him hugging those who clamoured to get their photograph taken with him.

I sat down with Channa and another garment worker. In Kunthea's absence, Channa was the one who talked most. She told me about the time she saw Hun Sen speak. About 19,500 workers from multiple factories attended the event, some bussed in by factory owners. Hun Sen was only there for an hour from 9.00am but workers got the whole day off.[10]

I asked what Hun Sen said in his speech, but Channa couldn't remember – she was far away from the stage and wasn't paying much attention. Some workers near her fell asleep, and others had their heads down, playing on their phones, prompting sharp words and glares from security guards. Channa saw Sen talk to some of the eager workers at the front, present $200 to each of the pregnant workers, shake hands and pose for selfies before being swept away by his entourage.

Afterwards, Channa and her friends didn't talk about having heard the world's longest-serving prime minister in the flesh. 'We just lined up in a long line to receive 20,000 riels,' said Channa. 'People weren't really excited or enjoying it. They just wanted it to finish so they could receive their money and go.'

Channa's friend said that she went because the money and time off was too tempting.

'Would you have gone if you were only paid 5000 riels?' I jokingly asked.

'No!' Channa's friend was adamant.

'What about 10,000 riels?'

Pausing, Channa's friend replied that the equivalent of $2.50 would maybe be worth it. Channa was less enticed, saying that she only went for 20,000 riels because it was close to where she lived. This was the same woman who had willingly *paid* 30,000 riels for a motorcycle taxi to take her kilometres across town to see Kem Ley's body.

It is estimated that at least $3.5 million was handed out to factory workers, who Hun Sen called his 'nieces and nephews', in the year leading up to the election. It is likely the money came from government funds, even though Hun Sen's speeches were focused on party politics.[11] Hang Puthea of the National Election Committee saw nothing wrong with this because 'as the head of the Royal Government, he has the right to organize things in society', and Hun Sen did pause gifting money during the official two-week campaign period.[12]

Elections in Cambodia are held on a Sunday, the only day factory workers have off, but many factory workers are still registered to vote at their family home. Poor roads and lack of public transport make it impossible for some to travel there, vote and return to Phnom Penh on the same day, in order to be back at work on Monday. The CPP's enthusiasm for a high turnout prompted the Ministry of Interior to declare three days of paid holiday, instructing employers to give workers time off the day before and after the election.[13] The government also strongly encouraged factories to give workers bonuses or advances to help cover the cost of travelling home. Both Channa and her friend received $100.

Hun Sen was winning support by returning to his old theme of providing better spoons, expanding the number of workers who would get free healthcare and ordering employers to treble their contribution to the National Social Security Fund.[14] The minimum wage had caused Cambodia to burn in 2013, but the government had increased it every year so that by the 2018 election, it had doubled to $170 per month. During an address to factory workers just before the election, Hun Sen dangled the carrot that the minimum wage could rise to $250 by 2023 if the CPP was re-elected.[15] Perhaps he hoped that if people had better spoons, and maybe even a bowl to themselves, they wouldn't notice that the spoons of some had been taken away.

CHAPTER 29

PRESSURE

Ou Ritthy had left Cambodia to study in the Netherlands two days before Kem Ley was killed. He returned on the day that Kem Sokha was arrested and *The Cambodia Daily* closed down. Ritthy had won a bet on the 2013 election, correctly predicting that FUNCINPEC would not win any seats, and he won a bet on the 2017 Commune election, guessing that the CPP would win, but only just. His predictive skills had waned, though, and he had to buy perfume for a friend after Sokha was arrested and lunch for another when the CNRP was dissolved.

'Kem Sokha is a big thing. They [the CPP] want him to resign. It seem to be very clear. Then the CNRP dissolve! Too much. I cannot … I still speak to some friends and say I don't believe it. It's like, it's too big, too impossible.' Commenting on how the CPP's tolerance of dissent had changed, Ritthy continued, 'The years 2013, 2014, it seemed to be … they allow the opposition to dance, to shout, scream. And then 2017, it's much … like a new guy, you know? It's like a ghost chasing you … it's very systematic, no hesitation.'

Ritthy said the CPP had created fear by changing the laws on political parties, trade unions and telecommunications. 'Even charities, they want to say something, but they look at the law and they think, *oh*. So the law controls them. The law makes them reconsider what to do. Then they start to target individuals. Kem Sokha … journalists. *Cambodia Daily*. Then civil society. We wait and see. Who is next?'

At the time of Kem Sokha's arrest, two charities heavily involved in campaigning against illegal corruption and land grabbing were shut down, others were investigated and two American charities that promoted democratic citizenship were banned. 'Civil society, we stay quiet,' whispered Ritthy. 'Sometimes … we would cancel the forums to avoid [displeasing government], because we don't know where they stop.'[1] Many charities had employment contracts that banned staff from taking part in political campaigns, particularly those not affiliated to the CPP.[2]

Just after the CNRP was abolished, Koul Panha, Executive Director of COMFREL, went into hiding abroad. He was still there two weeks before the 2018 election, when I spoke to him. COMFREL was the main independent monitor of elections in Cambodia but chose not to take part in the 2018 elections after the government accused it of being the headquarters of a 'colour revolution'. Their partners in monitoring previous elections had also pulled out: Transparency International because their American funders were banned from Cambodia, and ADHOC because they saw no point getting involved in an election where everybody already knew the outcome.[3]

'If you observed the elections and reported irregularities, do you fear that you would be punished for doing so?' I asked Panha.

'Yes, this is a really very severe attack by the ruling party and we are really concerned. It's unpredictable. We cannot predict what would happen to us. But we can see every attack from the ruling party. If we have a law, independent authority, independent court, it's relatively stable. We can predict what would happen to us. But now we are very concerned, we cannot predict anything ... If we found out something that affect their prestige or political image or criticise them, we can be punished by them ... Something wrong, they can just punish us immediately.'

Panha sounded dazed, like somebody stumbling away from a car accident. 'I never believe that they would dissolve the large opposition like that. There is not even a clear crime, you know. Very surprised ... I never expected that.'[4]

Panha returned repeatedly to the unpredictable nature of Hun Sen, comparing him to a volcano that could erupt while you slept. Rather than considering himself a minor figure compared to Kem Sokha and so less likely to be targeted, Panha felt his lower status afforded him less protection. 'They arrest Kem Sokha!' Panha's pitch rose. 'There is no law. Oh my goodness, how they implement that? And what happen to us? They dissolve the opposition, what could they do to us?! ... There is no prediction, especially in terms of legal.' Panha paused and heaved a sigh.

'Because there is no law and it is very unpredictable, do you —' I began to ask.

But Panha, agitated, cut me off. 'We have a constitution and we have laws, but they do not implement! They decide by themselves! For instance, they arrest Kem Sokha ... He is leader of the opposition! They dissolve the opposition. They dissolve the Members of Parliament. In our constitution, they cannot do that ... You cannot do that! It is impossible!' Spent by the stress, Panha finally exhaled and there was silence.

'Is that why you left?' I asked softly.

'Yes, I have very high risk to me. I cannot feel very safe. Unsafe. If we have law, reason, we can stay to talk. Argument. We can adjust. Impossible in current situation. Nobody predict what will happen. So you have to ...' Panha let out another sigh. 'I ... I am very pessimistic, very pessimistic, about the current situation.'

'Do you think you can go back [to Cambodia] next year or soon?'

'We'll see. I cannot predict. It's out of control. Before there were some problems, of course, but I could still manage. Respond to the different situations.'

'I am very sorry that you have had to go through this.'

'Yeah ...' Panha mumbled goodbye, still trying to make sense of where Cambodia had found itself.

Chen Sokngeng, the 26-year-old former commune chief, was one of 280 CNRP officials who crossed the border into Thailand after the CNRP was dissolved, but he returned before the election.[5] Warily, he agreed to meet me in a café in Siem Reap. Since returning, Sokngeng had avoided politics and felt that he was being followed and watched. His silence had kept him safe, but I was asking him to talk, which he agreed to as long as my questions were 'only about the past, which is already done'.

Sokngeng admitted to being scared, saying others were too. He was clearly feeling the strain: he was struggling without money and couldn't return to medical practice because he feared a fake medical complaint that could lead to him being sued; something similar had happened at a friend's clinic. He said he would have to pay $20,000 to get a doctor's role in a government hospital and his family couldn't afford that.[6] Instead, he had opened a restaurant to make ends meet.[7]

Sokngeng seemed to enjoy the chance to reminisce about the CNRP's rise and his part within it, even though he was cautious: at times, he extended his neck forward like a turtle to talk quietly with me. Over a meal of fish soup, Cambodian pancakes and *kor sach-chrook pong tay-a* (caramelised pork stew), I asked him if we could go to see his old commune office. With heaviness, he said that he could not go there as 'some people would not be happy'. He contented himself with showing me photos of walking up the stairs into the office for the first time after his election win and standing with the other, older, CNRP councillors. The photos were all he had left to show of his former life.

◈

In May, two months before the election, a cross-ministerial taskforce was created to 'take action against the dissemination of any content, information or SMS, images, videos' that threatened national security or disrupted public order. The Ministry of Information advised they would sanction anybody for using 'insulting words against leaders or any individual as affecting their reputation and public image': 'Such matters cannot be considered as an expression of opinion.' The Interior Ministry added that it would be looking out for people 'inciting colour revolution'.[8]

At the same time, Cambodia signed agreements with Russia and China to jointly fight what the government called 'cybercrime'. A step toward this was a requirement that all domestic and international internet network traffic be transmitted through a data management centre run by the government-owned Telecom Cambodia.[9] The government also demanded that every website register details with the Ministry of Information. The rationale for this was that 'fake news is not good for a real democracy',[10] which had become a common justification for repressing the media and online activism, even in countries deemed to be setting the standard for democracy.

Devoid of opposition in parliament, the CPP amended the constitution so that individuals and organisations 'shall primarily uphold the national interest' and 'shall not ... directly or indirectly affect the interests of the Kingdom of Cambodia'. The CPP also passed a new law which made it a crime to say or do anything that 'could affect the dignity of the King'.[11] The King, as he had done before to avoid signing controversial laws, immediately departed for a medical check-up in China, leaving royal assent to his delegate, the CPP President of the Senate.[12]

A 39-year-old widow, who had just been fired as a garment worker because she had complained about a lack of rights, was arrested after she posted a film of herself throwing a shoe at a CPP billboard. The mother-of-two was found hiding in Thailand and extradited back to Cambodia – despite the UN giving her official refugee status – and was jailed for two years.[13] A seventy-year-old barber and former CNRP activist spent ten months in jail for comparing the King unfavourably to ancient kings. A fifty-year-old primary-school teacher spent six months in jail because in a Facebook post he blamed the King for the CNRP's dissolution and loss of Cambodian land.[14] A woman was sentenced to a year in jail for accusing Hun Sen, via Facebook, of killing Kem Ley. A 29-year-old man was arrested on his wedding day for calling the government 'authoritarian', and another was charged for a Facebook post dating back to 2013. A young woman was even questioned by her Commune Chief because she wrote a poem about her homeland being spoiled by a 'brutal thief' who only had one eye.[15]

As well as the government monitoring dissent, online hackers were causing havoc for independent charities and those considered to be anti-CPP. ADHOC, reeling from the imprisonment of four of its staff and its Executive Director going into exile after receiving 'explicit threats', had its website hacked three days after being launched. Aware the government could access their internet servers, ADHOC had to stop using email and consider returning to paper and pen.[16] Another human rights organisation was also targeted by hackers, and the online catalogue of all *The Cambodia Daily*'s articles was blocked in Cambodia.[17] Ou Ritthy had his Twitter account hacked three times before the 2018 election, telling me that 'it feels that we are watched personally and electronically'.[18] May Titthara's wife, a teacher, had her Facebook account hacked and a porn film posted on it.[19]

The chess pieces were being moved into position for the endgame, and CNRP supporters were feeling the pressure tightening around them. They had lost their king and queen, one to exile and another in jail. Their knights and rooks were scattered and the CPP wanted to make sure the pawns couldn't lead an electoral boycott. Kannitha, my quick-witted former colleague, said that in Cambodia it is not enough to cut down a tree; you must destroy all of the roots, too.[20]

In a private meeting, Hun Sen warned union leaders not to organise protests in support of the CNRP or an electoral boycott. Rong Chhun, the former National Election Committee member, was seen as a chief instigator of the 2013 protests and given a warning.[21] Chhun had wanted to return to his job as a teacher but took more than one month to formally request this after leaving the NEC, so was sacked along with ten former CNRP officials who also wanted to return to teaching.[22] Sardonically, Chhun called every day a 'non-profit day for me' and became dependent on others for food and rice.[23] Another trade union leader who wanted the EU to withdraw the free trade agreement was forced to leave Cambodia after people broke into his house and officials threatened he would die like his brother, the slain Chea Vichea.[24]

The pressure was trickling through society, reaching those at the very bottom. It had stopped Channa from listening to the radio in her own home, and Kunthea confided that she would like to invite me to her house but she was afraid because 'people around there will wonder why we talk. Even something normal like this, is not.' Kunthea wanted me to meet her three sons, who were doing well in primary school, which, perversely, worried her. 'If they get high education like Kem Ley, they will go as Kem Ley.'[25]

As the election neared, Chamroeun found it difficult to answer when I asked him how many people he thought would vote, and he was unsure how he would vote himself. 'For me, I say 70 per cent will not go but a part of me, 30 per cent will. You know why? Because the rumours that they can spread through their network. They might stop your ID card. They might not recognise you. I believe this government can do anything. They can go this far' – he placed his hand on the table and added, 'they go even further,' extending his hand out into the middle.

'If you don't go to vote, you will be … enemy. During the election, I tell my wife to look at the neighbours. Listen. If so hard for us to stay at home, we have to consider to go and vote. And just … cross so that your finger [is inked], your name is still voting. But so far, 70 per cent I don't go. Not just me, my friends, my relatives. But it still possible that we might go because of the government. It is difficult to say. Let's see. The Prime Minister has not said anything about what happens to you if you don't go to vote.'[26]

It was not long before Hun Sen and the CPP did speak, though.

The head of the National AIDS Authority warned the crowd at a public event covered by the media: 'When going to vote, there is a mark, the finger is inked. But if you don't go to vote, you don't love democracy, you love dictatorship. Your finger is not inked, which makes it easy to recognise that you are supporting treasonous rebel groups.'[27] The ink had been changed since 2013 so that it couldn't be washed away.

Officials from Hun Many's youth organisation told people in Mondolkiri that they wouldn't be able to access government services if they didn't vote.[28] Garment workers were told not to show up for work unless their finger was stained, and workers at one company were warned their wages would be docked if they didn't vote.[29] A teacher was arrested because, caught between his principles and pressure, he stole ink so that he and his colleagues could pretend they had voted because they had been told they would not receive their wages otherwise.[30] Police terrified families in Banteay Meanchey, near the Thai border, by telling them that if their children working abroad didn't come back to vote, the government would take their land away from them.[31]

In case people still hadn't got the message, a few days before the election Hun Sen announced, 'Those who don't vote – due to provocation by the treasonous and destroyers – are those who destroy democracy, and will regret this.'[32] He issued an order that 'all National Police forces must also fulfil their duty to vote on July 29'.[33] Those employed by the government – teachers, soldiers, police, bureaucrats – knew that after the election they would be asked to line up with their colleagues, face their superiors and hold up their right forefinger. A lack of ink would be indelibly remembered.

Losing the fight, Rainsy invoked King Sihamoni, who as a neutral monarch does not vote, to persuade people to abstain from participating. 'Even though the King is being held hostage by Hun Sen, he has let us know that he would not go to vote on July 29. Let's follow his good example with regard to this fake election! On that particular day we just want to be neutral like him!'[34] Rainsy's ploy was undermined when the King signed a letter asking his people to vote.[35]

Sophal, once adamant that he would not vote, called me just before the election to say that the pressure was too great and that there was no choice but to vote, although he would make sure to spoil his ballot. Sreyleak, the midwife who had studied abroad, previously told me, 'Nobody can put pressure on me' but admitted she now felt 'very pressured'.[36] She and her husband decided they too would vote by spoiling their ballot, and maybe even write 'CNRP' on it.[37] Titthara, the investigative journalist, said that his sibling had been visited by the Village Chief, who made comments such as, 'Oh, I see that you will have two buildings on your land, why don't you come to vote?', inferring that the second building may not be given official planning approval. She didn't want to go but she had to 'follow'.[38]

Cambodians were receiving two mobile phone messages a day from their service providers urging them to vote. Users of WhatsApp were being invited to join groups that promoted voting for the CPP. A Veng Sreng shopkeeper said, 'We know what is going on, but we can't express it publicly.'[39]

Shortly before the election, I had breakfast with Rithisak, my friend who grew up in the refugee camps. He would pause the conversation when a waitress went past, and I noticed that he avoided using Hun Sen's name, only referring to the Prime Minister as 'him', as if we were back in 2012. He admitted that people were 'more scared now' because every village had a CPP person who was watching what they were saying and doing. 'Even if you say something little to criticise the government or something the government is responsible for, you will be visited by the CPP local leaders and they will interview you about what you said. You will be punished – your business or family will be criticised or excluded. You can't even criticise the state of the roads.'[40] Local authorities had visited Rithisak at his home about comments he had made, and his wife worried for their reputation with the CPP. He had previously been adamant that he would not vote, but was having second thoughts.

One month before the election, I met a group of fourteen young people who volunteered with the Youth Resource Development Program. They were all university students in Phnom Penh but had come from different provinces. In two groups, they had stayed for three nights with local villagers in Preah Vihear province, learning about the effects of illegal logging and mining. Most did not know what to expect before going, but one, Piseth, told me that he had read some information about a campaigner who had died six years previously: 'There was an activist, Chut Wutty. He was killed because of Prey Lang [Cambodia's biggest remaining forest]. According to the newspaper, the deforestation is just becoming higher and higher after his death.'[41]

The group was shocked to hear that chemicals that poisoned the fish in local rivers had been used to flush gold out. They were angry to see trees reduced to stumps and discarded trunks left by illegal loggers who only wanted the most valuable wood. Piseth was particularly angry: 'In every school, there are children [who] don't have enough chairs to sit on and we waste our forest.'

Local environmental activists explained that when they notify forestry officials that they will patrol the forest, they never catch illegal loggers, but when they don't, they always do.[42] Some of the youths actually came across illegal loggers, who were local indigenous people themselves. 'They felt scared when they saw us,' the group leader recalled, 'but we told them, "Don't be scared, we do not arrest you." We ask them, "Why are [you] cutting down the tree?" They said they knew it was illegal, but they wanted to make money to support their families and children going to school.' These loggers, unlike others who carried guns,[43] were ashamed of what they were doing and lied to their families about where they got their money from. They sold wood to a company who had arranged with the police not to arrest them.[44]

The group was told not to post photos to avoid alerting authorities to their trip. Some posted on Facebook when they got back, but most kept their trip a secret from their parents. Piseth explained that his mother thinks these trips are 'too dangerous': 'She starts to worry about me when Chut Wutty and when Kem Ley is killed.' One girl said her parents thought it was dangerous for her to get involved in politics, and a boy said his father forbade it because 'he has experience from Pol Pot regime … he feels very frightened for what happened in the past'. The group leader said that parents ban their children from participating 'because they hear the threats from politicians. And some, they hear about people who were killed … Kem Ley. There is the news that makes people feel scared and afraid of being in political action.'[45]

The fourteen members of the group, including the leader, were all in their teens or early twenties. They had innocent faces with wide eyes and a nervous air of courage. Many of them had told their parents that they would not vote, sometimes causing family ruptures. Piseth's mother blurted out, 'You are crazy! You are in the CPP Family Book!' Cheang Sokha, the leather-skinned leader of the Youth Resource Development Program, had told me that in 2013, when the CNRP was riding through Phnom Penh, the young people had 'killed a political fear' that the old generation had, but their own fears were now written across their faces.[46]

One boy, with a surprisingly deep, husky voice, admitted, 'I have thought about Chut Wutty. When I go to the field, I think about this.' Piseth shared that he often felt scared: 'You know, once, I had a dream of being killed. Being tangled. One dream I was shot. Three times in that dream. And really, I scared of that. Everybody is scared of death. But I cannot let my fear occupy my life. Maybe we can escape, but we cannot stop fighting.'[47]

CHAPTER 30

YOUR AIM IS ONE

Not all those opposed to the CPP supported Sam Rainsy's call for an election boycott. Ou Ritthy told me, 'I am so disappointed – our democracy is young and we keep telling people to go to vote as it is part of democracy. Now the situation has changed, and now we tell them not to vote. For less-informed citizens, they could be confused – what is democracy about?'[1]

Kannitha, a long-time admirer of Rainsy, was stern when I asked what she thought of the boycott: 'I don't support that action. To appeal for people not to vote, it is something we should not do, something like abuse the rights of people. To me, citizen should vote.'[2] She thought Rainsy was wrong to ask people to boycott the election when he wasn't living in Cambodia experiencing the pressure everybody else was.[3]

Rotha, the youthful husband who rode a motorbike in support of the CNRP in 2013, had also become disillusioned.[4] Rotha had supported Sam Rainsy since high school. I asked him if he would have still voted CNRP if Rainsy was in Cambodia. 'If he still in the country, united with Sokha and had not joined the assembly, yes, would still have supported. He was away in South Korea when they issue an arrest warrant. He said that he would come back even if he would die, but at the last moment, he changed his mind and went to France. He always changed his mind.'

'Was it then that you changed your mind about supporting him?' I asked.

'Uh-huh. He is not real with the supporters. When the CNRP was dissolved by the CPP, he said that the CNRP would never be dissolved. He said it right at the last minute. Then he said that even if dissolved, they would set up a new CNRP before the election. It did not happen. Then he said, "Stay home and win." It changed every time so we cannot trust him.'

He told me, 'I will go to vote. It's my right. CPP could win all seats and change the constitution ... But he [Sen] needs a two-thirds majority, so if we go to vote and deny them two-thirds, we can stop them. Another thing, it can keep people to practise their rights. Even though we will not win the election, they know that they go to vote every five years. We know that CPP will win this election, but not by 100 per cent, and that is important.'

Across Cambodia, support for Rainsy among those opposed to the CPP was beginning to waver, even splinter. A splinter had already occurred in 2014 when, before he was assassinated, Kem Ley and six others formed the Grassroots Democratic Party. Yeng Virak, a human rights campaigner who had been jailed along with Kem Sokha, became its president. Virak, Ley and other party founders had been influential activists within the CNRP but became disillusioned in the aftermath of the 2013 election. They were disappointed that the CNRP had not prepared for the inevitable post-election disputes, failing to gather evidence for their complaints and denouncing the results too quickly 'because they felt so proud' about how much support they had, as Virak put it. When the CNRP began to negotiate with the CPP, Virak felt the CNRP had focused on attaining positions, such as chairmanship of five largely powerless parliamentary committees, rather than negotiating policies and legal amendments: 'The sad thing was the behaviour of the leader. It's like, "Okay, guys, I've got this. You can trust me. We've got the main messages and can explain to people about everything later."'[5]

Virak watched laws being passed without discussion or debate. The National Assembly became 'like a machine'. He and others concluded that the CNRP 'will always be an opposition party, because of how they structure themselves – a one-man show'.[6] The Grassroots Democratic Party began building political participation at a local level, with members deciding on policies and leadership. 'These parties [CPP and CNRP] only produce followers,' said Virak. 'Our mission is to produce good leaders.'[7]

Lacking resources, candidates and a well-known spokesperson after Kem Ley returned to being an independent commentator, the Grassroots Democratic Party only contested twenty-seven of Cambodia's 1600 communes in the 2017 local elections, winning just five councillors in total. It could have had more when the CNRP was dissolved but it refused to accept its share of the CNRP's redistributed seats.

In his fifties, Yeng Virak evoked a 1980s-era. Lech Wałęsa with his bushy grey moustache, rare in clean-shaven Cambodia. As we spoke, he kept shifting, unable to find a comfortable position while explaining why the GDP was participating in an election he did not believe was free or fair: 'The opposition party needs to be realistic. The election will go ahead. If you refuse to join, you unintentionally let the guy win forever. You give the guy a two-thirds majority and then [the CPP] do what they want.'[8]

Virak did not believe the boycott would be effective because foreign governments would recognise the new government regardless. 'Will foreign governments refuse to shake the hand of Hun Sen? Will they close their embassies? Will they cut diplomatic ties? If not, then CPP will be internationally recognised and will have a massive majority and things will carry on.'[9] An ambassador to one of the EU's most powerful nations had told Virak that some European countries will 'shake hands' with Hun Sen. Australia had already drunk champagne with him, after pledging $40 million in aid because Cambodia agreed to take six refugees from Iran, Syria and Myanmar who had made their way to Australia.[10] Virak said the scale of China's support rendered diplomatic objections largely impotent and that any 'economic embargo may have worked in the old days of the Cold War, but not now'.[11]

Virak had tried to persuade CNRP leaders and supporters to join the GDP, or at least vote for it, but was accused of betraying democracy and of being a CPP puppet.[12] I asked Virak if it would make a big difference if Rainsy encouraged people to support the GDP, to which he replied, 'Yes, but it will not happen.'

Sam Rainsy did not speak to Virak before calling for an election boycott. When I asked why, Virak could only say, 'Sam Rainsy is not the type.'

The chief executive of one of Cambodia's largest charities complained to me about the lack of cooperation between these parties: 'After the election, you can talk about your different aims, but before, your aim is one.' I asked him why the respective leaders had not worked together. Referring to Rainsy predominantly, he replied caustically, 'It is because they are full of elegance.'[13] May Titthara thought the opposition had returned to 2012 when, divided, they spent more time criticising each other than the ruling CPP.[14]

After consulting with local members, the GDP's ruling committee voted to participate in the 2018 election. They recognised that the CNRP's dissolution was an 'injustice' but they wanted to present Cambodians with an alternative to the CPP. There were more than half a million voters who had not voted for the CPP or the CNRP at the last election. Virak thought it reasonable to offer these voters, and former CNRP voters not joining the boycott, the option to vote for change.[15]

Many doubted the GDP's effectiveness, though, as its leaders were little known and, with few resources or activists, half of the country may never hear about its campaign. Chamroeun, ideologically close to the GDP, dismissed their chances. 'No, they are not credible enough to win any seat. They may win one or two because of the favour of the CPP,' he said, indicating the CPP may lend support to other parties to make it seem like a genuine multi-party election. 'If they come far, they will be crushed. If they gain 55 [seats] in 20 years maybe it would be okay, but if they gain that many in the next election, it will just be like that. Gone.'

Given what had happened to Kem Ley, I asked Virak what he thought would happen if the GDP did well. His reply was affable, but displayed hints of fear: 'Hope for the best and prepare for the worst.' Having been in jail before, Virak knew what the worst could entail and his tone became steely as he continued: 'If we get to be that popular, let them beat us up. We will let them arrest and jail us. That is fine. They can arrest us all. We will not go anywhere. We have an agreement if they arrest one, we will all go to be arrested the next day. If they dissolved the main opposition again, there would be an even bigger scandal.'[16]

Virak was doing his best to make a bad election good. He was calling old friends in charities, pleading with them to monitor the vote, but to no avail. The GDP had lost some support in recent times as Kem Ley's brother had created his own party and spoken favourably of Hun Sen, and Ley's widow vocally supported Rainsy's Clean Fingers campaign.[17] Dismissed by CNRP leaders, let down by its former friends and ignored by the national media, Virak's party faced an immense challenge. Virak did not talk about the number of seats they would win, saying only that they were endeavouring 'to maintain the democratic space to maintain hope'.[18]

Cambodia was reduced to hoping that hope could survive.

CHAPTER 31
ENDGAME

The evening before the election, I had doughy, thick-crusted seafood pizza with Maly, the woman in red who made friends with kangaroos outside her window in Australia. She had once brought her family to this chain restaurant to show them what pizza was, and it remained their favourite.

Slurping on a giant cola refill, elfin Maly told me about yet another Cambodian party leader: the League for Democracy's Khem Veasna, whom she said 'can win my heart with his speaking'.

Maly first heard Veasna speak in 2008, when a university professor recommended she listen to one of his speeches. 'Back then, I didn't care about politics. I was young and taught not to talk about politics. My mind opened when I start to listen to him. The way he explains is, to me, so clear. Somehow, it is logical.'[1]

Maly believed Veasna's eight-point vision for Cambodia was the path towards real change. Eschewing promises of higher wages or immediate benefits, Veasna proposed structural reform: term limits for the Prime Minister; MPs independent of party control; greater legal rights for individuals against the government; elections for village chiefs; and the Prime Minister's power to appoint army generals withdrawn.

Of the nineteen parties competing with the CPP, twelve had never competed in an election before, and it was only the more established League that appeared to be gaining support. On the last day of the campaign, tens of thousands attended a League rally in Phnom Penh. My friend Rotha said it echoed the early days of the CNRP when people contributed their own money and campaigned into the night. The League even copied the CNRP's call-and-response method: 'Is the League big enough?' someone would ask, with the masses bellowing, 'The League is very big now!'[2]

The League may have been getting bigger, but it was still dwarfed by the CPP.

A few weeks before the election, I was in Battambang, a relatively prosperous town where farmers in the surrounding countryside can sometimes harvest twice a year. Battambang does not have the tourists of Siem Reap or the chaotic bustle of Phnom Penh. It sits on a river, where locals enjoy picnicking and exercising. A concrete art deco market serves as the town's focal point, surrounded by shaded streets of French colonial architecture that house a mix of artists' galleries, tailors and hip cafés. The countryside is lush and expansive, dotted with the odd hilltop temple. One afternoon, I decided to ride along a back road towards Phnom Sampov, where there is a hilltop temple and a cave from which millions of bats fly at sunset. Driving along on my Honda Dream 125, every few seconds I passed a newly erected CPP sign stuck into the grass by the roadside. Hundreds of Hun Sens stared back at me.

Soon after, I met Bunroeun, the ageing councillor in nearby Banteay Meanchey. At his house I noticed a CPP sign beside his front gate, near his stockpile of rubber boots, which he sells at various markets. Bunroeun told me CPP officials put it up when he was away and he dare not take it down. I then noticed a small CPP poster stuck on the wall of his house near a CPP flag. Catching my glance, he explained that he took the poster and flag because 'I did not feel that I had power to deny. I took them to remain safe.'

Bunroeun had decided to vote. 'I must go to vote because of my safety. I am targeted by the CPP – the key people here [in his commune] get me to vote. They have the power to do whatever they want. I am important because I was CNRP.'[3] Bunroeun knew that some younger councillors had fled and his provincial CNRP director had left for France,[4] but he told me: 'I cannot. I don't know where to go. If they want me to be in jail, sure, I will be in jail.'[5]

Hunched on a small chair on his front porch, elbows leaning heavily on his knees, he told me that he thought Rainsy was wrong to ask people like him not to vote. 'Rainsy said that if we stay at home, we will win. He should not say like that. He puts people in positions of pressure. Now they have trouble ... Rainsy should not say bad things about people who go to vote. He is okay, but those in Cambodia are not okay.'[6]

With the CPP ascendant, Cambodians were preparing themselves for life post-election. Rithisak, my friend who had grown up in the refugee camps, told me that more people were trying to get a CPP card: 'If somebody comes to accuse you of something, if you have a CPP card, you are protected.' He did not have one and had been told he would have to wait a long time to get one. Trying to curry favour, his wife asked to help campaign for the CPP and was granted a CPP t-shirt in return.[7]

On the last day of campaigning, I went to the largest rally Cambodia had ever seen, with 250,000 people all wearing light blue or pristine white CPP polo shirts. The main stage was on Phnom Penh's Diamond Island, but there were too many people to fit into that vast plaza, so tens of thousands spilled out onto nearby boulevards and parks, watching Hun Sen give his address via gigantic screens.

'Recently we have taken legal measures to eliminate a group of traitors who attempted to topple a lawful government and to bring the country to war,' boomed Sen. 'If we didn't block them with an iron fist, the country would have come under another war.'[8]

I wandered through the rally, nodding and saying hello to people confused at my presence. Some waved their CPP flag and smiled. A couple stood near me, nearly building the courage to ask why I, a foreigner, was there as we nodded along to bands pumping up the crowd with pop music. The moto-taxi driver who used to sit outside the house I stayed in – the one the family never conversed with – was there for work. His hair was slicked back, with a side parting, and he wore shiny leather shoes. Smiling broadly, he shared his luck at becoming a driver for important people in government, a job he had got through his brother. Insisting that I share in his good fortune, he bought more food than we could possibly eat, urging me to try a little of everything.

After the speeches were done, people began to file away, and cavalcades of vehicles spread out in different directions throughout the city to spend the day campaigning. As they went, the concluding words of Hun Sen would have been ringing in their ears: 'Remember this: it is only people who go to vote that support democracy. Those who oppose the election destroy the nation and democracy, which should be handled with zero tolerance.'[9]

○

I asked Maly about the 2013 election. She said she had wanted to join the protests, but something had stopped her. She wasn't scared; it was more like an invisible force froze her, caused by her upbringing and culture.

Maly thought about asking her mother if she realised that her daughter wanted to be out there protesting too, but she found it too difficult to bring it up. She thinks it 'shameful' that she remained absent from the rallies while 'enjoying the fruits of other people's labour'. It is 'terrible that citizens do not care about politics in their own country' – even if she understands why.[10]

'Our current people are shaped by the education system of thirty years in the past,' explained Maly. 'They shape who they are nowadays. They just imitate each other and memorise the past.'

Maly said her mother has been brought up to be 'deaf and blind', dominated by her husband and then her sons. I was interested in hearing her mother's experience, but Maly said her mother would find it very strange to be asked for her reflections. If I asked for her mother's opinion, even on simple things, her mother wouldn't volunteer an answer as she has never learnt how to think for herself. She has never been allowed.

There is a book on Cambodia written by Swedish anthropologists in the 1990s called *When Every Household Is an Island*. It describes the deep obligations that people have to their family, but not necessarily to the wider community. I asked Maly if she thinks familial obligations come at the expense of societal ones. 'It's really difficult for people to protect other families. In our culture, we mind our own business, and when we see somebody else lower than us, we are happy. And when we see them higher, we are sad.' With an academic's detached curiosity, she observed, 'It is interesting.'

'What do people think when they see land activists in jail?' I asked. 'Do people see that and think *that it is bad and I need to do something*?'

'It is like somehow we are scared, so if there is no effect on us, we feel lucky ... Especially older people, they say "Don't interfere with politics!" Sometimes I tell my mum, "Because we are not affected it is easy for us not to do anything, but [if we] put ourselves in those situations ..."'[11]

One of Cambodia's few psychiatrists has written that Cambodians have learnt 'the one who survives is the one who is skilful at being deaf and blind', while another concludes that 'the permanent level of anxiety among Cambodians is unbelievable'.[12] Many are still living with the Khmer Rouge quite literally: the man who tortured one of Sophal's relatives lives just down the road from him, a common enough situation after the peace deal reintegrated Khmer Rouge officials, often into positions of local government. The widespread anxiety means that, according to a Norwegian specialist who trains Cambodian psychiatrists, 'the Cambodian perspective is very short-term. They can't believe in peace; they believe most conflict must lead to violence.'[13] Their fear is not just a fear of the past, but a fear that the past will return.

Kosal, the CPP official who employed a former CNRP commune chief, believes that the enduring effects of the Khmer Rouge regime has 'destroyed [the nation's] soul', making Cambodians 'like zombies': 'My mother-in-law said before [the Khmer Rouge] we have a lot of social order. Brother respect brother. Now it's different. Different mindset. The moral, the soul. My mum told me that in the Khmer Rouge, there's a line of starving people tied by a thread, a tiny rope. And they don't do anything! If they break the thread, they get shot. Twenty people in the line and a thirteen- or fourteen-year-old holding a gun, and nobody dare do anything because they lost soul.'[14]

Kosal is dismayed at this submission to authority, which the Director of the Documentation Center of Cambodia has said was learnt because in order to survive you could not react to violence, even when watching someone's execution. 'Everybody was passive ... You pretended to be dead [inside].'[15] Now, he believes the same behaviour has 'become the norm ... that's what's scary'. It is those who cannot feign indifference that face the wrath of government.

Reflecting on the fates that befall those who refuse to stay quiet, like his ADHOC colleagues and Chut Wutty, my friend Karuna told me, 'I feel such pity for those who have a conscience.'[16]

Dav Ansan, the man who works closely with Hun Many in his youth organisation, once worked as a legal practitioner in the Khmer Rouge Tribunal. He said that role was a 'privilege' because he discovered so much about Cambodia's history. 'Frankly speaking, the way we learn about our own history is limited ... Even the older generation who really got experience of the Khmer Rouge, they only knew about what happened in their own village. To go from village to another village, you needed a special pass. They didn't know what was happening elsewhere.'[17]

I recalled interviewing Heng, a retired provincial police chief who had worked in the police and security services for more than thirty years since the fall of the Khmer Rouge in 1979. When I asked what he did as a police chief, a position he attained latterly, he described fighting the Khmer Rouge in the 1980s and early 1990s. I asked him about the biggest challenges when working as police chief, and he returned to when he was an ordinary policeman fighting the Khmer Rouge, who 'kept coming'. I asked him why people join the police in Cambodia and he told me, 'Many people volunteered to fight Pol Pot.' Even when I began questions with 'Since the year 2000 ...', Heng would drift back to the Khmer Rouge.[18] In Cambodia, it is not that people hold onto the past, it is the past that holds onto people.

As I listened to Maly unburden her frustrations about Cambodian society, she twice mentioned an argument with her mother, whom she often feels talks in a different language to her, the day before. Taking the invitation to enquire, I got the full story. Maly revealed that her family was pressuring her to vote; she told them that the CNRP said you would be a traitor to your country if you voted. Her mother, supported by her sisters, told Maly to stop talking about politics – the government had said bad things may happen if you didn't vote. Maly exploded, yelling that her mother 'had a tumour on her brain from Pol Pot'.[19] There was silence, then hurt, then tears. Maly didn't mean to upset her mother, who, like many, is stricken by fear of the 'terrors' coming back. Even so, Maly is desperate for Cambodia to find its soul again.

Ansan has seen the same fear in his own family. 'If you reach out to the older generation, they still have some kind of trauma,' he told me. 'My parents, 6.00 or 7.00pm, they call: "Please get home." During my grandparents' time ... whenever the rain come, they tried to catch the water because, before, not enough water. And rice stock. Has to be full up. All the time. Afraid of the war, afraid of instability. Whenever they hear bad news anymore, they just call us up to come back home right away. They still have that way of thinking. That trauma.'

Unsurprisingly, Cambodia has incredible rates of post-traumatic stress disorder and suicide. More than half of people assessed in one province were classified as highly anxious.[20] The effects have been passed down from one generation to the next: a study found that the more children of Khmer Rouge survivors know about their parents' trauma, the more they 'parrot their parents' aberrant behaviour' and even begin to 'see danger when there is no danger'.[21] Ansan believes this has created emotional instability within Cambodians. 'Even though we have been in full peace since 1998, I see the mind of the people are not really stable yet. Look at what happened in 2013 ... Why after the counting at the polling station was there violence?'[22]

Ansan was not just saddened but scared by the recent violence against Vietnamese citizens: the cars being burnt and the hospital being ransacked on Veng Sreng Street. When Karuna told me he thought that the Veng Sreng protestors could have taken the whole city if they had guns, there was a trace of awe. CPP families would have felt quite differently, though.

Veng Sreng Street reminded Ansan of the Thai Embassy burning in 2003. 'A radio station broadcast a few words, a rumour only, that the Khmer Embassy in Thailand was under attack by Thai people and that a Thai movie star said that Angkor Wat was owned by Thailand,' he explained. 'That's all. But the students burned down the Thai Embassy.' Hundreds of Cambodians had ransacked the embassy before setting it alight. They moved on to loot and burn Thai-owned hotels and businesses, forcing 600 Thai people to be evacuated by Thailand's air force, as Cambodian police largely stood by. The episode still haunted Ansan: 'That was the first time that I saw the flames so high with my own eyes, and I can still see that. My house was next to the burning factories. And nobody cared because the sense of nationalism was too strong.

'And who did that?' he continued rhetorically. 'Law students! Not uneducated. From that example, I draw my own assessment. We need to do more about the minds of Cambodian people. The flames are still there and they can be excited quite easily … the opposition use the rhetoric of racial discrimination. It's really destructive. It's really dangerous for our society. They should be smarter about their politics and getting more votes. They should not use hatred. Class. The rich and poor.'

Ansan also mentioned the battle between CPP and FUNCINPEC in 1997. He had a class next to a hospital and when he arrived, there was a hole in the wall caused by a rocket and shrapnel littered the ground. 'That's the first time that I saw rocket landing on a roof. The first time that I heard rocket launchers and could feel them … People just ran away from the centre … It looked like the picture of 1975, like the evacuation [of Phnom Penh].[23] You see the smoke. You see the people running, walking, cycling. Getting whatever they could take with them.'

A young Ansan raced to the market, afraid that looters would pillage the family's stall. Over several trips, Ansan ferried as much as his small body could carry. 'It was bad. That was the first time that I experience it and it is still there.' His voice dropped. Referring to the flames that still burn inside Cambodians from decades of trauma, Ansan muttered to himself, 'It is still there.'

There was a long pause before Ansan explained that these experiences made his generation different from his children's. He doesn't believe his children would understand a world where adults had so little education they would shoot guns into the air to stop the rain. 'Myself, I am first generation since Khmer Rouge. I am 1G. My children are 2G. They now reach puberty. Their way of thought is quite different from my time, and my time is quite different from my parents'. My parents had to travel to escape war. Fear for their lives. I did not experience that but still felt effects from the war – malnutrition, poor conditions … In primary school, I need to queue to get milk that came from humanitarian Red Cross, Vietnam, the Soviet Union. I needed to save it for my sister at home. We didn't have milk at home because of the economic embargo in the 1980s.'

During Ansan's time at school, Cambodia moved from being a communist country in civil war, to administered by the UN, to a booming free-market economy. 'When I reach high school, the country changed from one-party state and planned economy to free market, and there were a lot of changes during that time. A new way of life had to be adopted. Open up: not just the country, but the people too. Influx of dollar because of UNTAC. The first time people saw the dollar. Millions of dollars came in. I myself saw a lot of new things that I had never seen before. Even the cans of milk imported from Thailand. I still remember the taste was very, very good. Sweet and tasty. One can was worth everything. You can imagine, during the economic embargo, not enough to eat. Just humanitarian food.'

The drive to support future generations had led Anasan to work with Hun Many's youth organisation. He was campaigning with Hun Many before the 2013 election when they encountered a raucous CNRP crowd, angry with the CPP. Their inflamed passions reminded him of the students attacking the Thai Embassy in 2003. 'On national road 5, the CNRP had many motorbikes, flags. They just stop there. They get more crowded and all converge. We get jammed and stuck and some of the activists insult my boss – "*chuon kbot cheeit*" (traitor), "*Yuon*". Shouting, throwing bottles. At that moment, the only way is to stay calm or if they get worse, run away. I did not expect that in 2013. My expectation was that this society, country, should be more civilised, more mature in exchanging ideas. Ten or twenty years ago, we exchanged bullets. Fighting … I did not want to see that anymore. In 2013, I believed that we would be much better.'

I asked if Ansan thought that the CNRP and their supporters had made clear in 2013 what change they wanted.

'That's what make it dangerous. Cambodia was the experiment in the 1970s when the Lon Nol regime led a coup against Sihanouk [which precipitated the Khmer Rouge]. The same rhetoric against Sihanouk when they said "*kbal Yuon, kluon Khmai*": "the head is Vietnamese even though the body is Khmer". Or too close to China. Repeating history … Unfortunately, it happened for some people in some countries that they want change and it has proved to be very destructive. Very unfortunate for them. That is another eye-opening experience.'

Ansan was referring to the colour revolutions that led to violence or civil war in countries such as Syria, Libya and Egypt. The Cambodian government distributed videos of these hellish infernos, warning the same could happen in Cambodia if the CPP was not in control. Ansan saw

Cambodia's youth as an 'opportunity for this country' but also 'a danger'.

One evening before the 2013 election, sitting on my balcony, I watched the grandfather of the household below me. He was on the pavement saying goodbye to a visitor when a small moto-parade of CNRP supporters weaved down our street noisily, thumbing their nose at the government, calling for change. The grandfather, a former senior government official and CPP member, watched impassively as they motored past. He stood for a moment looking down the street after them, then turned and walked back inside. That was the only time that I ever seriously thought about what CPP supporters were thinking when the massive protests swept across the country. I wanted to ask the grandfather what was in his mind as he watched the CNRP supporters, but shied away from broaching the subject of politics.

It was Ansan, firmly ensconced within the CPP by 2013, although politically moderate, who gave me this perspective. 'During the last election, the public sentiment was sooooo different, including with my parents, my neighbours. Everywhere. They told their children not to travel far. Stay close to family. Don't go out at night. Stock canned fish, dried food, rice.'

Talking more with Ansan, I learnt that you can tell what Cambodians, often stony-faced or hiding behind a fixed smile, are thinking by looking at the price of rice. Rice, synonymous with the word for food, is sacred to a people who still remember famine. Hun Sen knows this intimately, coming to power as the rice harvest of 1984 failed disastrously.[24] Rice has become a security blanket, with some Cambodians packing it into their suitcase when going overseas, just in case the destination doesn't have any. Rumours of impending discord fuels panic buying, sending the price skywards and the urban poor into hunger. Rice, next to water, is the staple of Cambodian life; its price can be the difference between one daily meal or two. Before the 2018 election, unlike in 2013, the price of rice remained steady.

'That to me is really positive,' said Ansan. 'In their thought, in their mind, some stability in their mind. And I am really happy to see that. I think it is a good foundation for society to move forward. An election is just one day. After an election, life continues. Need to go to work, earn money, go to school. That's what I want to see in the future.'

I wanted to talk again to Sin Rozeth, the ousted CNRP Commune Chief of the O'Char Commune in Battambang. Since being forced out, she had no party, an infirm mother and a guiding force who was in exile. In a country where the CPP dominates all, Rozeth had a black mark against her.

Rozeth's noodle restaurant in Battambang town had space for about sixty, but on the day I visited there were only two customers, with as many waitresses slumped over a table, resting their heads on their arms. Even so, she refused to take my money for *noom banh chok*, her speciality dish – a traditional Khmer rice-noodle curry that combines fish gravy, cucumber, banana blossom, lily stems, basil and mint.

The MP for Battambang had seen former CNRP officials – including Chea Chiv, who had taken the photo of clean fingers – talking with Rozeth in her restaurant. The MP accused her of using her restaurant as a base for a 'rebel movement', warning that it would be 'really dangerous for Rozeth and should not be tolerated'.[25] Tongue-in-cheek, Rozeth hung a banner outside that read, *Rozeth's shop welcomes all guests, but not rebels.* In the new Cambodia, this was enough to get her summoned to a meeting with the Governor of Battambang Province.[26]

People started to avoid Rozeth, scared to be seen near her. A taxi driver taking one of my friends from Phnom Penh to Battambang refused to drop him off at her restaurant in case the police took his registration number and gave it to police in Phnom Penh. Of the hundreds of interviews I did for this book, it was only for Rozeth that I struggled to find somebody willing to interpret for me. People would pull out when learning who I was meeting. I eventually hired an interpreter from a town hours away.

Despite such reactions, Rozeth was still giving interviews to journalists covering the election, and still posting photos on Facebook of her holding up a clean finger. She had begun selling handbags, doing anything to make ends meet.

Rozeth said that sometimes people from her old commune would visit, though not many. 'Some of them are sad and feel regret. Even today, some of them come to me for help. Come to my restaurant to talk. They know that I worked hard.'[27]

'Some former CNRP members have gone to live in Thailand. Have you considered doing that?' I asked her.

'I will not run away as I need to be here for my mother. My mother wants me to go to Thailand but I will not go. My mother is seventy-four now. Before, I could keep her with friends or relatives, but not now.'

A former senior CNRP politician, disaffected with Rainsy, had created the Khmer Will Party to contest the elections, garnering support from some former CNRP officials. Already knowing the answer, I asked Rozeth if she would join this newly formed party. Although her answers usually ran for minutes in an impressive display of lung capacity, this time she gave a short, curt 'No.' Her face was blank. There was no more to be said or asked about it.

Figuring that I may as well ask the unpopular questions together, I inquired if she would be voting in the upcoming election. Rozeth was slightly more expansive this time. 'For me, no.'

'What do you think about those parties that are participating?' I asked.

'A party that was supported by more than three million people and dissolved cannot be replaced by small parties. They are all just ... they are not important and just help the CPP gain legitimacy.'

Before I went to meet Rozeth, a porter at my hotel confided that he admired Rozeth because she was not scared, unlike him and everybody else.[28] Sitting in her near-empty restaurant, looking into her brown eyes as she spoke to me, I sensed a young woman alone, and asked if there were times when she was scared.

'Yes, I am scared. Everyone is scared and gets scared in this society, so it's no different for me. Sometimes, a gang comes at night and they curse at me. They shout, they threaten. I am a woman and I get a lot of intimidation.' I knew that police with AK-47s had patrolled slowly past her restaurant.[29]

'Everybody is scared a little, but not everybody does what you do,' I said. 'What do you think makes you different?'

'Personally, I put benefits for the entire nation as top priority. Of course we love our family, but we have one life, so we have to speak out about what we want and speak our true feelings, and not just for our family but for the whole country.'

'This time is the most important period,' Rozeth continued. 'Politics is more important now than at other times. Lots of intimidation. Pressure. People in jail. This is a critical time for people to be involved in politics.'[30]

After leaving her restaurant, my hard-found interpreter asked what I thought of Rozeth as we rode away on his Honda Dream 125 motorbike. An academic who does not care for the antics of politics, he showed surprising levels of concern for this woman he had never met before we began working together. He kept returning to Rozeth as we sat in a café, shaken himself by the visible stress that she was under. It was not just Rozeth, but all of Cambodia that was on edge as the election day drew closer.

CHAPTER 32

ELECTION DAY

Even at night, after the traffic had stopped and there was only the odd person picking at rubbish, Cambodia always filled me with wonder. The Independence Monument lit up in an empty boulevard; street children in Wat Botum park doing cartwheels; a barber shop transformed into a disco bar; a late-night restaurant crammed with people eating pig-intestine porridge at midnight. Phnom Penh is a city alive with possibility.

There were days when the city emptied, though. During Pchum Ben, when ancestors are remembered, everyone returns to their family homeland and you feel like an intruder on a deserted film set. Cambodian New Year can feel like that too, with markets closed and my favourite street-food seller absent from her corner.

The day of the 2018 election was like this.

Thousands of buses and minivans had left Phnom Penh, full of people pressed to the sides and hanging out the open back door, travelling back to their homeland to vote. The evening before, Maly and I had struggled to find a restaurant open for dinner. On election morning, I awoke to a Phnom Penh that felt sullen, like an overcast grey Sunday in England.

Polling stations opened at 7.00am. Shortly after, I cycled past Kab Ko Market, which would normally be buzzing with shoppers and people eating pork and rice for breakfast, but all was quiet. There was one girl in her early twenties taking a photo of her clean finger while the rest of her family stood a few metres away, just having voted, inked fingers to prove it. I cycled towards a Wat Botum park absent of morning exercisers.

I travelled along Sihanouk Boulevard, past Hun Sen's compound and the Independence Monument, towards Olympic Stadium. I could have cycled on the other side of the road, against the traffic, without even fearing a horn, so empty were the roads. I passed three small food stalls on the pavement. One seller sat on the ground picking at the underside of his foot, while another sat on a chair staring into space.

I turned the corner, approaching the back of Orussey Market, where there were normally stallholders selling spit-roasted ducks. The roads running alongside the giant indoor market were barricaded as I gently pedalled my old, upright-style bicycle towards the marquees that had been erected as polling stations.

A policeman standing at the perimeter rope looked towards me. I slowed and hopped off my bicycle, trying to smile innocently. I greeted the pot-bellied policeman in deliberately broken Khmer. Stony-faced, he raised his right hand, pointing to a side street. Looking beyond him, I saw five sombre Cambodians coming out of a tent with ink-stained forefingers. They did not even glance at each other as they started their motorbikes and left.

Cycling away from the market, down Street 166, where all the tailors with old Singers usually stitch and sew, I went to the riverside. It was deserted save for some people solemnly traipsing in and out of marquees.

Travelling back around to the Russian Market, after two hours of silence I was glad to meet Pich, the man who works with trade unions, and his wife for coffee. I watched other people in the café glance at Pich's clean finger.

Later that morning, Maly texted to say she had voted, her mother waking her up at 6.00am to make sure they were there for the polls opening at 7.00am.[1] All of her neighbours went to vote and then 'continued our living as usual', but she sensed everybody in the community watching each other: 'We just keep watching what's going on. What are other neighbours doing? Just trying to look around. Other people look at us and we look at them.'[2]

Rotha and Soveacha voted for their party. Rotha had previously said that people felt safe to vote for the CNRP in the 2017 commune elections because nobody could know how they voted, but many, especially those in small villages, now feared rumours that commune officials had told CPP members to mark the ballot in a certain way, making it possible to identify the ballots of CPP and non-CPP members.[3]

At the other end of the country, broad-shouldered Sophal had also heard this rumour, adding that CPP members had been given instructions on how to fold their paper. Originally planning to avoid the polling station, Sophal felt he had no choice but to vote. He wanted to write 'they force me to vote' on the ballot, but he didn't dare. Instead, he ticked every box, like his sister and brother did, and made sure that he folded the paper in the same way as those around him before dropping it into the box. Steeling himself for that moment, he told me, 'I always think my body will go, but my heart will remain the same.' CPP staff smiled and asked where his parents were. Sophal said they were too ill to vote and watched as a note was scribbled next to his parents' names on the roll.[4]

Rithisak could not take that risk after being visited at home and decided to stain his finger. Channa, the dimpled factory worker, voted and upon returning home told her brother-in-law to turn the television off so she didn't have to hear the results. Sreyleak, previously adamant that nobody could pressure her to vote, found herself at the polling station too. Piseth, the young man who had nightmares of being shot, avoided it by telling his mother that he couldn't find his identity card.[5] Leap, a man of both diplomacy and principle, was secure enough in his international job to refrain from voting, quietly answering others' questions that as his party was not on the list, there was nowhere for him to tick. 'This is the minimum I can do for democracy,' he told me.[6]

Conversely, Ou Ritthy voted in his first Cambodian election, finally freed from election monitoring and liaising with the media. Travelling back home to Pursat, he pondered whether he would spoil his ballot or support the party that his friend Kem Ley had established.

Sokngeng, the young CNRP councillor in Siem Reap, had come back from Thailand and shut himself in his room to sleep most of the day.[7]

Rozeth started the day by posting old photos in which she had been captured pointing, just happening to show a clean finger. She then took a day trip with four friends, finding some fresh air and an opportunity to post one more photo of her holding up a finger without ink.

Pen Raksa of Transparency International lives in a village near Phnom Penh where everyone knows each other. He felt he had to vote, otherwise he would be 'known as an opposition supporter' and his family 'would be affected by the authorities'. He was out in the morning and so only went to vote at 2.00pm. When he got there, the Village Chief was sitting outside and told him which desk to vote at. Then the Chief said, 'And your wife, she has not come to vote yet.' Raksa was shocked. 'I could not believe it. I called her and asked what she was doing and if she would be coming to vote. I thought, *wow, they know everything so clearly.* So clearly.' His wife hurriedly left the house.[8]

Multiple people described to me the same set-up at different polling stations: commune officials sitting outside, CPP party representatives monitoring voters as they came and went, and two soldiers standing guard, often in the shade of a nearby tree. A Nepali international observer said he saw CPP party representatives 'actively monitor people from places that were inappropriate' and expressed concerns about the military presence.[9]

Sophea was in the village she had spent months campaigning in, where she voted and kept a tally of how many others had, updating it hourly. The CPP had promised every village a post-election party if its turnout exceeded 90 per cent. Sophea had made sure that every villager had their voter registration card or letter authorising them to vote. Her boss had also messaged every villager, advising, *Don't let your children [returning from Phnom Penh] influence you. You must influence them.* Sophea watched the turnout rise with every hour and soar past 90 per cent. In her village, 166 people voted CPP and only fifteen voted for other parties. Every village in Sophea's commune had a turnout greater than 90 per cent.[10]

Khemera, the CPP official who had spent weeks living with villagers, never using his title of His Excellency, was in his rural commune fretting about the young people who had returned to vote: 'We spend weeks with their parents ... lots of time explaining and some were convinced and some were not. We don't mind. They have their own choice. Then the night before the election, these people come back from Phnom Penh and voila! Financially they provide to their parents. I had heard about it, but wow! And some people in Korea do the same. They call and say do not vote or we stop supporting you. Nothing we can do about it ... We had our time, and they had their bonding time. We could not force them.'

Khemera needn't have worried, as his commune had the highest increase in CPP votes in that district. 'I was surprised. I thought it would be more [than the last election], but this was beyond expectations. It wasn't what we expected because from CPP members, a few hundred increase only, but we got more than 50 per cent from CNRP people who we went to their houses and talked with.'

Khemera took a photo of himself and his colleagues on election day. There is a clear sense of camaraderie as they celebrate beside a whiteboard showing the running tally of votes from all the villages. He is in the middle, leaning back on his chair to see the camera, smiling triumphantly in a tight huddle with his friends. All the villages, having exceeded 90 per cent turnout, were guaranteed what Khemera, borrowing a phrase from his time in America, called a 'thanksgiving party'.[11]

May Titthara, who had become the editor of *Khmer Times*, went back to Svay Rieng, taking with him three old desktop computers for the school that he funds there, supporting 500 students.[12] He had been working from 6.00am to 9.00pm most days in the lead-up to the election but was interrupted two nights earlier when the government suddenly blocked all mobile phone access to the *Khmer Times* website, as well as to other news agencies that were often critical of the government. Titthara couldn't believe it and called his publisher, who was in Malaysia at the time, to see if he could help.

'He did not believe me! He said it is fine, but he looked on a desktop. I show him a picture from my phone. He said your network is not working. I said no, it is the whole country!'[13]

Other, more government-friendly news organisations were still posting online, as was the National Election Committee. In an impressive display of coordination, the NEC gave near-live updates throughout the day on the percentage of people who had voted. It also posted photos: of people queuing to vote before the polls opened; of a mother preparing to vote while holding two young children; of an old man struggling to enter the polling station being helped by two youngsters; of an old woman in a wheelchair looking confused as to why somebody wanted a photograph of her inked finger.[14] Television news stations even showed footage of people with IVs in their arms showing up to vote, and moto-taxi drivers were paid to ferry people to the polling station.[15]

The logic of 2013 had been flipped. Rainsy, the Western-educated democrat, now wanted people to stay at home; Sen, the authoritarian born from communism, wanted as many people to vote as possible. Both Rainsy and Sen saw their futures, and that of Cambodia, as dependent on one thing: how many people would vote?

Just before the polls closed at 3.00pm, I met two friends on the leafy terrace of a café, a relative oasis away from the sweaty streets. Vanna was the last to arrive, slinging his helmet over the mirror of his motorbike and casually ambling towards us, smiling at the story he had to share. When passing other motorcyclists on his way to meet us, Vanna would glance at their fingers to see if they had voted, just as everyone else was doing. Stationary at a red light, Vanna looked at the female driver to his left, and then looked again in a double-take. The top of her right forefinger was missing, and he thought to himself cheekily, *Wow, she must be a very strong supporter of Sam Rainsy.*[16]

My two friends began to show me photos of spoilt ballot papers that people had posted on Facebook. One had every box ticked; another had a big X across the page. One person had drawn a radiant sun, the logo of the old CNRP. I mentioned that the NEC had announced that 70 per cent of people had already voted by 1.00pm, prompting them to laugh in apparent disbelief. Just then, an orange Lamborghini roared down the narrow tree-lined street, ignoring the give-way junction. Vanna joked that the driver shouldn't have left it so late to get to the polling station. We laughed, knowing that such a person would have made sure their finger was stained already.

At 5.00pm, the NEC announced that the final voter turnout was 82 per cent, a figure that would later be revised to 83 per cent.[17] Fewer people voted in the 2018 national election than in the local elections of 2017, but only 150,000 less. Sam Rainsy's Clean Fingers campaign had been dashed, and with it his hopes of ever becoming Prime Minister.

I asked a few friends if anybody wanted to watch the result with me, but all politely declined. They were already bored with what they called a 'meaningless election'.[18] One or two, like Maly, watched *Radio Free Asia*'s Facebook Live showing members of the Cambodian diaspora protesting in Thailand and America from home.

I sat in a deserted rooftop bar, half-watching television coverage on my phone. The election program's host spent hours presenting graph after graph from different communes, each time following the same script: name of the first party on the list and total votes received; name of the second party on the list and total votes received, and so on, right down to the twentieth and last party on the list, the CPP. The graph showed a smattering of votes among the nineteen other parties, dwarfed by the CPP's tower at the end, which generally reached beyond 70 per cent.

When the host had gone through every commune, it was clear that the CPP had vanquished all opponents. Yeng Virak's Grassroots Democratic Party had garnered a paltry 1 per cent – one million people paid homage to Kem Ley at his funeral, but only 70,000 crossed a box in favour of his dream. The party set up by former CNRP politicians just before the election barely did any better, and even Khem Veasna's League for Democracy Party faltered, gaining only 5 per cent. Second place went to the one-in-ten people who destroyed their ballot paper in protest.

By now it was late, and I looked upon a city that for once seemed asleep. Beyond the Tonlé Sap and Mekong rivers, the glow of lights faded into darkness as concrete towers gave way to wooden houses and mud roads. Out there, fifteen million people had just put their heads down for the night, knowing that they now lived in a country where one party had won every seat in the election.

CHAPTER 33
THE NUMBERS

Yeng Virak, the President of the Grassroots Democratic Party, was despondent when I met him a week after the election. When we had last spoken, he thought voter turnout would be around 60 per cent, but he subsequently witnessed the same CPP campaigning tactics in his own village that Sophea, Khemera and Kosal used in other parts of the country. He saw the effectiveness of the 'machine' that 'pushed people to vote' and began to expect a turnout of 70 per cent.

'In my village, the Chief has a big party before election day. Big, big party. Hundreds of tables. Imagine that a village chief can organise this?! But he had staff from government to help ... including a senior officer from the national paediatric hospital who was there campaigning. The CPP pay for everything and during the concert time you could hear the names being read out of who had donated money. 10,000 riels per family. Except our house, of course.'

Virak would also avoid the post-election party to celebrate his village having a voter turnout above 90 per cent. He had hoped that former CNRP supporters who felt forced to vote would support the GDP, but over one million such voters switched to the CPP instead. Virak blamed this on vehement CNRP criticism of the GDP: 'Every day during the campaign, twenty-one days, there were voices to discredit GDP. They go too far. Really sad. We have these challenges. One is the climate of fear and the threats and intimidation. The big party has structures of power, money, uses state resources and structures to secure victory. On other hand, CNRP's Clean Fingers campaign is discriminating [against] us and colouring us. And civil society groups, our friends, who turn their backs on us, discriminate, create mistrust and doubt and suspicion.'[1]

Virak felt personally aggrieved by rumours that GDP leaders had received land from the CPP:[2] 'A close friend of mine from civil society, they question why and how GDP have money to campaign when they hear that [we] have no money. We save and collect from members – we make sacrifices! Activists make sacrifices …Very sad … We knew that this was not a free and fair election but join because, as I said before, whether we join or not, the election go ahead. CPP would win, and after election everybody would shake hands and continue.'

Virak was at pains to convince me that the GDP or the League for Democracy could have won three seats in Phnom Penh if people hadn't spoiled their ballots and had voted for them. Instead, the CPP had a clean sweep.[3] I reminded Virak that before the election he had hoped the GDP could do enough 'to maintain the democratic space' and asked if that was still possible without a seat in the National Assembly. Virak admitted that it would be 'difficult'. He was 'seriously concerned' that the CPP would hold every seat in the National Assembly and more than 90 per cent in the Senate, and have 99.5 per cent of all commune councillors. 'That's why we know we want to contest the election – to prevent [complete] CPP control. But now … they can do whatever they want.'

'Do you have hope that in the next five years, democracy will continue and human rights will be respected?'

'No, it's an ongoing struggle. Maybe before the election, we are too optimistic … but again, we have this culture of hope. We plan to work hard from now. Today, we already continue to educate people, raise awareness of a citizen's role, the role of parliament, our policies. We will recruit more members. And train people to be good candidates for commune council elections in 2022. We will contest in all communes.'

He fell into silence. We each looked out of the window of the Java Café, watching people sheltering from the torrential rain under the King Father's statue, contemplating what had just happened and what lay ahead.

∼

The next day, I met Hang Puthea in his office. Rather than buoyed by a high voter turnout, Puthea seemed stressed, even harassed. He was understandably tired from the demands of running an election, and he was forthright, less chatty than he had been a few weeks earlier.

Puthea quickly asserted that it had been a 'true election' that 'respected the will of the people'. He blamed Sam Rainsy for casting aspersions on the election, saying Rainsy 'confused the public' and 'continues to cause troubles'.

He recognised that people may think it 'weird' that one party won every seat, but the election followed 'the trail of democracy'. Puthea even said a few times that it was a better election than the 2017 commune council one. 'This election is better than before, in terms of the social situation being peaceful,' he said. 'Citizens do not have any concerns while going out to vote. In a previous election, cars were set on fire … This time, if the citizens are not happy, they don't need to burn cars. They just invalidate the ballot.'

Puthea dismissed the Japanese government's concern over the high number of invalid votes – nearly 600,000 – saying that even though it was 'more than before', it 'cannot be compared to the millions of valid ballots'. He also rejected the notion that there was coercion to vote. 'I observed that those who were determined not to vote, they could not maintain the stance. They went out and vote as well. It is like during Pchum Ben time … everyone goes to pagoda, you have to go too even though you don't want to … [This] cannot be considered as coercion because it is a cultural psychological issue of a nation.'[4]

Rong Chhun, Puthea's former colleague at the National Election Committee, thought the only similarity to Pchum Ben was that there had been a death. '2018 is a bad situation. It is the death of democracy in Cambodia,' he told me in a tone devoid of drama.

When I met Chhun in the small office of the Cambodian Independent Teachers' Association, he didn't, or couldn't, believe the voter turnout was so high. He had been following the National Election Committee announcements, which said that 37 per cent of people had voted by 9.00am and 58 per cent had voted by 11.00am. Chhun saw people voting first thing, but then it became 'quiet, very quiet', so he questioned how the turnout rose to over 80 per cent.[5]

He also didn't believe that only 600,000 people spoilt their ballot papers, finding it impossible that nearly five million people would vote for the CPP when less than 3.5 million did at the commune council election the year before. He called it a 'fake figure'.

May Titthara shared some of Chhun's disbelief. 'I still wonder if there is something, the black boxes, inside or not. [Turnout] is a lot …' he said. 'When I went to put my vote in the box, it was full. I wonder that maybe a lot of people come to vote … If quiet, it should be empty. I am still wondering who is going early.'[6]

Karuna from ADHOC drove out of Phnom Penh, visiting polling stations in three different provinces. He was struck by the number of police and soldiers and noted that people voted early in the morning and then left. 'We compare to previous time and not like this. [Before] they would continue to stand at the polling station. They would wait until the counting time. But this time, so silent.'

Karuna was gobsmacked by the announcement that turnout had reached 83 per cent. 'But how?' He could not square the official figure with the quiet polling stations he had witnessed.[7]

Maly doubted the results. Kannitha certainly didn't believe them, asking, 'How can I, when my eyes see something different?'[8]

The 2013 election only had a turnout of 69 per cent. It seemed inexplicable that more people could have voted in 2018 when it was so 'quiet' compared to the impassioned election of 2013. But the CPP was a victim of the erroneously inflated voter list in 2013, totalling 9.7 million people, compared to only 8.4 million in 2018. The number of people reported to have voted in 2018 was only slightly higher than in 2013, but the turnout rate in 2013 was being calculated using an inaccurate total number of voters. My explanation did little to dissuade Kannitha and Maly.[9] When I asked Rozeth for her opinion, she stated without equivocation, 'The result is not true. The election day was quiet and not many people go to vote. So it's not true.'[10]

There were also questions over how the votes were counted. Rotha watched the election results alone, as his wife and in-laws had no interest, and he observed, 'During the count, they not allow people to watch. A lot of security around.'[11]

Yeng Virak complained that many GDP members were not allowed to observe the counting, and that all polling stations stopped the public from watching too.[12] This contrasted with 2013, when people could watch votes being counted and there were a multitude of trained observers from Cambodian charities and places like Japan, the European Union and the United States. All of these groups had refused to observe this election in protest. In 2018, most observers came from Hun Many's youth organisation: they had little training and their independence was questionable. There were 500 international observers who generally praised the election, but Rotha, like many others, had no trust in them: 'We do not know where they are from. The news said they are all friends of Hun Sen. From Russia, China.'[13] A man from COMFREL voiced many people's thoughts when he ridiculed the idea that China could judge whether an election was free and fair when they didn't even have elections.[14]

As proof that proper procedures were not followed, at least some of the time, Karuna and Raksa showed me videos shared on Facebook. Sometimes, a vote counter would pick up a ballot, shout 'CPP' and then put it down without showing it to observers, as they are meant to.[15] Karuna also complained, as did Yeng Virak, that final tally sheets were not always posted on the walls of the polling station.[16] Rotha showed me photos on Facebook from one polling station that recorded the LDP as having thirty-one votes, but the final tally sheet showed zero for the LDP and thirty-one votes for another party. Rather than seeing this as a one-off mistake, Rotha saw it as the opposite: 'This is only one polling station. LDP don't have observers all around the country.'[17]

Despite sharing doubts, there was an acceptance from most of the minor parties and their supporters that their defeat was real. Titthara was 'surprised' the GDP got so few votes, while Karuna appeared disappointed that their performance was so 'weak'.[18] While the LDP submitted many complaints, they did not challenge the overall result.

If the results were generally accurate, it meant that the CPP vote had increased by around 1.5 million, which could only have happened if about that number of CNRP voters switched to the CPP rather than spoiling their ballot. Even more than the high turnout, this was proof of Hun Sen's remarkable success. Less than one year since he had banned the CNRP and imprisoned its leader, his government had persuaded, using pressure, fear, gifts and reform, over a million former CNRP voters that he was their next best choice. This baffled some Cambodians. A perplexed Rotha asked of CNRP supporters, 'Why they do like that?'[19]

The result was not a surprise for everyone, though. Both Rong Chhun and Rozeth had predicted that the CPP would win every seat as the other parties were too small, too unknown and too lacking in credibility to win enough votes.

The CPP had not been so sure. In his office three days after the election, Khemera told me that the CPP would have preferred fewer seats, and people were scratching their heads to see if there was a constitutional way not to take them all.[20] A week later, Ansan reiterated to me that the CPP leadership did not expect to win all 125 seats; he was surprised the opposition parties had not done better. Ansan's friend described the predicament that the CPP was in: it looked undemocratic that they had won every seat, but it would be even more undemocratic if the rules were amended so that seats could be shared with other parties.[21]

Phirun, the loyal civil servant, had spent many hours campaigning for the CPP. During the campaign, his wife feared their children would forget what he looked like. Phirun and his CPP colleagues felt they had worked hard and had earned the massive victory. 'The strength of the CPP is that we are not too proud of our achievements,' he told me. 'We are always careful. We always keep going to the constituency to meet people. The city members always go to the provinces to meet the people even though it's not election time. And the CPP network is *very* active, *very* organised. And they do their job.'

Modest, diligent Phirun was proud of the turnout. 'You know, before the election, there were two opposing views. One was asking people to stay home, not to cast a ballot, while the ruling party and other legitimate institutions, including the King, asked people to go and vote. Yeah, so now the turnout is very high, eighty-two point something.' Phirun paused before cheerily asking me a question he already knew the answer to. 'So, what is the voter turnout in your country?'

Phirun's good cheer changed to indignation when he brought up US- and EU-issued statements criticising the election. 'They have their right to make their statements but, I mean, what about when Donald Trump implement immigration policy that separates parents from children? The USA is the father of democracy and … they accuse Iraq of having weapons of mass destruction and then it was nowhere to be found. So? How the US explain that? "Okay, because I am a superpower, so everything I do is good, but Cambodia, small, poor country, if you don't listen to me, I don't support everything you say." Is that it?'

Phirun was clearly irked so I let him continue. 'Or the European Union. The CNRP have good connections with European Union and America. It is easy to understand [why they criticise the election]. You know, I think we [are] very lucky to have international observers to witness the real election here … Without those international observers, the former CNRP will say more. See?! CNRP are politicians. You know what politicians are like. They are good at talking, criticising, but when they become leader of the country themselves, you think they are perfect?'[22]

For Phirun and the CPP, the election had become a matter of national pride, and international criticism was offending their honour.

The next day I had lunch with Maly, who, like most Cambodians, was mystified by my questions about the veracity of the election results. My interest was odd to her because most Cambodians had known what the result would be ever since the CNRP was banned: the CPP would remain in government and Hun Sen would be Prime Minister. It didn't really matter if the CPP won every seat or only 90 per cent of them; they could still do whatever they wanted. The real question, Maly told me while looking up from a bowl of pasta, was 'what is the story behind the numbers?'[23]

CHAPTER 34

CAMBODIA CHANGING

I have known Davuth since my first day in Cambodia. He is a compact man who always moves with purpose. When he is not working long hours, spending time with family or attending weddings to maintain his networks, he dances in aerobic exercise groups at Phnom Penh's outdoor stadium. These activities represent the four responsibilities that guide his life: leading his organisation and staff; being a good husband and father; securing his family's position and safety; and maintaining his health so that he can accomplish the other three.

Cambodia's civil war in the early 1970s forced many to leave their villages and head for the sanctity of Phnom Penh. Davuth's family made this move in 1974, just a year before the Khmer Rouge took over. Davuth was not even a teenager when the regime forced every single Cambodian to leave Phnom Penh to work in the rice fields, in a mass evacuation of more than one million people.

Davuth's parents were killed immediately, and he was separated from his nine siblings. Put to work sowing rice, he was often starving and could see tiny fish in the paddy but knew he would be killed for trying to quickly gulp one. He survived by eating rice gruel and whatever insects he could find.

When the CPP and the Vietnamese Army freed Cambodia from the Khmer Rouge three and a half years later, Davuth trod back to his old village, hoping to find his family. Amid the desolation, an old woman pointed him in the direction of his older sister. He found her near death and spent three days nursing her back to life. It was only after those three days that his sister finally recognised who had been caring for her. She gradually regained strength and the two children realised they needed to find somewhere to live. With no place to go, they began a long walk back to Phnom Penh.

The countryside was full of bony bodies in rags struggling to find their way back to a time and place before the Khmer Rouge. Amid this country-wide criss-crossing of the lost, Davuth and his sister stumbled into their younger sister. Reunited, the three set up life in Phnom Penh, remembering their parents and seven brothers and sisters who didn't make it.

Davuth earned a prized scholarship to study in the Soviet Union during the 1980s. After UNTAC began, he worked for an international aid organisation, impressing the expatriate leaders and progressing into more senior roles. Now an experienced executive director of a large charity, Davuth also donates time to help other charities with their governance.

Davuth is one of few leaders in the aid sector who support the CPP, although this does not blind him to their failings. After I met Duong Virorth in the Council of Ministers, Davuth took me for lunch. I shared that Virorth said the government was not trying to control charities but provide a framework for coordination and dialogue. He laughed, incredulous that Virorth could even pretend such a thing. He also dismissed Virorth's comment that some charities 'had been too quick to take to the streets', saying they had little choice.

Davuth and his family had always voted CPP, but by 2013 they were beginning to reconsider, increasingly unhappy with Vietnamese state-controlled companies gaining huge land concessions. However, they doubted that the CNRP could change the course of Vietnam's influence in Cambodia and trusted the CPP to develop and manage the country better.

After the election, Davuth felt a change in his family as they saw 'more and more terrible' things through social media. There was more 'corruption, nepotism … scrapping the people's land, logging' and the gap between rich and poor was becoming 'really huge'. By 2017, both Davuth and his wife were ready to switch to the CNRP and found it 'really, really bad' for Cambodia when the CPP disbanded it. Davuth believes Hun Sen realised he was cornered: 'If they allow the CNRP for this election, there is no way for CPP. No chance.'

Davuth's wife works in government but has never been an active campaigner for the CPP. Before the 2018 election, Davuth would tease her about voting for one of the new opposition parties, but she always pushed him away, saying, 'No, no, no.' Davuth's sister-in-law, the eldest in the household, would never countenance voting against Hun Sen and the CPP. 'Many people are the same. And older people are very much like this and I cannot blame them,' explained Davuth. 'They have lived through many regimes and are scared of it turning again. Fear of fighting. They already have suffering. Like me, families killed by Khmer Rouge. Escape from one area to another during civil war. Nobody wants to go back. They see the development of the country – peaceful. That's why people still support CPP.'

Davuth said his son, who also works for a charity, 'doesn't understand that much' about Cambodia's past. His son does not believe that civil war or the terror of the Khmer Rouge could happen again because he thinks that the UN and international community would not let it. Instead, his son spars about politics with his ageing aunt, knowing he can do so because he is her favourite. When talking about young people's understanding of the Khmer Rouge, Phirun, the loyal civil servant, said they are 'naïve' and 'don't fully understand ... Only once you experience things yourself do you know.'

Davuth sees the disagreements between generations arising from how they view present-day Cambodia. The old people, who have never been outside Cambodia's borders and did not have internet or television for most of their lives, can only compare Cambodia to what it was, to the days of civil war and the Khmer Rouge. Young people, who may have visited Thailand or Malaysia and dream of an imagined West they see in films or on social media, compare Cambodia to what it could be. His son believes Sam Rainsy could develop Cambodia along the lines of a Western country, whereas voting for the CPP was like voting for Cambodia to become a 'Chinese colony'. Two days before the election, Davuth sensed his son still had strong loyalties to the CNRP and was not sure if he would vote or not. Davuth was certain his wife would vote, as she would have to show her finger at work, and while he considered abstaining, Davuth knew that he would vote too.

Come election day, Davuth, his wife, his son and his elder sister-in-law all rose early and went to the polling station. 'It seemed like a lot of people went in my voting station. They think as Cambodian citizens, [they should] come to vote. Compared to five years ago, probably the same number of people come to vote, but people can come and vote quickly, easily and leave.'

Davuth was surprised by the overall voter turnout but didn't see any evidence of wrongdoing. 'It seems like this is actually what happened. The people are surprised but I don't think there is a lot of complaints.'

I asked him what he thought about the numbers who voted for the CPP, and he paused, taking a breath before explaining: 'No really big party that is able to compare. Even myself, I did not interest at all to look at the other parties. I knew that, actually, they don't have the capacity to manage the country ... Younger people, they never lived through this time [Khmer Rouge]. They think that those politicians, the way they treat people, not really treat fairly. But we actually have to think, who have capacity to manage the country, to make it stable? Even myself, sometimes I might change my mind but in the end I voted for CPP because I think only they are able to lead the country at this stage.'[1]

'What did your son think about it all?'

'He did not say which one he voted for but I could see that he probably changed his mind as well. He probably voted for CPP. Because there is not any political party that he wanted to vote for. Given that example of myself, of my son, possibly the vote the CPP receive is true.'

Channary was another young person who voted for the CPP, and not because of *khnorng*, fear of the Khmer Rouge or a lack of education. She voted for them because of the change she saw happening all around her.

Channary had lived in Phnom Penh's White Building, once the longest building in Cambodia. Claustrophobic flats crammed hundreds of families into a series of concrete blocks connected by unlit walkways and stairwells. As well as having a strong community of artists, especially classical dancers, there were rumours of drug users and people who sold their bodily wares. During my first weekend in Cambodia, I had nervously struggled to find the safety of an art exhibition amid the dark clamour of the White Building, having been warned by a tuk-tuk driver not to venture inside. Winding my way through alleyways, I passed a flat with its door wide open, even though nobody looked to be home. I could see a small blackboard above the kitchen table with the words *past perfect tense* and various English phrases beneath. Scrawled in chalk on the flat's concrete outside wall was a list of English words and grammatical rules. The whole house had been given over to their children's betterment.

In 2014, the government announced that the White Building was unsafe and residents would have to leave. *The Phnom Penh Post* photographed a girl looking out from her home at the demolishment that had already begun. Channary is that girl's aunt and helps raise her. The girl calls her 'Mum'.

Channary had spent her whole life, nearly thirty years, living in the White Building. Her mother had been there since the fall of the Khmer Rouge in 1979. Channary still works nearby, feeling the memories of her old life every day. When she takes her niece to work, as they walk past the former site of the White Building her niece will look up and say, 'Mum, look at the house. I miss our house.'[2]

The compensation Channary's mother received was not enough to buy a new home, so Channary organised a bank loan, much against her mother's wishes. Her mother, like many older Cambodians, doesn't trust banks and wanted her compensation to be paid in cash so she could store some in the house and some on her body. Channary was flabbergasted. '"Oh my god," I say. "What?! It's so dangerous, easy to be robbed. Take the cheque, go to bank, put in the bank. That's all. So easy!"'

We were sitting outside a bar not far from where the White Building once stood. I commented that the land, in a prime city location, must have been very valuable.

'They give us a little money but they can earn a lot,' replied Channary, as she pushed her large round spectacles upwards with a forefinger.

At a meeting with White Building residents, the Minister for Land Management asked if anybody had any questions. 'My mum, she keep silent and not say anything. She doesn't know I want to ask. I didn't tell anyone. I didn't write it down. I just listen and think ... and then I go up to the microphone. My first time. I feel that I will regret if I don't speak at that time. Actually, it's the last chance to do something. I was nervous and hesitated. When I stand up to talk, I say my name and say, "I don't ask a question but this is what I request."' Channary was still surprised by her own impetuosity. 'I said that they give us limited time to move and you cannot limit us, like, one week, two weeks. "You have to give us three months. Not easy to find somewhere else. Two, for the [compensation] fee, do we get as the net fee or have to cut for tax? We get little money and if you cut the tax, no, cannot. Please give us it as the net fee [after tax]."'

Channary laughed in disbelief at herself, slapping my forearm, before returning to her story. '"And if you agree that, please make sure you put it in the contract. I want to make sure. This is an important point. You have to put it in the contract. Please."'

The Minister agreed to change the contracts and give one month's notice of the exact date of eviction. Many residents thanked Channary, admitting that they had not thought about such points.

'That's why after the White Building, the CPP win. Because they say, "We help you, you have to help us win. Don't break your promise. We have to win." Everyone say, "Yes, yes, yes." Before, my mum voted CPP. Even me, I voted CPP. This year too – still.'

I had been friends with Channary for a few years but never knew that she supported the CPP. She began to explain. 'For me, another party, there is no other. No show. They don't give us feelings of trust. If they want to change, show something. What they want to change? For me, they should show us that if they become government, this is the first thing they would change: traffic or rubbish. Don't say about big things; say small things to show us. They just want to change the country, but to what? What? They just speak about politics. Just blah, blah.'

I asked Channary if she thought it was difficult to talk about politics publicly. She replied that it was not now, but 'five years ago, maybe more'. Five years ago, Channary was one of few young people supporting the CPP and the inhibition she felt was in contrast to the liberation CNRP supporters experienced.

'Why did so many young people vote CNRP five years ago?'

'Five years ago, we had a choice and many bad things were happening [with forced evictions in the neighbourhoods of] Boeung Kak, Borei Keila … that's why we wanted change.' Channary cited the CPP's handling of the White Building as evidence of change. 'This is the first time that government actually not fighting, not Boeung Kak or Borei Keila. Smoothly. We talk and negotiate. Even me, I joined the meeting and I stand up and talk … I see more change now, and CPP is much better – do much better to make changes.'

I asked Channary if she watched the White Building being demolished. She did, with her mother and her niece, sitting on the pavement across the road. 'My mum was crying, me too. We have many memories there. Hard to leave but also good to leave. They go together – good and bad change go together. You cannot pick one.' Channary, her mother and her niece now live in a new suburb that she describes as 'quite quiet … relaxed', where her niece can play with friends on the empty roads.

It initially struck me as odd that Channary wanted change yet had voted CPP. But as we sipped cocktails in a trendy riverside bar, metres from the corner where I had eaten noodles with Neary five years earlier, we looked upon a thriving Phnom Penh, full of flashing lights, bustling traffic and gleaming buildings. A lot had changed, and after two decades of rapid growth, Cambodia had officially become a lower-middle-income country.

Channary remembered the art exhibition at the White Building I visited during my first weekend in Cambodia. Some young men had once discounted her as marriage material because of where she lived, but exhibitions like those made her feel proud of the people she lived with. Those boys now had to prove they were good enough for her.

Channary's sparkly iPhone buzzed as her eight-year-old niece called to ask when she would be home. Finishing our drinks, I rode Channary to her motorbike some streets away. She sat side-saddle on my pannier rack with a dancer's poise. Then she hopped off, donned her helmet, revved her moto and sped down the road to her new home.

CHAPTER 35

HUN SEN'S RIGHT TO RULE

A few nights after the election, I met Dav Ansan in a dimly lit bar with chic waitresses in black dresses. He had just come from dinner with a friend and he still appeared to be lost in that conversation, or the one he was having inside his own head. Knowing that Ansan saw himself as part of the 'new blood' that had helped the CPP institute reform, I tried to engage him by asking if he thought Cambodia would continue to change in the next five years. Brightening, he leaned forward, stating that even greater progress would be made and, hopefully, at a faster rate than ever. He joked that I should write a book about the five years following 2018, not those preceding it.[1]

Ansan was sure that the next five years would proceed without Rainsy, who he thought was finished. The day after the election, Rainsy, from his garden terrace in France, had said the turnout was 'impossible' given the 'atmosphere' around the polling stations. He alleged that at least 20 per cent of ballots had been spoiled, rather than 10 per cent, with those votes being incorrectly allocated to the CPP. He even called Cambodia's current situation 'reminiscent of the situation under Pol Pot, with China the only backer of such a totalitarian regime'.[2]

I had once asked Ansan if he thought Hun Sen would ever trust Sam Rainsy to govern Cambodia. He had paused, meeting my eyes for what felt an eternity, before unfavourably comparing Rainsy's bourgeois upbringing and foreign residence with Hun Sen's knowledge of rural Cambodia and management of the military.[3] Perched on my stool now, listening to Ansan, it occurred to me that the real question was not if Hun Sen trusted Sam Rainsy but whether Hun Sen trusted Cambodians to choose the right person to be their Prime Minister. I put the question to Ansan and he thought for a second, cocked his head to one side, and reflected that maybe Hun Sen does now, as if Sen believed that his overwhelming election victory proved that the country had finally seen sense. As when we last met, Ansan invoked the burning of the Thai Embassy and high trauma rates among the population, suggesting that it was still too risky to let the Cambodian people decide everything for themselves.[4]

Huy Vannak, the President of the Union of Journalist Federations of Cambodia and Ansan's friend, was more explicit about the need for Cambodians to be ruled for their own good: 'Cambodia ... we just learn how to walk last 20 years ... We just emerge ... You don't have the [educated] people in the developing country. The core of the judgement is different. They just start to learn. They just find ability.'

Vannak thinks that Western people who query why developing countries haven't quickly established effective government need to understand that it can take decades to re-build a country after complete devastation: 'You see some Western people asking, "Why? Why?" You [Western people] want to follow a set of values, of standards. [Then] you put yourself in the shoes of others, and "Oh!" You can't force or tell children six years old, ten years old, to do technical or high school ... The majority of people, they are not smart enough.'[5]

The average Cambodian adult has had less than five years of schooling, and Vannak sees this as the main reason for poverty and poor government administration.[6] Enrolling late in school or dropping out early are still very common in Cambodia, but now three-quarters of children complete the six grades of primary school, and nearly half complete lower secondary school.[7] There is a flourishing tertiary education sector – admittedly of varying quality, but a whole new generation of university graduates are entering Cambodia's workforce.

Kimchhay is the young, languid student who told me that Hun Many's youth organisation is open to him as the son of a government official but he preferred to be involved with the informal political forum Politikoffee. The first time I met him, he was sitting in a swanky café in jeans and a loose t-shirt, buried in Albert Camus's *The Outsider*. A 2014 survey of Cambodians found that most see the government's role as akin to a father's, while the citizens are its children, creating a parent-state.[8] Some saw the relationship between government and citizen as more equal, but the idea that the government is a servant of the people was not even considered as a possible answer. Four months before the 2018 election, Kimchhay penned an essay about political paternalism in which he wrote: 'Assuming that people are capable of being rational, but they are currently living in the state of irrationality, then an external coercive force can justifiably intervene to make sure that the society is moving in the right path.'[9]

I wondered if the trauma that Ansan saw in the population and the low levels of education Vannak described had created a Cambodian 'state of irrationality', justifying government coercion. A few weeks after the election, I met Kimchhay again and asked him about this. In response, Kimchhay practised the Cambodian art of avoiding a direct answer: 'If we rule and always have to show the people the way, then we think of them as being incapable of rationality. If we really think that people can be rational, then I would say that there is a way to make them rational, instead of just telling them what is good for them.'[10]

'Do you think that aim of educating people to become rational is happening at the moment in Cambodia?' I persisted.

'I was never taught how to think. Because from grade 1 to 12 … we were told to express the lessons and what the book said, not what we think about it. The education system is not tuned in a way to make people think. It makes people remember and repeat, but not ask why.'

'In your essay, you write about perpetual paternalism. Do you think that a paternalist will always think that paternalism is necessary, or is it possible for a paternalist to recognise that they can relinquish power?'

'If the paternalist doesn't severely affect the population while making the population prosperous, and that country wants to be prosperous and not to become democratic, then I would say the paternalist would have legitimacy to rule over people. But if we think what they are doing is not to our values or to our benefit, then it cannot be justified.'

Cutting to the chase, I asked, 'Where there is only one party in parliament, do you think that makes it more likely that paternalism will continue?'

'Even if in a pluralistic country and people remain silent, people just vote once every five years, then it would be like paternalism.'

Traditional notions of paternalism, including male authority, are reinforced in Cambodia by the teaching of moral codes that men and women are expected to follow. Centuries ago, a Cambodian poet wrote *chbap pros* and *chbap srey* – rules for men and rules for women – that are still taught in some schools today, even if they were officially withdrawn from the curriculum in 2007. Maly was made to recite these codes as a girl and yearned for a life different to that of her mother. She characterises *chbap pros* as being all about what boys can do, while *chbap srey* is all about what girls cannot do.

The different moral codes have created one of Cambodia's most famous proverbs, 'Men are gold and women are linen.' A bar of gold can be bumped, grazed, even melted down and re-shaped, and it is still valuable. A white linen cloth, however, is ruined as soon as a spot of colour stains it. This proverb, detested by Maly, takes on a physical truth when a white cloth is used to confirm a new wife's purity after her wedding night. In the run-up to the 2018 election, I began to see graffiti scrawled along different laneways that read *Women are gold*. I took Maly to see one section of it and she beamed with pride. 'We begin to fight back a lot,' she said.

I told her that I had talked with a government official who justified the need for a paternalist government by describing the flames of the Thai Embassy and the trauma of war. As I spoke, I watched an intelligent, educated, caring woman squint, trying to understand what I was talking about. The more I spoke, the more the notion of Cambodians being unable to choose a government for themselves felt ridiculous. Reaching peak embarrassment, I asked her if it was okay for a government to make decisions for the people's own good.

'But do you think the current government does that?' Maly exploded.

'This man thinks that the people need to be looked after.'

'I doubt that.'

I prodded again. 'He is saying that Cambodian people cannot be trusted to govern themselves. Can you be trusted?'

'Yes, I can be trusted!' Her whole body rose in tandem with the pitch of her voice. I smiled, looking at the graffiti, pretending not to notice Maly's glare.[11]

Leap knows Dav Ansan, believing him to be 'a good guy', and asked if Ansan tried to convince me of the CPP's perspective. I told him how Ansan continued to be haunted by the burning of the Thai Embassy, and that he thinks there is still trauma in the minds of Cambodians, justifying Hun Sen's level of control.

'Yes ... but I do not agree with [this reasoning]!' Leap laughed as he knew this would be no surprise. 'I think keeping social order is important, but it needs to be systematic, by rule of law and implementation of law, not rule by one person. Interesting views. Interesting.'[12]

'Another point made was that in 2013, when the opposition was strong, there was a lot of tension.' Leap murmured in agreement as I continued. 'The price of rice went up, people hoarded food and so on. This election? Peaceful. Order. The price has not gone up, people can move without fear.'

'These are very interesting things, but I don't agree with this justification either. It's you [the CPP] who create the threat. It's you who control the system.'

'It's you who create the fear?' I offered.

'The one who create that is you! Keeping the social order is important but you need to ... currently, it is not about keeping, it is about suppressing.'

It is suppression that gives Maly the feeling of being in a straitjacket. She wants to be a prominent female role model, maybe even in politics, but confided that this prospect is 'scary': 'Seeing our people in a very worrying situation and we can't do anything to help, and at the same time we think it is none of our business – sometimes I feel sad, cry, about nepotism, discrimination and aggressiveness of rich people and how they treat the poor. And I think, how about those people? How much do they suffer and struggle in their life? There must be something we can do. One day, I feel that if I have the urge, then I risk my life, just one time.'

Seeing parallels, I asked Maly what she thought of Sin Rozeth.

'Sometimes I think, *how can she speak when I cannot?* Sometimes, I really appreciate them [activists] for speaking up and doing some amazing things that I should do as well. Sometimes, we are waiting to gain benefit from other people's effort. We tell our children not to go there to protect ourselves, to be safe, when the protestors go there and endanger themselves. The majority of them are from rural poor, factories and construction. They are so affected to the extent that they cannot live anymore. Sometimes I feel guilty for getting the food at the end without being there. But what can I do? If I speak up, what would happen to me? What would happen to my family? Sometimes I think that I would be better to be an orphan. Then things would only affect me. I would have nothing to lose.'[13]

Ansan was disappointed at the intolerance of opposing views, believing Cambodia had become 'too politicised' and 'fragmented ... even at the community level'. He was depressed that CNRP supporters could not think of one good reason to vote for the CPP, despite Cambodia's national income growing fifth-fastest in the world between 2013 and 2018.[14] 'This 7 per cent [average annual growth] does not happen automatically,' Ansan stressed. He wants neighbours, even those who voted differently, to be able to sit down after an election and eat Khmer noodles together, agreeing to disagree. 'Wherever I go [during the election campaign] I meet people, and in my speeches, I ask them a favour. Those who are members of CPP, if or when CPP win and if they have a gathering, a party, as a CPP family, please invite your neighbour even if you know that they didn't vote CPP. Ask them to join. Invite them. Because the election is only one day. We should not define our society by one day. We should move on.'¹⁵

I sympathise with Dav Ansan's vision of depoliticising Cambodian life. The blind squabbling of people wedded to political parties can be corrosive, and even Leap agreed that many Cambodians believe that making steady progress with schools, roads and jobs is more important than democratic freedoms. The problem is that the absence of argument was due to suppression. When the second-largest political party is banned, free media compromised, human rights activists jailed, garment workers shot and a social commentator killed, is it possible to sit and eat Khmer noodles together and pretend these events are of no significance? This is what Hun Sen expected as he urged a nationwide series of Khmer noodle parties to foster reconciliation among Cambodians across the political divide.¹⁶

Cambodia's most famous seller of Khmer noodles, Sin Rozeth, did not take part in this feast of contrived reconciliation. She shared a different vision with me, one that asked people to think beyond what spoon they have to eat with. 'We should not just be born to eat and live,' she said. 'We should do something greater. It's not the Party [the CNRP] that rescues the country. We want the word "rescue" in their hearts and taking back the country by taking back their freedom.'¹⁷

Cambodians decided that the 2018 election was not the time to stand up, though. Putheara, Kem Ley's childhood friend, described it best when he told me, 'The people are quiet now. They are not quiet in their hearts, but it is quiet now.'¹⁸

⁂

Shortly after the 2018 election, I had dinner with Neary, who I had sat with at the corner restaurant when we heard those first shouts for change five years previously. Exhausted, she had given up working for human rights charities and was now working in design. She avoided the election, spending the weekend in tranquil Kampot, where the river and forests provide refreshingly clean air. Her mother had stayed in Phnom Penh to vote CPP for the first time ever, having been pressured into completing a CPP Family Book six months earlier.

Neary and I caught up with each other's lives before talk inevitably turned to the election. The conversation faltered, with awkward silences between our observations. We knew there was nothing left to say: Hun Sen would be Prime Minister for the next five years, and likely more. Neary sighed and imagining that she was addressing Hun Sen. 'Okay. Fine. You win.'[19]

The spirit of opposition had been defeated. Kannitha, my former colleague, returned to the despondency that had enveloped her after the CPP's overwhelming 2012 local election. 'If I care, what can I do?' she asked. 'If I can do, I will care, but there is nothing that I can do.'[20] Davuth's friends had complained, 'I don't vote for CPP but they are still in power, so it doesn't matter what I do. There is no point, why bother?'[21]

Being forced to endure another CPP government was eating Chamroeun up inside: 'When they started to close down *The Cambodia Daily* and close down the CNRP, I decided to stop. To stop listen to the radio. To stop reading the government newspaper. I don't want to hear anything. When they close down the CNRP, I was so upset. So frustrated. It's like it drove me crazy. So, I don't want to care. To listen. To hear any political development. Because it made me so sick.' Chamroeun spat out the word 'sick' as though trying to rid himself of bile. 'I was sickened by the government when they close down the CNRP.'

'Did you feel as though part of your Cambodia had been taken away from you?' I asked.

'Yep.' Chamroeun paused, taking a heavy breath. 'I feel like they really try to go to dictatorship. They don't care about the freedom of people anymore. So, they can do anything. You know, they can do anything. They don't care. Even killing people. So, like, freedom has been removed.'

'Did you think it was possible that they would do that?'

'I never believe that they would do that. Never believe that they could do that. It's like they are moving back. They could undermine their achievement, their reputation so far. I think it is just crazy for a person who achieve a lot in the past. Even if he has done a lot of bad to the country, he has achieved a lot too. But he has done this move. It could destroy his achievement. I never thought that he could have done this. Very surprised. I talk to my friends and they feel the same way. It's not just me who wants to stop listening or stop understanding with this government. They also have the same feeling. If they listen too much, they cannot sleep, they have a bad feeling, you know ...'[22]

Davuth believed that people 'don't care so much' about the 2018 election, burying their feelings. Instead they switched their energy to 'really focus on their own business and their work'. He felt that citizens were displaying greater 'maturity' in accepting what they could not change, recognising the pointlessness, as the Cambodian proverb teaches us, of trying to hit a stone with an egg.[23]

I explained to Davuth that in a liberal democracy, we would think it strange that a Prime Minister could say he was willing to kill 200 of his citizens and still gain so many votes. There was a pause before Davuth, a man who has endured so much, responded. 'Well, really hard to say. It seems that people enjoy the peace, but it doesn't mean that they are happy.'[24]

CHAPTER 36

THE SACRIFICE OF SIN ROZETH

Vanda, the ADHOC human rights worker who wrote songs in jail, was surprisingly upbeat about democracy in Cambodia, in marked contrast to the post-election gloom of others opposed to the CPP. Noticing my confusion, he explained that rather than seeing this as the zenith of the CPP's power, dissolving the CNRP had showed that it was 'scared of the people and the movement'.[1]

'I have my own belief that this country has changed already,' he told me. 'You may challenge me – the government has just won every seat. But because of this, because the government has created fear in people, I can see that the movement has moved in the right direction because the government cannot pretend it is a democratic country. It shows the real attitude, the real leadership of this government. This is what I saw when I worked there: the giant eating the young. Those outside the government, they did not see this. They saw the pretty, handsome giant. But now, the giant has been forced to reveal itself.'

One person in the grip of the giant was Rozeth. I met her at her restaurant just after it had closed one evening. Seeing me step out of a tuk-tuk, Rozeth came out to unchain two of the three tall metal gates barricading the front, separating them so I could squeeze through the gap. Smiling broadly, she welcomed me, and I felt a moment of relief to see her looking well.[2]

She was wearing a brown shirt with black cuffs and collar that was buttoned right to the neck. She wore light blue trousers and platformed sandals that inched her over five feet. The only make-up was a light brushing of face powder, and her hair was tied back tightly. For Rozeth, a Saturday evening was just like any other.

She brought us tea and I looked around the restaurant, noticing there were fewer tables and more handbags, which she was now selling online.

Two weeks before the election, Rozeth had shared a post by a CNRP leader holding up a clean finger, which gained 693 likes and sixty-one shares. On that same day, she posted a video of handbags for sale, which garnered 21,000 views, 1400 likes and 235 shares.

I asked her if she was worried that the CPP had won all 125 seats. She had anticipated it but she did not believe the election results anyway. I asked her what it would mean for democracy and freedom in Cambodia.

'We can hear, we can see, but we cannot talk.'

She did not believe it would be like that forever, though, pointing out that there was little hope in 2012 but then the parties merged, Rainsy returned and the country woke up. 'This shows that they [the people] will do something for the country.' Her optimism comes from a belief that discontent has been suppressed but not destroyed. 'People seem to be quiet, but they feel frustrated, depressed. Hun Sen probably understands this and that will worry him.'

I asked what future lay waiting for her. 'This business,' Rozeth said with a smile, 'is a holiday for me. When CNRP come back, I will go back to politics. At this time I need to earn money, but no party will stand forever.' Even if it was said with tongue in cheek, only Rozeth could ever think of calling her situation 'a holiday'. In the months that followed the election, Rozeth was summoned to court multiple times to answer accusations that her restaurant was a site of rebellion. Rozeth was not one of the 118 CNRP officials banned from politics, but that did not matter to the courts. They accused her of hosting a 'conference', demanding to know who had attended and what was talked about. They harangued her with questions about who her customers were and criticised her posts in support of Sam Rainsy, to which she replied, 'There is no law to stop people missing their leader.'

Rozeth felt that she was in a 'deadlock situation', conceding, 'Friends, neighbours, relatives do not dare to come to my restaurant. If they come here, they always get a summons to the court. I lose a lot of guests.' One of her close friends was pressured into signing a contract agreeing to 'cut the relationship', as Rozeth put it. The police surveilled her, even taking photos of her giving clothes to poor people in her former commune. Just before I visited, a man she had never met had been shouting outside her restaurant, pretending to be an ex-lover and accusing her of being a harlot. 'There is no freedom for me. It feels like I live in a prison, a jail without walls.'

Deep into a long conversation with Ansan, who had once told me that Cambodia must avoid returning to the days of the Khmer Rouge and civil war 'at all costs', I asked what he thought of criticism that order and stability had come at the price of democracy. 'I think the balance is right,' he answered without hesitation, before adding, 'but I also understand at the same time local people may not see this balance.'[3]

The Polish journalist and author Ryszard Kapuscinski wrote that the politics of a country happens on a scale that eliminates the individual.[4] When we look at the grand questions of a nation's future, the woes of an individual are too small to be seen. Focusing on what is right for the entire country, an abstract whole, allows us to ignore the parts that make up that whole. A young woman like Rozeth can be discarded, lost in a quest for 'balance'.

One evening, I was sharing a bottle of wine with Kosal in a bar that was playing Cannonball Adderley's jazz totem 'Mercy, Mercy, Mercy' – which further encouraged Kosal's tendency towards melancholy. Clinking his glass, I asked if he remembered to pay for all the food and drinks when he celebrated his recent birthday with friends. Smiling ruefully, he feigned annoyance that he also had to pay for his team because their collection didn't quite cover the bill for his birthday lunch at work.

I mentioned to him that I had recently met Rozeth, the enemy of his party.

'Is she converted now?' Kosal asked sarcastically, knowing she never would. 'Honestly, to be fair,' he continued, 'she is quite talented. Yeah ... She just happens to be on the wrong side.'

'She believes one thing and you believe —' I started.

'Exaaactly,' he interrupted. 'But if she were on the right side, it would be a different story. I appreciate Rozeth, her soul. I appreciate this kind of commitment ... I have nothing against that ... Anyone who got a soul can get along with me.'

Rozeth was paying a heavy price for being 'on the wrong side', but the CPP did not even give her much thought, Kosal told me. 'Honestly saying, we wouldn't recognise her anyway. You know, on our side she is not important.' I met one CPP official who could not remember her name, referring to her merely as the 'Battambang Khmer noodle owner'.[5]

Rozeth is not Rainsy. She could quietly recant her views and live a normal life in Cambodia, or cross the border in search of a new life, but she refuses to submit. 'I do not go to Thailand. I stay here. Even when they call me again, I am happy to go to the court.' Rozeth is aware that people now look to her as a model for how they should act. 'There are about forty people who get called to court,' she explained. 'They are motivated to go to court because I am still here. I say that I am just like anyone else. I am scared but my fear does not stop me. I want to show this role model cannot be bought by money. What I can do is that.'

Rozeth cannot sit down after the election with CPP supporters to eat noodles, like Ansan wishes; the strangling of democracy is not something she can swallow. Her freedom, and that of other CNRP activists who refuse to yield, is the price Hun Sen is willing to pay for order and stability, for Cambodia's progress. But it is also a sacrifice that Rozeth is willing to make, hoping that it may shake, awaken, us all before it is too late.

CHAPTER 37

PLAYING WITH COAL

Putting politics aside, the mix of CPP and CNRP supporters in Chen Sokgeng's soccer team all went to the opening of his restaurant. But as the election neared and Hun Sen's accusations of treason heightened, the CPP footballers became afraid to be seen with Sokngeng. 'If they see me in the street, they just look right and left, shake hands and then say goodbye. They are frightened that people will accuse them of having some connection with me. If they open a business, they will lose [customers]. And if they hold any position with the government, they will not be promoted.'

As we ate grilled fish with shredded ginger and soybeans in his near-empty restaurant, Sokngeng told me that 'the old concept' of not being able to speak to people from other parties is 'being removed bit by bit'. I told him of Chamroeun's belief that a CPP and a CNRP supporter could never have a harmonious marriage, but Sokngeng sees this becoming more normal in Cambodia's future: 'When the democratic concept reaches the heart of all people, they will see people have the right to support any party. You have the right to support the party you like, but make sure the family do not fight.'[1]

I jokingly asked Sokngeng if he could foresee marrying a CPP supporter and with a twinkle in his eye he told me about the 28-year-old daughter of a high-ranking CPP official who sent him a Facebook friend request when he first became a commune leader. She told him on Facebook that she 'fully supports' his work and that she and her sister secretly support the CNRP. They have even met for clandestine cups of coffee.

I left Sokngeng's restaurant hopeful that his Cambodian Romeo and Juliet tale would have a happy ending, symbolising a wider reconciliation within Cambodian society. Naïvely, I hoped that a book, written by a Westerner seeking to increase his own understanding, could assist by stitching together a dialogue of perspectives from both sides. I even had daydreams of inviting Kosal and Ritthy, Ansan and Rozeth, and all the others, to sail on the Mekong at sunset with me – not to talk about politics, simply to understand each other as people. It is a notion touching arrogance that Cambodians could not arrange this themselves if they thought it would do any good.

Kosal once told me, 'The thing is, you know that no one can fix it but us.' He said that charities and international development agencies were outside of government, unable to change what is happening on the inside.[2] He was sitting behind his large wooden desk, facing the open-plan office where thirty of his staff sat. Papers were piled on different corners of the desk and a man shuffled up, head lowered and knees slightly bent, placing more documents for him to sign. Kosal at work is serious, commanding even, as he tries to drag his department forward. While I waited, I looked at his shelves full of family photographs, gifts and books and wondered where he found the time.

Recapping his pen, Kosal dived straight into an explanation of why years of foreign advice had often gone unheeded. 'If you say, "Okay, Kosal, come on, let's change it," but you are the enemy or on the outside … even if you are a normal friend and you say, "Kosal, come on, let's do this," [I think] *What the hell?*'

'"Why are you telling me what to do?"'

'Exaaactly.' Kosal nodded.

When Kosal returned from abroad, he was an outsider. Colleagues didn't like it when he told them that their way of doing things was wrong. He realised that the government is like a family and only those in the family can suggest what should happen.

Kosal believes Cambodian people can see change occurring, albeit slowly. He remembers one of his early bosses putting his arm around his shoulder, counselling him that his proposed project was a good idea, but the old man was going to retire in two years and didn't have the energy or ability to make it happen. Kosal had to wait. But he feels the clock ticking, time running beside him, sometimes ahead of him, going so quickly he can't catch it: 'I realised many years ago that we do not have much time. Seven years? Ten years? Right?' Kosal had calculated that in the early years of your career, you are climbing the ladder and unable to influence, and in the later years, you are past your peak, unable to keep improving. 'That's why I want to keep moving. I am here for a reason and I try to do my best. In the end, there's nothing else.'[3]

It is only outside of work that Kosal stops moving long enough for melancholy to visit him. A previous night, sitting having a quiet drink together, Kosal admitted, 'To be honest ... I know there's some unjust and it's hard for me. Even though I'm on this side, because of unjust ... Hard to swallow, to chew on it ... this is why we say we need deep reform to salvage the nation. The nation going in this direction, sooner or later it loses itself. It's a sad thing.'[4]

Kosal's mother and wife had both asked him why he worked for the government when he could get a more highly paid job with an international aid charity, but that would mean he was on the outside, unable to make change, unable to help his country. The opposition disappoints him for failing to even identify the simple things that could be improved. Kosal remains determined because of his admiration for his minister and his belief that Hun Sen wants reform too. Kosal sees that Sen sometimes struggles to get his ministers and secretaries of state to support reform, but Kosal supports the gradual process of moving older people out and young reformers in. For Kosal, sitting at his desk looking out onto his staff, the biggest problem facing governance of Cambodia is not the lack of financial resources, but the lack of skilled, educated people willing to work in government.[5]

Listening to this, I thought of Ritthy, who I would be eating dinner with that evening. There were 130 people in Ritthy's class when he was doing his Master of Public Policy in the Netherlands, nearly all having enjoyed an education far surpassing his. In group work, his fellow students would direct him, fearing that he would present poorly and bring the group's mark down. Eventually, Ritthy's good humour wore thin and he told them that he had four years' experience working in public policy while they had none. Ritthy was one of only forty-five people to graduate.

He was already sipping a beer, tucking into grilled beef and morning glory vegetables by the time I came down the alleyway to the deserted restaurant. The waitress smiled when I walked in, glad of the interruption to her boredom, giving me a menu as I sat down opposite Ritthy. I smiled as I read some of my favourite dishes from lunchtimes past, and couldn't resist ordering chicken and fried ginger in homage to my old boss, who had heard me ordering this on my first lunch break and proceeded to ensure the restaurant always had it available, assuming it was my favourite rather than just the one I could pronounce.

Thinking back to Kosal, I asked Ritthy if he had ever considered joining the government.

He laughed. 'Like playing with coal. If it is hot, you get burnt. If it is cold, you get dirty. Either way, don't touch it.'[6]

'So, even if the Minister of Education and Youth came to you and offered you a special role within government, you would not take it?' The Minister of Education was a star of government, although he would always be too modest to admit it. Highly educated and extremely hard-working, he was handpicked by Hun Sen in the wake of the 2013 election to transform Cambodia's failing education system. With zeal, he was determined to get around vested interests that blocked progress.[7]

'They try to get rational people to go in to change from within, but they are just a small light. One that can be blown out at any time.'

I imagined Hun Sen putting his lips together and the whole of Cambodia feeling the hurricane.

'Like Hang Puthea,' Ritthy continued, 'you go in with good intentions. Then you get accustomed to the system, the climate. Then you make a little compromise to be in the system. And you end up defending the system.' Ritthy's brow wrinkled as he put a finger to the bridge of his glasses to adjust them. 'Because you feel this is your legacy. You start with principles, professionalism, then have fear, pressure, interest, personal [connection] ... The person is corrupted – not in terms of financials but their values and respect. Bit by bit you end up being turned to defend the system. It is not just Puthea, many people. It happens to many people.'

'So you don't think it is possible to change the direction of the country from within?'

'It would take too long. Too long for the purposes of living! It would be like the evolution into being a human!'

I smiled at Ritthy's laughter. 'You know,' I began, 'Cheang Sokha thinks the next generation of CPP leaders will be more progressive. He has a little hope for this.'

'So he sees some bright in the dark, gloomy place?'

I admitted that despite Sokha's cautious optimism, he too warned that currently 'the sky is very dark'.[8] His phrase was almost the same as that used by Kannitha, my former colleague, when I asked about Cambodia's next five years: 'I have less hope. Or, to put another way, I am hopeless. The future is dark. Dark.'[9] It was so dark she would send her children abroad 'with no hesitation' if she could find somewhere for them.

For a few moments, Ritthy and I sat in silence, looking out into the night as the rain bounced off the road. People scurried past, balancing on the kerb to keep under the shelter of the roof's overhang, while tuk-tuk drivers opportunistically offered rides.

'Do you think a small bright light can be seen in the dark gloom?' I asked, unsure of the answer myself.

'The little light can be put out at any time! How can it survive against the heavy rain? Puthea is a victim too. There are no winners. Only everybody is a victim. A victim of the way we construct society. He is in a trapped position. Even the one who suppresses becomes the one who is a victim. Who is the winner? Villagers suffer. They lack food, poor governance affects their lives … Puthea suffers.'

'So, in terms of leaders, do you see any acting as good role models?'

'No, not really. We may have some who seem to be nice people but they serve the government. Like Mr Education. "Yes, we don't blame you. We understand."'

Ritthy took a swig of beer as I argued for the defence. 'He would say that – he is trying to achieve change from within.'

Ritthy told me his father hoped to retire the following year as school director, but even his replacement had become politicised. 'The guy who should succeed him, the deputy, will not because he is not CPP. So, they will give it to a very young guy to do. If he complains, they will send the right guy to a rural place. Far away.'

I imagined the deputy telling his wife and parents that his time would not be coming. Not unless he touched the coal.

'He [the Minister of Education] has a list of shortcomings, limitations, and cannot do more.' He made a big change to [reform] Grade 12 exams but then many [students] failed them.' Ritthy paused, so I asked what happened next, knowing that many universities were privately owned by CPP members. 'All these government people said, "No! Must do re-exam. We own these universities and need students." Now, it becomes like, even if people want to serve society, have a good head, a good mind, it's not possible. Even if good intentions to reform, cannot do and take too long. So difficult. The enabling environment is not there. One person is willing but the surrounding are not. That is why we question whether they can reform and make change.'

Rong Chhun, one of ten CNRP officials sacked by the Minster for Education for failing to return to quickly enough to work as teachers after the CNRP's dissolution, agreed. For Chhun his sacking was proof that the Minister's 'left hand is the Ministry and right hand is the Party'. He said that this politicisation stretches 'from the Ministry to the school', which restricts reform. 'There is a political structure inside. If he wants to reform the education system, it is not possible because of the political effects.'[10] The focus on politics detracts from the tasks of governing, which had prompted one of my interviewees to comment ruefully that if the CPP spent as much time planning reform as they did preparing for the 2018 election, health and education services wouldn't be in such a mess.[11]

I told Ritthy that Kosal believes Cambodia's biggest problem is a lack of educated people working in government. He acknowledged that a lack of educated professionals had been a problem for the country, but he now sees many accomplished people in Cambodia. The problem is that they are not being used by the government because they are not CPP members. This was the reason Ritthy would never get involved. Looking up from his grilled beef, he declared, 'If you touch the coal you will end up burnt or dirty, and I don't want to be either.'[12]

CHAPTER 38

CAMBODIA'S WAY

In 1995, Hun Sen was asked what he thought about liberal democracy and he replied, 'It's good for America. I'm not sure it's good for others.'[1]

In a later interview, a journalist cited other South-East Asian leaders who had argued that liberal democracy is incompatible with Asian values and asked Hun Sen if it could work in Cambodia. 'The geography, traditions and psychology differ from country to country and region to region,' began Sen. 'Even within ASEAN there are differences in culture, religion and race. Except in sports, there is no international standard which you can apply universally ... I always object when people talk to us about international standards. Even in the Francophone and Anglo-Saxon judicial systems there are big differences.'[2]

Western journalists have used this denial of international standards to argue that Hun Sen isn't a democrat,[3] but in the same interview he also said: 'Liberal multi-party democracy is how we choose to put a complete end to armed struggle. Sometimes we face and accept criticism, insults and cursing in the newspapers. But that's better than allowing people's blood to be shed. Democracy is good for Cambodia, but I'm not sure it would work in Vietnam, Laos and Burma.'[4]

Hun Sen is devoted to a relativist perspective where culture and history shape the way that politics operate within a country. When the Cambodian government justified the dissolution of the CNRP, it said, 'Democracy and human rights are country-specific and the forced transplantation of these principles [from the West] are bound to fail if the process disregards the national context.' The government said that it wanted to create a 'Cambodian Way' of developing democracy.[5]

This Cambodian Way appears to be informed by what have been labelled 'Asian values', with themes of consensus, harmony, unity and community. Since the 1990s some Asian leaders have claimed that Asian values, including the family being more important than the individual and economic rights trumping political rights, made liberal democracy unsuitable for their countries. Instead, they advocated for a version of paternalistic democracy – government for the people but not by the people, with liberal freedoms constrained. They attested that economic development requires social cohesion and stability, justifying limits to freedom of expression in case it brewed discord and disorder.[6]

Confucianism has been cited as the source of Asian values, with its emphasis on the collective good and hierarchical social relations, and a belief that a wise leader should rule unrestrained by a separation of powers.[7] Cambodia is predominantly Buddhist, but culturally influenced by Confucianism. It also has Brahman Hindu heritage from its fabled Angkor period, which has traditions of god-kings ruling the masses uncompromisingly.[8] The ideas of Asian values recur in Hun Sen's language: collective order precedes personal freedom; consensual governance is appreciated over adversarial politics; loyalty to and respect for authority is fundamental. Rights, rather than being owned by citizens, are granted by government and can therefore be taken away.[9] When the CNRP was taken away from Cambodians, the CPP said that liberal democracy was an unattainable 'pure and perfect democracy' that was 'imposed' on Cambodia.[10] The CNRP's dissolution marked the moment that the CPP unshackled itself from Western norms introduced during UNTAC.

Embracing a model of consensus-seeking after the 2018 election, Hun Sen invited each political party to send two representatives to join a newly established Supreme Consultative Council. These representatives were offered salary and rank equal to ministers, although they lacked any powers. Hun Sen said he would meet with the body twice a year to discuss ideas for national development, in a demonstration of Cambodia's 'unity and solidarity'.[11]

When I asked Phirun about the role that competition can play in democracy, he recognised that Cambodians, as Buddhists, highly value cooperation, but he stressed they also value competition, even in government, because without it 'people feel too comfortable'. Similarly, Kosal didn't want the CPP to win every seat. He thinks a good opposition could help Hun Sen challenge vested interests blocking reform and push the government to improve.[12] Ansan agreed, saying that Hun Sen cannot continually criticise ministers or he becomes weaker, so a constructive opposition helps him to hold government officials to account.[13] In all these instances, however, it was understood that competition would always be for second place. Those unwilling to cooperate on Hun Sen's terms – such as Yeng Virak's Grassroots Democratic Party, who declined to join the Supreme Consultative Council because they feared losing their right to criticise – were labelled 'enemies' and 'rebellious'.[14]

Phirun blamed the CNRP for their own demise: they 'forgot that Cambodia is not like Western culture'. He told me: 'They need to learn the art of criticising the government ... find way to talk and then approach it softly. They have to balance. If they want Point A, they need to think how they reach that point without confronting too much.'[15]

Chamroeun and Davuth talked of a gradual transition away from the CPP over five years, maybe ten. Leap thought it was the only 'realistic' option given so many feared that a sudden change in government would destroy the connections their businesses relied on.[16] Grains of sand would need to shift over time, imperceptibly tilting the scales towards change. Fewer people believe Sam Rainsy to be the man who can accomplish this. Phirun emphasised that taking power from Hun Sen would require fortitude: 'I mean, to be able to gain the power, you must continue. If you continue, if you are fighting, criticising, and then at the time your popularity is gaining more and more, you stop, you afraid, you fear? ... If you want to win against Hun Sen, you have to really fight, even you have to die. Not fight and then stop and then start again. Keep going. See?'[17]

Ever since UNTAC, Cambodians have seen their future as a democratic one. Even if they recognised Cambodia did not always live up to its constitutional status as a liberal democracy, many believed that this status was the promise of what Cambodia would become. The dissolution of the CNRP shocked people because it broke that promise. Instead, the CPP announced, 'Liberal democracy can wait!'[18] But for how long? If another political party rose to be as popular as the CNRP, would Hun Sen simply ban that party too? Sen has made it clear that he wants one of his sons to succeed him as Prime Minister, which has led people to question what Cambodia is becoming if it is no longer becoming a democracy.

With only one party in the National Assembly, Rong Chhun felt that Cambodia was 'turning back towards the situation of the 1980s', when it was a communist country. This was partly because of Hun Sen's commitment to cooperate with China.[19] Chhun found the CPP's monopoly 'scary' and feared that the government may try to abolish some of the larger trade unions, like the one he headed, just as they had done with the CNRP.[20]

Ou Ritthy did not think that Cambodia had returned to communism but did believe its leaders were 'using a communist style of working'.[21] Koul Panha, the frazzled head of COMFREL living in exile, had previously called Cambodia 'electorally authoritarian' but, for him, the uncompetitive 2018 election meant that it now couldn't even be termed that. He didn't know if Cambodia would follow 'Chinese model, Vietnamese model ... Russia model. We are not sure.'[22] Kannitha felt Cambodia was on a precipice: 'If we go a little further, we could fall over [the edge].'[23]

Not long after the election, I spent an afternoon with Soveacha and Rotha and asked them what kind of country they wanted Cambodia to become. Rotha's phone rang – and a Cambodian will always answer his phone – so Soveacha went first, enthusiastically declaring that he wanted Cambodia to become like the United States or the United Kingdom. I asked him what it was about those countries he liked. 'Democracy. Justice at the courts. Cambodia is unfair. The rich man wins, and the poor ...'

'You don't want to be like Singapore or China?' I quizzed.

Soveacha responded unequivocally, 'No. More rights.'

Rotha came back and Soveacha asked his sidekick what future he wanted for Cambodia.

'Rule of law, *nytoroth*.' I smiled at Rotha's response, remembering that was what Ny Sokha from ADHOC had named his newborn son while in prison. 'People live under that. Everyone. Even the Prime Minister. We have checks and balances so not just one person can order everything – the courts, the assembly. The three powers should be separate – courts, executive and legislative – as stated in the constitution.'

Soveacha asked him which country he would like Cambodia to emulate, keen to see if Rotha would give the same answer he had.

'Democratic country, like South Korea.' His answer surprised me, pricking my Western bias. Rotha explained the removal of President Park Geun-hye in 2017 for corruption was an example of what should happen in a democracy. 'Even though she abuses the power, she cannot rule the military to protect her. Not have the full power to do everything. We want change. You imagine a country that the son can order the troops and his father is the Prime Minister?'[24]

Years earlier, just after I joined the organisation Soveacha and Rotha worked for, I was at a staff meeting where we discussed working hours. The chief executive wanted to retain a 7.30am start time as it allowed two hours for lunch. Traditionally, people would return home to eat and sleep during this time, but most people stayed at the office because travelling home took too long in city traffic. These people wanted to start at 8.00am and take a shorter lunch break. Unable to reach a consensus, we held a vote. Rotha was trusted to collect the slips of paper and tally them on the whiteboard. The staff overwhelmingly voted to start at 8.00am, and with minimal fuss the chief executive accepted this change. I thought of my previous bosses back home and doubted they would ever have embraced democracy so well.

I met many Cambodians who yearned for democracy and, like Soveacha, dreamed of their country becoming like the United States or the United Kingdom. I often wondered what they would think if they could ever experience these democracies up close, where social ills and corruption remain and there are plenty examples of governments removing people's rights.[25]

Chamroeun had seen these countries through his time studying abroad and was still entranced by this 'different world', even if 'they are a bit cold to foreigners'. 'Yeah, at that time I was very optimistic about my country,' he told me. '1996 was only three years after UNTAC. I was very motivated to help Cambodia to be like those countries. I really wanted Cambodia to develop fast. I had an opportunity to live in the UK but I didn't want to stay there, I just wanted to come back, to help my country. 1997, there was a coup d'etat and big fight in the government. I thought, *oh!* I started to doubt.'

Two decades after being crestfallen at democracy being replaced by tanks and guns, Chamroeun witnessed Cambodia's second-largest party dismantled and the ruling party win every seat in the National Assembly. I asked him what he thought of people who say that South-East Asian cultures, including Cambodia's, may not be compatible with democracy.

'Yeah, I think that they might be correct. The current mindset, or culture, or way of thinking, may not be compatible with Western democracy or Western values of fairness, transparency and good governance. But, you know, this is because people are not exposed to quality education. They don't have enough knowledge about a different world, the outside world. This is why their old mindset, their culture, cannot be changed. But through education, over time, it can be compatible. Currently, they are right, at the moment. It doesn't mean that forever it will still be like this, but because people are not well educated, they don't do research, they don't try to learn more, they stick to the old mindset.'[26]

Maly may have successfully resisted her family's promptings of marriage, but two of her close friends complied with arranged marriages. She is frustrated that cultural change is happening so slowly it is like watching rice grow, even though she experiences Cambodia's rapid economic transformation every time she visits her mother's village. In the early 1990s, when Maly was a child, it took three days and three nights from Phnom Penh to reach her mother's remote village in Kratie province. Part of the journey was by boat, and once, while in the middle of the Mekong, there was a gunfight between boats. Bullets flew over Maly's head as her mother threw herself on top to protect her. Nowadays, Maly can buy a ticket online for a bus that will reach the village in six hours.

Given the immense change Maly had witnessed in twenty-five years, I asked what she imagined would happen in the next ten or fifteen years.

'Good question. I can see a better, happier Cambodia.'

'What does it look like in your head?' Maly paused, looking skyward, so I mistakenly tried to help. 'Does it look like Singapore? Australia? Japan?'

'Why do we not look like a future Cambodia without imitating others?' Maly replied with indignation. 'Of course, we can learn from others. But we try to be ourselves. I just want a country where everyone is equal, no matter where you are from or what you are doing. A society where we can speak freely, express our opinion and be treated fairly.'[27]

Not long afterwards, as I sat with Ou Ritthy in a sleek café with his MacBook on the table in front of us, he dismissed arguments that Cambodian culture meant democracy is an inappropriate form of government. 'It is an excuse. Culture does play a role, but culture comes from practice. If you agree to practise a new way, an acceptable way, like democratic culture, you can start changing families, schools, media, pagoda. Change in a way to make sense. It is not about copying Western values but making our sense of what we do. It is not that democracy cannot be applicable in South-East Asia but [some] people are not ready to change. In this country, we have a lot of older leaders who have been in power a long time and preach this concept. They create their own democracy and they try to adjust [the system so] they can control power. It is more like an excuse.'[28]

In 2017, a few months before the CNRP was dissolved, Ritthy had written an article published by the Asian Human Rights Commission in which he stated: 'Just as everything changes in life, I believe Hun Sen can change. And I insist he should change. It's neither impossible nor ever too late for him to change. He is very smart, far-sighted.'[29] Ritthy had been trying to appeal to Sen, hoping that he could be convinced it was possible to govern in a different way. Just one year later, Ritthy saw the impossibility of this. '[Now] I cannot say like that. It's completely changed.'[30]

Given Hun Sen's remarkable ability to endure, many Cambodians were not expecting change anytime soon. Ritthy shared some black humour on this point. When the government granted a Chinese company a fifty-year lease on Phnom Penh's river port, one of Ritthy's friends, disgusted, said: 'In fifty years, we don't know what the Chinese will do with it. In fifty years, long time, I die, we die, all die. Nobody knows.' With mock alarm, Ritthy responded, 'We die in fifty years? We have to die after Hun Sen!'

Perhaps it is only this natural fate that Cambodians believe can bring any meaningful change to their leadership. Rong Chhun once said that he would not marry until Cambodia had a new Prime Minister. A week after the 2018 election, I asked Chhun, in his fifties and still single, about this. It was one of the few times that Chhun let himself laugh before responding. 'Yes, until Cambodia has real, stable freedom.'

'Do you still believe that it is possible?'

'I still have hope that there may be change. If people cannot change him, nature will change him. He cannot go against nature.'[31]

Ritthy may joke about Hun Sen reigning for another fifty years, but he also recognises that Hun Sen cannot live forever. He urged young Cambodians to return from abroad so that Cambodia can prepare 'for when Hun Sen is no longer and we can contribute and play a role in Cambodia'.[32] 'I have strong argument with people,' he said, 'because who will do if you will not do yourself? You need to start – you cannot expect politicians to do things for you but you do not contribute. This is the country that you were born in. I don't agree with the idea of leaving – I always want to stay and see lots to do here. Education, art, agriculture. Everything is possible here and we need people to do. Everything abroad is already settled. In Cambodia, everything is happening. I feel like I want to contribute to build something.'[33]

When Chamroeun told me that he had stopped reading newspapers, listening to the radio or following politics, I asked if he had given up hope for change. 'I not give up hope,' he said. 'You know, I still have hope ... Somehow, even I stop [following politics], I decide to forget as much as possible about the current politics in Cambodia, I still hear. I still know the development. I still know what is going on.'

Chamroeun may have stepped back into the shadows, as many have, but they, and the hope that burned for five years, was still there. Flickering. Ritthy saw this light, arguing that democracy had not left Cambodia entirely. Rather, it was entering a second chapter. 'If we look at the leader, it seems to be pessimistic. Some friends look at the leader, the state institutions, and they become pessimistic, disappointed and stop. Don't do anything. If you look at the current leaders, they cannot change. We cannot expect them to, so it is like we have to forget. But I look at young people. The knowledge of democracy has been increasing [even if] the physical infrastructure of democracy has been destroyed. The knowledge, the spirit of democracy, the spirit that people understand about human rights, the sprit that people understand about freedom of speech, has been increasing. I call 1991 to now chapter one of democracy in Cambodia. Now, the new chapter has just started.'[34]

PART IV
2022

'The bamboo shoots succeed the bamboo.'
ទំពាំងស្លឹងបូស្សី

Cambodian proverb

CHAPTER 39

CANDELIGHT

'Hello! Please meet my husband.'

Rozeth had never spoken English to me before, and despite being three years since we had last met, she was smiling unabashedly.

'Nice to meet you. Thank you for coming. Yes, I am Rozeth's husband,' Ratanak greeted me in clear English.

Ratanak and Rozeth had married just three months earlier, in March 2022, although they had known each other for fifteen years as Ratanak is the son of Eng Chhai Eang, a former Vice-President of the CNRP. He too grew up in a family supporting Sam Rainsy. Traditionally, weddings take place in the home town of the bride, but they chose to have theirs in Phnom Penh, where many of their family friends lived.

'How many people attended your wedding?' I asked.

'Fifty tables,' Ratanak replied, meaning that there were 500 guests, which is normal for a wedding in Phnom Penh, although this one was full of members from the new Candlelight Party.

Turning to Rozeth, I asked if her ageing mother, now eighty, had travelled to Phnom Penh for the wedding, and she replied without waiting for my interpreter to translate. 'Yes! She went to the wedding.'

'And how many different dresses did you have?'

Cambodian weddings begin shortly after dawn with a procession of gifts from the groom's family to the bride's and continue throughout the morning with different Buddhist ceremonies, including one where the parents cut strands of hair from the wedding couple. The bride and groom change outfits for each ceremony, so it was no surprise when Rozeth said they changed seven times during the day and again for the dinner.

'Your mum must have been very happy to see you get married,' I said.

'Yes, she was very happy to see her child get married, but she has one more wish – to see Sam Rainsy return. Sam Rainsy wanted to become Prime

Minister, but now he wants to make the road for the new generation. We are without Sam Rainsy as a campaigner, but he is still with me in the country,' said Rozeth, placing her palm on her heart, moving from romance to politics in a single beat.

'Rozeth, was it a difficult choice to get involved in politics again and stand in this election?'

'For me, I faced very strong challenges to be involved in this election, because I am a symbol of opposition to the CPP.'

'Were you nervous? Because you have experienced a lot of pressure. Were you nervous, deciding to stand again?'

'For me, from my heart, I don't feel scared too much because I am the one who will reach the villagers and the villagers will stand behind me. Recently, there was a serious case when a member of Candlelight was arrested and sentenced to jail. Although we do nothing, we are still accused of betraying the nation. For me, though, although I know that tomorrow there could be an arrest, I still try to face the challenge. So, the fear that I had built from the past has disappeared.'

'The other Candlelight people, when did they ask you to stand or when did you decide to stand?'

'Near the end of 2021, they have the assembly, the party assembly, and they knew there would be commune elections and required candidates. In Battambang, there are ten communes and in all of those all the candidates from 2017 come back to stand again this year. Just changed from CNRP to Candlelight. And the Candlelight Party is a new party but was established a long time ago. Just changed its name from the Sam Rainsy Party, but the symbol is still the candle.'

'Has everybody from the CNRP come to the Candlelight Party, or have some gone to other parties?'

'Some went to different parties, to the small parties. Some created new parties. But 90 per cent from the CNRP come to the Candlelight. We have candidates in more than 1600 communes, nearly in all 1652 communes.'

I asked Rozeth what her mother thought of her getting involved in politics again. Rozeth's response was ringing. 'She will join the campaign tomorrow! She encouraged me to stand as a candidate.'

Tomorrow would be the last day of Rozeth's campaign to win back her role as O'Char Commune Chief. She had paused her campaigning only to get married. She told me that the people in her commune supported her when she announced that she would stand. 'When I went house to house, I heard the voices of villagers directly and they encourage me and wish me success in this election. It seems that they are happy,' Rozeth said. 'The CPP target O'Char Commune, though, really target to make sure that they win. They try to threaten the people not to involve with me. The absence of our party for five years makes the people feel nervous to support us, to show their support.'

'Have people become less nervous or more nervous in the last few weeks?' I asked.

'The people have seen what the CPP did to our party, so people feel nervous and do not dare to say whether they support us or not. But they will reveal the truth on election day.'

Four years after choosing to boycott the national election because the CNRP had been dissolved, Sam Rainsy and some former CNRP officials decided that they needed to form another party to stand against Hun Sen's CPP. In August 2021, they took the first steps to re-form the old Sam Rainsy Party, lying in abeyance since the formation of the CNRP, now called the Candlelight Party after its candle logo. Its leaders asked Rozeth to become a candidate in the national elections in 2023, but she demurred, saying she wanted to prove herself at the local level first, where she believed she could make a bigger difference to people's lives.[1]

Two weeks before the commune elections, Candlelight Party leaders came to a campaign event in O'Char and Rozeth was given five minutes at the beginning to address the few hundred people. Stepping forward and grasping the microphone, she began by hailing the people of O'Char and their bravery: 'I walked to give letters and used a loudspeaker to invite people. Still, one party was worried; they sent letters to people yesterday to hinder them from coming to this meeting. But I do not feel despair. Those who do not attend today whispered to the organiser, "Please tell Rozeth not to be upset; on the day of the election, June 5th, in the secret room, Candlelight will shine, my dear Rozeth." Some villagers asked their husbands to attend this meeting. Some villagers asked their wives to participate in this meeting. Some people asked their children to follow to get the job done. Win or lose?'

'Win!' the crowd chanted in reply.

'Change or no change?!'

'Change!!!'[2]

When I met with Chea Chiv, the broad-smiling, round-shouldered former CNRP leader of Battambang, he did not hesitate to give his thoughts on whether Rozeth would win: 'Yes, she will. I know this clearly. Money cannot buy hearts, and Rozeth has taken her heart to the villagers.'

The day before the election, Chamroeun told me that his wife had talked on the phone with Rozeth a couple of times previously. 'We buy oranges from her. We see online, she sells handbags. We do not want oranges but we buy them. We want to support. My wife wants to express her admiration. Just to speak, support. Say she inspires. Then she got a phone call from the telephone company. "How do you know Rozeth? Why do you speak to her? What do you speak about?" I think everyone who contacts Rozeth has like this. She wants to change her number, but I say, "No, you have done nothing wrong. So no need."'

'What do people admire about Rozeth?'

'Courage. And she speaks logically. She explains. She is not extremist, not racist. If she's just aggressive against the ruling party, like other opposition, then nobody care, but she speaks from situation, explanation. Courage and rationality. Amazing how she does not have high education but speaks like that. Amazing.'

'What is the Candlelight candidate like in your commune? Do you know them?'

'I see them – they ride through, but I don't know them. No idea. But I know the CPP Commune Chief. He is good. He is popular. He never tries to do bad things. But people who like Sam Rainsy … it could be an uneducated person, a tuk-tuk driver, and we still vote for them. We think about the country.'

Sam Rainsy was still in France. The government had cancelled his Cambodian passport and would not grant him a visa on his French one. The government had also changed the constitution in 2021 so that Cambodians with dual citizenship could not become Prime Minister. Furthermore, as a convicted criminal, he could not even be involved with the political party that once bore his name lest it give the government grounds to dissolve this party too. His endorsement of the Candlelight Party, however, was enough to win the support of Chamroeun and swathes of Rainsy loyalists.

'Do you think the Candlelight Party will do well?'

'Not as well as CNRP did. Only began to organise four months ago. And difficult to get candidates because of the pressure. Actually, my wife wants to stand and I would support her. But she is scared. Maybe later, but not now. I think if she stands, no problem for personal safety, would be fine. But her family … She doesn't want to undermine them.' His wife's family have strong connections to the CPP, including an uncle who is an Excellency.

'Are your children old enough to vote now?' I asked.

'Yes, both of them. I am excited to vote tomorrow. We will go as a family.'

'Do you think it will be a high turnout?'

'At work, we do not discuss. Nobody. But I see yesterday, some people talk about the election and they will go to vote … We've all been waiting five years for this.'[3]

CHAPTER 40

A CHICKEN HOUSE

Rozeth's husband had organised for me to spend the afternoon of the election at the Candlelight Party's headquarters in Phnom Penh, where I was to meet Sar Longdeth, the Party's Chief for Phnom Penh. The office is actually a townhouse in a new concrete suburbia with no sign above the door and only two small candle logos on the wall. Longdeth greeted me as I crept into the front room, unsure if I was in the right place for the headquarters of the main opposition. He ushered me through to a room at the rear, which would normally be a kitchen and have small chicken coops outside the back door. Instead, I found the nerve centre of the Candelight Party's results-gathering operation for Phnom Penh. It had one computer, a printer/scanner, a stack of coloured markers and a few walkie-talkies. I was given a plastic chair beside one of the younger staff members, who was sitting at the elbow of the Deputy Chief at the computer.

While others would come into this back room to sit down and talk, Longdeth was always standing – sometimes leaning against the wall, sometimes going upstairs to check results from other provinces, sometimes seeing who was arriving in the front room. Moments after rain began to clatter down, he burst into the room, still on the phone, to ask the Deputy Chief about the weather forecast. Thirty minutes before the polls closed, the heavens opened across Cambodia. Longdeth was worried that polling stations would close doors and windows, preventing people from seeing the counting of votes.

Some polling stations did close their windows and doors, but not all. With the young man at the elbow of the Deputy Chief, I watched a Facebook Live feed showing ballots being counted at one of Phnom Penh's polling stations. A man held up the ballot paper for a woman to see; she shouted the number of the party that received the vote, while another woman chalked it up on a blackboard: '*Pee, Pee, Pee, Pee, Muoy, Pee, Pee, Muoy, Pee, Pee, Pee, Pee, Pee, Muoy ...*'

Pee, the Cambodian word for the number two, was the CPP in this commune and it was garnering four times as many votes as the Candlelight Party.

Candlelight Party agents stationed at each polling station were to take photos of the final tally and send it via Telegram, the encrypted messaging service, to the Deputy Chief and the young man at his elbow. Waiting on these photos, the young man twisted one of his forefingers nervously while watching Facebook Live, which was now showing another polling station with similar results. He got up and stood in the corner, facing the wall like a naughty school child, staring up at the ceiling. His phone buzzed with a result and he read the numbers out for the Deputy Chief to enter into their tally. He sat down again, restless, rocking backwards on the chair legs, before rising to shelter in his corner with his back to the computer.

By 5.00pm, a council of male candidates, plus Sar Longdeth, was gathered in the front room. I began to hear the phrase '*sangkat Rozeth*'. At first people were eager to hear if the result was in, and then they were asking their colleagues if they had heard the news. Soon, it was just me and the Deputy Chief sitting near the computer, the young man now sitting on the floor, leaning against the wall. At 5:35pm, *Fresh News*, widely viewed as a government mouthpiece, declared that the CPP had won O'Char Commune, with 64 per cent of the vote in the two-horse race. Rozeth would return as Deputy Commune Chief only.

More photos were coming in and the young activist recited numbers of votes polling station by polling station as the Deputy Chief faithfully recorded their defeat in the spreadsheet. The colourful markers remained untouched.

Longdeth came in and scrutinised the spreadsheets over the Deputy Chief's shoulder. Straightening, he smoothed his hair, sweeping his palm over his side parting, and left. Just before 6.00pm, *Fresh News* reported that the CPP, informed by their own staff with photos, spreadsheets and walkie-talkies, were on course for a landslide election win.

I looked out to the front room and the council of men sitting at an imaginary roundtable, each offering their insights into why defeat had been inevitable. One came into the back room, hands deep in his pockets. He nodded to us but said nothing as he stood behind the Deputy Chief, who was still tapping away on the keyboard. He bent over to see more closely and shook his head, leaving without a word. A few minutes later, at 6:45pm, the Deputy Chief got up from his chair and turned the computer off.

I was packing things into my bag when Longdeth returned to the back room, sliding the door closed behind him. He stood with his back against the wall. 'The problem was that we needed 4000 observers but we didn't have enough. We didn't have enough to cover all polling stations. This is a big problem, and we didn't have time to train them, train them to be observers.'

'This was just for Phnom Penh?' I asked. 'How many did you need?'

'We needed another 570. Been difficult to recruit them. Some people don't want to do [it] and some people agree but then feel intimidated so pull out. Also, some people don't have ID card so cannot vote and others miss getting registered. The Cambodian Reform Party made things difficult for Candlelight. People think the opposition are disunited and people feel unsure. They are unsure about who these parties are, where they come from, who leads them. Pol Ham was important in CNRP but now he is Reform Party. And then there is the Khmer Will Party too.'

'I read that Kem Sokha announced that he would not vote.'

'This is a big thing! Very important. Had a big effect. He said he did not support Candlelight so people are unsure and many Kem Sokha supporters don't go to vote or vote for another party, like Reform Party. If Sokha votes, people will follow him. This was a big thing.'

'It looks like you may get about 20 per cent or 25 per cent of the vote. Were you expecting to get more?'

'I think we may get about 30 per cent. I'm not surprised by this result. I could see during the campaign. People were unsure, people didn't know who Candlelight was, where we come from. Fewer people join in the rallies and campaigning. Normally, when we have the big ones ... people would join as it goes by, but this one, no. We had spoken to police about traffic management before the rally, they knew the time, the route, the roads, but we got no help. We had to do it. There were many traffic jams so the campaign wasn't moving. Before, the campaigns were maybe three times as big. It didn't feel like 2017. Plus, people weren't clear who the leader was. You need to be able to say and show who the leader is.

'At the moment, they feel disappointed,' he continued, referring to the young activists in the office and the candidates in the front room. 'They have lost confidence. They thought it would be a different result. But the leaders, we know, we can tell what the result will be. We will encourage and try for next year. This is just a start, though. A start for Candlelight. We are an old party and older people know us but the young never hear of us so we have to tell them about Candlelight and they will begin to realise our history and connection to CNRP. Then we gain more young voters. More of them will vote for Candlelight in 2023. This is a start – we will prepare again. We gained more people as the campaign went on. And at the moment, we have few resources. There was no time to prepare, just three to four months before we decide to join the election, and not many people. Look at our house for chickens – this is our headquarters!'[1]

The young and old filtered out of the townhouse to the chorus of frogs and crickets greeting the night in the field opposite. They climbed onto their motos and went home to their families.

On the way home, I stopped at a food stall and ordered *khtieu*, Cambodian noodles. I sat alone at a table for six. Before my food arrived, a man with three children on his moto pulled up and sat down at the table beside me. He spoke English, as well as some Chinese – because his grandfather was Chinese, he told me. The two youngest children were also learning Chinese, and spoke some English too – the boy told me that he would be six the following month and the daughter piped up that she would soon be ten. The third child, an older girl who bore no resemblance to the others, sat mutely.

As we all began to tuck into our *khtieu* and fried rice dishes, the father told me about his brother abroad, his relative studying in America and his elderly mother here in Phnom Penh. He enquired how common it was in the West for couples not to marry. I was enjoying his curiosity.

As he had been born in Phnom Penh, just after the Khmer Rouge, I asked him what his family does at New Year when people leave the city to return to their homeland. 'Usually, we stay and enjoy Phnom Penh being quiet, although it feels strange. It can be difficult to go away – expensive and busy. Sihanoukville has changed a lot since you were last there, maybe. Many casinos and Chinese people … You know, you may like Cambodia and think it is good, but it can be difficult for politics in this country. We give 99-year leases to Chinese companies and people fear that they may not leave afterwards or won't give back. Same with Vietnam. Sometimes the Prime Minister may be under their influence. We borrow from China a lot so have to sometimes do things to give back.'

'Yes, I couldn't recognise Sihanoukville when was I there three years ago. Didn't even know where I was standing.'

He explained that things had improved since some Chinese left during the pandemic and the government closed online gambling operations. There was a pause before he said, 'You may not know, but there was an election today.'

'Have you been watching the results?'

'No, no point. There is only one. No other party. Even I, I vote for them.'

'Were there other parties in the election, though? I heard about a Candlelight Party.'

'People don't know it well. They are unsure about it. It is not strong. No leader. Rainsy is away and Sokha is in trial. There is nobody like them.'

'So who is the leader of the party?'

'Ehh ... I don't know, I don't know, actually.'[2]

He poured jasmine tea into cups of ice for his two children and insisted on serving the older child too, who turned out to be the family's helper. We continued talking while his children practised their English on me.

Rising to leave, the man secretly paid for my food before putting his son in front of him on the moto, with the two girls behind. They waved goodbye – including the helper, who was by now smiling broadly – and I sat back down, watching as they joined the swirl of motos.

CHAPTER 41

THE ELEPHANT AND A MOUSE

'When did you find out the result?'

'It was about 5.30pm. We know, we get from each place. Our people [at each polling station] tell us the results and then we get official results about 7.00pm. We get over 80 per cent. Six [councillors] for us.'

'Over 80 per cent? That is more than the average. That's really good,' I offered.

'I thought, I thought we would get 70, you know. But people come back who we don't know. You know, factory workers. People coming back [to vote] for the election.'

'They were not there when you were campaigning?' I asked.

Despite the overwhelming victory, Kosal was annoyed about the one commune seat that had got away. 'No. Exactly.'

'What was the result at the 2017 election, though?'

'It was 5–2 to them,' replied Kosal, as if it was a football score.

'That is an impressive turnaround. 5–2 them, now 6–1 you.'

'Yes, but still … my boss is happy, though. 6–1 is okay. And I guess it is good they have one. One who, you know, can question.'

'What turned it around? You've been working hard there, helping people a lot?'

'I took a risk. That man, the former chief. I tell my boss that we need to get him. The villagers love him. He is like something special for them. He is not an old man, maybe younger than me, like forty or something. You should meet him, you know. So I ask him to join and stand for Chief. I went to his house.'

'You, an Excellency, went to the house of a former CNRP commune chief?'

'Yes, I went to his house and ask him. I don't go as an Excellency, I just go as a normal person. Person committed, want to work, work for the people.

Tell him we both want the same thing.'

'What did he say?'

'He said he would think about it. Actually, he said he was going to ask God and think about it.'

I couldn't hold my laughter in anymore.

'He is a Christian, you know. He is not a priest, but the one who organise the church. Everybody in that church, they know him. He is like the lead of the church. Many go to that church. He came back after a few days and said, "Okay, I spoke to God," and he say something about sending a message, and then say, "I will do it." I don't know why. I don't know. He just said yes, he would.'

'You went to his house and asked the former CNRP chief. That must have been difficult for you to do. What about the existing CPP chief – what did he say?'

'I tell my boss that if we want to win, we need to get him back. But there was pressure, not just from him, but people even more, you know, even more at the top. They say, "What are you doing?! Can't do that." If it went wrong, you would not see me. I would be gone, bye-bye, I would not be sitting here tonight.'

It was the night after the election, and I had joined Kosal and three of his colleagues in an outdoor restaurant where they were celebrating the victory, one with especially abundant joviality. His colleagues, initially wary, asked what I was doing in Cambodia and I explained that I was writing about the election. 'I swear on my drunkenness that it is a true and fair election!' said the jovial celebrator. Turning to Kosal, he queried, 'True and fair? Is that what they say?'

'Ummm ...' Kosal tapped his temple. 'Free and fair. You say free and fair.'

'Free and fair! I swear that it was free and fair. No one can say it was not. Everyone can see. This was true. I promise. No one can deny. The Village Chief not there. No forcing people to vote. It is secret, people can vote whoever. Yes, there will be small issues. Some bad people. But small. Not big, not everywhere.'

'Good on bad side and bad on good side,' mused Kosal.

'You have to see whole wildlife. Can't just look at one tree. See whole wildlife.'

We were all momentarily confused before Kosal worked out what his colleague meant. 'Forest, you mean forest. Can't look at one tree, look at whole forest.'

'Eh? Yes, forest. *Jul muy!*'

We all laughed while clinking glasses. Kosal and his colleagues had spent fourteen days campaigning continuously in their commune. Indeed, Kosal had supported the council greatly since first being assigned that commune five years previously. Kosal told me that the living conditions have been transformed and there are now systems in place that will continue when he moves on. He and his colleagues had worked for years to bring about progress, so it frustrated them that people doubted their victory was 'true and fair'. Earlier that day, the Candlelight Party had refused to recognise the result, saying that some of their party representatives were not allowed to observe ballot counting, which 'indicated vote-rigging'.[1] The jovial one could not understand their doubts. 'People criticise the election, or make complaints, say the counting not right. How they say that?'[2]

That morning, I had breakfast with Kimchhay, the languid student. We talked about his final university thesis on populism and the promotion of falsehoods in politics.

'You talk about how populists, to rally people, may denigrate minority groups, like ethnic minority groups,' I said. 'It made me think about what some people say about some of the opposition parties here in Cambodia – that they are populist in the way that they try to discuss …'

'Vietnamese people,' Kimchhay interrupted.

'Yeah.'

'I can see that. It also part of my thinking how opposition parties use race as a ticket to rally people. Vietnamese this, Vietnamese that. But is it really the core of the problem in Cambodia? Everything can be attributed to Vietnamese? Or is the problem somewhere else? It's not a right choice, but maybe a correct choice to try to get power.'

'Do you find it disappointing? The use of race?'

'I mean, I find it disappointing.'

'What did you think about the campaigning for this election?'

'This election is different to the national one. It's about those commune leaders and how effective they are at processing my documents. One time, I went to get my identity card copied and they did not even ask me for any money. They said, "Come back in three days," and I come back in three days and I ask "How much is that?" And they say, "No, we don't take it." That's why I find that it is good, so I vote for them.'

Like every other commune before the election, Kimchhay's commune had been run by the CPP. I asked him if the running of his commune had improved in recent years. 'Yeah. If you want documents fast, you can give some extra compensation. But if you don't need it fast, you just go, "Here are my documents" and then come back one week or something. This is how I think about my vote in this recent election.'

'You are educated, very educated.'

'Hopefully,' Kimchhay joked.

'You once told me you are liberal. You are a thoughtful person. You know about society and you think about it. The opposition would say that you would be their target voter. Why do you think they fail to engage with people?'

'People like me?'

'Yeah.'

'I don't see what they are going to do for the country. What are they planning to do? And all I see is more us-against-them politics. All I see is their rallying cry.'

'When I think about the opposition, about falsehoods, it seems to me that they are ignoring the truth that there are a lot of people who want to support, who want to vote for, the ruling party,' I volunteered.

'Yeah, it is not all about compulsion. I mean, we have to believe in something, we would feel naked if we don't have reasons, even if those reasons are not valid.'

The Candlelight Party announced that the election results 'did not reflect the will of the people',[3] and Karuna from ADHOC said the same, word for word, when having lunch with me. I wondered how they knew what the real will of the people was.

Karuna explained that people felt pressured when voting, or even to vote, pointing out that public servants were being asked to send a photo of their inked finger to their boss – Davuth's wife was told to show her head and torso in the photo to prove it wasn't someone else's finger. And other people were influenced by gifts, especially because a list was kept of who received gifts, who voted and how many votes the CPP got. Intimidation and gifts created pressure which, according to Karuna, meant that some people did not have free will when voting.

Ou Chanrath, a former CNRP politician who leads the Cambodian Reform Party, admitted it was not his 'will' to vote, even for his own party: 'Voters were not really excited with the election. They seemed to come unhappily. Like me; I also went to vote but it was not voting from my real will but voting out of consideration of what's the next-best option.'[4]

While some voters may have been induced by gifts or intimidation to vote CPP, and some may have been voting half-heartedly, this does not equate to a CPP victory being *against* the will of the people. Two days after the election, I was out with Channary, the young woman who moved from the White Building, and four of her friends.[5] All voted CPP, praising their handling of the pandemic, and found the alternatives laughable.

That same night, Ritthy (who was now married) told me that the CPP 'get credit for COVID, vaccine, social protection scheme increasing – it's quite generous'.[6]

Small Rotha, nearing forty and with high blood pressure, did not doubt the results: 'Some people were for CNRP last time, but when no more CNRP, they vote CPP. The Candlelight come but don't know who's the leader. Like, my parents at the province, yeah, just follow majority in the village.' His uncle, a CNRP demonstrator who camped at Freedom Park during the protests of 2013–14, had shown no interest in the Candlelight Party; he and other CNRP officials in the area had moved district, giving up politics and concentrating on farming.[7] Even Rong Chhun acknowledged that there wasn't a majority wanting the Candlelight Party to win.[8]

Accepting a genuine CPP victory does not mean that the election was free and fair, though. Most citizens were free to vote, but not all were free to stand for election. Kem Sokha was on trial, Chea Chiv and 100 former CNRP politicians were banned, and many more, like Chen Sokngeng, were abroad avoiding jail. Dozens of candidates were rejected from the ballot, and Sam Rainsy was prohibited from entering the country. None of these people was free to compete with the CPP, and no one could vote for them.

Rozeth's burning defiance is stoked by these injustices. I watched as she discovered one of her banners cut down. She found it dumped behind a bin down an alley.[9] A few days later she was searching for another banner, and then another, and then another. She was not the only Candlelight Party candidate to experience this, which is of course something that would never happen to the CPP. The preponderance of funds the CPP has, the media influence, the government resources and the conscription of public servants, never mind judicial bias, means that, as Leap said, the election was a competition between an elephant and a mouse.[10]

It was for these reasons that the Candlelight Party claimed the election was not free and fair. One of its vice-presidents, Son Chhay, went further by claiming votes had been 'bought and stolen',[11] which incensed the CPP and the National Election Commission. The CPP sued him for $1 million in defamation, while the NEC sued for a public apology. The NEC declared 'There may be no election more honest than Cambodia's.'[12]

I asked Hang Puthea, the NEC member, how he defined 'free and fair', as it was clear the NEC and CPP had a very different opinion to the Candlelight Party. Puthea, who had always talked freely in my previous interviews with him, reached into his blazer pocket, pulled out a notebook and began to read from it: 'For free and fair in Cambodia, free means that every citizen who can vote has free decision to vote for any party they like and fair means that everyone has the same period to prepare and campaign.'[13]

The former campaigner for free and fair elections, who had come onto the NEC in 2015 as its lone neutral member, then put the script back in his pocket and looked at me, ready for the next question.

CHAPTER 42

ENMITY RETURNS

Kem Sokha, arrested on 3 September 2017, had still not received a verdict in his trial. There had been a pause during the pandemic, and when the case resumed, the hearing was limited to once a week, on a Wednesday morning. Banned from politics and foreign travel while under trial, Sohka was aware the judiciary seemed in no rush to hear the case. He had been charged with conspiring with a foreign power to foment hostilities or acts of aggression against Cambodia. The prosecution, however, had still never named which foreign power Sokha had conspired with, although did list a range of implicated parties that included the United States, Australia, Taiwan, the EU and even Yugoslavia.[1] The prosecution instead focused on his partnership with Sam Rainsy, probing possible complicity in the crimes of which Rainsy had been convicted.

A year after the CPP's clean sweep in the 2018 national election, and with the CNRP dissolved, Rainsy decided in 2019 that there was no option but to return to Cambodia and risk arrest. Unlike in 2013, Rainsy announced his return months in advance and declared his mission as 'to arrest Hun Sen'.[2] He even challenged Sen to step down if more than one million people greeted him at the airport. Sen responded by promising Rainsy that his supporters would only be able to see him in prison.[3]

Hun Sen did not wait for Rainsy to arrive, though, and dozens of Rainsy's supporters were arrested in the weeks leading up to the promised return on 9 November 2019, Cambodia's Independence Day.[4] Driving home from a café, Chea Chiv was stopped by authorities, who told him to exit his car as he was under arrest. He asked what for and was met with: 'They want you arrested.' His shirt was ripped in the ensuing scuffle as they handcuffed him, bundled him into a car and took him to Battambang's police headquarters. Chiv said that they deliberately shamed him by leaving him shirtless and pettily refused to return his Sam Rainsy Party membership card, which he had held in his wallet since 2003. He was then taken to Phnom Penh with many other former CNRP staff and held in Prey Sar prison for a couple of weeks. He wasn't allowed to call a lawyer or his wife, who was told by police that he was in a car accident and had injured two people.[5]

Characterising Rainsy's return as an attempted coup, Sen declared that the army lay in wait for Rainsy and ordered soldiers to 'attack' his supporters 'wherever you see them': 'You don't need arrest warrants at all ... Our troops should be deployed with all kinds of weapons. This is not a normal demonstration or protest – it has become an armed conflict.'[6] The army erected checkpoints along the border, patrolling roads.[7]

On 7 November, Rainsy made his way to Charles de Gaulle airport in France but Thai Airways refused to allow him on the plane because Thailand's Prime Minister had promised Hun Sen to prevent his arrival.[8] The Laos Prime Minister had done the same,[9] and Vietnam would never let him in, meaning all land crossings into Cambodia were blocked. Rainsy managed to get to Malaysia but found no way of departing for Cambodia.[10] He chose Indonesia next,[11] but again found no route to Cambodia, so by the end of the month Rainsy was back in Paris.[12] Cambodia's courts sentenced him in asbentia and eight other CNRP leaders, including Rozeth's father-in-law, to twenty-plus years for 'plotting an attack'.[13]

Kem Sokha was not one of those charged, however. Indeed, the day after Rainsy was stopped boarding a flight from Malaysia to Cambodia, Sokha was released from house arrest, although under strict conditions.[14] Sokha's closest advisers had been absent from Sam Rainsy's campaign to return,[15] and Sokha distanced himself by announcing that he would 'never do something that could cause turmoil and chaos' and 'never leave my motherland at all as I have chosen her as a base for my political career'.[16]

Their old mistrust was reignited when the CNRP was dissolved. Sokha still called himself President of the Cambodian National Rescue Party but Rainsy appointed himself President of the Cambodian National Rescue Movement, then Acting President of the CNRP while Sokha was under arrest.[17] When Rainsy called on CNRP supporters to support the Candlelight Party, Sokha denounced it: 'I would verify that I am not involved. Rainsy and his colleagues have walked away from the principles and spirit of unity.'[18] Rainsy responded that Sokha only said this because he was being held prisoner by Hun Sen,[19] which provoked Sokha's daughters to brand Rainsy a liar with a history of exploiting Sokha for his own ends.[20]

The division was exacerbated by the proliferation of parties with links to the CNRP: former members created the Cambodian Reform Party and headed the Kampuchea Niyum Party, the Cambodian National Love Party, the Khmer Conservative Party and the Khmer Will Party. Rainsy blasted all of these groups for playing into Hun Sen's hands.[21]

Just a month before the June 2022 commune election, Sokha testified in court that he had nothing to do with the Candlelight Party and would not be friends with those who 'harmed the interests of the nation'.[22] He had also been filmed telling villagers not to vote, but it still shocked many when he announced on the day of the election that he and his close supporters would not vote.[23] Days later, Rainsy criticised Sokha for 'making a serious mistake', telling the media 'I really regret … his speech',[24] which prompted Sokha's chief adviser to accuse Rainsy of 'betraying the will of the Cambodian citizens by running away from the spirit of unity'.[25] There was little semblance, never mind spirit, of unity: Sokha had spent more time speaking with Hun Sen in the previous month than he had with Sam Rainsy in years. Sokha's lawyer downplayed the importance of Sokha's four-hour conversation with Sen at the funeral of Sen's brother; he said they only talked about 'normal, general things … COVID, family'.[26]

Since I had last met with Rong Chhun in 2019, he had spent fifteen months in jail for alleging the government allowed Vietnam to encroach on Cambodian farmland at the border. Actually, Chhun corrected me, it was fifteen months and twelve days, as every day in prison counts. His nephew, always at his side when I had met him before, had died in an unexplained moto accident, so Chhun was meeting me alone. Looking older than his early fifties, he poured me tea but, with his bad eye getting worse, nearly missed my cup. Chhun had previously exempted Sokha when criticising CNRP leaders for not standing up against its dissolution, but he thought Sokha's attacks on the Candlelight Party were wrong. 'We have not learned the lesson of 2013. The opposition is split and it is not just the votes that are being split … the effect is more than that. The voters do not see a strong opposition. They see weak parties – small parties that cannot compete against the strong one. So they see no choice. And all the small parties, they divide their resources, their people, their effort.

'The Candlelight Party has to be open-minded to accept other parties, to include other parties and their leaders. If the Candlelight Party is too proud and does not include, does not reform with other parties, then it will still say the same. It will not grow. It will fail. It will fail at the national election. A good soup is one that is based on a mix of ingredients. With only one ingredient, it is not as delicious as when the right ingredients are mixed together. If the Candlelight Party continues like this, it will win only ten to twenty seats in the National Assembly elections of 2023.'²⁷

CHAPTER 43

CHAPTER TWO

The question of who will succeed Hun Sen was finally settled when, in December 2021, the CPP's Central Committee endorsed Hun Manet as the CPP's next leader. Hun Sen will lead the CPP into the 2023 national elections and possibly even the 2028 elections, before handing over to his eldest son.

During an Australian interview in 2015, Manet was almost bashful trying to avoid questions about whether he would follow his father as Prime Minister. The interviewer suggested that Manet – the first Cambodian graduate from America's West Point Military Academy, with a Master and PhD in economics from New York University and Bristol University respectively, and the Commander of the Royal Cambodian Army – had been groomed from a young age to become Prime Minister. Manet replied coyly that it is the Cambodian people who choose their Prime Minister.[1]

Manet had also played a leading role in Cambodia's management of COVID-19. The World Health Organization dubbed Cambodia's response 'remarkable'.[2] While Thailand charged citizens for a vaccine and Vietnam experienced shortages, many Cambodians I met during the election campaign had already been vaccinated four times and Cambodia had even donated vaccines to Laos, Myanmar, Timor Leste and Nepal.[3] To convince people of the vaccine's safety, Manet stepped forward to be its first recipient.[4] In charge of quarantine management, he led – along with this wife, who has a PhD in Public Health – the establishment of a large Phnom Penh treatment centre as cases increased.[5] Dav Ansan told me Manet had impressed many during this time: 'I observe the way he manage COVID, himself and his wife, that was so amazing. People really appreciated his sacrifice. He stayed out late, most of the time had to stay away from his children. He managed all this logistics arrangement, armed forces to control situation, managed medical doctors, volunteers: quite a challenging job.'[6]

Manet's youngest brother, Hun Many, has also continued his rise to prominence. He was profiled in a book written by the co-founder of the independent *Thmey Thmey News*. The journalist found that the more he learnt about Many, who had completed a degree in New York and a Master of International Relations at the University of Melbourne, the more he saw him as a potential great leader.

Phirun, who has spent time in delegations with Hun Many, has been 'impressed' by the children of Hun Sen, who have all learnt the value of responsibility: 'The younger generation have new ways of thinking. Their knowledge, their skill – compared with the opposition party, they are better. The opposition ... they don't – some of them don't – have experience with government, don't have experience with parliament, don't have experience with foreign affairs. I remember one time when the National Assembly hosted an international event, it was an event for Asia Pacific Parliamentary Forum ... Hun Many was the chair of the meeting and sometimes spoke about issues very controversial. Wow, he handle the meeting so well. And I look at him, he did the job so confidently.'[7]

Chamroeun has conversed briefly with Manet a couple of times, during which Manet said that, like his father, he fears that Cambodians are quick to anger and need to be controlled. Manet shared his father's vision of Cambodia becoming like Singapore, although sometimes disagreed on the means of getting there. Chamroeun believes that the CPP's new generation may love the country but when pushed, they will put the Party first.[8] Leap also thinks there are young CPP leaders who have 'genuine care for the country' and 'want to shift to a new model' but, crucially, concludes, 'they also want to make sure their party remains. They are not quite yet true to the real pluralism.'[9]

Ritthy had spent a day with Many at a Politikoffee seminar just before the election and described him as a 'nice guy' and 'quite reasonable', but was unimpressed when Many told attendees that the priority in politics is winning. 'Win for what?' Ritthy asked me. 'Just to keep winning? Winning for power and do what?' While admitting that with age he is beginning to understand the CPP's balance of responsibilities to the nation, to its own members and to international relations, Ritthy is not hopeful the CPP's new generation will be different: 'CPP want change but they don't want to be changed.'[10]

It is difficult to see who could force them to change. When I asked Chamroeun about the next generation of leaders in Cambodia, he immediately said, 'I only see the CPP.' Without Rainsy and Sokha, the leaders of the Candlelight Party were struggling to cut through.

Thach Setha was one of the 118 CNRP politicians banned from politics for five years in 2017 but was pardoned in April 2021.[11] Setha had worked closely with Sam Rainsy since 1995 and quickly set about reactivating the Candlelight Party by travelling the country to recruit candidates for the commune election. The President of the Candlelight Party is Teav Vannol, now living in America and a figurehead only, meaning Setha was often assumed to be the party's leader; indeed, it was in the 'President's office' where I met him.

With Rainsy in France and Sokha unwilling to join the Candlelight Party, I asked him who the Party's prime ministerial candidate in the 2023 election would be. Son Chhay, a former CNRP Senator, had recently returned to Cambodia from Australia, where he is a dual citizen. He became a Candelight vice-president, meaning that Setha and Chhay were jointly leading press conferences and party duties. Setha, smiling at my question, said nothing had been decided yet.[12]

Rong Chhun knows Setha and Chhay, both in their sixties and involved in politics since the early 1990s, so I asked him who he thought would be the Party's candidate. He implied that neither Setha nor Chhay, even if Chhay relinquished Australian citizenship to be eligible, may be the right answer. 'I don't know, but there will be discussions. The leaders have to reflect on the result and what it means. Twenty per cent is not good enough and the current leaders have to reflect on that.'

'Do you see who the next generation of leaders may be?'

'I don't see a new generation of leaders. Cannot see who they are or who they will be. They have not been identified. Naturally, bamboo has bamboo shoots, but I cannot predict if the shoots will be stronger or weaker than the old bamboo.'[13]

The CPP won 1648 of 1652 councils, a victory that, combined with an opposition in disarray, has made it 'dominant', as Phirun explained: 'The ruling party, they have position everywhere. And their network inside the country ... no question. Everything is under control.'

But the people in the rural communes of Doung, Kraya, Chamna Leou and Pdao Chum had voted no to the CPP and yes for the Candlelight Party. What was happening in these villages that the absence of Rainsy and Sokha was not felt? What sort of people lived there who could defy the CPP machine?

Rithisak and I turned off the main road in Pdao Chum and drove between lush green rice fields, where water buffalo grazed with birds on their backs, to meet Chang Phalla, who was standing outside a school waiting for us. He took us down a mud road to his home, a traditional wooden house built on impressive four-metre-high stilts. In the early 1980s, after the Khmer Rouge was overthrown, Phalla was given responsibility for helping to settle fifty families in Pdao Chum. The local authorities were impressed so gave him another fifty, and then more again, and before long, Phalla, still in his twenties, was Deputy Village Chief. In the 1993 election he stood as a CPP member, although drifted away in the years after. Shortly before the 2002 commune election, Phalla, a rice farmer, saw a sign outside a house: 'The sign had three words on it. It said *Integrity. Honesty. Justice.* I thought, "I have these three in my heart so maybe that's the party." It was the Sam Rainsy Party and they asked me to join. In 2007, I stood as the Party's second candidate and was elected, and then in 2012, I was elected Deputy Commune Chief.'

'Why did you leave the CPP?' I asked.

'The ruling party was not addressing the problems of the people. They were not focusing on them. The rich people become richer, much richer. They twist and lie for their own benefit. With them, white becomes black.'

'Did they ever pressure you or try to stop you from standing?'

'They put a lot of pressure. A lot of pressure. Others may have run away because the pressure was so great. They would try to bribe me as well. Offer me money or positions, but I only need three meals a day – that is all I can eat.'

'Why did you not run away? Did you think about it?'

'I don't want the villagers to think that I am like a dog that runs away.'[14]

Phalla sat square to the table with a mammoth book in front of him. His eyes barely flickered at my questions as if nosy foreign visitors in his home were a normal occurrence.

'In 2017, when it was the CNRP, you won the election and became Commune Chief.'

'Yes, in 2017, we won six of the nine seats and I became Chief.'

'And then the party was dissolved. Were you surprised?'

'There was a meeting three days before the court decided. I said we should stand up but the leaders said no, we should not, we should let the international community put pressure on the government to solve it. It was a wrong decision. Terribly wrong. We should have done the opposite.'

'What happened to you? When did they come to tell you to leave?'

'The clerk came and told me I had to collect my things and leave. They actually asked me to leave the week before the CNRP had even been dissolved.

CHAPTER TWO

I asked them to show me the law, the document, but they couldn't show me anything. The ruling party asked me to join with them, but I cannot. I would not join with them.'

Despite being replaced as Chief and no longer even a councillor, it was Phalla, and his digger, who villagers went to for help when there was flooding. It was he who gathered villagers, many of whom he had assisted to settle during the 1980s, to build a road from rice fields to the village, raising $2500 and contributing $500 of his own money. I asked him if it was an easy decision to stand for the Candlelight Party.

'It wasn't an easy decision, but I'm used to things being difficult. The CPP told me I wouldn't win. They try to warn me I won't win.'

'Were there any problems when you were campaigning?'

'There were no problems for me during the campaign. It was fine.'

I looked at him, barely shifting in his seat, thinking he would remain steady in a hurricane. 'What was it like on election day?'

'There were lots of people at the polling stations. The Village Chief. Local authorities. All there. It was like a net to catch people at the polling station.'

'Were people intimidated by that?'

'Villagers not really intimidated. Kind of normal. They were being told to vote for the angel, though. That's what they were being told.' The angel is the logo of the CPP.

'Do you think people believe that the vote is secret?'

'That is what I tell people. When I am campaigning, I tell people that their vote is secret. That they cannot know how they voted.'

'What did the villagers say to you when you were campaigning?'

'They said I was brave, brave because I stand even though I could be killed.'

'Did you think you were in danger?'

'I thought I could be attacked. Something could happen to me. The villagers, they were too scared to be seen talking with me. I could not go house to house. I had to use a loudspeaker and give out leaflets along the street. But after I win, they congratulate me. They are happy I win.'

'What would you say when you were shouting through the loudspeaker?'

'I would tell people they will have freedom, not like the last four and a half years. That a group of people just sitting [around a table] like this would not be alleged of doing something.'

'What did you feel when you won?'

'That now I had the opportunity to help people.'

'Did you celebrate at all?'

'Some villagers want a party and dance, but I said no. It will make the other side unhappy so we don't do it.'

'Do you think it will it be easy to work with authorities like education, health?'

'It will not be easy. It will be difficult to work with those government authorities. But I will persist. I will try to get along with the clerk. Try to work together.'

Hun Sen seemed in no mood for conciliation, though. The day before I met Phalla, thirty-one people were sentenced to six years or more, with another twenty given suspended sentences for 'plotting' Sam Rainsy's return. Just two weeks earlier, Chea Chiv had told me that his court case seemed dormant, possibly because Sen wanted to avoid bad press before an election. Chiv was in Battambang when he heard that he had been sentenced to six years, and immediately went into hiding just before the police searched his house. Seng Theary, an American-Cambodian human rights lawyer, was less fortunate, being dragged off the street and taken to prison.[15] This was the same day that the CPP sued Son Chhay for $1 million in defamation damages, in what many saw as a ploy to encourage Chhay to stay in Australia, where he was visiting. Failure to pay if found guilty could result in Chhay's imprisonment. The sentencing and defamation case sent shockwaves throughout Cambodia. I asked Phalla if it made him feel different.

'It makes no difference. I read about that and know about Seng Theary and the court case, but no difference for me.'

Before leaving, I asked the married father of four what the book was on the table in front of him.

'It is the book of all the criminal laws. I have read most of it so that I can refer to it in case people want to challenge me. Want to look down on me.'

Rithisak and I rose from our chairs, gave Phalla a *sampeah* and bade farewell before setting off for Kraya commune, where the diminutive Yab Yot had triumphed for the Candlelight Party. We arrived at Yot's house, similar to Phalla's but smaller and with noticeably shorter stilts, while Yot was still making his way back from his five-hectare mango and cassava plantation. We knew it was his house as it was bedecked in Candlelight banners and logos, and we soon saw him chugging along on his old black Honda 125 that was missing a piece of bodywork. He jumped off his moto and bounced into the stilted area under the house to quickly change his shirt and wipe down the wooden table for us.

Yot grinned in welcome, showing off the whiskers at each side of his moustache. He took off his wide-brimmed hat, putting it down on the table, and I noticed the soil engrained in the wrinkles of his palms and under his nails. Yot straightened his weathered beige shirt before sitting down and then scrambled to find his glasses, which were folded at the bridge like a pocketknife. He picked them up along with a notebook and pen, ready for our conversation.

'Of all the communes in the country, there were only four Candlelight Party candidates that managed to win and become chief. Why do you think you managed to win when so many others couldn't?' I asked.

'They know me very well. The villagers all know me. I have lived here all my life and they know that I will work for them. We won four seats and the CPP won three. The election was not fair in other communes, we would have won more. Even just there in Samaky [neighbouring commune], we only lost by thirty to forty votes.'[16]

'And of the four, three of them are in Kampong Thom province and all close to each other. That is interesting,' I observed.

'The candidates are honest, good people. They don't talk a lot. They don't just talk, they do. And the people in Kampong Thom, they are straight, honest people.'

Yot first stood in 2012 as a last-minute replacement because the existing candidates were prosecuted, one for murder. He led the Sam Rainsy Party to victory, spurred by widespread anger at 8000 hectares of farmland being given to a Vietnamese rubber company, the forced removal of a whole village,[17] and police beatings of protestors.[18] Yot spoke to the provincial Governor and rubber company to broker the return of some land to villagers, quickly gaining respect.

Yot won again in 2017 – unsurprising given he had raised contributions from villagers to build roads, improve irrigation and construct four dams that cost $20,000 to $30,000 each. The benefits were immediate, as farmers could grow rice during the dry season too, doubling harvests. That all came to an end in 2017, though, when the CNRP was dissolved. 'I was at home when I heard. I was surprised. I wanted to know why. Why was the party dissolved? What had the party done wrong?'

'At that time, there were no protests. What do you think about that?'

'The leaders should have stayed. They should have stayed and protested. Not flee abroad. They should stand and say they haven't done anything to break the law.'

'Do you know the CPP man who took over from you?'

'Yes, he was my deputy.'

'Was he sad about what happened to you – losing your job? Did he show any remorse?'

'He's a lovely person.'

'A lovely person?' I asked, taken aback by a description rarely used in Cambodian politics.

'Yes. Not a friend, but ...'

'He was sorry for you?'

'Yes, he said he doesn't want to replace me but has to follow instructions from the top. Four months that guy and district officials try to persuade me to join them. They offer me jobs, positions. They warned I would be pressured if I don't join.'

'What did other people say?'

'Villagers were upset but they didn't know what to say. Didn't know what to do.'

'When the Candlelight Party returned, began to re-form, was it a difficult decision to join?'

'I talk with a few others. We talk about it, about taking the risk to participate in politics again. If you join, then you have to be prepared to go to jail. To be pressured. To be harmed or even die.'

I asked what his wife thought.

'She was with me. She is fine. She doesn't mind me joining the Candlelight Party. She knows I do it to support the community.'

I mischievously asked if he thought his three children had voted for him, which caused to him stop and think for a moment. 'My oldest child is married and lives nearby. The middle one is eighteen years old and lives here with us, and the younger one too. I don't know if they voted for me. I don't know. Could have voted CPP.'

I smiled, doubting politicians in other families were so casual about how their children voted. 'Did you have people helping when you were campaigning?'

'There were seven Candlelight Party candidates and we all worked together. We supported each other and helped each other. When we were campaigning, villagers would tell me about the Commune Chief. They said he could not solve their issues. Could not fix the problems. This was why they didn't vote for him.'

During the last five years, three of the dams had become weaker and one had fallen into complete disrepair.

CHAPTER TWO

'The authorities did not try to stop me. In fact, as soon as they knew I was standing, they knew they would lose. The CPP would give money to villagers, sarongs, gifts, but no difference.'

On election day, tensions were less high than anticipated. 'The situation was fine here in this commune. It was not in others, but the situation here was okay. But one day before, they went to villagers and told them that if Candlelight win, it won't be able to do anything. They said it can't do anything – no power. They then showed them on ballot forms how to vote Cambodian People's Party.

'When I found out I had won, I was here at home. We had party agents at the polling stations and they update me very quickly. They send me photos of the tallies from the polling stations. I knew quite quickly.'

'Did you celebrate? Have a little party? Have a beer?' I asked with a smile.

'Ha, look at me! Look at my moto there! I have no money to celebrate or organise a party … My neighbours came to my house. They were very happy. We drank tea, coffee and talk.'

Our conversation was interrupted for the second time by *Voice of America*, calling to interview him. He was also being asked to use Telegram, so Rithisak showed him how to send text and audio messages, even photographs. When we resumed, I asked Yot if he had heard about the arrest of Seng Theary and the CPP suing Son Chhay. He raised his head and his whiskers twitched a little. 'I see this and it worries me. I think about it. But I will continue. It doesn't change. To do politics, you have to be prepared to go to jail or other things. I want real democracy. I want power away from the centre, decentralisation. I want people to have freedom, people to have rights. Important people, high people, they have power and they pressure lower people. They try to grab land, take from us. I will try to protect people from businesses and people who grab land. I don't have land but will protect the villagers. I could support rich people. Some leaders work with businessmen and they get rich. I could do that. If you have the right will to serve people honestly, to work according to fairness, then you will be poor. Look at my clothes, my appearance, my moto.'

I had been checking my phone regularly while talking to Yot. Being a Wednesday, I knew that Kem Sokha would have been in court that morning and wondered what had happened, given the mass sentencing of Rainsy supporters and Rainsy's criticism of Sokha for not voting.

As the session ended, the prosecutor asked Sokha to clarify who he was referring to when he had said that he would not be friends with people who harmed the nation. 'If I take this opportunity to talk everything about politics, it is over between Sam Rainsy and I. It is clear that there is no more "one Kem Sokha–Sam Rainsy." No more! He chose a different approach; he let the Candlelight Party take part in the election. He recently criticised me that I did not go to vote for the Candlelight Party. He announced about 9 November to ... come back to arrest the Prime Minister. I have never ever supported that. I never support that! Whenever the judge allows me to have political rights, I would immediately start a press conference to talk about this.'[19]

I asked Yab Yot what he thought about the news that the union between Kem Sokha and Sam Rainsy – the union that ten years previously had inspired Chamroeun to ride with the young, that had given Rotha and Soveacha hope the poor would be respected, that had caused Kunthea to chant for Hun Sen to step down and that had catapulted Sokngeng and Rozeth to become Commune Chiefs – was over.

'I regret that the two are separating. I'm not angry, I just feel disappointed. I wish it was not like this. But I will serve the people according to my plan and what I have said.'

I thanked Yab Yot, Commune Chief of rural Kraya in the heart of Cambodia, and gave him $2.50 for petrol, as he had to return to the fields that afternoon. We shook hands and walked the few metres together up to the road, pausing as a chicken wobbled past our feet.

Just before leaving, Rithisak asked to take a photo of Yot in front of his house, so he straightened his shirt again, smoothed his moustache, and remembered to throw his cigarette away just before being snapped, standing under the banner of a large Candlelight.

POSTSCRIPT

If you are patient in a moment of anger, you will spare yourself 100 days of tears.
បើអ្នកអត់ធ្មត់ក្នុងពេលខឹងមួយភ្លែត អ្នកនឹងមិនស្រក់ទឹកភ្នែកក្នុង រយៈពេលមួយរយថ្ងៃខាងមុខ។

Three months after the 2022 Commune Council election, Sam Rainsy was tried in absentia for planning to cede land to a foreign state.[1] This related to an agreement he signed with the Degar (or Montagnard) people, a minority ethnic group straddling the mountainous Cambodian–Vietnamese border, that if the CNRP won the election in 2013, it would return forests and land to them and provide them autonomy within Cambodia.[2] Despite the agreement not appearing to cede land to a foreign state, Rainsy was sentenced to life. Hun Sen said he would rather 'cut off my hand' than ever pardon Rainsy again.[3]

In March 2023, Kem Sokha's longstanding trial came to an end. He was found guilty of conspiring with a foreign power after the 2013 elections 'for a colour revolution to overthrow the government'. The judge declined to name which foreign power Sokha had conspired with, explaining this was to 'maintain good communications with the foreign countries'.[4]

Sokha, aged sixty-nine, was sentenced to twenty-seven years' house arrest and is only allowed to meet with family members. Upon receiving the judgement, Sokha remained silent, raising his fist above his head before pressing his palms together in a *sampeah*. Police then led him away and still remain guard outside his house.

Thach Setha, a Vice-President of the Candlelight Party, was arrested and imprisoned for allegedly issuing five cheques in 2019 without having funds to pay them, and for failing to appear for questioning in 2021. His lawyer argued that the matter of the cheques had already been settled in a separate case, but bail was denied and Setha remains in jail.[5]

Rong Chhun, the union leader and former NEC member, joined Candlelight and was elected as a Vice-President. He sought to challenge Hun Sen in his constituency seat in the July 2023 national elections and was a potential prime ministerial candidate. Chhun, however, was barred from standing because he remains under court supervision due to a suspended sentence.[6]

The exclusion of Setha and Chhun became moot when the Candlelight Party was entirely excluded from contesting the elections because it could not provide its original registration certificate. Candlelight said that the original may have been lost during a police raid when documents were confiscated but could provide photocopies. The NEC rejected photocopies as inadequate – despite accepting them for the 2022 Commune Council elections – and the police were unable to help find the original document.[7] The Ministry of Interior confirmed that the Candlelight Party was a registered political party and claimed it had returned the original certificate after processing the registration, suggesting that Candlelight may have 'pawned it in exchange for money'.[8] On 31 May, Hang Puthea, Chhun's former colleague at the NEC, announced registration for the election had closed without the Candlelight Party.

Rong Chhun initially declared a protest but postponed it, advising that Candlelight needed more time to prepare and to consider options if authorities did not permit the protest. Hun Sen warned potential protestors that the 'prisons are prepared' and told Rong Chhun that it was time for him to get married.[9] Hang Puthea threatened that the NEC would take legal action if anybody called for a boycott of the national elections, and the National Assembly warded against it by passing a law requiring future candidates to have voted in the two elections prior.[10]

Eighteen political parties will contest the national election on 23 July 2023.

Despite mounting arrests of Candlelight Party members and defections to the CPP, Yab Yot and Chang Phalla continue as Candelight Party Commune Chiefs, and Sin Rozeth, now a mother, remains Deputy Chief in O'Char, Battambang.

ACKNOWLEDGEMENTS

I have never known kindness like I experienced in Cambodia, and this book is only possible because of Cambodians generously giving me extraordinary amounts of time, interrupting their work and sacrificing family time to speak with me. Their generosity was such that I could have written a second book containing stories from indigenous people in Mondolkiri, families living in shacks next to Angkor Wat and those trying to hold onto the Sihanoukville they once knew. I am sorry that I have taken their stories and not been able to include them in this book. Several of these 'lost chapters' are on the book's website, and I urge you to read them: www.atigerrules.com.

Many friends helped make this book possible, some of whom prefer not to be named. Nobody worked harder than Sok Saren, who arranged interviews, translated documents and helped get me around rural Cambodia. I could not have done this without him. In Samrithy introduced me to many people, assisted during interviews and helped inspire the book's title (see website for full story). Kul Midy connected me with ADHOC and was my man in Mondolkiri, driving us through the night on a decrepit moto with my phone torch as our only light. Savann juggled work and family to help, and reached out to many people for me. I cherished conversations with Lay Vutha and Hoeurn, who provided rich insights, and I owe Nibpun a night in a fancy hotel after he worked all weekend and only got a shack to sleep in. Kheang Thida added final enrichment with the proverbs that open each part.

Of those featured in the book, Ou Ritthy was indispensable, and I would like to thank H.E. Dav Ansan for giving me huge amounts of time, sharing extensively. I think it is important to give the CPP's side of the story and Sal, a good friend, aided immensely with this.

My favourite sessions reviewing drafts were with The Inkermen on a Wednesday night in the pub, whose forthrightness was always wrapped in support. Any praise for my writing is due to their feedback on my match reports. John McGuinness gets a special mention for spending hours producing the book's incredible video trailer.

ACKNOWLEDGEMENTS

John Weber read many drafts, giving me welcome encouragement. Sue Coffey is the book's greatest cheerleader and also steered me with valuable advice. Emily Mann's belief in the book kept me going when I was beginning to doubt, and she prompted crucial improvements to early chapters. James Morgan's wisdom ensured the story did not become about the person wielding the pen. I would not have met some of the key people in this book without John Friend Pereira's help.

Julia Carlomagno took a chance on this book and I want to thank her, as well as Sarah Cannon, Sam van der Plank and Duncan Blachford for their work to publish and promote it. The eye-catching cover is due to Erika Piñeros, who provided an amazing archive of images, and the wonderful design is by Tom Francis, who also helped with the book's website.

It was a privilege to receive support from Sebastian Strangio, Sophal Ear, Tom Doig, Mary Ann Jolley and Gareth Evans. Gareth made valuable recommendations on the manuscript. I am humbled by what they have said.

Nobody has been more involved in reading drafts, helping me think about style, direction and content, and listening to my self-involved struggles, than Claire. The journey of this book began when we touched down in Cambodia more than ten years ago, and she has been part of it ever since.

It was the late Than Dara who taught me Khmer, and he opened Cambodia to me. Without him I would not have heard the stories I've been told in the same way, and I am deeply indebted to all my interviewees for what they have shared. I have admiration for each and every one of them. My name may be on the front cover, but this book has been written by Cambodians.

NOTES

Chapter 2: Injustice Burns

1   Boyle, D. & May, T., 'A history of violence', *The Phnom Penh Post*, 14 November 2012.
2   May, T. & Boyle, D. 'Bloody day in Svay Rieng', *The Phnom Penh Post*, 21 February 2012 and Khuon, N. & Chen, D., 'Three demonstrators shot during violent protest in SEZ', *The Cambodia Daily*, 17 February 2012.
3   Tep, N., 'Strike spins new deal for cycle factory crew', *The Phnom Penh Post*, 15 February 2012.
4   Boyle, D. & May, T., 'CCTV shooting footage reviewed', *The Phnom Penh Post*, 24 February 2012.
5   ibid.
6   May, T., 'Bavet governor implicated', *The Phnom Penh Post*, 2 March 2012.
7   ibid. and May, T. & Boyle, D., 'Victim rejects "pay-off"', *The Phnom Penh Post*, 8 March 2012.
8   May, T. & Boyle, D., 'Shooting in Bavet at PUMA supplier "unintentional"', *The Phnom Penh Post*, 20 April 2012; Chenda quoted in May, T., 'Investigation into former Bavet town governor closed, but still no trial', *The Phnom Penh Post*, 26 November 2012; Sakhorn quoted in May, T. & Boyle, D., 'Shooting victims fight on', *The Phnom Penh Post*, 20 December 2012.
9   Chhay, C., 'Witness duo no-show amid safety concerns', *The Phnom Penh Post*, 25 June 2015.
10 May, T., 'Bandith hearing concludes', *The Phnom Penh Post*, 1 March 2013.
11 May, T., 'Witnesses say they saw shots from Bandith', *The Phnom Penh Post*, 14 June 2013.
12 Boyle, D & May, T., 'Blind eye to forest's plight', *The Phnom Penh Post*, 26 March 2012.
13 ibid.
14 'Carving up Cambodia', *The Cambodia Daily Weekend*, 11 March 2013, pp. 4–11 and Global Witness, 'Country for Sale: Welcome to Cambodia', Global Witness Publishing Inc., Washington, D.C., 5 February 2009.
15 Pye, D & May, T., 'The calculus of logging', *The Phnom Penh Post*, 10 October 2014.

16 'Deforestation statistics for Cambodia', Mangobay, date unknown, https://rainforests.mongabay.com/deforestation/archive/Cambodia.htm and May, T., 'To honour Chut Wutty', *The Phnom Penh Post*, 21 April 2014.
17 'Carving up Cambodia', op. cit.
18 May, T. & Boyle, D., 'Teenage girl gunned down by security forces in eviction', *The Phnom Penh Post*, 17 May 2012.
19 Plokhii, O., 'Death of a forester', *Newsweek*, 27 August 2012.
20 Wray, L. & Battersby, S., International Women's Media Foundation, 2013, www.iwmf.org/2013/09/bopha-phorn-2013-courage-in-journalism-award/; Phorn Bopha, Author's interview, no. 225; and 'In the Cardamom Mountains, two deaths recounted', *The Cambodia Daily*, 28 April 2012.
21 Saing, S. & Seiff, A., 'Chut Wutty, prominent environmental activist, shot dead in Koh Kong', *The Cambodia Daily*, 26 April 2012.
22 Khuon, N., 'Court drops case of murdered environmentalist', *The Cambodia Daily*, 5 October 2012.

Chapter 3: The Man in Charge

1 Information in this opening from Mehta, H. & Mehta, J., *Strongman: The Extraordinary Life of Hun Sen*, Marshall Cavendish International, Singapore, 2013.
2 See for example Erlanger, S., 'Cambodia's Hun Sen; in Phnom Penh, Vietnam's "puppet" is finding his voice', *The New York Times*, 27 August 1989.
3 Events surrounding the Ambassador's wife taken from Coffey, S., *Seeking Justice in Cambodia*, Melbourne University Press, Carlton, 2018.
4 Hun Sen's salary in Mehta, H. & Mehta, J., *Strongman*, op. cit. Quote from Strangio, S., *Hun Sen's Cambodia*, Yale University Press, New Haven & London, 2014.
5 Strangio, S., *Hun Sen's Cambodia*, op. cit.
6 Erlanger, S., 'Cambodia's Hun Sen', op. cit.
7 Emmons, K., 'Chess player, philosopher, a leader of the country', *The Phnom Penh Post*, 1 December 1995.
8 Strangio, S., *Hun Sen's Cambodia*, op. cit.
9 Roberts, D., 'Meddling while Phnom Penh burned: The US role in the Cambodian secession', *Critical Asian Studies* 30 (3), 1998, pp. 14–24.
10 Vickery, M., *Cambodia; A Political Survey*, Editions Funan, Phnom Penh, 2007.
11 This proverb was told to me by Chen Sokngeng, Author's interview, No. 091.
12 Adams, B., *Cambodia: July 1997: Shock and Aftermath*, Human Rights Watch, 27 July 2007.

NOTES

13 Shaw, W., 'Battle for Phnom Penh: 10th anniversary of the 1997 factional fighting', *The Cambodia Daily*, 1 July 2017.

14 'CPP Congress: Hun Sen rapped on style while party expands', *The Phnom Penh Post*, 7 February 1997.

15 Brinkley, J., *Cambodia's Curse*, Black Inc., Melbourne, 2011.

16 Information on events of July 1997 taken from Adams, B., *Cambodia: July 1997: Shock and Aftermath*, op. cit.; Shaw, W., 'Battle for Phnom Penh', op. cit.; Willemyns, A., 'Making of a strongman: in July 1997, Hun Sen took full control of the country – and his party', *The Phnom Penh Post*, 5 July 2007; Adams, B., *30 Years of Hun Sen*, Human Rights Watch, 2015; Thayer, N., 'Cambodians describes atrocities by Hun Sen's forces', *The Washington Post*, 28 July 1997.

17 Willemyns, A., 'Making of a strongman', op. cit. and Adams, B., *Cambodia: July 1997*, op. cit.

18 Strangio, S., *Hun Sen's Cambodia*, op. cit.

19 Emmons, K., 'Chess player, philosopher, a leader of the country', op. cit. and Krishner, Bloss & Lor, 'The interview granted to *The Cambodia Daily*', *The Cambodia Daily*, 1–4 January 2002.

20 In May 1989, Hun Sen was asked what his ideology was. He replied, 'Ideology doesn't matter right now. What the people want is peace and development.' Erlanger, S., 'Cambodia's Hun Sen', op. cit.

21 Department of Planning, 'Education statistics and indicators 2011–12', Ministry of Education, Youth and Sport, Cambodian Government, Phnom Penh, 2012.

22 International Republican Institute, *Survey of Cambodian Public Opinion, January 12 – February 2*, 2013, www.iri.org/sites/default/files/Cambodian%20Poll%209%20Final%20PUBLIC.pdf

23 Chhay, Author's interview, No. 003.

24 Phan Kimsorn, Author's interview, No. 025.

25 International Republican Institute, *Survey of Cambodian Public Opinion, October 28 – November 10*, 2013, www.iri.org/sites/default/files/2014%20January%2023%20Survey%20of%20Cambodia%20Public%20Opinion%2C%20October%2028-November%2010%2C%202013.pdf

26 Brinkley, J., *Cambodia's Curse*, op. cit.

27 Strangio, S., *Hun Sen's Cambodia*, op. cit.

28 Global Witness, *Hostile Takeover*, Global Witness, London, 2016.

29 Committee for Free and Fair Elections in Cambodia (COMFREL), *Phnom Penh: Committee for Free and Fair Elections in Cambodia*, Final Assessment and Report on 2012 Commune Elections, 2012.

NOTES

Chapter 4: To the Rescue

1. Information in this opening from UN High Commissioner for Human Rights, 'Grenade Attack in Phnom Penh and Extrajudicial Executions, 1997', 13 May 1998, https://cambodia.ohchr.org/sites/default/files/Thematic-reports/Thematic_CMB13051998E1.pdf; Rainsy, S. with Whitehouse, D., *We Didn't Start the Fire*, Silkworm Books, Chang Mai, 2013; Biegun, S. & Hall, E., 'The March 30, 1997 grenade attack in Cambodia: a staff report to the Committee on Foreign Relations United States Senate', US Government Printing Office, Washington, 1999; Garella, A. & Pape, E., 'A tragedy of no importance', date unknown, www.cambodiagrenade.info/
2. Rainsy, S., *We Didn't Start the Fire*, op. cit.
3. For a full account, see ibid.
4. 'Cambodia 1994 – the News in Review', *The Phnom Penh Post*, 30 December 1994.
5. Rainsy's biography based on Rainsy, S., *We Didn't Start the Fire*, op. cit. See also 'The ambassador, the maid and the spankings – end of an envoy', *The Phnom Penh Post*, 18 August 2000.
6. Amnesty International, 'Kingdom of Cambodia: the killing of trade unionist Chea Vichea', 3 December 2004, www.amnesty.org/en/documents/asa23/008/2004/en/
7. Human Rights Watch, 'Cambodia: opposition politicians arrested, forced to flee', 6 February 2005, www.hrw.org/news/2005/02/06/cambodia-opposition-politicians-arrested-forced-flee and Samean, Y., 'Sam Rainsy Sentenced to 18 Months', *The Cambodia Daily*, 23 December 2005.
8. Sopheng, C., 'Exiled Cambodian opposition leader returns home', *The Irrawaddy*, 10 February 2006.
9. Kannitha, M., 'Rainsy sentenced to two years', *The Phnom Penh Post*, 26 April 2011.
10. Kannitha, Author's interview, No. 006.
11. Coffey, S., *Seeking Justice in Cambodia*, op. cit.

Chapter 5: Shifting Currents

1. Population Division of the Department of Economic and Social Affairs of the United Nations Secretariat, *World Population Prospects Data Booklet, 2017 Revision*, 2018, www.un.org/development/desa/pd/sites/www.un.org.development.desa.pd/files/files/documents/2020/Jan/un_2017_world_population_prospects-2017_revision_databooklet.pdf
2. Soeng, S., 'Social media's growing influence on Cambodian politics', *Asia Pacific Bulletin*, East-West Center, Washington, 23 July 2013.

NOTES

3 ibid.
4 Strangio, S., *Hun Sen's Cambodia*, op. cit., p. 180.
5 Barnes, W., 'Cambodia chooses Prince Sihamoni as new king', *Financial Times*, 14 October 2004.
6 McPherson, P., 'Reign of the quiet king', *The Phnom Penh Post*, 29 October 2014.
7 Strangio, S., *Hun Sen's Cambodia*, op. cit., p. 210.
8 Lipes, J., 'Cambodian opposition petitions EU, UN on fair election', *Radio Free Asia*, 20 May 2013 and Finch, S., 'Sam Rainsy', *The Diplomat*, 7 June 2013.
9 Meyn, C. & Phorn, B., 'Sam Rainsy promises return before election', *The Cambodia Daily*, 8 July 2013; Boyle, D. & Meas, S., 'Rainsy pledges return', *The Phnom Penh Post*, 7 July 2013; Boyle, D. & Meas, S. 'Mixed signals over Rainsy return', *The Phnom Penh Post*, 11 July 2013.
10 Yun, S. & Vandenbrink, R., 'Hun Sen warns of "war" if he loses election', *Radio Free Asia*, 19 April 2013; Boyle, D. & Meas, S., 'Rainsy pledges return', op. cit.; Ponnudurai, P., 'Cambodian opposition chief Sam Rainsy gets royal pardon,' *Radio Free Asia*, 12 July 2013.
11 'Cambodian opposition leader pardoned at request of PM', *Radio Free Asia*, 12 July 2013.
12 Chamroeun, Author's interview, No. 104.
13 'Rainsy returns' (video), *The Phnom Penh Post*, 19 July 2013, www.youtube.com/watch?v=0PdCP8zCfj8
14 Kannitha, Author's interview, No. 006.
15 Rotha and Soveacha, Author's interview, No. 197.
16 'Rainsy returns', op. cit.
17 May, T., 'At border, Rainsy plays old tune', *The Phnom Penh Post*, 25 July 2013.
18 Strangio, S., *Hun Sen's Cambodia*, op. cit.; Chandler, D., *A History of Cambodia*, 4th ed., Westview Press, Colorado, 2008; Brinkley, J., *Cambodia's Curse*, op. cit.
19 Chandler, D., *A History of Cambodia*, op. cit and Kamm, H., *Cambodia: Report from a Stricken Land*, Arcade Publishing, New York, 1998.
20 Strangio, S., *Hun Sen's Cambodia*, op. cit.
21 Rithisak, Author's interview, No. 073.
22 Rotha and Soveacha, Author's interview, No. 197.
23 Leap, Author's interview, No. 101.
24 Quoted in COMFREL, *Final Assessment and Report on the 2013 National Assembly Elections*, December 2013, https://comfrel.org/english/2013-national-assembly-elections-final-assessment-and-report/
25 Chen, D. & Meyn, C., 'Come election time, xenophobia proves expedient', *The Cambodia Daily*, 26 July 2013.

26 Sokha, C., 'Return sparks CNRP', *The Phnom Penh Post*, 21 July 2013.
27 Sophal & Serey, Author's interview, No. 024.
28 Brinkley, J., *Cambodia's Curse*, op. cit., p. 20.

Chapter 6: Election Eve
1   COMFREL, *Final Assessment and Report on the 2013 National Assembly Elections*, op. cit.
2   ibid.
3   Ou Ritthy and Dara, Author's interview, No. 149.
4   COMFREL, *Final Assessment and Report on the 2013 National Assembly Elections*, op. cit.
5   Soeung Saroeun, Author's interview, No. 102; Human Rights Watch, 'Cambodia: land titling campaign open to abuse', 12 June 2014; Ben, S. & Robertson, H., 'Hun Sen's student volunteer land-titling program under fire', *The Cambodia Daily*, 1 August 2014.
6   Yun, S. & Vandenbrink, R., 'Hun Sen warns of "war" if he loses election', op. cit.
7   'Cambodia media ownership monitor', Cambodia Centre for Independent Media and Reporters Without Borders, 16 January 2018.
8   COMFREL, *Final Assessment and Report on the 2013 National Assembly Elections*, op. cit.
9   'Cambodia media ownership monitor', op. cit. and Global Witness, *Hostile Takeover*, op. cit.
10 COMFREL, *Final Assessment and Report on the 2013 National Assembly Elections*, op. cit.
11 Meyn, C., 'Will Hun Sen's threat of war translate into votes?', *The Cambodia Daily*, 27 June 2013.
12 Human Rights Watch, 'Cambodia: army, police campaign for ruling party', 22 July 2013.
13 Seiff, A., 'Gunshot fired through opposition headquarters' window', *The Phnom Penh Post*, 20 July 2013; Human Rights Watch, 'Cambodia: army, police campaign for ruling party', op. cit.; COMFREL, *Final Assessment and Report on the 2013 National Assembly Elections*, op. cit.
14 Yun, S. & Vandenbrink, R., 'Hun Sen warns of "war" if he loses election', op. cit.
15 Neou, V., 'Rainsy says climate in Cambodia is ripe for civil war', *The Cambodia Daily*, 10 June 2013.
16 Yun, S. & Vandenbrink, R., 'Hun Sen warns of "war" if he loses election', op. cit.
17 Kannitha, Author's interview, No. 006.
18 COMFREL, *Final Assessment and Report on the 2013 National Assembly Elections*, op. cit.

NOTES

Chapter 7: Ghosts and Nobodies

1. COMFREL, *Final Assessment and Report on the 2013 National Assembly Elections*, op. cit.; Koul Panha, Author's interview, No. 172.
2. Transparency International Cambodia (TIC), *Final Election Observation Report on Cambodia's 2013 National Election*, September 2013, https://ticambodia.org/library/ti_resource/final-election-observation-report-on-cambodias-2013-national-election/ and Population Division of the Department of Economic and Social Affairs of the United Nations Secretariat, *World Population Prospects Data Booklet, 2017 Revision*, op. cit.
3. Giry, S., 'Autopsy of a Cambodian election', *Foreign Affairs*, September/October 2015.
4. COMFREL, *Final Assessment and Report on the 2013 National Assembly Elections*, op. cit.
5. Sen, D., 'Angry voters riot in Stung Meanchey,' *The Phnom Penh Post*, 28 July 2013; Strangio, S., 'Poll loosens Hun Sen's grip on Cambodia', *Asia Times*, 29 July 2013; De Carteret, D., 'Angry voters riot in Stung Meanchey (video)', *The Phnom Penh Post*, 28 July 2013, www.phnompenhpost.com/video/video-angry-voters-riot-stung-meanchey
6. TIC, *Final Election Observation Report on Cambodia's 2013 National Election*, op. cit.
7. L.H., 'Cambodia's election: feeling cheated', *The Economist*, 28 July 2013.
8. Sen, D., 'Angry voters riot in Stung Meanchey,' op. cit.; De Carteret, D., 'Angry voters riot in Stung Meanchey (video)', op. cit.; Strangio, S., 'Poll loosens Hun Sen's grip on Cambodia', op. cit.; Pineros, E., 'Riots in Phnom Penh after national elections 2013', 28 July 2013, http://erikapineros.com/stories/elections-2013/#1
9. Veng, S. et al., 'Big opposition gains', *The Phnom Penh Post*, 29 July 2013 and Ou Ritthy and Dara, Author's interview, No. 149.
10. Vanna, Author's interview, No. 163; Ou Ritthy & Leap, Author's interview, No. 240; Rong Chhun, Author's interview, No. 016.
11. Ou Ritthy & Leap, Author's interview, No. 240.
12. National Election Committee, *White Paper: The 2013 General Election for the 5th Mandate of the National Assembly of the Kingdom of Cambodia*, Cambodian Government, Phnom Penh.
13. 'Unofficial: CNRP won 76 seats out of 123', *Khmerization*, 28 July 2013, https://khmerisation.wordpress.com/
14. 'In preliminary results, ruling party seats diminished in election win', *Voice of America*, 28 July 2013, www.voacambodia.com/a/in-pre-results-cpp-seats-diminished-in-cambodia-election-win/1711736.html

NOTES

Chapter 8: Drop by Drop, the Bucket Fills

1. BBC, 'Cambodia election: opposition party rejects results', 29 July 2013.
2. COMFREL, *Final Assessment and Report on the 2013 National Assembly Elections*, op. cit. and 'Opposition rejects election result', *The Phnom Penh*, 29 July 2013.
3. Yun, S. & Lipes, J., 'Sam Rainsy claims his party won enough seats to form government', *Radio Free Asia*, 30 July 2013.
4. Quoted in COMFREL, *Final Assessment and Report on the 2013 National Assembly Elections*, op. cit.
5. Veng, S. et al., 'Big opposition gains', op. cit. and Yun, S. & Lipes, J., 'Sam Rainsy claims his party won enough seats to form government', op. cit.
6. Hunt, L. 'Cambodia's eerie silence', *The Diplomat*, 11 August 2013 and Murdoch, L., 'Hun Sen breaks silence, backs election fraud investigation', *The Sydney Morning Herald*, 1 August 2013.
7. Hunt, L. 'Cambodia's eerie silence', op. cit. and 'In Cambodia, political instability threatens economic prosperity', Stratfor, 19 August 2013.
8. COMFREL, *Final Assessment and Report on the 2013 National Assembly Elections*, op. cit. and 'In Cambodia, political instability threatens economic prosperity', Stratfor, op. cit.
9. Murdoch, L., 'Hun Sen breaks silence, backs election fraud investigation', op. cit.
10. Prak, C., 'Defiant Hun Sen says to form government despite Cambodia poll row', *Reuters*, 2 August 2013.
11. Prak, C., 'Cambodia election crisis deepens as opposition rejects results', *Reuters*, 2 August 2013.
12. COMFREL, *Final Assessment and Report on the 2013 National Assembly Elections*, op. cit.
13. ibid.
14. ibid.
15. Daniel, Z., 'Cambodian opposition's Sam Rainsy leads three-day protest over election win', *ABC News*, 16 September 2013; Ponnudurai, P., 'Deadly post-election violence erupts in Phnom Penh', *Radio Free Asia*, 15 September 2013; Hodal, K., 'Cambodian election protests grip Phnom Penh', *The Guardian*, 16 September 2013.
16. Huot, V., 'International support growing for Cambodian polls probe: Sam Rainsy', *Radio Free Asia*, 17 October 2013; Khy, S., 'Sar Kheng rebukes Sam Rainsy over negotiations', *The Cambodia Daily*, 10 October 2013; Ponnudurai, P., 'Deadly post-election violence erupts in Phnom Penh', op. cit.
17. A national survey of 1000 people conducted in May 2014. Everett, S. & Meisburger, T., *Democracy in Cambodia: a survey of the electorate*, The Asia Foundation, Phnom Penh, 2014.

NOTES

18 Strangio, S., 'Veneer of democracy in Cambodia', *Asia Times*, 16 July 2013.
19 Ou, S. & Kim, S., *20 Years' Strengthening of Cambodian Civil Society*, Working Paper Series No. 85, Cambodian Development Research Institute, October 2013.
20 Prak, C., 'Cambodia election 2013: government rejects opposition's call for probe into alleged fraud', *Reuters*, 28 September 2013.
21 Prak, C., 'Defiant Hun Sen says to form government despite Cambodia poll row', op. cit.
22 Yun, S., 'King convenes Cambodia's parliament amid opposition boycott', *Radio Free Asia*, 23 September 2013.
23 ibid.
24 TIC, *Final Election Observation Report on Cambodia's 2013 National Election*, op. cit. and COMFREL, *Final Assessment and Report on the 2013 National Assembly Elections*, op. cit.
25 ibid. COMFREL found 9000 instances and NGO-CEDAW found 1772.
26 Pen Raksa, Author's interview, No. 150.
27 In a survey conducted in May 2014, 60 per cent of Cambodians did not think the NEC was free from political influence and only one-third were satisfied with its performance. Everett, S. & Meisburger, T., *Democracy in Cambodia*, op. cit.
28 Electoral Reform Alliance (ERA), *Joint Report on the Conduct of the 2013 Cambodian Election*, November 2013, Phnom Penh, https://comfrel.org/english/joint-report-on-the-conduct-of-the-2013-cambodian-elections-the-electoral-reform-alliance-era/
29 ibid. COMFREL found 13.5 per cent of people surveyed were not on the list (1.25 million). TIC found 8.88 per cent, which the NEC initially recognised before saying that only 3 per cent of people were missing.
30 ibid.
31 ibid.
32 ibid.
33 Chamroeun, Author's interview, No. 104.

Chapter 9: Veng Sreng Street

1 Savchenko, Y. & Acevedo, G., *Female Wages in the Apparel Industry Post– MFA*, The World Bank Policy Research Working Paper 6061, May 2012, https://elibrary.worldbank.org/doi/epdf/10.1596/1813-9450-6061.
2 D'Amico, S., *Cambodia's Trade Union Law: A Necessity*, Employers' position paper, Cambodian Federation of Employers and Business Associations, 2015, www.camfeba.com/legal/Report%20%26%20Press%20

NOTES

release/20150520_CAMFEBATULPolicyPaper_LongVersion_(v15)_FINAL2September2015.pdf

3   Xinhua, 'Cambodia's opposition to protest daily to call for reelection', *Global Times*, 14 December 2013.
4   Channa and Kunthea, Author's interview, No. 226.
5   Ou Ritthy and Dara, Author's interview, No. 149.
6   This system of mutual aid is traditionally known as *brovas day kinear*. Slocomb, M., 'The nature and role of ideology in the modern Cambodian state', *Journal of Southeast Asian Studies*, 37 (3), 2006, pp. 375–95.
7   Ou Ritthy and Dara, Author's interview, No. 149.
8   Mech, D. & Meyn, C., 'CNRP holds biggest demonstration in decades', *The Cambodia Daily*, 23 December 2013.
9   ibid.
10 Mom, K. & Teehan, S., 'Strike numbers swell', *The Phnom Penh Post*, 27 December 2013.
11 ibid.
12 Fuller, T., 'Rally draws a diverse group of protesters in Cambodia', *The New York Times*, 29 December 2013.
13 Heijmans, P., 'In pictures: Cambodians take to the streets', *Al Jazeera*, 30 December 2013.
14 ibid.
15 Taing, R., 'Upholding freedom of the press in the Kingdom', *Khmer Times*, 6 September 2019 and Mom, K. & Teehan, S., 'Take it or leave it offer', *The Phnom Penh Post*, 30 December 2013.
16 Moeun Tola, Author's interview, No. 129,
17 Soeng Sen Karuna, Author's interview, No. 219.
18 Channa and Kunthea, Author's interview, No. 226.
19 Soeng Sen Karuna, Author's interview, No. 219.
20 Rotha and Soveacha, Author's interview, No. 197 and Wallace, J. & Neou, V., 'Cambodia protests unmask anti-Vietnam views', *Al Jazeera*, 24 January 2014.
21 Soeng Sen Karuna, Author's interview, No. 219.
22 Chan, C. et. al., *A Week that Shook Cambodia*, Asia Monitor Resource Centre, Hong Kong, February 2014.
23 Moeun Tola, Author's interview, No. 129.
24 Chan, C. et. al., *A Week that Shook Cambodia*, op. cit.
25 Willemyns, A., 'Threat of force hangs over "culture of dialogue"', *The Cambodia Daily*, 23 January 2015.

26 Channa and Kunthea, Author's interview, No. 226.
27 Soeng Sen Karuna, Author's interview, No. 219.
28 Moeun Tola, Author's interview, No. 129.
29 Chan, C. et. al., *A Week that Shook Cambodia*, op. cit.
30 Mech, D. & Doyle, K., 'Police kill 5 during clash with demonstrators', *The Cambodia Daily*, 1 April 2014.
31 Channa and Kunthea, Author's interview, No. 226.

Chapter 10: The Third Hand

1 Rotha and Soveacha, Author's interview, No. 197.
2 Channa and Kunthea, Author's interview, No. 226.
3 Mech, D. & Robertson, H., 'Union leaders charged over nationwide protests', *The Cambodia Daily*, 3 September 2014.
4 Ou Ritthy and Dara, Author's interview, No. 149.
5 Channa and Kunthea, Author's interview, No. 127.
6 Ou Ritthy & Leap, Author's interview, No. 240. Ritthy used the word 'tank' but the type of vehicle seen was more likely an armoured vehicle with a machine gun mounted on top. Licadho, 'When freedom meets oppression: timeline of recent events', 9 February 2014.
7 Meas, S., 'Freedom Park braces for violence', *The Phnom Penh Post*, 15 July 2014.
8 Ou Ritthy & Leap, Author's interview, No. 240.
9 Cuddy, A. & Meas, S., 'Tables violently turned', *The Phnom Penh Post*, 16 July 2014.
10 Ou Ritthy and Dara, Author's interview, No. 149.
11 Sum, S., 'Cambodia's ruling, opposition parties agree to end year-long deadlock', *Radio Free Asia*, 22 July 2014.
12 ibid.
13 ibid.
14 Boyle, D., 'Rainsy after the deadlock (video)', *The Phnom Penh Post*, 24 July 2014.

Chapter 11: A Culture of Dialogue

1 Rotha and Soveacha, Author's interview, No. 197.
2 Chamroeun, Author's interview, No. 104.
3 ibid.
4 Vaulerin, A., 'Au Cambodge, une politique d'ouverture ébréchée', *Liberation*, 22 July 2015.

5   Leap, Author's interview, No. 147.
6   Leap, Author's interview, No. 101.
7   Ou Ritthy, Author's interview, No. 057.
8   Ker, M., 'Cambodia prime minister's nephew arrested', Associated Press, 25 November 2003.
9   Berthiaume, L., '"Iron fist" court reform seizes one of its own', *The Cambodia Daily*, 19 August 2005.
10   Rong Chhun, Author's interview, No. 018.
11   Rong Chhun, Author's interview, No. 016.
12   Meas, S. & Pye, D., 'Rong Chhun ready to scrap', *The Phnom Penh Post*, 13 April 2015.
13   Hang Puthea, Author's interview, No. 023.
14   'CSOs call for the immediate release of opposition Senator', press release, 18 August 2015, https://comfrel.org/english/ and Johnson, C., *Cambodia: New Election Laws*, Global Legal Monitor, 24 March 2015.
15   TIC, *Final Election Observation Report on Cambodia's 2013 National Election*, op. cit.
16   Rong Chhun, Author's interview, No. 017.
17   Hang Puthea, Author's interview, No. 023.

Chapter 12: Dialogue Unravels

1   Chamroeun, Author's interview, No. 104.
2   Wathanakam, K., 'Hun Sen plays hardball while CNRP faces conundrum', *Khmerization*, 30 July 2015.
3   Pav, S. & Chea, T., 'Jailings test the "culture of dialogue"', *Khmer Times*, 21 July 2015.
4   Vaulerin, A., 'Le pouvoir cambodgien fait tout pour diffuser la peur', *Liberation*, 23 July 2015.
5   ibid.
6   Hu, H.C., 'The Chinese conceptions of face', *American Anthropologist*, vol. 46, no. 1, Part 1, 1944, pp. 45–64.
7   ibid.
8   Meas, S., 'Dinner lives on for PM, Rainsy', *The Phnom Penh Post*, 27 August 2015.
9   Hang Puthea, Author's interview, No. 023.
10   As part of the July 2014 agreement between the CPP and CNRP, Sam Rainsy was officially recognised as Leader of the Opposition Group in the National Assembly, giving him rights to raise issues and call for debates. This was modelled on the role of the Leader of the Opposition in the UK Parliament.

NOTES

11   Dav Ansan, Author's interview, No. 125.
12   Ting-Toomey, S., 'Facework/facework negotiation theory', in J. Bennett (ed.), *Sage Encyclopedia of Intercultural Competence, Volume 1*, Sage, Los Angeles, 2015, pp. 325–30 and Oetzel, J.G. and Ting-Toomey, S., 'Face concerns in interpersonal conflict a cross-cultural empirical test of the face negotiation theory', *Communication Research*, vol. 30, no. 6, 2003, pp. 599–624.
13   Hinton, A., 'Head for an eye: revenge in the Cambodian genocide', *American Ethnologist*, vol. 25, no. 3, August 1998, pp. 352–77.
14   Dav Ansan, Author's interview, No. 125.
15   Hinton, A., 'Head for an eye', op. cit.
16   Ngor, H., *A Cambodian Odyssey*, MacMillan Publishing, London, 1987.
17   Hinton, A., 'Head for an eye', op. cit.
18   Dav Ansan, Author's interview, No. 112.
19   Dav Ansan, Author's interview, No. 125. CNRP activists fed rumours that Hun Sen's eldest son was born from a relationship between his wife and former Vietnamese leader Le Doc Tho.
20   Dav Ansan, Author's interview, No. 112.
21   Meas, S., 'PM pushes for more Freedom Park arrests', *The Phnom Penh Post*, 4 August 2015.
22   Meas, S., 'SRP's Sok Hour arrested', *The Phnom Penh Post*, 17 August 2015.
23   Hong, S. et. al., 'Two Cambodian opposition lawmakers attacked by protesters', *Radio Free Asia*, 26 October 2015.
24   Human Rights Watch, 'Cambodia: stop cover-up of political violence', 4 May 2016, www.hrw.org/news/2016/05/26/cambodia-stop-cover-political-violence
25   Mech, D. & Turton, S., 'Third member of PM's Bodyguard Unit seen kicking head of MP promoted', *The Phnom Penh Post*, 26 January 2017 and Mech, D. & Turton, S., 'MP attackers promoted', *The Phnom Penh Post*, 28 December 2016.
26   Human Rights Watch, 'Cambodia: stop cover-up of political violence', ibid.
27   Chhay, C., 'CPP ousts Sokha from Assembly post', *The Phnom Penh Post*, 31 October 2015 and Kuch, N., 'Kem Sokha removed as Assembly Vice President', *The Cambodia Daily*, 30 October 2015.
28   Cochrane, L., 'Cambodia's opposition leader Sam Rainsy delays return amid arrest fears', *ABC*, 17 November 2015.
29   National Assembly Official, Author's interview, No. 056.
30   Human Rights Watch, 'Cambodia: drop case against opposition leader', 13 November 2015, www.hrw.org/news/2015/11/13/cambodia-drop-case-against-opposition-leader

31 Murdoch, L., 'Opposition leader Sam Rainsy delays returning to Cambodia', *The Sydney Morning Herald*, 17 November 2015.

Chapter 13: A Game of Chess
1   Soeung Saroeun, Author's interview, No. 102.
2   Doung Virorth, Author's interview, No. 126.
3   Kunthea, Author's interview, No. 127.
4   Doung Virorth, Author's interview, No. 126.
5   Soeung Saroeun, Author's interview, No. 102 and National Assembly official, Author's interview, No. 056.
6   Phirun, Author's interview, No. 054.
7   *Law on Associations and Non-Governmental Organisations*, Cambodian Government, Phnom Penh, 2015, https://cambodia.ohchr.org/sites/default/files/Unofficial_Translation_of_5th_LANGO_ENG.pdf
8   Cheang Sokha, Author's interview, No. 035.
9   Labor Rights Thematic Group, *Submission to the United Nations Universal Periodic Review*, UN Human Rights Council, 2019, www.ohchr.org/EN/HRBodies/UPR/Pages/KHIndex.aspx
10 Cambodian Center for Human Rights (CCHR), *Fundamental Freedoms Monitoring Project 1st Annual Report*, April 2016 – March 2017, https://cchrcambodia.org/admin/media/report/report/english/2017-08-10-CCHR-FFMP-Annual-Report-Eng.pdf
11 AHDOC, *Land Situation in Cambodia in 2013*, 27 May 2014, www.adhoc-cambodia.org/report-land-situation-in-cambodia-in-2013-2/
12 Kimsorn, Author's interview, No. 034.
13 Information on arrests in ADHOC, CLEC and LICADHO, *Call for the Release of Activists and Monitors* (Joint Statement), 2 September 2015, www.licadho-cambodia.org/pressrelease.php?perm=391; Aun, P., 'After arrests, environment NGO defends tactics', *The Cambodia Daily*, 26 August 2015; INI, *Survey of Cambodian Public Opinion, October 28 – November 10*, op. cit.; CCHR, *Fundamental Freedoms Monitoring Project 1st Annual Report*, op. cit.
14 Doung Virorth, Author's interview, No. 126.
15 *Constitution of the Kingdom of Cambodia*, Cambodian Government, Phnom Penh, 1993. Retrieved from https://www.refworld.org/docid/3ae6b5428.html
16 *Tearing Apart at the Seams*, Allard K. Lowenstein International Human Rights Clinic, Yale Law School, April 2011.
17 Chuon Momthol quoted in Yun, S., 'Inclusion of pro-government union at conference opposed', *The Cambodia Daily*, 28 April 2003.
18 Pich, Author's interview, No. 156.

NOTES

19 Of 233 factories monitored as part of Better Factories Cambodia, which is about half of all factories, six controlled unions and seven prevented workers from joining the union of their choice. Sophal, C., 'Labor rights and trade unions: a chapter in Cambodian constitutional law' in Hor, P. (ed.), *Cambodian Constitutional Law*, Konrad-Adenauer-Stiftung, Phnom Penh, 2016, chapter 22.

20 Pich, Author's interview, No. 156.

21 *Tearing Apart at the Seams*, op. cit. and Sophal, C., 'Labor rights and trade unions', op. cit.

22 Chhay, C., 'Union leader convicted of drug charges', *The Phnom Penh Post*, 27 June 2011.

23 Channa and Kunthea, Author's interview, No. 127.

24 The probationary period is three months.

25 Report of the Committee on the Application of Standards, 'Information and reports on the application of conventions and recommendations', International Labour Conference, 107th Session, Geneva, May–June 2018 and *Tearing Apart at the Seams*, op. cit.

26 Human Rights Watch, 'Cambodia: garment factories thwarting unions', 2 February 2014, www.hrw.org/news/2014/02/02/cambodia-garment-factories-thwarting-unions.

27 Teehan, S. & Mom, K., 'Union reps fired after strike', *The Phnom Penh Post*, 28 January 2014.

28 Ministry of Labour and Vocational Training, *Law on Trade Unions*, Cambodian Government, Phnom Penh, 2016.

29 Labor Rights Thematic Group, *Submission to the United Nations Universal Periodic Review*, op. cit. and Pich, Author's interview, No. 156.

30 'Arbitral awards', The Arbitration Council, 2023, www.arbitrationcouncil.org/arbitral-decision/arbitral-award/ and Kong, M., 'Report from labour council says Kingdom disputes down in 2017', *The Phnom Penh Post*, 28 August 2018.

31 Labor Rights Thematic Group, *Submission to the United Nations Universal Periodic Review*, op. cit.

32 'Individual Case (CAS) – Discussion: (2017)', 106th ILC session: Freedom of Association and Protection of the Right to Organise Convention, 1948 (No. 87), Cambodia.

33 Better Factories Cambodia, *Annual Report 2018: An Industry and Compliance Review*, International Labour Organization (ILO) and International Finance Corporation, Geneva, 2018.

34 Ministry of Labour and Vocational Training, *Law on Trade Unions*, op. cit.

35 Hun Sen did not name the opposition woman by name but gave clear reference to her and said she had 'strong legs', slang for being a prostitute.

Schlein, L., 'UN denounces defamation case against politician in Cambodia', *Voice of America*, 12 July 2010.
36 Cheung, B., 'Criminal Code (2009): Khmer – English Translation', Sithi, January 2014.
37 Aun, P., 'Government accuses NASA of incitement over deforestation data', *The Cambodia Daily*, 16 January 2017.
38 Sen, D., 'Unionists arrested over Kampong Speu demonstration', *The Phnom Penh Post*, 3 February 2016.
39 Sen, D., 'Trio jailed for leading Kampot strike action', *The Phnom Penh Post*, 7 July 2016.
40 Mech, D. & Robertson, H., 'Union leaders charged over nationwide protests', *The Cambodia Daily*, 3 September 2014.
41 Amnesty International, *Taking to the Streets: Freedom of Peaceful Assembly in Cambodia*, London, May 2015, www.amnesty.ca/sites/amnesty/files/cambodiareport4june15.pdf
42 Hul, R., 'Hun Sen threatens legal action against rights activist', *Voice of America*, 5 January 2016.
43 Ministry of Post and Telecommunications, *Law on Telecommunications*, Cambodian Government, Phnom Penh, 17 December 2015.

Chapter 14: Here Is My Son
1 UYFC Deputy Provincial Leaders, Author's interview, No. 049.
2 Angkor Sankranta Map, http://angkor.com.kh/wp-content/uploads/2018/04/Map-Angkor-Sangkrata-2018.jpg
3 Phirun, Author's interview, No. 232.
4 UYFC Deputy Provincial Leaders, Author's interview, No. 049.
2 Sothea, Author's interview, No. 235.
3 Kimchhay, Author's interview, No. 132.
4 Identity retained, Author's interview, No. 152.
5 Identity retained, Author's interview, No. 050.
6 Ou Ritthy, Author's interview, No. 114.
7 Ou Ritthy, Author's interview, No. 057.
8 Ou Ritthy, Author's interview, No. 114.
9 Kosal, Author's interview, No. 231.

Chapter 15: *Khnorng*
1 Sotheavy, Author's interviews, No. 176 and 212.
2 Maly, Author's interview, No. 124.

NOTES

3   Maly, Author's interview, No. 142.
4   Maly, Author's interview, No. 141.
5   Maly, Author's interview, No. 141 and Maly, Author's interview, No. 124.
6   Sreyleak, Author's interview, No. 011. All subsequent quotes are from the same interview.

Chapter 16: A Slave to One Side

1   Chhay, Author's interview, No. 003.
2   *A Human Rights Analysis of The Amended Law on Political Parties (2017)*, Office of the United Nations High Commissioner for Human Rights in Cambodia, March 2017.
3   Identity retained, Author's Interview, No. 066.
4   Vanna, Author's interview, No. 196.
5   Ouk Chhayavy, Author's interview, No. 058.
6   Phirun, Author's interview, No. 232.
7   Phirun, Author's interview, No. 143.
8   Phirun, Author's interview, No. 232.
9   Chamroeun, Author's interview, No. 104.
10   Koul Panha, Author's interview, No. 172.
11   Vanna, Author's interview, No. 196.
12   Vanda & Sokha, Author's interview, No. 162.
13   'In the Cardamom Mountains, two deaths recounted', op. cit.

Chapter 17: Rule of Law

1   Neou, V., 'Anti-terror police question woman embroiled in Kem Sokha affair allegations', *Voice of America*, 11 March 2016.
2   Kuch, N., 'Woman admits to affair with Kem Sokha', *The Cambodia Daily*, 20 April 2016.
3   Taing, V., 'Sister in law of Srey mom responds to investigation', *Khmer Times*, 3 April 2016.
4   Vanda & Sokha, Author's interview, No. 162.
5   Niem, C., 'Detentions extended for officials in "bribery" case', *The Phnom Penh Post*, 28 October 2016.
6   Lay, S., 'Alleged mistress files complaints against Sokha, ADHOC', *The Phnom Penh Post*, 25 April 2016.
7   Vanda & Sokha, Author's interview, No. 162.
8   All quotations from Vanda and Sokha from Vanda & Sokha, Author's interview, No. 162, unless otherwise noted.

NOTES

9 Boliek, B., 'Cambodian court sentences opposition leader Kem Sokha to five months in jail', *Radio Free Asia*, 9 September 2016.
10 Mech, D., 'Breaking: royal pardon for Kem Sokha', *The Phnom Penh Post*, 2 December 2016.
11 ADHOC staff member, Author's interview, No. 159.
12 Vanda & Sokha, Author's interview, No. 162 and ADHOC staff member, Author's interview, No. 159.
13 Vanda & Sokha, Author's interview, No. 162.

Chapter 18: The Man in the White Shirt with a Black Heart

1 Global Witness, *Hostile Takeover*, op. cit.
2 Sophal, Author's interview, No. 021.
3 Kou Sina, Author's interview, No. 157.
4 Willemyns, A. & Sek, O., 'Moniker a morbid fit for Kem Ley's fables', *The Cambodia Daily*, 18 July 2016.
5 The close associate was Soy Sopheap, CPP-aligned journalist. Ou Ritthy & Leap, Author's interview No. 240; Ou Ritthy, Author's interview, No. 057.
6 Ou Ritthy, Author's interview, No. 057.
7 Ou Ritthy & Leap, Author's interview, No. 240.
8 'កិច្ចពិភាក្សាលើការគ្របគ្បាប់ជនញេរបសក្រុល «ហ៊ន» នៅកម្ពុជា (video)', *Radio Free Asia*, 12 July 2016, www.youtube.com/watch?v=ASK5L8m6i-8
9 INI, *Survey of Cambodian Public Opinion; October 28 – November 10*, op. cit.
10 Global Witness, *Hostile Takeover*, op. cit.
11 Yeang Sothearin, Author's interview, No. 252.
12 Ou Ritthy & Leap, Author's interview, No. 240.
13 Yeang Sothearin, Author's interview, No. 252.
14 Tes Putheara, Author's interview, No. 239.
15 Tes Putheara, Author's interview, No. 133.
16 101 East, 'Cambodia's deadly politics (video)', *Al Jazeera*, 12 January 2017.
17 Phorn, B., 'Meet the alleged killer of Cambodia's Kem Ley', *Voice of America*, 23 July 2016.
18 ibid.
19 May Titthara, Author's interview, No. 099,.
20 Ou Ritthy & Leap, Author's interview, No. 240.
21 ibid. and Ou Ritthy, Author's interview, No. 057.
22 Ou Ritthy & Leap, Author's interview, No. 240.
23 Pen Raksa, Author's interview, No. 150.

NOTES

24　Tes Putheara, Author's interview, No. 133.
25　Willemyns, A., 'Kem Ley's final fables', *The Cambodia Daily*, 6 July 2016.
26　Channa and Kunthea, Author's interview, No. 217.
27　Phak, S. et. al., 'Kem Ley laid to rest at home in Takeo', *The Phnom Penh Post*, 26 July 2016.
28　Kou Sina, Author's interview, No. 157.
29　Identity retained, Author's interview, No. 128 and Tes Putheara, Author's interview, No. 133.
30　Channa and Kunthea, Author's interview, No. 217.
31　Ou Ritthy, Author's interview, No. 057.
32　Yeang Sothearin, Author's interview, No. 252.

Chapter 19: The Rise of Rozeth

1　Shaviv Strategy & Campaigns, *Public Opinion Research Cambodia*, October 2016.
2　COMFREL, *Final Assessment and Report: The 2017 Commune Council Election*, October 2017, https://comfrel.org/english/final-assessment-and-report-the-2017-commune-council-eelection/October
3　ibid.
4　ibid.
5　ibid.
6　ibid.
7　Niem, C., 'Head of state promotes nearly 200 RCAF officers', *The Phnom Penh Post*, 5 June 2018; Dara, M., 'More than 300 RCAF officers promoted, including 178 new generals', *The Phnom Penh Post*, 1 March 2018; COMFREL, *Final Assessment and Report: The 2017 Commune Council Election*, op. cit.
8　COMFREL, *Final Assessment and Report: The 2017 Commune Council Election*, op. cit.
9　All quotations from Sin Rozeth, Author's interview, No. 042 and Sin Rozeth, Author's interview, No. 222.

Chapter 20: A Transfer of Power

1　Bun, S., 'ERA raises concerns for voter registration', *The Phnom Penh Post*, 8 September 2016.
2　Rong Chhun, Author's interview, No. 016.
3　COMFREL, *Final Assessment and Report: The 2017 Commune Council Election*, op. cit.
4　International Institute for Democracy and Electoral Assistance, *Voter Turnout Database*, https://www.idea.int/data-tools/data/voter-turnout

NOTES

5   COMFREL, *Final Assessment and Report: The 2017 Commune Council Election*, op. cit.

6   Soeng Sen Karuna, Author's interview, No. 219. The COMFREL official was Korn Savang.

7   COMFREL, *Final Assessment and Report: The 2017 Commune Council Election*, op. cit.

8   Mondolkiri CNRP Activist, Author's interview, No. 118.

9   Chamroeun, Author's interview, No. 104.

10   Sophal, Author's interview, No. 019; Rotha and Soveacha, Author's interview, No. 197; Channa and friend, Author's interview, No. 217.

11   Ou Ritthy and Dara, Author's interview, No. 149.

12   Chamroeun, Author's interview, No. 104.

13   Sotheavy, Author's interview, No. 176.

14   COMFREL, *Final Assessment and Report: The 2017 Commune Council Election*, op. cit.

15   Sin Rozeth, Author's interviews, No. 222 and No. 042.

16   Chen Sokngeng, Author's interview, No. 091.

17   Pav, S., 'Commune chief wants to end culture of revenge', *Khmer Times*, 14 August 2017.

18   Niem, C. & Touch, S., 'Siem Reap chief locked out of office by predecessor', *The Phnom Penh Post*, 11 July 2017.

19   Sun, N., 'New opposition commune chief on the move to make area corruption free', *Voice of America*, 12 July 2017.

20   Chen Sokngeng, Author's interview, No. 091.

21   Chen Sokngeng, Author's interview, No. 094.

Chapter 21: To Catch a Tiger

1   Identity retained, Author's interview, No. 128.

2   Shaviv Strategy & Campaigns, *Public Opinion Research Cambodia*, op. cit.

3   May Titthara, Author's interview, No. 145.

4   Hang Puthea, Author's interview, No. 062.

5   Phirun, Author's interview, No. 232.

6   Kuch, N., 'Hun Sen goes on tirade against opponents', *The Cambodia Daily*, 26 May 2017.

7   Van, R., '"Prepare your coffin": Hun Sen repeats bloody power promise', *The Cambodia Daily*, 22 June 2017.

8   'Cambodian PM calls for loyalty from security officials', *The Straits Times*, 25 July 2015.

NOTES

9   Sok, S.R., 'Cambodia's armed forces "belong" to the ruling party: four-star general', *Radio Free Asia*, 29 July 2015.
10 Ouch, S., 'Student gets 18 months for call for "color revolution"', *The Cambodia Daily*, 16 March 2016.
11 IRI, *Survey of Cambodian Public Opinion; October 28 – November 10*, op. cit.
12 'Intelligence chief talks about protests and regime change', *Khmer Times*, 1 June 2016.
13 Lor, S., 'ស្វែងយល់ពី៖ បដិវត្តពណ៌កកើត និងដំណើរការដោយរបៀបណា?', 10 May 2016.
14 Mech, D., 'Key cop warns of coming revolts', *The Phnom Penh Post*, 17 March 2016.
15 Ben, S., 'Hun Sen orders investigation into situation room', *The Cambodia Daily*, 28 June 2017.
16 Touch, S., 'PM files lawsuit against analyst', *The Phnom Penh Post*, 14 February 2017.
17 Leap, Author's interview, No. 039.

Chapter 22: Radio Silence
1   Millar, P., 'Without fear or favour: *The Cambodia Daily*', *Southeast Asia Globe*, 3 October 2017.
2   Phorn Bopha, Author's interview, No. 225.
3   Quinn, F., 'The free press in Cambodia is under attack and we should be paying attention', *Irish Examiner*, 17 September 2017.
4   Phorn Bopha, Author's interview, No. 225.
5   Paviour, B., 'Branding *Daily* a "thief", Hun Sen says pay tax or leave', *The Cambodia Daily*, 23 August 2017.
6   Muyhong, C., 'Former *Cambodia Daily* readers left hungry, shift news diet', *Voice of Democracy*, 4 September 2019.
7   Ball, M., 'When the presses stop', *The Atlantic*, January/February 2018.
8   Phorn, B., 'Journalists behind prison bars in Cambodia', *Voice of America*, 3 May 2019.
9   Phirun, Author's interview, No. 232.
10 Bastard, D., *Cambodia: The Independent Press in Ruins*, Reporters Without Borders, Paris, 2018.
11 '*Post*'s bill from tax authority business as usual, says CEO', *The Phnom Penh Post*, 21 March 2018.
12 O'Byrne, B. & Baliga, A., '*Phnom Penh Post* sold to Malaysian investor', *The Phnom Penh Post*, 6 May 2018.
13 'Leaked emails from Deputy PM Sok An's office', *Khmerization*. 6 May 2017 and LICADHO, *Attacks and Threats Against Human Rights Defenders 2007:*

NOTES

A Briefing Paper, 2008, www.licadho-cambodia.org/reports/files/126LICAD HOHumanRightsDefendersReport2007Eng.pdf

14 Nachemson, A., 'The end of Cambodia's free press', *New Natarif*, 5 July 2018, https://newnaratif.com/journalism/end-cambodias-free-press/ and '*Post* senior staff out in dispute over article', *The Phnom Penh Post*, 8 May 2018, www.phnompenhpost.com/national/post-senior-staff-out-dispute-over-article

15 Ministry of Commerce Business Registration, 'Entry for POST MEDIA CO., LTD. (00012053) Private Limited Company', www.businessregistration.moc.gov.kh/

16 Bastard, D., *Cambodia*, op. cit.

17 Yeang Sothearin & Cheang Sokha, Author's interview, No. 230.

18 Liu, L., 'Statement of *Radio Free Asia*'s president on Cambodia', *Radio Free Asia*, 12 September 2017.

19 Bastard, D., *Cambodia*, op. cit.

20 Huy Vannak, Author's interview, No. 238.

21 Reporters Without Borders, 'World Press Freedom Index'. In 2018, Cambodia was ranked 142nd and Singapore, 151st.

22 Socheat, Author's interview, No. 053.

23 Huy Vannak, Author's interview, No. 238 and Kijewski, L., 'Group warns of "ruthless crackdown" on Cambodian journalists', *Voice of America*, 24 April 2019.

24 Huy Vannak, Author's interview, No. 238.

25 Yeang Sothearin, Author's interview, No. 252.

26 Baliga, A. & Mech, D., 'RFA confirms office closure', *The Phnom Penh Post*, 14 September 2017.

27 'Journalists in Cambodia – persecution and hell', Reporters Without Borders, 14 November 2018 and Prak, C.T., 'Two Cambodian journalists facing spying charges freed on bail', *Reuters*, 21 August 2018.

28 Yeang Sothearin & Cheang Sokha, Author's interview, No. 230. All quotations are from this source unless noted.

29 'Journalists in Cambodia – persecution and hell', Reporters Without Borders, op. cit.

30 Handley, E., 'The James Ricketson trial', *The Lowy Institute*, 7 September 2018.

31 Yeang Sothearin & Cheang Sokha, Author's interview, No. 230.

Chapter 23: *Chhob*

1 Office of the United Nations High Commissioner for Human Rights in Cambodia, *A Human Rights Analysis of the Amended Law on Political Parties (July 2017)*, July 2018, https://cambodia.ohchr.org/

2 CCHR, *Fundamental Freedoms Monitoring Project 1st Annual Report*, op. cit.

NOTES

3 Cambodian Centre for Human Rights, *Annex 1: Legal Analysis of the July 2017 Proposed Amendment to the LPP*, Office of the United Nations High Commissioner for Human Rights in Cambodia, March 2017 and OHCHR, 'A human rights analysis of the amended law on political parties', 2017, https://cambodia.ohchr.org/

4 Meas, S., 'King again in Beijing for contested Party Law's signing', *The Phnom Penh Post*, 24 July 2017.

5 Meas, S., 'Opposition completes removal of Rainsy signs', *The Phnom Penh Post*, 7 August 2017.

6 Meas, S., 'Dinner lives on for PM, Rainsy', *The Phnom Penh Post*, 27 August 2015.

7 Jolley, M., 'Threats and corruption: behind the scenes of Cambodia's election crackdown (video)', *Al Jazeera*, 14 July 2018.

8 'Sokha arrested for "treason", is accused of colluding with US to topple the government', *The Phnom Penh Post*, 4 September 2017.

9 Sam Sokong, Author's interview, No. 223.

10 Pheng Heng, Author's interview, No. 269.

11 Sam Sokong, Author's interview, No. 223.

12 'Sokha arrested for "treason", is accused of colluding with US to topple the government', op. cit.

13 Sam Sokong, Author's interview, No. 223.

14 Ben, S. & Mech, D., 'Death of democracy', *The Phnom Penh Post*, 17 November 2017.

15 Mech, D., 'Government-aligned *Fresh News* seemingly a bludgeon for ruling party', *The Phnom Penh Post*, 28 August 2017.

16 Mech, D. 'Breaking: Interior Ministry files complaint to dissolve CNRP', *The Phnom Penh Post*, 6 October 2017 and May, T., 'PM hints end in sight for CNRP', *Khmer Times*, 12 October 2017.

17 'Sokha arrested for "treason", is accused of colluding with US to topple the government', op. cit.

18 Niem, C., 'Hun Sen offers ultimatum for CNRP officials: defect or risk a five-year ban', *The Phnom Penh Post*, 6 November 2017 and Sam Sokong, Author's interview, No. 223.

19 Quotes in this paragraph from Hang Puthea, Author's interview, No. 023 and Hang Puthea, Author's interview, No. 062.

20 'Sokha arrested for "treason", is accused of colluding with US to topple the government', op. cit. and Kong, M., 'CNRP's "free Sokha" signs taken down', *The Phnom Penh Post*, 9 October 2017.

21 Niem, C., 'CPP rewrites rules again, with amendments planned to political laws to redistribute CNRP seats', *The Phnom Penh Post*, 11 October 2017.

22 Mech, D., 'CPP set to amend laws to take all of CNRP's commune chief seats', *The Phnom Penh Post*, 13 October 2017.
23 Soeng Sen Karuna, Author's interview, No. 140.
24 Soeng Sen Karuna, Author's interview, No. 219.
25 Soeng Sen Karuna, Author's interview, No. 140.
26 Ben, S & Mech, D., 'Death of democracy', *The Phnom Penh Post*, 17 November 2017.
27 Sam Sokong, Author's interview, No. 223.
28 ibid.
29 Soeng Sen Karuna, Author's interview, No. 219.
30 Soeng Sen Karuna, Author's interview, No. 140.
31 Sam Sokong, Author's interview, No. 223.
32 Hang Puthea, Author's interview, No. 023.
33 ibid.
34 Hing Thirith, Author's interview, No. 228.
35 Rong Chhun, Author's interview, No. 016.

Chapter 24: Clearing the Table
1 Sin Rozeth, Author's interview, No. 042.

Chapter 25: Flattened
1 Niem, C., Chen, D. & Kijewski, L. 'Surveillance up ahead of CNRP verdict', *The Phnom Penh Post*, 16 November 2017.
2 Cheang Sokha, Author's interview, No. 199.
3 Soeng Sen Karuna, Author's interview, No. 219 and Niem, C., Chen, D. & Kijewski, L. 'Surveillance up ahead of CNRP verdict', op. cit.
4 Bunroeun, Author's interview, No. 032.
5 Bunroeun, Author's interview, No. 029.
6 Kannitha, Author's interview, No. 006.
7 Chea Chiv, Author's interview, No. 221.
8 Chen Sokngeng, Author's interview, No. 094.
9 Bunroeun, Author's interview, No. 029.
10 Rong Chhun, Author's interview, No. 018.
11 Vanna, Author's interview, No. 196.
12 Muong, N. & Lipes, J., 'Opposition members quit Cambodia's electoral body in protest of party's dissolution', *Radio Free Asia*, 20 November 2017.
13 Freedom House, 'Freedom on the Net – Cambodia 2018', https://freedomhouse.org/country/cambodia/freedom-net/2018

14   Chen Sokngeng, Author's interview, No. 094.
15   Chen Sokngeng, Author's interview, No. 091.
16   Sun, N. & Wallace, J., 'The reluctant defectors of Cambodia', *Voice of America*, 16 December 2017.
17   Chea Chiv, Author's interview, No. 221.
18   Sun, N. & Wallace, J., 'The reluctant defectors of Cambodia', op. cit.
19   Chen Sokngeng, Author's interview, No. 091.
20   Chen Sokngeng, Author's interview, No. 094.

Chapter 26: What the West Fails to See
1   Willemyns, A., 'Don't compare me to Suu Kyi, Sam Rainsy tells supporters', *The Cambodia Daily*, 24 June 2016.
2   Vietnamese repairman, Author's interview, No. 096.
3   Dav Ansan, Author's interview, No. 125.
4   Huy Vannak, Author's interview, No. 238.
5   Ministry of Foreign Affairs and International Cooperation, *Cambodia: Stability and Development First*, Cambodian Government, Phnom Penh, February 2018, www.mfaic.gov.kh/wp-content/uploads/2018/02/4T2-Stability-12-February-2018.pdf and Ministry of Foreign Affairs and International Cooperation, *Cambodia, Democracy and Human Rights: To Tell the Truth*, Cambodian Government, Phnom Penh, 30 September 2017, https://pressocm.gov.kh/en/archives/13782
6   Associated Press, 'Hun Sen derides "democracy"', *The Bangkok Post*, 29 December 2018 and 'PM Hun Sen tells US not to destroy happiness of Cambodian people', *Fresh News Cambodia*, 29 December 2018.
7   Ministry of Foreign Affairs and International Cooperation, *Cambodia*, op. cit.
8   Merimee, J. & Wisnumurti, N., 'Letter from the permanent representatives of France and Indonesia to the United Nations addressed to the Security Council', United Nations General Assembly, 30 October 1991.
9   Ministry of Foreign Affairs and International Cooperation, *Cambodia*, op. cit.
10   Kosal, Author's interview, No. 001.
11   Kosal, Author's interview, No. 231.
12   Phirun, Author's interview, No. 232.
13   Neou, V., 'Hun Sen: CNRP dissolution, NEC resignations, and aid cuts will not affect 2018 election', *VOA Khmer*, 23 November 2017 and Graham, L., 'S. 1468 (116th): Cambodia Accountability and Return on Investment Act of 2019', United States Congress, Washington, 14 May 2019.
14   Muong, N. & Lipes, J., 'Opposition members quit Cambodia's electoral body in protest of party's dissolution', *Radio Free Asia*, 20 November 2017.

15   ibid.
16   'Joint motion for a resolution on Cambodia: notably the dissolution of the CNRP party', European Parliament, Strasbourg, 13 December 2007, www.europarl.europa.eu/doceo/document/RC-8-2017-0686_EN.html?redirect
17   Hor, K. & Baliga, A., 'As Hun Sen goads West, minister quietly notes massive cost of sanctions', *The Phnom Penh Post*, 19 December 2017 and May, K., 'Garment makers demand "amicable" end to political row', *Khmer Times*, 19 December 2017 and 'Hun Sen has bigger worries than elections', *The Asean Post*, 27 July 2018.
18   Phirun, Author's interview, No. 232.
19   Channa and Kunthea, Author's interview, No. 127.
20   Pich, Author's interview, No. 156.
21   Graham, L., 'S. 1468 (116th)', op. cit.
22   Bunroeun, Author's interview, No. 029.
23   Ou Ritthy & Leap, Author's interview, No. 240.
24   Leap, Author's interview, No. 039.
25   United Nations General Assembly, 'United Nations charter', 1945, www.un.org/en/about-us/un-charter
26   Ou Ritthy & Leap, Author's interview, No. 240.
27   Leap, Author's interview, No. 039.
28   Leap, Author's interview, No. 147.
29   Leap, Author's interview, No. 101.
30   Neou, V., 'Hun Sen: CNRP dissolution, NEC resignations, and aid cuts will not affect 2018 election', op. cit.
31   Information on South China Sea in Mhatani, S. & San, S., '"My vote is useless": some refuse to cast ballots in Cambodian election', *The Washington Post*, 29 July 2018.
32   Thayer, C., 'ASEAN'S code of conduct in the South China Sea: a litmus test for community-building?', *The Asia Pacific Journal*, vol. 10, issue 34, no. 4, 19 August 2012.
33   ibid. and Chheang, V. & Heng, P., 'Cambodian perspective on the Belt and Road Initiative', NIDS Joint Research Series, No.17, National Institute for Defense Studies, Tokyo, 2019, Chapter 1.
34   Bower, E., 'China reveals its hand on ASEAN in Phnom Penh', Centre for International & Strategic Studies, Washington, 20 July 2012.
35   Kozlovski, M., 'Sea dispute lingers at ASEAN summit', *DW Akademie*, 22 November 2012.
36   Szep, J. & Pomfret, J., 'Tensions flare over South China Sea at Asian summit', *Reuters*, 19 November 2012.

37   Thayer, C., 'ASEAN'S code of conduct in the South China Sea', op. cit.
38   Query Wizard for International Development Statistics, Organisation for Economic Cooperation and Development, date unknown, https://stats.oecd.org/qwids/#?x=2&y=6&f=3:51,4:1,1:2,5:3,7:1&q=3:51+4:1+1:2+5:3+7:1+2:29+6:1993,1994,1995,1996,1997,1998,1999,20
39   Tran, M., 'World Bank suspends new lending to Cambodia over eviction of landowners', *The Guardian*, 10 August 2011.
40   Strangio, S., *Hun Sen's Cambodia*, op. cit.
41   Dreher, A. et al., 'Aid, China, and growth: evidence from a new global development finance dataset', AidData Working Paper #46, AidData, Williamsburg, 2017.
42   'Countries and regions profile: Cambodia', European Commission, 2020, https://ec.europa.eu/trade/policy/countries-and-regions/countries/cambodia/
43   'ASEAN investment report 2019 – FDI in services: focus on health care', The ASEAN Secretariat, October 2019 and International Telecommunications Union, 'Number of people using the internet statistics', 2019, www.itu.int/en/ITU-D/Statistics/Pages/stat/default.aspx
44   Mhatani, S. & San, S. '"My vote is useless"', op. cit.
45   This term was first used to describe what could be a string of military naval bases that China are building across Asia and Africa, but many consider them to be purely commercial ports, although they could be dual-use in the future.
46   Po, S. & Heng, K., 'Assessing the impacts of Chinese investments in Cambodia: the case of Preah Sihanoukville province', *Pacific Forum*, vol. 19, Working Paper 4, May 2019; Prasso, S., 'Chinese influx stirs resentment in once-sleepy Cambodian resort', Bloomberg, 21 June 2018; Murdoch, L. & Geraghty, K. 'The next Macau? China's big gamble in Cambodia', *The Sydney Morning Herald*, 20 June 2018.
47   Po, S. & Heng, K., 'Assessing the impacts of Chinese investments in Cambodia', op. cit.
48   ibid.; Sopheak, Author's interview, No. 108; Pech, Author's interview, No. 109.
49   Murdoch, L. & Geraghty, K. 'The next Macau?', op. cit.
50   Chheang, V. & Heng, P., 'Cambodian perspective on the Belt and Road Initiative', op. cit.
51   'Cambodia: Obama, Hun Sen in "tense" talks', *Radio Free Asia*, 19 November 2012.
52   Emmons, K., 'Chess player, philosopher, a leader of the country', op. cit.
53   Slocomb, M., 'The nature and role of ideology in the modern Cambodian state', op. cit.
54   Phirun, Author's interview, No. 232.

55 Strangio, S., *Hun Sen's Cambodia*, op. cit.
56 Dav Ansan, Author's interview, No. 125.
57 Phirun, Author's interview, No. 232.
58 ibid. and Phirun, Author's interview, No. 054.
59 Phirun, Author's interview, No. 232.

Chapter 27: Clean Fingers

1   May, T., 'Rainsy vows to compete in next election', *Khmer Times*, 5 December 2017.
2   Mech, D. & Nachemson, A. 'PM, military officials say Rainsy will face "treason" suit over Facebook post', *The Phnom Penh Post*, 7 December 2017.
3   Chhorn, C., 'Cambodia's Sam Rainsy found guilty of defamation, ordered to pay $1 million', *Reuters*, 29 December 2017.
4   Hutt, D., 'Does Cambodia's new opposition movement really matter?', *The Diplomat*, 17 January 2018.
5   May, T., 'CNRM creates rift between Sokha and Rainsy', *Khmer Times*, 22 January 2018.
6   Hutt, D., 'Can Cambodia's fractured opposition survive?', *Asia Times*, 5 April 2017 and Cheang Sokha, Author's interview, No. 199.
7   Hutt, D., 'Does Cambodia's new opposition movement really matter?', op. cit.
8   Nachemson, A., 'CNRM calls for boycott of water linked to Huns', *The Phnom Penh Post*, 19 February 2018.
9   Nachemson, A., 'Election body threatens legal action over Sam Rainsy's boycott leaflets', *The Phnom Penh Post*, 2 May 2018.
10 'Law on Election of Members of the National Assembly, NS/RKM/0315/003', Cambodian Government, Phnom Penh, March 2015.
11 Nachemson, A., 'Election body threatens legal action over Sam Rainsy's boycott leaflets', op. cit.
12 Hang Puthea, Author's interview, No. 023.
13 Smith, R., 'Report of the Special Rapporteur on the situation of human rights in Cambodia', United Nations General Assembly Human Rights Council, September 2018.
14 ibid.
15 Chea Chiv, Author's interview, No. 221.
16 Dim, S. & Hang, P., 'Chea Chiv, Thorng Saroeun and Kruy Kimsiang agreed to pay a fine', National Election Committee, 22 January 2019.
17 ibid. and Soth, K., 'Preah Sihanouk woman accused of insulting Hun Sen with Facebook poem', *The Phnom Penh Post*, 3 May 2018.

18 Taing, V., 'Five more fined over election boycott campaign', *Khmer Times*, 8 August 2018.
19 Kimsorn, Author's interview, No. 025.
20 Sun, N. & Wallace, J., 'Cash, oaths and holy water: inside the CPP's quest to identify its own true supporters', *VOA Khmer*, 15 November 2017.
21 Meas, S., 'Leaked document spells out CPP's plan to monitor members', *The Phnom Penh Post*, 29 August 2017.
22 Sophal, Author's interview, No. 019. Quotation in following paragraph also from this interview.
23 Meas, S., 'Leaked document spells out CPP's plan to monitor members', op. cit.
24 Sun, N. & Wallace, J., 'Cash, oaths and holy water', op. cit.
25 ibid.
26 Sophal, Author's interview, No. 019.
27 Pen Raksa, Author's interview, No. 150.
28 May Titthara, Author's interview, No. 145.

Chapter 28: Charm Offensive

1 Sophea, Author's interview, No. 151.
2 Kosal, Author's interview, No. 001.
3 Kosal, Author's interview, No. 231.
4 Kosal, Author's interview, No. 002.
5 Khemera, Author's interview, No. 158.
6 ibid.
7 ibid.
8 Kosal, Author's interview, No. 231.
9 Khuon, N., 'Garment workers help CPP overtake CNRP strongholds', *Khmer Times*, 2 August 2018; 'Samdech Akka Moha Sena Padei Techo Hun Sen, Prime Minister of the Kingdom of Cambodia, meets this morning with more than 10,000 workers in Por Sen Chey district', *Fresh News Cambodia*, 8 January 2018.
10 Channa and friend, Author's interview, No. 217.
11 Kann, V., 'PM reportedly gifted $3.5m to 700,000 working class voters at unofficial campaign events', *VOA Khmer*, 6 July 2018 and Prak, C. & Allard, T., 'Crackdown and cash: Hun Sen's recipe for victory in Cambodian poll', *Reuters*, 15 June 2018.
12 Prak, C. & Allard, T., 'Crackdown and cash', op. cit. and Mom, K., 'PM to curb garment worker visits during election campaign', *Khmer Times*, 31 May 2018.

13   Hang Puthea, Author's interview, No. 023.
14   Chheang, V. & Heng, P., 'Cambodian perspective on the Belt and Road Initiative', op. cit. and Spiess, R., 'Employers required to pay more into NSSF for workers', *The Phnom Penh Post*, 9 January 2018.
15   Yin, S. & Baliga, A., 'PM muses on minimum wage growth', *The Phnom Penh Post*, 29 March 2018.

Chapter 29: Pressure

1   Ou Ritthy & Leap, Author's interview, No. 240.
2   Sophal, Author's interview, No. 019.
3   Pen Raksa, Author's interview, No. 212 and Soeng Sen Karuna, Author's interview, No. 219.
4   Koul Panha, Author's interview, No. 172.
5   Smith, R., 'Report of the Special Rapporteur on the situation of human rights in Cambodia', op. cit.
6   He also said that a provincial governor role cost $2 million every five years.
7   Chen Sokngeng, Author's interview, No. 094.
8   Morgenbesser, L., 'Cambodia's transition to hegemonic authoritarianism', *Journal of Democracy*, vol. 1, 2019, pp. 158–71; Mech, D. & Hor, K., 'Three ministries set up web-monitoring group to look out for "fake news"', *The Phnom Penh Post*, 7 June 2018; Kann, V., 'Cambodia forms task force to monitor "fake news" on social media', *VOA Khmer*, 6 June 2018.
9   'Freedom on the net – Cambodia 2019', Freedom House, 2019.
10   Lamb, K., 'Cambodia "fake news" crackdown prompts fears over press freedom', *The Guardian*, 6 July 2018.
11   CCHR, 'The human rights situation in Cambodia in 2018', 2019 and 'Freedom on the net – Cambodia 2019', Freedom House, Washington, 2019.
12   Keo, S. & Gerin, S., 'Cambodian king leaves signing of controversial constitutional amendments to ruling party', *Radio Free Asia*, 22 February 2018.
13   CCHR, *Cambodia Fundamental Freedoms Monitor – 2nd Annual Report*, Freedom House, Washington, 2018; 'Freedom on the net – Cambodia 2019', op. cit.; Pheak, S., '"Shoe thrower" Sam Sokha sends apology to PM', *The Phnom Penh Post*, 12 September 2018.
14   Human Rights Watch, 'Political prisoners Cambodia', 24 January 2020, https://www.hrw.org/
15   Soth, K., 'Preah Sihanouk woman accused of insulting Hun Sen with Facebook poem', *The Phnom Penh Post*, 3 May 2018.
16   ADHOC staff member, Author's interview, No. 159.

NOTES

17 Cochrane, L., 'Vietnamese hackers trigger software trap after Australian sale of newspaper in Cambodia', *ABC News*, 15 May 2018 and 'Freedom on the net – Cambodia 2019', op. cit.
18 Ou Ritthy, Author's interview, No. 057.
19 May Titthara, Author's interview, No. 099.
20 Kannitha, Author's interview, No. 006.
21 Yon, S. & Nachemson, A., 'PM warns unions ahead of poll', *The Phnom Penh Post*, 23 April 2018.
22 Niem, C., 'Sacked teachers testify at court', *The Phnom Penh Post*, 28 February 2019.
23 Rong Chhun, Author's interview, No. 018.
24 CCHR, *Cambodia Fundamental Freedoms Monitor – 2nd Annual Report*, op. cit.
25 Channa and Kunthea, Author's interview, No. 226.
26 Chamroeun, Author's interview, No. 104.
27 Niem, C., 'Nonvote a vote for "rebels", AIDS authority chief slams Rainsy's call to boycott national elections', *The Phnom Penh Post*, 9 May 2018.
28 Nachemson, A., 'Cambodia's election: against Hun Sen, only way to win is to not vote', *South China Morning Post*, 28 July 2018.
29 Beech, H. & Sun, N., 'In Cambodia, dissenting voters find ways to say "none of the above"', *The New York Times*, 31 July 2018 and Smith, R., 'Report of the Special Rapporteur on the situation of human rights in Cambodia', op. cit.
30 ibid.
31 'Hun Sen needs strong poll turnout to save face', *The Bangkok Post*, 28 July 2018.
32 Yee, T.H., 'Cambodian PM Hun Sen: those who don't vote in election will "destroy democracy"', *The Straits Times*, 27 July 2018.
33 Mech, D., 'Hun Sen praises National Police, while ordering them to vote in poll', *The Phnom Penh Post*, 15 March 2018.
34 'CNRP points to King in call for vote boycott', *The Phnom Penh Post*, 17 July 2018.
35 'Royal message calls for Khmer people to vote', *Fresh News*, 28 July 2018.
36 Heng, Author's interview, No. 130.
37 Sreyleak, Author's interview, No. 011.
38 May Titthara, Author's interview, No. 145.
39 San, S. & Mahtani, S., '"My vote is useless"', op. cit.
40 Rithisak, Author's interview, No. 073.

NOTES

41 Youth Resource Development Program participants, Author's interview, No. 135.
42 ibid.
43 Lamy, Author's interview, No. 187.
44 Youth Resource Development Program participants, Author's interview, No. 135.
45 ibid.
46 Kimsorn, Author's interview, No. 034.
47 Youth Resource Development Program participants, Author's interview, No. 135.

Chapter 30: Your Aim Is One
1 Ou Ritthy, Author's interview, No. 057.
2 Kannitha, Author's interview, No. 006.
3 Kannitha, Author's interview, No. 008.
4 Rotha and Soveacha, Author's interview, No. 197.
5 Yeng Virak, Author's interview, No. 103.
6 ibid.
7 Poree, A.L., 'Cambodia's direct democracy weakened but not broken', Swiss Broadcasting Corporation, 25 August 2016.
8 Yeng Virak, Author's interview, No. 103.
9 ibid.
10 'Champagne with dictators', *ABC*, 30 July 2018.
11 Yeng Virak, Author's interview, No. 103.
12 Rong Chhun, Author's interview, No. 016 and 'GDP slams vote boycott calls', *The Phnom Penh Post*, 7 June 2018.
13 Soeung Saroeun, Author's interview, No. 102.
14 May Titthara, Author's interview, No. 145.
15 Yeng Virak, Author's interview, No. 103.
16 Yeng Virak, Author's interview, No. 206.
17 Khy, S., 'Kem Ley's wife refuses to support new party', *Khmer Times*, 16 March 2018.
18 Yeng Virak, Author's interview, No. 206.

Chapter 31: Endgame
1 Maly, Author's interview, No. 141.
2 Rotha, Author's interview, No. 009.
3 Bunroeun, Author's interview, No. 032.

4	Sophal & Serey, Author's interview, No. 024.
5	Bunroeun, Author's interview, No. 029.
6	Bunroeun, Author's interview, No. 032.
7	Rithisak, Author's interview, No. 073.
8	Ono, Y., 'Cambodia's Hun Sen slams boycott calls as "destroying democracy"', *Nikkei Asia*, 27 July 2018.
9	Sok, K., 'Election campaign ends as Cambodians prepare to vote', *Voice of America*, 28 July 2018.
10	Maly, Author's interview, No. 124.
11	Maly, Author's interview, No. 141.
12	Brinkley, J., *Cambodia's Curse*, op. cit.
13	Kamm, H., *Cambodia: Report from a Stricken Land*, op. cit.
14	Kosal, Author's interview, No. 231.
15	Brinkley, J., *Cambodia's Curse*, op. cit.
16	Soeng Sen Karuna, Author's interview, No. 140.
17	Dav Ansan, Author's interview, No. 125.
18	Heng, Author's interview, No. 130.
19	Maly, Author's interview, No. 124.
20	Schunert, T. et al., 'Cambodian mental health survey 2012', Royal University of Phnom Penh, 2012 and Dubois, V. et al., 'Household survey of psychiatric morbidity in Cambodia', *International Journal of Social Psychiatry*, vol. 50, no. 2, 2004.
21	Brinkley, J., *Cambodia's Curse*, op. cit.
22	Dav Ansan, Author's interview, No. 125.
23	Ansan is referring to the forced evacuation of all inhabitants from Phnom Penh by the Khmer Rouge. Even the frail and sick were ordered to march hundreds of kilometres, with many dying on the way.
24	Slocomb, M., 'The nature and role of ideology in the modern Cambodian state', op. cit.
25	Soth, K., 'CPP lawmaker accuses Sin Rozeth of supporting Rainsy's movement, using restaurant as front for political activity', *The Phnom Penh Post*, 29 January 2018.
26	Soth, K., 'Joking "rebel" sign at Sin Rozeth restaurant attracts governor's warning', *The Phnom Penh Post*, 6 February 2018.
27	Sin Rozeth, Author's interview, No. 042.
28	Identity retained, Author's interview, No. 047.
29	Jolley, M., 'Threats and corruption', op. cit.
30	Sin Rozeth, Author's interview, No. 042.

NOTES

Chapter 32: Election Day

1. Maly, Author's interview, No. 141 and Messenger chat.
2. Maly, Author's interview, No. 142.
3. Rotha, Author's interview, No. 009.
4. Sophal, Author's interview, No. 021.
5. Piseth, Author's interview, No. 236.
6. Leap, Author's interview, No. 147.
7. Chen Sokngeng, Author's interview, No. 095.
8. Pol, P., 'ANFREL unveils plan to destroy democracy', *Khmer Times*, 25 June 2018.
9. 'Press conference by international observers 5', *Khmer Times*, 30 July 2018, www.youtube.com/watch?v=lb-Y3KkjysU
10. Sophea, Author's interview, No. 151.
11. Khemera, Author's interview, No. 158.
12. May Titthara, Author's interview, No. 099.
13. May Titthara, Author's interview, No. 145.
14. All Facebook posts, saved to my Facebook.
15. See TVK video saved in Facebook and Sophal, Author's interview, No. 022.
16. Vanna, Author's interview, No. 163.
17. National Election Committee of Cambodia, 'Voter turnout – press release', 29 July 2018.
18. Pen Raksa, Author's interview, No. 150.

Chapter 33: The Numbers

1. Yeng Virak, Author's interview, No. 040.
2. Kannitha, Author's interview, No. 006.
3. Hutt, D., 'Spoilt ballots tally a major protest at Cambodia's poll', *Asia Times*, 30 July 2018.
4. Hang Puthea, Author's interview, No. 062.
5. Rong Chhun, Author's interview, No. 018.
6. May Titthara, Author's interview, No. 145.
7. Soeng Sen Karuna, Author's interview, No. 140.
8. Kannitha, Author's interview, No. 007.
9. ibid. and Maly, Messenger 29/7/19.
10. Sin Rozeth, Author's interview, No. 043.
11. Rotha, Author's interview, No. 009.
12. Yeng Virak, Author's interview, No. 040.
13. Rotha, Author's interview, No. 009.

14 Soeng Sen Karuna, Author's interview, No. 219.
15 Soeng Sen Karuna, Author's interview, No. 140 and Pen Raksa, Author's interview, No. 150.
16 Soeng Sen Karuna, Author's interview, No. 140.
17 Rotha, Author's interview, No. 009.
18 May Titthara, Author's interview, No. 145 and Soeng Sen Karuna, Author's interview, No. 140.
19 Rotha, Author's interview, No. 009.
20 Khemera, Author's interview, No. 161.
21 Dav Ansan, Author's interview, No. 112.
22 Phirun, Author's interview, No. 143.
23 Maly, Author's interview, No. 142.

Chapter 34: Cambodia Changing
1 Davuth, Author's interview, No. 205.
2 Channary, Author's interview, No. 136.

Chapter 35: Hun Sen's Right to Rule
1 Dav Ansan, Author's interviews, No. 125 and No. 112.
2 Sok, K., 'Hun Sen vows to arrest Sam Rainsy if he returns, or step down as PM', *VOA Khmer*, 31 August 2019; Taing, V., 'Sam Rainsy disputes invalid ballot results', *Khmer Times*, 2 August 2018; 'Opposition leader Sam Rainsy denounces Cambodia's "sham election"', *The Daily Mail*, 31 July 2018, www.youtube.com/watch?v=Y7Oq1EA6kpU
3 Dav Ansan, Author's interview, No. 125.
4 Dav Ansan, Author's interview, No. 112.
5 Huy Vannak, Author's interview, No. 238.
6 'Human Development Indicators – Cambodia (to year 2019)', United Nations Development Programme Human Development Reports, 2020, http://hdr.undp.org/en/indicators/103006 and Huy Vannak, Author's interview, No. 238.
7 Ministry of Education, Youth and Sport, 'Public education statistics and indicators 2018–19', March 2019, www.moeys.gov.kh/index.php/en/emis/3069.html#.YJ75zqgzY2x
8 Everett, S. & Meisburger, T., 'Democracy in Cambodia', op. cit. The phrase 'parent-state' is taken from Hoon, C.Y., 'Revisiting the Asian values argument used by Asian political leaders and its validity', *Indonesian Quarterly*, vol. 32, no. 2, 2004, pp. 154–74.
9 Citation withheld to protect privacy.

NOTES

10. Kimchhay, Author's interview, No. 202.
11. Maly, Author's interview, No. 141.
12. Leap, Author's interview, No. 147.
13. Maly, Author's interview, No. 141.
14. 'GNI per capita – world development indicators', The World Bank, 20 December 2019, https://databank.worldbank.org/source/world-development-indicators
15. Dav Ansan, Author's interview, No. 125.
16. 'PM Hun Sen urges people to host "Khmer noodle" party for national unity', *Fresh News Cambodia*, 3 June 2019.
17. Sin Rozeth, Author's interview, No. 042.
18. Tes Putheara, Author's interview, No. 133.
19. Neary, Author's interview, No. 192.
20. Kannitha, Author's interview, No. 008.
21. Davuth, Author's interview, No. 005.
22. Chamroeun, Author's interview, No. 104.
23. Davuth, Author's interview, No. 205.
24. Davuth, Author's interview, No. 218.

Chapter 36: The Sacrifice of Sin Rozeth
1. Vanda & Sokha, Author's interview, No. 162.
2. The following section is mainly from Sin Rozeth, Author's interview, No. 042 and Sin Rozeth, Author's interview, No. 043.
3. Dav Ansan, Author's interview, No. 125.
4. Kapuscinski, R., *Imperium*, Granta Books, London, 1993.
5. Kosal, Author's interview, No. 231.

Chapter 37: Playing with Coal
1. Chen Sokngeng, Author's interview, No. 095.
2. Kosal, Author's interview, No. 002.
3. Kosal, Author's interview, No. 001.
4. Kosal, Author's interview, No. 231.
5. Kosal, Author's interview, No. 002.
6. Ou Ritthy, Author's interview, No. 114.
7. Ouk Chhayavy, Author's interview, No. 058.
8. Yeang Sothearin & Cheang Sokha, Author's interview, No. 230.
9. Kannitha, Author's interview, No. 007.
10. Rong Chhun, Author's interview, No. 018.

11 Sophal, Author's interview, No. 019.
12 Ou Ritthy, Author's interview, No. 114.

Chapter 38: Cambodia's Way

1   Emmons, K., 'Chess player, philosopher, a leader of the country', op. cit.
2   Krishner, Bloss & Lor, 'The interview granted to *The Cambodia Daily*', op. cit.
3   Strangio, S., *Hun Sen's Cambodia*, op. cit.
4   Krishner, Bloss & Lor, 'The interview granted to *The Cambodia Daily*', op. cit.
5   Ministry of Foreign Affairs and International Cooperation, *Stability and Development First*, op. cit.
6   Park, C.M. & Shin, D.C., 'Do Asian values deter popular support for democracy? The case of South Korea', Asian Barometer Project Office, National Taiwan University, 2004; Barr, M., 'Lee Kuan Yew and the Asian values debate', *Asian Studies Review*, vol. 24, no. 3, September 2000; Hoon, C.Y., 'Revisiting the Asian values argument used by Asian political leaders and its validity', op. cit.; Ojendal, J. & Antlov, H., 'Asian values and its political consequences: is Cambodia the first domino?', *Pacific Review*, vol. 11, no. 4, 1998.
7   Park, C.M. & Shin, D.C., 'Do Asian values deter popular support for democracy?'; Barr, M., 'Lee Kuan Yew and the Asian values debate'; Shin, D., 'Reassessing the Confucian Asian values debate in Confucianism and democratization in East Asia', Cambridge University Press, Cambridge, 2011, pp. 317–34.
8   Peang-Meth, A., 'Understanding the Khmer sociological-cultural observation', *Asian Survey*, vol. 31, no. 5, May 1991, pp. 442–55.
9   Slocomb, M., 'The nature and role of ideology in the modern Cambodian state', op. cit.
10 Ministry of Foreign Affairs and International Cooperation, *Stability and Development First*, op. cit.
11 Taing, V., 'Opposition parties meet with Hun Sen', *Khmer Times*, 22 August 2018 and 'Cambodian political parties unanimously agree on draft royal decree on the establishment of Supreme Council of Consultations', *Fresh News*, 4 September 2018.
12 Kosal, Author's interview, No. 002.
13 Dav Ansan, Author's interview, No. 112.
14 Yeng Virak, Author's interview, No. 040 and 'Only half of opposition to attend PM's forum', *The Phnom Penh Post*, 21 August 2018.
15 Phirun, Author's interview, No. 232.
16 Leap, Author's interview, No. 039.

17 Phirun, Author's interview, No. 232.
18 Ministry of Foreign Affairs and International Cooperation, *Stability and Development First*, op. cit.
19 Rong Chhun, Author's interview, No. 016.
20 Rong Chhun, Author's interview, No. 017.
21 Ou Ritthy, Author's interview, No. 114.
22 Koul Panha, Author's interview, No. 172.
23 Kannitha, Author's interview, No. 006.
24 Rotha and Soveacha, Author's interview, No. 197.
25 Surveys have found that Cambodians have a greater desire for the rule of law than OECD countries. Gibson, J., Sonis, J. & Hean, S., 'Cambodians' support for the rule of law on the eve of the Khmer Rouge trials', *The International Journal of Transitional Justice*, vol. 4, no. 3, 2010.
26 Chamroeun, Author's interview, No. 104.
27 Maly, Author's interview, No. 141.
28 Ou Ritthy, Author's interview, No. 057.
29 Ou, R., 'Cambodia: Prime Minister Hun Sen was a successful wartime leader but certainly not one in peacetime Cambodia', Asian Human Rights Commission, 26 April 2017.
30 Ou Ritthy, Author's interview, No. 057.
31 Rong Chhun, Author's interview, No. 018.
32 Ou Ritthy, Author's interview, No. 131.
33 Ou Ritthy, Author's interview, No. 114.
34 Ou Ritthy, Author's interview, No. 057.

Chapter 39: Candlelight

1 All Sin Rozeth, Author's interview, No. 256.
2 Sin, R., 'មិនឱ្យញាតិកាណបក្សភ្លើងទៀន', Facebook Post, 23 May 2022.
3 All Chamrouen, Author's interview, No. 258.

Chapter 40: A Chicken House

1 Sar Longdeth, Author's interview, No. 259.
2 Identity unknown, Author's interview, No. 283.

Chapter 41: The Elephant and a Mouse

1 Sorn, S., 'Candlelight Party cries foul as CPP appears to have won landslide at polls', Cambodian Journalists Alliance Association, 6 June 2022.
2 All Kosal & colleagues, Author's interview, No. 261.

NOTES

3   Sorn, S., 'Candlelight Party cries foul as CPP appears to have won landslide at polls', op. cit.
4   Ouch, S., Mech, D. & Dickison, M., 'Voter sentiment or irregularities? Theories abound over landslide election', *Voice of Democracy*, 6 June 2022.
5   Channary, Author's interview, No. 264.
6   Ou Ritthy, Author's interview, No. 277.
7   Rotha, Author's interview, No. 281.
8   Rong Chhun, Author's interview, No. 265.
9   Sin, R., 'ចោរលួចកាត់បងារនៅភូមិអញ្ញាញ សង្កាត់អូរចារយកមកផ្ទះដាចោល នៅក្រោយសំណល់ឡានគេចោះចោល', Facebook Post, 28 May 2022.
10 Leap, Author's interview, No. 263.
11 'NEC files lawsuit against Son Chhay for public defamation, requests for public apology', *Fresh News Asia*, 17 June 2022.
12 Ouch, S., Mech, D. & Dickison, M., 'Voter sentiment or irregularities?', op. cit.
13 Hang Puthea, Author's interview, No. 268.

Chapter 42: Enmity Returns

1   Niem, C., 'Sokha's treason trial begins', *The Phnom Penh Post*, 15 January 2020.
2   Niem, C., 'CNRP support will not be tolerated', *The Phnom Penh Post*, 29 August 2019.
3   Sok, K., 'Hun Sen vows to arrest Sam Rainsy if he returns, or step down as PM', *VOA Khmer*, 31 August 2019.
4   Khan, L. & Nhim, S., 'Three charged for plotting CNRP "coup" over support for Rainsy's return', *Voice of Democracy*, 1 October 2019.
5   Chea Chiv, Author's Interview, No. 255.
6   Niem, C., 'CoM: Rainsy has crossed "red line of democracy"', *The Phnom Penh Post*, 1 October 2019; Eckert, P & Keo, S., 'Cambodian PM threatens to use army to prevent Sam Rainsy return', *Radio Free Asia*, 2 October 2019; Keo, S., Sok, R. & Lipes, J., 'Cambodia's PM Hun Sen orders military to "attack" exile opposition leaders on sight', *Radio Free Asia*, 7 October 2019.
7   'Live blog: Cambodia's opposition returns', *VOA Khmer*, 7–10 November 2019, www.voacambodia.com/
8   Hul, R., 'Prime Minister Hun Sen sends another warning to CNRP supporters', *VOA Khmer*, 8 November 2019.
9   Yun, S. & Whong, E., 'Hun Sen gains Laos' support in preventing Sam Rainsy return to Cambodia', *Radio Free Asia*, 12 September 2019.
10 Kijewski, L., 'Cambodian opposition leader doesn't return as promised', *VOA Khmer*, 9 November 2019 and Nor, R. & Teh, Y., 'Sam Rainsy to meet government backbenchers tomorrow', *New Straits Times*, 11 November 2019.

NOTES

11 'Cambodian opposition leader Sam Rainsy arrives in Indonesia', *The Free Press Journal*, 14 November 2019, www.freepressjournal.in/

12 Yun, A. & Finney, R., 'Cambodia's Hun Sen thanks US President Trump for his "understanding, patience"', *Radio Free Asia*, 17 November 2019.

13 Hul, R., 'Cambodia opposition leaders receive "outrageously harsh" jail terms for alleged coup plot', *VOA Khmer*, 3 March 2021. Likely articles 451 and 453 of the criminal code.

14 'Rainsy's in Malaysia, Sokha's out of jail. Is Cambodia's Hun Sen in a pickle?', *South China Morning Post*, 11 November 2019.

15 Travouillon, K., 'Rainsy's point of no return', *New Mandala*, 14 November 2019.

16 Khuon, N., 'Kem Sokha's cabinet chief denounces claim over Sokha–Rainsy phone call', *Fresh News Asia*, 28 November 2019 and Khuon, N., 'Kem Sokha reaffirms path of non-violence', *Khmer Times*, 26 November 2019.

17 Tin, S., 'Chantha calls out Rainsy for using Sokha as tool', *Khmer Times*, 25 August 2021.

18 'Kem Sokha and Sam Rainsy are not as one, Sokha reiterates', *Fresh News Asia*, 15 June 2022.

19 Khuon, N., 'Kem Sokha's message shows Rainsy–Sokha split after Candlelight Party congress', Cambodian Journalists Alliance Association, https://cambojanews.com/

20 Khuon, N., 'Kem Sokha's cabinet chief denounces claim over Sokha–Rainsy phone call', op. cit.

21 Ben, S., 'Rainsy ignored: breakaway party leaders brush aside ex-CNRP chief's rhetoric', *Khmer Times*, 23 September 2021.

22 Khuon, N., 'Kem Sokha insists he has no connection to Sam Rainsy', Cambodian Journalists Alliance Association, 26 May 2022 and Morn, M., 'Kem Sokha: "I have stopped having any connection with Sam Rainsy"', *Voice of Democracy*, 15 June 2022.

23 K&K Post, 'Kem Sokha requests people don't vote for any party', 30 March 2022, www.youtube.com/watch?v=dO8BVttmo-A and 'Kem Sokha will not go to vote due to no political party of his choice', *Fresh News Asia*, 5 June 2022.

24 Mao, S. & Sam, S., 'Sam Rainsy criticizes Kem Sokha for not voting in the commune elections', *Cambodianess*, 11 June 2022.

25 'Kem Sokha's confidant calls Sam Rainsy a culprit, mad dog', *Fresh News Asia*, 10 June 2022.

26 'Detained former opposition chief meets with Cambodia's Hun Sen', *Radio Free Asia*, 9 May 2022 and Pheng Heng, Author's interview, No. 269.

27 Rong Chhun, Author's interview, No. 265.

NOTES

Chapter 43: Chapter Two

1. 'Hun Manet on ABC's *The World*: in full', *ABC Pacific*, 19 October 2015.
2. World Health Organization, 'WHO Regional Director commends Cambodia's COVID-19 response and strong commitment to investing in health for the future', 6 June 2022, www.who.int/cambodia/news/detail/06-07-2022-who-regional-director-commends-cambodia-s-covid-19-response-and-strong-commitment-to-investing-in-health-for-the-future
3. Dav Ansan, Author's interview, No. 274.
4. 'Cambodia begins COVID-19 vaccination, PM Hun Sen's eldest son gets first shot', China Global Television Network, 11 February 2021.
5. Ry, S., 'Manet recalls urgent establishment of Covid treatment in capital', *The Phnom Penh Post*, 13 April 2022.
6. Dav Ansan, Author's interview, No. 274.
7. All Phirun, Author's interview, No. 279.
8. Chamrouen, Author's interview, No. 258.
9. Leap, Author's interview, No. 263.
10. Ou Ritthy, Author's interview, No. 277.
11. 'Thach Setha, a former CNRP lawmaker now rehabilitated and allowed to be involved in politics again', *Khmer Times*, 13 April 2021.
12. Thach Setha, Author's interview, No. 280.
13. Rong Chhun, Author's interview, No. 265.
14. Chang Phalla, Author's interview, No. 275.
15. Ouch, S. & Khan, L., 'Updated: mass trial sentences 31 to jail, Cambodian-American detained', *Voice of Democracy*, 14 June 2022.
16. Yeab Yoth, Author's interview, No. 276.
17. Gironde, C. et al., 'Working paper: large-scale land acquisitions in Southeast Asia', Swiss Network for International Studies, August 2014.
18. Global Witness complaint against Vietnam Rubber Group, 'Recommendation to the FSC Board of Directors', June 2015, https://connect.fsc.org/actions-and-outcomes/current-cases/vietnam-rubber-group-vrg
19. 'Kem Sokha and Sam Rainsy are not as one, Sokha reiterates' (translation of audio recording), *Fresh News Asia*, 15 June 2022 and Morn, M., 'Kem Sokha: "I have stopped having any connection with Sam Rainsy"', op. cit.

Postscript

1. Associated Press, 'Cambodian court convicts opposition leader of land giveaway', *AP News*, 20 October 2022.
2. Niem, C. & Baliga, A., 'Rainsy's vow of "autonomy" for ethnic group sets off treason probe', *The Phnom Penh Post*, 8 Mar 2018.

NOTES

3   'PM: "'No way" "traitor" Sam Rainsy will ever be pardoned', *Khmer Times*, 20 October 2022.

4   Khuon, N., 'Court sentences ex-opposition leader Kem Sokha to 27 years incarceration for treason and lifetime ban from politics', *Camboja News*, 3 March 2023.

5   Khuon, N., 'Court of appeal denies Thach Setha bail request', *Camboja News*, 31 March 2023.

6   Khuon, N., 'NEC rejects Rong Chhun's candidacy, unionist to withdraw from July election', *Camboja News*, 10 May 2023.

7   Sovann, S., 'New policy may prevent opposition Candlelight Party from registering for elections', *Camboja News*, 3 May 2023.

8   Khuon, N., 'NEC refuses to register Candelight despite Interior Ministry document', *Camboja News*, 12 May 2023.

9   Sovann, S., 'Candlelight leader Rong Chhun postpones mass protest after Hun Sen threatens to arrest him', *Camboja News*, 2 June 2023 and Khuon, N., 'PM Hun Sen threatens Candlelight members with arrest if they protest party's inability to participate in elections', *Camboja News*, 15 May 2023.

10 Khuon, N., 'National assembly approves election amendments, changes made to four laws', *Camboja News*, 23 June 2023.